David and Denise Cross have   leagues in the ministry for over twenty-five years. Their profound knowledge and experience of Christian discipling and healing is beyond dispute. And this amazing reference book is the physical evidence of the pilgrimage of faith they have walked together with the Lord.

David is an engineer by training and as an engineer he knows that accuracy of design and construction is critical if a bridge, for example, is going to be safe and fulfil its purpose. But as a Christian leader he also knows that faithfulness to the Word of God is an absolutely essential prerequisite for living the Christian life. And it is this commitment to the truth and application of Scripture which underpins this remarkable book.

The *A-Z Guide to the Healing Ministry* is much, much more than a dictionary to refer to when you want to know something. It is in itself a life-transforming challenge to living the Christian life in relationship with the Lord and in the power of the Holy Spirit. For every entry not only contains the information you might be looking for, but it also challenges the reader to apply the knowledge in their own life. It is only by applying the truth, in this way, as Jesus said in John 8:32, that the truth can indeed set you free.

This book will be an essential tool in the hands of every person who has any responsibility for, or involvement in, prayer ministry. It's a pastor's gold mine! It will be required reading for all our staff and ministry teams at Ellel Centres around the world. I unreservedly commend this book to you.

Peter Horrobin
Founder and International Director
Ellel Ministries International

A-Z GUIDE
TO THE
HEALING MINISTRY

A–Z Guide to the Healing Ministry

DAVID CROSS

Illustrations by Gillian Louise Cross

Sovereign World

Published by Sovereign World Ltd

PO Box 784, Ellel, Lancaster LA1 9DA United Kingdom

www.sovereignworld.com

Copyright © March 2016 Ellel Ministries

The right of Ellel Ministries to be identified as author of this work has been asserted by them in accordance with the Copyright, Designs and Patents Act 1988.

All rights reserved. No part of this publication may be reproduced, stored in a retrieval system, or transmitted in any form or by any means, electronic, mechanical, photocopying or otherwise, without the prior written consent of the publisher. Short extracts may be used for review purposes.

ISBN: 978-1-85240-843-5

Unless otherwise stated, all Scripture quotations are taken from the New American Standard Bible®, Copyright © 1960, 1962, 1963, 1968, 1971, 1972, 1973, 1975, 1977, 1995 by The Lockman Foundation Used by permission. (www.Lockman.org)

Other Bible versions used are:

NIV – NEW INTERNATIONAL VERSION®. Copyright © 1973, 1978, 1984 by Biblica, Inc. All rights reserved worldwide. Used by permission.

NIrV – NEW INTERNATIONAL READER'S VERSION®. Copyright © 1996, 1998 Biblica.

NEW INTERNATIONAL VERSION® and NIV®; NEW INTERNATIONAL READER'S VERSION® and NIrV® are registered trademarks of Biblica, Inc. Use of either trademark for the offering of goods or services requires the prior written consent of Biblica US, Inc.

KJV – From The Authorized (King James) Version. Rights in the Authorized Version are vested in the Crown. Reproduced by permission of the Crown's patentee, Cambridge University Press.

NKJV – New King James Version. Copyright © 1979, 1980, 1982 Thomas Nelson, Inc.

NRSV – New Revised Standard Version. Copyright © 1989 by the Division of Christian Education of the National Council of the Churches of Christ in the USA.

NLT – Scripture quotations marked NLT are taken from the Holy Bible, New Living Translation, copyright 1996, 2004. Used by permission of Tyndale House Publishers, Inc., Wheaton, Illinois 60189. All rights reserved.

GNB – Good News Bible © 1994 published by the Bible Societies/HarperCollins Publishers Ltd, UK Good News Bible © American Bible Society 1966, 1971, 1976, 1992. Used with permission.

NCV – New Century Version®. Copyright © 2005 by Thomas Nelson. Used by permission. All rights reserved.

The Message – Copyright © 1993, 1994, 1995, 1996, 2000, 2001, 2002. Used by permission of NavPress Publishing Group.

YLT – Young's Literal Translation, public domain.

GW – GOD'S WORD®, © 1995 God's Word to the Nations. Used by permission of Baker Publishing Group.

TLB – The Living Bible. Copyright © 1971 Tyndale House Publishers

LITV - Literal Translation of the Holy Bible Copyright © 1976 - 2000, by Jay P. Green, Sr.

NET - New English Translation, © 2005 Biblical Studies Press, L.L.C.

Illustrations by Gillian Louise Cross (gillian@tigerx.co.uk)
Cover design & typesetting by Zaccmedia.com

Printed in the United Kingdom

ACKNOWLEDGEMENTS

I am so very grateful to Jesus for the countless fellow workers in the Body of Christ who have made it possible for me to hear and apply God's truth, received through their inspired advice, teaching and writing. Since 1993, my wife Denise and I have had the immense privilege of being part of Ellel Ministries, seeing many lives, including our own, significantly changed through walking in the truths which God has revealed in His Word. My thanks go especially to Peter and Fiona Horrobin for pioneering and sustaining this Ministry, under the Lord's direction, over so many years, and for their encouraging me in the writing of this book.

I have tried to condense into these pages as many as possible of the precious principles of the healing and deliverance ministry of Jesus, which have been gleaned over the years by the worldwide family of Ellel Ministries. Thank you all for your determination to seek the Lord for these biblical principles, and for using them to bring restoration to broken and captive lives.

Thanks also to Gillian Cross for perseverance in providing the delightful illustrations, to Rosalinde Joosten and all the Sovereign World publishing team, and finally to those who have been kind enough to read through the text of this A to Z book and give such helpful advice. Your contributions and support have been truly invaluable. Alison Scarborough, Brenda Rankin, Sue Griffiths, John Marshall, Pauline Turner, Julie Smith, David Kyle Foster, and especially Grace Marshall, thank you all so much for helping me. I pray that all the work put in to these pages will bear much fruit in God's Kingdom.

David Cross
March 2016

FOREWORD

By Stuart McAlpine
Senior Pastor, Church of Christ our Shepherd,
Capitol Hill, Washington, DC

Ellel Ministries has already given the world-wide body of Christ an incredible library of teaching resources, and is arguably one of the most significant prophetic voices in this generation to call the church back to a biblical proclamation of the kingdom of God, accompanied by healing of the sick and deliverance from demons. Through its training and equipping centers around the world, it has raised up thousands of healed healers and consequently impacted the church and the nations wherever it has been established.

The indispensable book, *Healing through Deliverance* by the Ellel Ministries Founder, Peter Horrobin, was a breakthrough theological and pastoral textbook on the subject. And the book now in your hands is an essential, empowering contribution to the development and furtherance of the healing ministry in the church at large, and in your local church.

Other books by David Cross, and his wife Denise, have become vital teaching tools for hundreds of pastors like myself, and we have always kept spare copies of them on our shelves to be able to give them immediately to those who need their instruction and direction. Out of a lifetime of experience and gifting, and extraordinary tutelage by the Holy Spirit, David has once again prepared a ground-breaking, life-healing resource for the Body of Christ.

It is absolutely unique. An A-Z is a dictionary, a reference book, right? It is going to be comprehensive, and hopefully comprehensible, right?

FOREWORD

It is going to give you the irreducible minimum that you need to know, and it is going to be succinct, instructive and sensible, right?

Yes, you are completely right on all counts and this book satisfies all those expectations. But here's the thing. This is the only A TO Z that I have ever read as an A THROUGH Z! Yes, it will be your best and most invaluable 'go-to' biblical and pastoral reference resource for all things related to healing, for almost any relevant phrase or term, topic or theme that you could possibly think of...but by the way, there will still be more that you will find within its pages that has never been on your spiritual radar.

My point, and my strongest recommendation, is that instead of putting this volume in your reference section, you immediately go to 'A' and begin to read it from cover to cover, to 'Z', as you would read any other book.I know that's not how you read the normal A-Z but this is not your ordinary dictionary!

Far from feeling that you are jumping from one thing to another, governed by the alphabetical sequence, you will find, as I did, an amazingly inter-connected, multi-layered presentation of truth. The lay-out of the book forces you to make the connections yourself, and invites you to thoughtfully and eagerly cross-reference, between this truth and that one, between this explanation and your experience, between their need and that provision, between that prayer and this answer, between that sickness and this healing, between that bondage and this deliverance.

I am so thankful to David, and to Ellel Ministries, for the thoroughness and integrity of their A-Z commitment to the whole A-Z teaching of scripture about healing and deliverance. They don't miss any of the letters that many would rather skip or ignore altogether.

As a pastor, and as an encourager of a new generation of pastors, I would urge you not only to buy this volume, but to immediately order others, especially for your pastor and elders, who hopefully will ensure that every member of their healing prayer and counseling teams has a copy, and all the congregants to boot! Also, buy a copy for any and every library that you know: public, seminary, school, college, church. Of course, they will be grateful for another reference book but they will not know that those who open its pages will not be able to stop reading it like a normal library book, and that they will encounter Father, Son and Holy Spirit.

You can hear the gentleness but the persuasiveness of a pastor's voice as you read it. It is grounded in scripture, and it is not simply about definitions but about applications. You will be counseled and you will receive ministrations of the Holy Spirit as you follow each letter.

A word-dictionary teaches you about the meanings of a word, but it does not necessarily help you to speak well. Of course, this book will exposit the meaning of the words related to healing, but it will also make things well – both by bringing you healing as you respond to its scriptural insights and pastoral instructions, and also by equipping you as one who can bring Jesus' healing to others.

This is no ordinary A-Z dictionary. This is a compendium of truth that will bring you to the person and presence of Jesus, the ultimate Alpha and Omega when it comes to our salvation, our healing and our deliverance. But enough…Get reading and discover what I found!

Stuart McAlpine
February 2016

INTRODUCTION

Jesus started His healing and deliverance ministry 2,000 years ago, and it is wonderful to find that He is still setting people free today. At Ellel Ministries, we have been privileged to see God bring true healing in many precious lives since the ministry was founded in 1986. We have experienced both successes and failures, learning and growing with each. From all that has been seen and learned, the ministry now offers teaching, founded on the Word of God, available through hundreds of courses and retreats around the world. These are designed to give increasing understanding of the biblical principles that bring God's healing into damaged lives. In fact, we believe that disregarding the counsel of God in the Bible both does us harm in this life and affects our eternal well-being. It is therefore the aim of Ellel Ministries, and indeed the aim of this book, to teach only what the Bible teaches and to share from our experience of implementing that teaching in practice.

We have discovered that both understanding and applying the truth of important concepts from the Word of God, such as forgiveness, freedom from generational iniquity and soul-ties, restoration from inner brokenness and dissociation, deliverance from spiritual captivity, and many other significant principles, have been the gateway to God's healing into countless lives.

This book has been written to provide concise definitions and explanations of significant biblical words, concepts and principles which have become part of the teaching and tool-kit of Ellel Ministries' teams around the world. Of course, such a tool-kit on its own is useless without the divine expertise and direction of the Holy Spirit, but just as Jesus taught his first disciples the keys to healing as He walked this earth, so we, His disciples today, also need to explore these concepts so that we are ready to be faithful apprentices under the Master's direction.

INTRODUCTION

The definitions given in this book are not intended to match the precision of a dictionary. Instead, they are designed to be of practical relevance to those who want to understand how God heals lives today. If you are seeking for techniques in Christian healing, you will not find them in this book. If, however, you want to get a basic grasp of the meaning and application of particular biblical concepts, which are dynamic keys to wholeness and freedom, then the pages of this book will provide a useful reference and guide to the practice of Christian healing and deliverance.

Each entry in this book comes with a short definition developed out of the teaching, a further explanation of the meaning and some biblical references to anchor the principle described. Where appropriate, there are also a few lines on how the healing of Jesus can be received today for the particular issue being considered. Along with the written explanations, there are some simple illustrations. We know that a picture can often bring revelation, even better than words, and I am indebted to Gillian for her creative pictures.

When Jesus defeated Satan on the cross, He opened the prison doors that were constraining our lives, so giving us the opportunity to find freedom and restoration from all the damaging effects of sin and spiritual captivity. It was a finished work of liberation from the vicious *ruler* of this world, and it is for all those who will acknowledge Jesus as the perfect *Savior* of this world.

> Isaiah 49:9... I will say to the prisoners, "Go free!" and to those who are in darkness, "Come out to the light!" They will be like sheep that graze on the hills ... (GNB)

In a nutshell, for each believer, the healing and deliverance ministry of Jesus is the important journey through those open doors into the abundant life which He came to give us. When someone has lived in the twilight world of a prison for many years it can be hard to have the full understanding of how to walk, and even the courage to move at all, from what is known into what is unknown.

Discarding the familiar routines of an imprisoned life can take time. There is a perverse comfort in hanging on to something of a long-standing identity, however wrong it may have been. We may need help from fellow-believers who are able to point out the path to freedom and to encourage us to shed the constraints of the past.

xiv

INTRODUCTION

There is an enemy who desires to keep us in the dark, but Jesus is ready to take our hand and lead us into increasing light. He often uses those of His followers who have already walked something of this challenging pathway to give support to those who are taking early steps. Jesus tells Peter to strengthen his brothers once he has discovered for himself more of the pathway of faith.

> Luke 22:31–32... Simon, Simon! Listen! Satan has received permission to test all of you, to separate the good from the bad, as a farmer separates the wheat from the chaff. But I have prayed for you, Simon, that your faith will not fail. And when you turn back to me, you must strengthen your brothers. (GNB)

It is to provide a little of this assistance that this book has been written, in order that the blessings of our covenant relationship with God can be increasingly enjoyed by all those who are seeking, or helping others, to move further into wholeness and freedom.

A-Z GUIDE
to the
Healing Ministry

Aaronic Blessing – words that Aaron and his sons were commanded, by God through Moses, to speak in blessing over the children of Israel.

It seems appropriate to start this alphabetical list, of topics associated with the healing ministry of Jesus, with these powerfully healing words. God chose to speak these over His covenant people, through those He called to be ministers of His blessing. In the Body of Christ today, we can both speak and receive these words, because they are exactly God's heart for every one of His children. Many people are looking for inner peace. As we seek truth and resolution for some of the disorder in our lives, we can rest in the certain assurance that such a desire for peace is fully in line with God. He is our heavenly Father and He is for us. He is carefully watching over us and His face shines with joy as we surrender our lives to Him.

> Numbers 6:22–26… Then the LORD spoke to Moses, saying, "Speak to Aaron and to his sons, saying, 'Thus you shall bless the sons of Israel. You shall say to them:
> 'The LORD bless you and keep you;
> The LORD make His face shine on you, And be gracious to you;
> The LORD lift up His countenance on you, And give you peace.'
> "So they shall invoke My name on the sons of Israel, and I then will bless them." (NASB)

Abdication (Abdicate) – unwillingness to walk in a position of God-given authority.

God's plan is that there should be structures within human relationships. They are there to give provision and protection for all those who walk in obedience to Him. Under the New Covenant, the foundational structure is the Body of Christ, but there is also a need for rightful order within marriage, within families and in nations. This is a very important part of how God provides spiritual covering over people's lives.

Within the Body of Christ, as well as in families and nations, certain people are called to exercise positions of God-given authority for the benefit of all, not least in the role of leadership.

> Romans 12:4-8... For just as we have many members in one body and all the members do not have the same function, so we, who are many, are one body in Christ, and individually members of one another. Since we have gifts that differ according to the grace given to us, each of us is to exercise them accordingly: if prophecy, according to the proportion of his faith... he who leads, with diligence. (NASB)

> Romans 13:1... Every person is to be in subjection to the governing authorities. For there is no authority except from God, and those which exist are established by God. (NASB)

Unfortunately the sin of humankind has distorted God's intentions of delegated authority, particularly with leaders, resulting sometimes in crushing control and sometimes in dangerous abdication. The best-known biblical example of this withdrawal from rightful responsibility is in the record of Ahab, who was unwilling to walk fully in his ordained position as a husband and king, frequently deferring to his wife Jezebel, who increasingly adopted powerful and even demonic control in the affairs of the royal household and of the nation of Israel.

> 1 Kings 19:1-2... Now Ahab told Jezebel all that Elijah had done, and how he had killed all the prophets with the sword. Then Jezebel sent a messenger to Elijah, saying "so may the gods do to me and even more, if I do not make your life as the life of one of them by tomorrow about this time." (NASB)

> 1 Kings 21:7... Jezebel his wife said to him, "Do you now reign over Israel? Arise, eat bread, and let your heart be joyful; I will give you the vineyard of Naboth the Jezreelite." (NASB)

The serious lesson today from the story of Ahab and Jezebel is that the avoidance of rightful leadership responsibility in families and churches can open a door to destructive control by others who may show powerful human ability, but not with God's anointing. Many husbands and fathers draw back from exercising rightful authority, looking for a "quiet life", but this has led to much frustration and disorder in families, just as in the royal household of Ahab.

Of course, God is not looking for tyrannical leadership. Every ship on the high seas needs a captain willing to hear all the advice of wise crew-members, but then able to take the full responsibility of giving clear direction. Perhaps it is time in your family or church to bring confession, repentance and forgiveness to the Lord, with regard to the issue of abdication, so that His order can be restored, allowing the fullness of His protection and provision.

See Authority, Body of Christ, Control, Headship, Jezebel, Marriage, Order

Abandonment (Abandon) – See Isolation

Abortion (Abort) – premeditated killing of a child between conception and birth.

We will refer to a fetal death which happens unexpectedly as a miscarriage. By contrast, in this section, we are considering the death of a fetus which happens by choice.

The life of every human being begins at conception. God forms us in our mother's womb by combining the physical matter of this earth with the breath of life from Himself.

> Zechariah 12:1... Thus declares the LORD, who stretches out the heavens, lays the foundation of the earth and forms the spirit of man within him. (NASB)

A fetus may not have intellectual awareness in the womb but his or her human spirit is present and is very well able to engage with the spiritual environment. For example, the Bible records that John the Baptist experienced this when he was still in the womb of his mother, the day Mary arrived, carrying Jesus in her womb (Luke 1:44).

The precious nature of our existence in the womb is nowhere better described than in Psalm 139. Our life is given by God, and only He can rightfully take it away.

> Psalm 139:13–16… You created every part of me; you put me together in my mother's womb. I praise you because you are to be feared; all you do is strange and wonderful. I know it with all my heart. When my bones were being formed, carefully put together in my mother's womb, when I was growing there in secret, you knew that I was there – you saw me before I was born. The days allotted to me had all been recorded in your book, before any of them ever began. (GNB)

To destroy a life, at any time, in rebellion to the will of God, gives significant authority to the enemy. When a womb is the place of such a death, there is license for the enemy to cause barrenness rather than fruitfulness in the future. An abortion brings the opportunity for spiritual defilement, not just to affect the mother's womb, but also affecting any future children formed there. Without the resolution that comes through Jesus, there can be demonic activity, such as a spirit of death affecting the womb in the future (Hebrews 2:14). There can even be situations where the unresolved presence of the human spirit of the aborted child can still affect the womb. Jeremiah describes this very thing. In his desperate anguish, Jeremiah spoke out a (wrong) desire to have been aborted, describing how this would have left him always in his mother's womb, spiritually abandoned.

> Jeremiah 20:15,17… Cursed is the man who made my father very happy with the news that he had just become the father of a baby boy. … If only he had killed me while I was in the womb. Then my mother would have been my grave, and she would have always been pregnant. (GW)

Thankfully, God longs to restore us and bring His healing and deliverance from every defilement of the past. If we have had an abortion, we can repent of taking this innocent life and receive God's complete forgiveness and cleansing from every power of darkness, such as an unclean spirit of death. We should then commit the human spirit of any life lost in the womb safely into the hands of Jesus, so that God's order is restored to the mother. Some people even find it helpful to ask the Lord what name to give the child, as he or she is given over to Jesus.

If we have given agreement to someone else's abortion, we can also know God's forgiveness and healing, through repentance. If we have been the subject of an attempted abortion, or we were born after the loss of a previous sibling in the womb, we can forgive those who were involved, seek the Lord for healing from all damage caused, and pray for release from any harmful soul-tie that might exist with the aborted child.

See Authority, Birth, Conception, Contraception, Fruitfulness, Full Fragmentation, Identity, Miscarriage, Soul-tie

Abuse (Abusive) – wrongful use of a person in a way that disrespects their true value and identity in God.

Abuse can be physical (such as violent attack), verbal (such as speaking threats), emotional (such as demanding sympathy), sexual (such as lustful behavior), or spiritual (such as false prophecy).

The Bible is clear that each one of us was born with an intrinsic and precious value, in which God delights, irrespective of our behavior. God does not love our sin, but He sees us as being of such immense value that He was willing to give the life of Jesus as payment for the redemption of every human being (1 John 4:10). When that value is rubbished through the words and actions of others (Mat 5:22), there can be deep wounding in the heart of those so treated. We were made to be cherished and protected like a priceless work of art, so abuse is shocking, painful and destructive, like a knife slashing the canvas of a magnificent painting.

Abuse is frequently associated with wrong control in a relationship, holding the victim into an emotional and spiritual bondage to the abuser. It is the realm of the bully. It causes deep distress and dysfunction in many lives, especially where the abuse has happened to vulnerable,

and often young, people, by those who should have been a means of protection rather than abuse.

Neglect can be as abusive as active harm. It is very destructive to the human heart to experience a careless and unsafe environment, in particular where parents have not provided the physical and spiritual protection over the children that God has entrusted to them. Withholding rightful love from the hungry heart of a child, constant disapproval, or thoughtless dismissal of gifting can lead to a distorted sense of value and identity, Even if the damage we sustain is unintended, like Mephibosheth (2 Samuel 9:8), it can leave us believing as he did, that we are no better than a dead dog!

As we forgive those who have been the source of abuse in our lives, not least where the offenders were our parents, there is a wonderful opportunity for healing through the covenant relationship which God has now renewed with all His children.

> Psalm 27:10… My father and mother may abandon me, but the LORD will take care of me. (GNB)

However serious the abuse has been in our lives, God has made a way to bring us into a new place of comfort and self-respect. He wants no issue to remain wrongly hidden. The abused person often feels shame, despite the fact that the wrongdoing lies with the abuser. God wants to cleanse us from any defilement and to lift all that shame from our lives. He wants us to know deep in our hearts the true value and identity which He has placed upon us. He says that we are His children, and well worth even the death of His Son on the cross.

See Affirmation, Belief, Control, Disapproval, Human Spirit, Identity, Neglect, Shame, Value

Acceptance (Accept, Acceptable) – acknowledgment of personhood and value.

In this world, the best that we usually experience is *conditional* acceptance, which declares that we are only acceptable, or wanted, if we meet the requirements or standards of those who are of significance in our lives. Actually, this is just a form of rejection. However, the way of the Kingdom of God is *unconditional* acceptance which declares that I am wanted, loved and valued simply for who I am, despite my unrighteousness and despite the needs I might have for healing or deliverance.

> Romans 5:8... But God demonstrates His own love toward us, in that while we were yet sinners, Christ died for us. (NASB)

Unconditional acceptance is what God designed us to experience from the earliest moments of our life, but it has been lost through humankind's rejection of the covenant relationship which God intended He would have with humanity. True acceptance is a place of deep security and a sense of belonging within His family. This can only be fully restored in the life of a believer through the witness of the Holy Spirit, who brings revelation to the human spirit about God's acceptance of us.

> Romans 8:15–16... For the Spirit that God has given you does not make you slaves and cause you to be afraid; instead, the Spirit makes you God's children, and by the Spirit's power we cry out to God, "Father! my Father!" God's Spirit joins himself to our spirits to declare that we are God's children. (GNB)

Walking in a Kingdom of God lifestyle of unconditional acceptance means accepting God as He really is, believing that He is full of truth and grace, exactly as demonstrated in the life of Jesus. It means accepting that God accepts us just as we are, despite our need of healing and cleansing. It means accepting ourselves just we are, embracing even those parts of our lives which have seemed inadequate or shameful, whilst still acknowledging the need to deal with our wounding and sin. It means accepting others just as they are, whilst being willing to help them to change more and more into the likeness of Christ. If we hold back the outflow of acceptance from our lives, it will stagnate the inflow! Acceptance is fundamental and essential to all relationships in God's family.

See Belief, Belonging, Identity, Inadequacy, Mindset, Personhood, Rejection, Relationship, Unconditional, Wounding

Accident – sudden and unexpected incident, which can cause damage to any part of our being.

Those who have suffered an accident may have received excellent medical care, but sometimes there is a lingering issue of disorder due to an inner unhealed place, which can only be fully restored by Jesus. Any unresolved damage in the soul and human spirit will inevitably be reflected in the physical body, in particular where there is inner brokenness or fragmentation caused by the sudden impact and shock of the accident.

> Proverbs 17:22... A joyful heart is good medicine, But a broken spirit dries up the bones. (NASB)

Jesus said that He came to bind up the brokenhearted (Luke 4:18). As we seek His healing, we need to bring the full truth of an accident before Him, acknowledging where there has been any sin by ourselves or by others. We need to forgive those who carried any of the responsibility for the accident, and receive God's forgiveness for any way that we might have personally been outside His covenant protection through our own sin.

Also, it can sometimes be helpful to recognize that defiled ground can be, at least in part, a cause of hostile spiritual activity. Sin in the past at a particular location, for example by destroying a life, will spiritually pollute the land (Numbers 35:33). When ground is defiled spiritually, this can give the enemy a right to hold that ground in a state of spiritual hostility, such that the land itself seems to be against us (Leviticus 18:26–28). Motorists are familiar with the concept of *accident blackspots*, which sometimes exist for no obvious practical reason.

When we have been injured in an accident which occurred on spiritually defiled ground, healing begins with our forgiveness of those who have sinned on the land in the past. Deliverance from territorial spirits may be an important part of the process of healing.

Then we can bring to the Lord any inner part of our lives that has been shattered by the trauma of the accident, asking for His deliverance from any hold that the enemy might have had on the place of brokenness. In the name of Jesus, we can ask for healing and declare a binding up of all that was broken in the soul and the human spirit, and so discover a new wholeness and freedom in every part of our body.

See Binding Up, Brokenness, Full and Partial Fragmentation, Human Spirit, Reclaim Ground, Trauma, Wholeness

Accusation – See Blame

Addiction (Addict, Addicted, Addictive) – unhealthy dependence on something.

The *something* could be, for example, drug abuse, smoking, gambling, television, exercise, sex or electronic games, and is likely to be rooted in a desire to find peace, comfort, escape or pleasure. However, what may start as a pursuit for euphoria can quickly become a desperate quest simply for relief from inner distress. The Bible warns us of the classic problem of the misuse of alcohol, which can destroy our effectiveness in the Body of Christ:

> 1 Timothy 3:8... Deacons likewise must be men of dignity, not double-tongued, or addicted to much wine or fond of sordid gain (NASB)

Addiction has been described as the enemy hijacking the brain's God-given 'feel-good' reward system (which rewards behaviors beneficial to the body). This reward system releases important chemicals such as dopamine. When control of some aspect of our being is handed over to an addictive practice, the hold on our lives will be a combination of chemical, emotional and spiritual bondage.

Secular help for addictions, whilst seeking to manage the dependence, often fails to recognize and deal with the roots of deep inner-healing needs, as well as the issues of powerful spiritual bondage. There is an ongoing worldwide debate in the treatment of many addictions as to whether the issue is primarily one of disease or of wrong behavior. In fact it is best seen as both of these, strengthened by the spiritual rights given to the enemy.

Humankind has always looked for a painkiller. Pain is the consequence of a wound in the body. It can come from physical, emotional or spiritual disorder. The main cause of wounding in the life of humanity is sin, whether done by us or to us. There are many kinds of wrong dependencies, ranging from pornography to heroin, and these can so easily seem to comfort our inner needs. In fact, heroin comes from opium, a substance which has been used for thousands of years as a painkiller.

Without God, we desperately try to deal with the pain, to kill it or to dull it, by any means at our disposal, including a dependence on substances or behaviors which we believe will help us to cope (Proverbs 23:35). More often than not they leave us feeling much worse than we did at the start, once the immediate effects have worn off. Unfortunately, many of these self-applied coping mechanisms are costly, sinful, shameful and sometimes illegal.

Prescribed medication from the doctor can manage pain for a while, and we thank God for this relief, but there is only one ultimate painkiller, Jesus Christ, who can get to the heart of humanity's problem in the human spirit and bring a permanent solution. Healing from addictions comes by fully facing the reality of the dependency issue, receiving the Lord's help and comfort for the underlying issues of insecurity, and also by making a powerful will choice in agreement with God (Mark 14:36). In Christ Jesus we can be completely dependent on the Father for every need in our lives, allowing us to be released from the soul-ties to those who have been our 'addiction family', such as fellow drug users or those providing the content of a pornographic internet site.

Any demonic hold of the enemy on all the distorted physical systems of the body will need to be specifically addressed and removed. This is necessary because our internal adjustment (tolerance) to the addictive practice will not just have been physical and emotional but also spiritual.

See Alcoholism, Coping Mechanisms, Deliverance, Drug Abuse, Gambling, Pain, Pornography, Soul-tie, Smoking

Adoption (Adopt) – parenting of a child by those who are not the biological parents.

This happens for many different reasons, for example death of parents, children given away by unmarried mothers, or children taken away by authorities who deem the parents unfit. Being given away under such circumstances was not God's intention for the nurture of children, but He knows about every dysfunction of human existence that has led to adoption and to the resulting problems that can so often occur. Our God is a redeemer who can restore lives from whatever has affected us in the past.

Moses was given away, and struggled with the conflicting identities which related to his adoptive and natural families (Exodus 2:11–14). Yet God called him, even in the place of his wounding, to walk in a remarkable destiny of leading the children of God out of slavery.

The pain of deep rejection is very common in those who have been adopted, even where all concerned have acted with the very best of intentions. This is because the separation from a biological mother and father, particularly at an early age, is a trauma to the human spirit, affecting the foundations of security and identity within the life of a child.

From the moment of conception to the critical time of being taken away from a birth-mother, the emotional atmosphere around a baby – for example, fear, deception or shame, as well as abusive words or violence – will all have a significant effect on the spiritual well-being of the child. This will often bring rejection, anxiety, insecurity, and a likely vulnerability to the effects of generational iniquity.

Whilst not minimizing the huge challenges of being raised by adoptive parents, many other people have also been effectively orphaned as a result of extremely poor or abusive parenting. In fact, the deep needs for true spiritual protection and nurture have not been adequately met in countless lives. However, God has made a way for adoption into His family for every human being who responds to His call (Ephesians 1:5). It is the answer to all the pain of absent or abusive parenting.

> Psalm 27:10... For my father and my mother have forsaken me, but the LORD will take me up. (NASB)

As we forgive those who have knowingly or unknowingly caused us pain through the process of earthly adoption, and as we make a choice to let Father God meet our deepest needs of self-worth and identity through His divine adoption (Ephesians 1:3–6), He can transform the security of our hearts and lead us into the fullness of a destiny which He has prepared, just as He did for Moses.

See Family, Father, Identity, Mother, Orphan Spirit, Rejection, Security

Adultery (Adulterous) – breaking of a marriage covenant through sexual intimacy with someone who is not the marriage partner.

The joining of a man and woman in sexual intercourse is not only a very intimate union of two people but a profound demonstration of the marriage covenant. When such intimacy takes place outside the boundaries of this covenant, there will be emotional and spiritual damage in the lives of those involved.

> Malachi 2:15... Hasn't he made the two of you one? Both of you belong to him in body and spirit. And why has he made you one? Because he was looking for godly children. So guard yourself in your spirit. Don't break your promise to the wife you married when you were young. (NIRV)

Throughout the Bible, God has also used the word *adultery* to describe the worship of false gods by the people with whom He had entered into covenant, just as a husband covenants with his wife (Jeremiah 3:8). In both worship and sexual union there is a giving of ourselves to another that touches the core of our identity, the human spirit.

Breaking covenant brings disorder, but thankfully Jesus has stepped into this world with the opportunity for forgiveness, cleansing and release from the ungodly soul-ties that result from the wrongful joining of our body, soul and spirit to another person, or even to false gods.

The world today increasingly dismisses the seriousness of the sin of adultery. Jesus neither belittled the sin nor held in condemnation the woman caught in adultery in John chapter 8. If we truly confess the breaking of the marriage covenant, Jesus is able to pay the cost of sin on our behalf and release us to walk in freedom from all defilement.

> John 8:10–11... [Jesus] straightened up and said to her, "Where are they? Is there no one left to condemn you?" "No one, sir," she answered. "Well, then," Jesus said, "I do not condemn you either. Go, but do not sin again." (GNB)

There is healing also for those betrayed. As we choose to forgive the one who has broken covenant, God's comfort can come to the deep places of our wounding. It will take time but, where appropriate, and by the grace of God, trust and confidence can be restored if there is determination and humility by both husband and wife.

See Betrayal, Covenant, Marriage, Sexual Sin, Soul-tie

Affirmation (Affirm) – supportive words or actions which edify the heart of the one receiving.

To those people who were open to the teaching of Jesus, as He walked the earth, every word was life-giving, always affirming the God-given identity and destiny of the hearers, to know that they were God's precious children, despite the reality of sins and wounds.

In the same way, God calls us to be instruments of His affirmation to one another. For example, one of the most important things that a father can do for his son or daughter is to speak into their hearts his approval of their God-given identity. Our heavenly Father demonstrated this in a powerful way at the baptism of Jesus.

> Luke 4:22... and the Holy Spirit descended upon Him in bodily form like a dove, and a voice came out of heaven, "You are My beloved Son, in You I am well-pleased." (NASB)

These words were intended to be heard and replicated by every earthly family which seeks to walk in God's ways. Much damage can be done to the human spirit, not least to sexual identity, when a father, in particular, fails to affirm his children with rightful words of acknowledgment and encouragement. Our human spirit is like a tender plant needing to be fed and watered in order to flourish.

We need to forgive those who have failed to give the nourishment of affirmation to us, particularly as we grew from childhood into adulthood. Sometimes we may also need to confess that we have sought to make up for this lack in ungodly ways. We can then ask our heavenly Father to supply our hearts with all that was missing in our growing years. It is never too late for God's redeeming work of affirmation in our lives.

Zephaniah 3:17... The LORD your God is with you; his power gives you victory. The LORD will take delight in you, and in his love he will give you new life. He will sing and be joyful over you ... (GNB)

See Approval, Disapproval, Human Spirit, Identity

Aggression – See Violence

Agreement (Agree) – unity of thoughts, words, actions or beliefs between two or more people.

There is spiritual power when two or more followers of Jesus agree on earth.

> Matthew 18:19... Again I say to you, that if two of you agree on earth about anything that they may ask, it shall be done for them by My Father who is in heaven. (NASB)

The Greek word, translated *agree* in this verse, literally means to be in *symphony* or *harmony* with one another, as in an orchestra. This is only possible when each person is following the same spiritual director. When we agree with one another, following the Holy Spirit, there is an impartation from God of spiritual authority and power which brings supernatural change to the issues of life. Unity of belief and purpose, in accordance with God's Word, brings the extraordinary command of His blessing and a rightful bonding within His family.

> Psalm 133... Behold, how good and how pleasant it is For brothers to dwell together in unity! It is like the precious oil upon the head, coming down upon the beard, Even Aaron's beard, Coming down upon the edge of his robes. It is like the dew of Hermon Coming down upon the mountains of Zion; For there the LORD commanded the blessing – life forever. (NASB)

But we need to take care! The enemy is always prowling with the desire to devour our lives, not least by uniting us in wrongful agreement with others in pursuit of sinful behavior. A conspiracy to commit a crime is recognized, even in secular law, as a very powerful instrument of social disorder. An agreement to sin can give significant authority to the enemy and bring bondage through the wrong relationship. We will need to seek the Lord for His forgiveness and for freedom from any such agreements which have been contrary to His commands, for example in ungodly fraternities (brotherhoods) or lifestyle groups.

See Bond, Bondage, Conspiracy, Iniquity, Soul-tie

Alcoholism (Alcohol Abuse, Alcoholic) – unhealthy dependence on alcohol.

Although alcohol is a God-given substance, useful as a disinfectant and commonly provided as an aid to celebration, even by Jesus at the wedding of Cana (John 2:1–11), it has always been misused by some people in order to escape from reality.

> Proverbs 23:29–35… Who has woe? Who has sorrow? … Those who linger long over wine … "They struck me, but I did not become ill; They beat me but I did not know it. When shall I awake? I will seek another drink." (NASB)

Unhealthy use of alcohol (Titus 2:3) is destructive to the body, distorting to the mind, will and emotions. It is divisive in families and it steals finances, self-worth and integrity. Organizations such as *Alcoholics Anonymous* have always advocated the need for a higher spiritual authority to overcome the deep hold of excessive alcohol use in people's lives. The highest spiritual authority that exists, and the only one that will ensure true freedom, rather than just management of this issue, is the authority of Jesus Christ.

When someone who has become too dependent on alcohol for comforting the inner distress of their lives faces the truth of their problem and the truth of the answer that lies in Jesus, then His grace and healing can restore all that has been damaged and stolen through alcoholism.

See Addiction, Coping Mechanism, Shame, Truth

Allergy (Allergic) – over-response from the body's immune system, when it is exposed to something which is harmless to most people.

Many people these days are seriously affected by substances which should be harmless, such as pollen and food proteins. The body's amazing immune system was designed by God to protect us against

harmful organisms, by detecting any threat and producing defensive antibodies. Throughout the Bible, God makes it clear that His covenant promises with humankind include our protection, both spiritually and physically (Exodus 15:26).

So how has this part of His system of protection got out of balance? God has certainly not broken His covenant with humankind, but unfortunately we have constantly separated ourselves from His protection. The immune system is God's way of ensuring that the countless organisms that exist around us and within us are not able to gain a harmful control over our lives. Interestingly, before the Fall in the Garden of Eden, God gave humankind authority over every other living thing (Psalm 8:6; Genesis 1:28).

A particular allergy may of course simply be rooted in a physical dysfunction in the body, but there is also the problem that humankind's sin and misuse of God's creation have upset God's order, and men and women find themselves subject to a hostile rule of spiritual darkness in this world (1 John 5:19). To counteract this rule, we will need to forgive those, including our ancestors, who have been the cause of this disorder. They may have worshipped creation (in fertility rites, for example) rather than the Creator (Romans 1:25), so giving the enemy a license to control our lives through allergic reactions to plants and animals.

We may need to confess our own sinful attitudes too. I remember the testimony of a lady who described how a long-standing allergic skin rash disappeared overnight when she brought to God the unforgiveness and bitterness she still felt about a betrayal that had occurred many years before. It is always worth asking the Lord what the roots are of any problems in our bodies with allergies.

See Covering, Foothold, Generational Iniquity, Reclaim Ground

Alternative Medicine (Alternative Healing or Therapy)
– medication or therapy which invokes a power to heal, which is not scientifically quantifiable or repeatable.

Also called complementary medicine or holistic medicine, such medical procedures are not regarded by the majority of doctors as sound practice, but are nevertheless gaining increasing general acceptance. The main question for Christians is whether the power being used is spiritually safe. False healing can be one of the deceptive and destructive activities of the enemy, if we seek an unseen power to heal which is not subject to the authority of Jesus.

Some alternative diagnostic methods and medicines have a very clear occult foundation, such as acupuncture, homeopathy, reflexology, reiki and iridology. The spiritual roots of other practices, such as aromatherapy, herbal medicine, chiropractic, osteopathy or applied kinesiology may not seem so clear. However, there should always be concern, for every follower of Jesus, as to what is the spiritual basis of any healing method, especially when the beliefs of the founding practitioners were completely contrary to biblical truth as, for example, with chiropractic.

If healing is sought from a spiritual source which is not consistent with the teaching of Jesus, the enemy can be given authority over the healing process and can hold the person in demonic bondage. Although there might be changes in the person's symptoms, this is achieved by use of an unclean spiritual power. Such false healing will block the true healing that God desires for our lives.

In God's view, the diagnosis of our spiritual condition needs the plumb line of His truth against which to compare the righteousness of our lives. Many alternative treatments purport to diagnose spiritual imbalance as being the cause of sickness, even using instruments like a pendulum to divine the problem. We need to keep to God's instruction for spiritual diagnosis, to acknowledge His view of sin and to follow His way of true restoration.

> Jeremiah 6:16... Thus says the LORD, "Stand by the ways and see and ask for the ancient paths, Where the good way is, and walk in it; And you will find rest for your souls." (NASB)

From the beginning of humanity's existence, we have searched for pathways of living that will lead to health and well-being. In fact, many alternative therapies have clear roots in an ancient Chinese philosophy called Taoism. The word *Tao* means the way. Jesus, by whom all things were created, predates even the most ancient of human philosophies.

He alone is *the* Way, *the* Truth and *the* Life. Praise God that the search for the good path is complete in Jesus, for those who follow Him.

See Deception, Discernment, Healing, Occult, Power, Sin, Spiritual

Ancestral Worship – worshipping or invoking the dead for the purpose of bringing well-being to the living.

This practice, still common in many cultures, is demonstrated through private devotions, public rituals and festivals, and particularly, but not exclusively, during funerals. Any reverence for the dead which involves communication of any kind with them opens a door in the spiritual realm in a way that God has forbidden for those in a covenant relationship with Him. The Bible refers to this as the sin of necromancy and such practice can intensify the effect of inherited generational iniquity.

> Deuteronomy 18:10–11… There shall not be found among you any one that maketh his son or his daughter to pass through the fire, or that useth divination, or an observer of times, or an enchanter, or a witch. Or a charmer, or a consulter with familiar spirits, or a wizard, or a necromancer. (KJV)

Ancestral worship has been prevalent in Eastern religions, animism, Native American and aboriginal beliefs. In addition, some historical individuals, such as Buddha and Confucius, have been a focus for devotion. As a consequence, the worshippers can be wrongly joined, not just to the demonic realm but also to the human spirits of dead people, whether those people are ancestors or the idolized founders of a false religion. God would not forbid His people to consult with the dead if it were not possible to do so. It is also worth noting that the worship of ancestors is often closely tied up with a distorted reverence of ancestral ground, opening the worshipers to the influence of territorial spirits.

Any wrong ties formed in the spiritual realm can make us vulnerable to being influenced by those to whom we become joined, whether these individuals are living people, family ancestors or deified historical figures. We can be affected spiritually, emotionally and even physically by the defilement of their lives. God wants us to be joined to the one who is life (Jesus) and not to be bound to dead people, nor to be controlled by demonic powers promoting the characteristics of the enemy, such as death, disease, false religion, pride, rejection and false duty.

See False Religion, Generational Iniquity, Human Spirit, Necromancy, Soul-tie

Angel (Angelic) – spiritual being created by God to serve Him.

The Hebrew and Greek words used in the Bible indicate that the primary role of angels is to be messengers for God, but they also appear in Scripture involved in worship (Revelation 5:11–12), teaching law (Hebrews 2:2), releasing punishment (Acts 12:23), guarding God's people (Psalm 34:7), working miracles (Acts 12:7) and assisting believers.

> Hebrews 1:14... What are the angels, then? They are spirits who serve God and are sent by him to help those who are to receive salvation. (GNB)

Some names and positions are specifically described, such as the warrior archangel (ruling angel) Michael and the messenger angel Gabriel, who famously came to Mary. Part of the angelic host joined Satan in his rebellion against God, and these fallen angels are active in the realm of spiritual darkness (Revelation 12:7–9; Jude 6). Fallen angels do not appear to be the same as the unclean spirits (Acts 23:8) which particularly seek to inhabit the lives of human beings, but it is clear that they occupy a destructive hierarchy of territorial and rebellious rule in the spiritual realms, an authority conferred on them through the sinfulness of humanity.

> Ephesians 6:12... For we wrestle not against flesh and blood, but against principalities, against powers, against the rulers of the darkness of this world, against spiritual wickedness in high places. (KJV)

It is not for us to call on angels, but we can always call on God, who clearly uses them in the affairs of humanity, including the task of bringing about His purposes of healing and deliverance. We should therefore not be surprised if sometimes the presence of holy angels is evident and significant, especially when there is a need to deal with unclean spirits, or when God sees particular need for our protection (Psalm 91:11).

See Powers of Darkness, Ruling Spirit, Unclean Spirit, Spirit, Satan

Anger (Angry) – a God-created emotion in response to perceived injustice, intended to motivate us to bring about a godly resolution.

Feeling angry when we experience something that is contrary to God's laws is not sin. The problem comes because we often fail to express that anger in a righteous way. Either we give license to destructive rage or, very commonly, we suppress the anger because it appears to be unacceptable and therefore do not allow it to motivate us toward resolving the injustice. Paul warns the Christians in Ephesus that these wrongful ways of dealing with anger can even give opportunity for the enemy to get a measure of control.

> Ephesians 4:26–27... Be angry, and yet do not sin; do not let the sun go down on your anger, and do not give the devil an opportunity. (NASB)

In this verse, we are being encouraged to express righteous anger, and indeed to be willing to confess those times when we have pushed such anger into the dark, for whatever reason. Of course, our carnal nature frequently presses us to be angry, not because God's laws are being broken, but rather because we are not getting our own way! This is unrighteous anger and needs to be confessed as such, but remember there is often a difficult mixture of anger within us, some godly and some ungodly. The good news is that God understands our anger. He knows the feeling (Psalm 103:8-9) and expresses it in righteous wrath when He sees human beings refusing to walk in truth.

> Romans 1:18... For the wrath of God is revealed from heaven against all ungodliness and unrighteousness of men who suppress the truth in unrighteousness ... (NASB)

Jesus expresses this same divine emotion when He sees His Father's house being used for commercial gain rather than communion with God (John 2:15–16). It is interesting that Jesus felt it important to release the rightful emotional and physical stress within His body by wielding a whip and overturning tables. When we are dealing with buried anger, even from a distant past issue, it can be extremely liberating to express the trapped emotions with spoken words and appropriate actions, such as beating our fists on a pillow or tearing up redundant telephone directories, while not harming others in the process.

It is very common for people to be carrying the hidden anger of childhood injustice. In fact, Paul warns parents to be careful that godly discipline of their children does not become a place of harshness or injustice (Ephesians 6:4), which can then remain unresolved into adulthood, even leading to inner disorders such as depression. If we experience outbursts of inappropriate anger today, it is very likely that there is some injustice from the past yet to be dealt with. It is sometimes easier to wrongly show some anger rather than to rightly face a deeper pain. If we are to find real freedom, we will need to forgive the people who provoked us to anger, and our wrongful suppression of emotions will need to be confessed so that true peace can be restored, and any grip by an unclean spirit of anger removed.

See Control, Denial, Depression, Emotion, Foothold, Injustice

Anointing (Anoint) – marking out of someone, or something, in order to denote the ownership and authority of God, for a purpose.

The Hebrew and Greek words for *anointing*, used in Scripture, mean to rub on oil.

This was the physical way by which the kings, priests and prophets of the Old Testament were frequently marked out as coming under the delegated spiritual authority of God, for the purpose of ruling over, or ministering to, His people. Such anointing was sometimes the passing of authority from one servant of God to another, and sometimes the establishing of a new position of divine authority.

> 1 Samuel 10:1... Then Samuel took a jar of olive oil and poured it on Saul's head, kissed him, and said, "The LORD anoints you as ruler of his people Israel. You will rule his people and protect them from all their enemies ..." (GNB)

Anointing with oil is also referred to in the New Testament as a powerful way of declaring the presence of God operating in people's lives, particularly in healing (James 5:14; Mark 6:13). However, it is, of course, the Holy Spirit, not the oil, that imparts such supernatural authority and power.

This is an important issue for followers of Jesus, if we are truly seeking to represent Him in this world. In other words, if we minister to others, in any capacity, without the anointing of God through the Holy Spirit, we are simply bringing human wisdom and human ability. Such ministry may be well-intentioned and may even be helpful, but it is not the supernatural intervention into this needy world that God has purposed through the Body of Christ. Jesus warns us, His disciples, that it is only when we have a wholly submitted relationship with God that we can be sure that He is truly the source of our spiritual authority when we minister to those in need (Matthew 7:21–23).

Jesus is revealed in Scripture as *the* Anointed One, the one to whom all authority has been given in heaven and on earth (Matthew 28:18). Only in Him can we receive and exercise true anointing. When we give our lives to Jesus, the Holy Spirit marks us out as God's children, declaring in the spiritual realm that we are men and women walking in a delegated, divine authority for specific purposes within the Body of Christ.

> 1 John 2:20... But you have an anointing from the Holy One, and you all know. (NASB)

This divine anointing and delegated authority begin as we are born again of the Holy Spirit, through acknowledging Jesus as Lord of our lives, but it becomes an empowered authority through baptism in the Holy Spirit, as He is given the freedom to operate *throughout* our lives rather than just *over* our lives. The gifts of the Holy Spirit can then flow through each of us for the common good of the whole Body of Christ.

If we have received Jesus as Lord of our lives, the anointing of God is surely upon us. We are marked out in the spiritual realm and known to belong to Him. He then waits for us to walk on in our lives under this divine anointing, increasingly manifesting the fruit, gifting and ministry of the Holy Spirit, as we allow Him to fill us and change us into the likeness of Christ. To be an effective member of the Body of Christ and to find the fullness of our destiny, we don't need *more anointing* but rather *more willingness* to walk in total submission to the commands of Jesus and therefore walk under the anointing that already does rest upon us. It is walking rightfully *under* authority that will make us effective to walk *in* authority (Luke 7:8; John 12:49).

See Authority, Baptism in the Holy Spirit, Fruit, Gifts of the Holy Spirit, Supernatural

Antichrist – demonic spirit or group of spirits counterfeiting the Holy Spirit.

This spirit is active in all false religion and is likely to be even more active in these end days of enemy deception. It has the characteristic of focusing attention on itself rather than on Jesus. For believers, recognizing the interaction and rightful order of the Godhead – Father, Son and Holy Spirit – is essential for discernment of what spiritual authority and power is being manifested in any particular situation.

> 1 John 2:22... Who is the liar but the one who denies that Jesus is the Christ? This is the antichrist, the one who denies the Father and the Son. (NASB)

In people's desperation for an experience of the supernatural, it can be surprisingly easy to be deceived and drawn by a demonic spirit, which may show remarkable power but which is not the Holy Spirit, the one who will act only in harmony with the Father and the Son. Jesus tells us how the Holy Spirit will always operate so that we need not be deceived. He will give glory to Jesus, not to Himself:

> John 16:13–15... When, however, the Spirit comes, who reveals the truth about God, he will lead you into all the truth. He will not speak on his own authority, but he will speak of what he hears and will tell you of things to come.
>
> He will give me glory, because he will take what I say and tell it to you. All that my Father has is mine; that is why I said that the Spirit will take what I give him and tell it to you. (GNB)

See Deception, Discernment, Holy Spirit, Power, Ruling Spirit, Trinity

Anti-Semitism (Anti-Semitic) – hostile prejudice against Jews.

God made a powerful pronouncement over Abraham and his descendants as He entered into covenant with this unique people-group, the Jews.

> Genesis 12:3... And I will bless those who bless you, And the one who curses you I will curse. And in you all the families of the earth will be blessed. (NASB)

Although the word *Semitic* can refer to a number of different people-groups, the phrase anti-Semitism most often relates to prejudice against Jewish people.

The Bible tells us that God chose the Hebrew nation to have a special covenant relationship with Him, declaring that He would be their God (Genesis 17:7), and He later gave them laws and commands by which to enjoy the blessings of His covenant (Deuteronomy 4:13).

He also promised land for His people to possess for all time (Genesis 17:8), a land from which they would actually be dispersed through disobedience, during the Assyrian and Babylonian exiles and again after the time of Jesus. It is a land to which they have returned in an extraordinary way, as we saw when God's promised restoration of the state of Israel (Ezekiel 36; 37) actually occurred in 1948.

Although they were dispersed for many centuries, the Jewish people retained a strong and unique identity. Many times, and in many nations, this has attracted extreme hostility and prejudice toward their culture, their success in business, their religious observance, their close-knit communities and, for some, their difference from Christianity. Down through history, Gentile (non-Jewish) believers have frequently been determined to reject the reality of the Jewish root of Christianity, the olive tree, into which they have been grafted (Romans 11:1–24).

Still today, anti-Semitism can be a very strong mindset, conscious or unconscious, in individuals, families and nations. Jews are, in fact, no more and no less sinful than many other people-groups, but they are frequently held in a place of deep enmity, empowered by unseen spiritual contention, for Satan knows that God will bring about His end-time purposes, in part, through this people to whom He has made unbreakable covenant promises (Zechariah 8:22–23).

As with anyone's wrongdoing, it is right to confront, with grace, the sin of individual Jews or even the nation of Israel, but to hold a

ANXIETY

place of judgment or hatred against the Jews, as a people-group, is to contend with the heart of God, and it can bring defilement, and even cursing, upon those whose hearts are bound by anti-Semitism. However, personal confession of these heart attitudes can bring powerful freedom and cleansing. If we are in a place of leadership of a family or Christian organization, it can often have a significant effect on the group if we confess and repent on their behalf.

See Covenant, Curse, Judgment, Reconciliation, Restoration

Anxiety (Anxious) – generalized fear which causes distress to the human spirit, soul and body.

The root meaning of the Greek word, translated as *anxiety* (or *worry*) in the New Testament, implies a divided mind, meaning that when anxiety gets a hold we find it difficult, like Martha, to be rightfully focused (or single-minded) on the issues of priority (Luke 10:41). Anxiety is the result of unresolved inner disorder (Psalm 139:23–24), which may be caused by past trauma, personal sin, lack of spiritual covering (Matthew 9:36), including lack of parental bonding, or even generational iniquity, together with the consequence of choices we make about how much we trust God in the present and for the future.

Jesus gives His disciples a clear command not to give a place to anxiety or worry, relating the issue to the question of where they have truly put their trust: is it in God, or in human provision?

> Matthew 6:24–25... You cannot be a slave of two masters; you will hate one and love the other; you will be loyal to one and despise the other. You cannot serve both God and money. This is why I tell you: do not be worried about the food and drink you need in order to stay alive, or about clothes for your body. After all, isn't life worth more than food? And isn't the body worth more than clothes? (GNB)

Freedom from anxiety is found in making radical new choices about trusting God for the future, as well as receiving His spiritual covering, healing and peace for the traumas and distress of the past. When forgiveness has been given to those who have been careless with our protection, and when God's forgiveness and covering has been applied to the exposed, wounded and defiled places in our soul and spirit, His

25

peace can transform our lives. Healing for any physical infirmity caused by anxiety comes as part of this overall freedom.

> Philippians 4:6–7... Do not be anxious about anything, but in every situation, by prayer and petition, with thanksgiving, present your requests to God. And the peace of God, which transcends all understanding, will guard your hearts and your minds in Christ Jesus. (NIV)

See Bonding, Covering, Fear, Human Spirit, Mind, Peace, Trust

Approval (Approve) – acknowledgment, acceptance and affirmation of a person, both in who they are and what they do.

Irrespective of our abilities, each one of us needs approval in the core of our being, received from those who are significant in our lives, just as essentially as a plant needs water. In fact, approval is one of the primary needs of our human spirit. This nurture should start from the first day we are known about in the womb, coming from parents who express unreserved delight in our existence. Even in the womb, we receive this parental approval into our human spirit, and we continue to need it, particularly throughout childhood and into adulthood. It deeply affects the spiritual wholeness of our lives. A father's approval of his children is of immeasurable importance in the development of a secure identity.

Of course, this is a fallen and imperfect world where disapproval of our innate personhood is sadly more common than approval. But God can redeem us from the wounding of this neglect in nurture. Despite all our faults and failings that need resolution, He truly approves of you and me.

> Zephaniah 3:17... The LORD your God is with you; his power gives you victory. The LORD will take delight in you, and in his love he will give you new life. He will sing and be joyful over you ... (GNB)

Out of a growing personal confidence in God's approval there comes an ability to help others. Within the Body of Christ, we can be powerful instruments of God's approval of each other as His children. We can help one another to deal with the pain of the past and increasingly know the certainty of our individual significance in God's family.

See Acceptance, Affirmation, Disapproval, Father, Identity, Significance

Atonement (Atone, Atoning) – reconciliation of God and humanity through the forgiveness of sin.

The Hebrew word for *atonement* describes God's spiritual covering of our lives. We need His covering to restore us from the damaging exposure that results from sin. The *Day of Atonement* described in Leviticus chapter 16 (known by Jews today as Yom Kippur) literally means the *Day of Covering*, a day each year when God, under the Old Covenant, recovered and cleansed His chosen people.

Sin separates us from God. The good news is that Jesus has made available for all humankind God's forgiveness for sin, by shedding His blood through His death on the cross. Jesus provided the final perfect sacrifice that had been foreshadowed by God's instructions to the Children of Israel.

> Leviticus 17:11... For the life of the flesh is in the blood, and I have given it to you on the altar to make atonement for your souls; for it is the blood by reason of the life that makes atonement ... (NASB)

It is because of this once-and-for-all atoning work of Jesus that there is today the opportunity for His followers to be reconciled to God and to His protective covering. This is the good news of the New Covenant.

We become spiritually exposed and damaged through our own sin and also through the sin of those who have carried responsibility for our lives (such as parents) and through the defiled spiritual inheritance that comes down to us from the iniquity of our ancestors. Because of the restoration of covering which Jesus' sacrifice offers us, we can be healed and delivered from the disorder in our lives caused by sin.

See Blood, Covenant, Cross, Covering, Forgiveness, Protection, Reconciliation

Attention Seeking – inappropriate drawing of attention to oneself, trying to fix the inner pain of rejection or disapproval, for example.

We were all made by God to know personal significance, as His covenant children. However, the disorder of this world has frequently sown a very different message into our hearts. Dysfunctional family life as children can leave many people emotionally and spiritually hungry for acknowledgment and affirmation.

> Luke 22:24... And there arose also a dispute among [the disciples] as to which one of them was regarded to be the greatest. (NASB)

In the absence of rightful relationships with others who truly appreciate their God-given identity and destiny, some people will do things, even extreme things, to receive the desired attention of others. This is done as a coping mechanism. Interestingly, some people say about their lives as children, that they would have preferred even the negative attention of a physically aggressive response from their father rather than the pain of constant neglect. When people are obviously looking for attention through inappropriate appearance or behavior, it will be helpful to encourage them to look at the root of unresolved emotional pain, rather than just confronting them with today's behavior, which can simply compound the underlying rejection.

It is particularly important, when relating to those needing help with this issue, to seek the Lord for a wise balance of truth and grace. Jesus was perfect in such ministry (John 1:14) and so the Holy Spirit will guide us if we ask Him. Jesus needed to challenge His disciples with the radical ways of His Kingdom, in regard to their need for significance. He might need to challenge and teach you and me.

> Luke 22:26b–27... but the one who is the greatest among you must become like the youngest, and the leader like the servant. For who

is greater, the one who reclines at the table or the one who serves? Is it not the one who reclines at the table? But I am among you as the one who serves. (NASB)

See Affirmation, Coping Mechanism, Disapproval, Humility, Neglect, Pain, Rejection

Attitude – position or view that we hold about ourselves or the world around us.

Formed out of our core beliefs, these views of life develop as we experience the good and the bad in relationships with other people and even with God. When such attitudes become fixed and begin to regularly control our behavior, an unconscious spiritual hold becomes established on our thinking, sometimes referred to as a mindset. God wants to reshape our attitudes so that we might increasingly reflect the image of Christ.

Philippians 2:4–5... do not merely look out for your own personal interests, but also for the interests of others. Have this attitude in yourselves which was also in Christ Jesus ... (NASB)

See Behavior, Belief, Core Belief, Mind, Mindset

Authority – given right or entitlement for a purpose.

Jesus sent out His disciples specifically with power (the ability) and authority (the right) to carry out the healing and deliverance ministry on His behalf.

Luke 9:1... And He called the twelve together, and gave them power and authority over all the demons and to heal diseases. (NASB)

Here's a simple picture to show the difference between authority and power. A quarry manager may have been given permission (authority) by the quarry owner to remove rock from the ground, and legally that's very important, but it is only when he has dynamite (power) that he is able to complete the task!

We need to realize that our enemy, Satan, cannot attack anyone without entitlement; he needs authority (or rights). God is in overall authority (Romans 13:1), but He also gave authority over the earth to humanity (Genesis 1: 26–28). When you obey someone, you give them authority over you (Romans 6:16). When we sin, both individually and as a group (family, nation etc), we are giving away the authority that God gave us, and giving it to the one we obey – Satan. Since Satan already has power, once he has authority as well, he can begin to steal, kill and destroy (John 10:10).

Because of the disobedience of humankind, considerable spiritual authority has been handed over to Satan and his powerful demonic realm. It is only by walking under the authority of Jesus (obeying Him), and also operating in the power distributed by the Holy Spirit, that disciples today have any opportunity to exercise a true healing and deliverance ministry (Luke 10:19).

Jesus makes it very clear that you cannot discern His true authority in the lives of His disciples by measuring the amount of power being manifested there, but rather by the fruit of His character being displayed in their lives.

> Matthew 7:20,22–23… So then, you will know them by their fruits. … Many will say to Me on that day, "LORD, LORD, did we not prophesy in Your name, and in Your name cast out demons, and in Your name perform many miracles?" And then I will declare to them, "I never knew you; DEPART FROM ME, YOU WHO PRACTICE LAWLESSNESS." (NASB).

When challenging the enemy's control in someone's life, it will be necessary to first remove the authority that was given to him through the activity of sin (whether that is sin by the person themselves or by others misusing their place of responsibility in the person's life). This should be done before tackling and evicting the powers of darkness, so that they cannot return. Acknowledging the truth of iniquity in our lives (the places where we are out of line with God) *exposes* the places where the enemy may have a measure of spiritual authority. Action such as repentance, forgiving others and receiving God's forgiveness for our own sin, *removes* that authority.

See Discernment, Control, Foothold, Forgiveness, Fruit, Power, Rebellion, Right

Badness (Bad) – not goodness.

When something is bad it is regarded as evil, wicked, worthless or faulty. The problem for some people is that through the abusive and wounding experiences of their lives, they have concluded, albeit unconsciously, that these words aptly describe their own core identity. Somewhere within, a voice declares, "I am bad." In the day-to-day of life, they may have dissociated from this unwanted inner place, but it can deeply affect their beliefs and behaviors. Jesus has come to declare something very different – that in Him, we are made perfect through and through. As we forgive those who damaged the person that God made us to be, and as we repent of our own sinful responses to the wounding caused by others, increasingly we can lay hold of our new faultless condition, through Him who is all goodness.

> 1 Thessalonians 5:23... May the God who gives us peace make you holy in every way and keep your whole being – spirit, soul, and body – free from every fault at the coming of our LORD Jesus Christ. (GNB)

See Belief, Evil, Goodness, Sin, Wrong

Baptism (Baptize) – symbolic washing, by dipping in water, to declare repentance and cleansing from sin.

For followers of Jesus, water baptism identifies the believer with the death and resurrection of Jesus, the means by which God's forgiveness and cleansing from sin has been achieved.

> Romans 6:4... By our baptism, then, we were buried with him and shared his death, in order that, just as Christ was raised from death by the glorious power of the Father, so also we might live a new life. (GNB)

Interestingly, early church writers, such as Hippolytus of Rome, tell us that it was common for baptism to follow a lengthy period of instruction, healing and deliverance, sometimes up the three years, so that immersion in water could truly represent the start of a new and cleaner life.

It is significant that Jesus, although completely sinless, considered it right to be baptized Himself, despite John's protests, so endorsing the ministry of the Baptist, completely humbling Himself before people and before His Father, and giving an example to those who would be His followers (Matthew 3:13–15).

See Baptism in the Holy Spirit, Cleansing, Repentance, Sin

Baptism (Baptize) in the Holy Spirit – immersion in the Holy Spirit, empowering followers of Jesus to walk under His anointing.

Jesus baptizes His disciples in the Holy Spirit, giving Him access to operate *throughout* our lives rather than just *over* our lives. The gifts of the Holy Spirit can then flow through each of us for the common good of the whole Body of Christ.

> Acts 1:5,8... John baptized with water, but in a few days you will be baptized with the Holy Spirit. ... when the Holy Spirit comes upon you, you will be filled with power, and you will be witnesses for me in Jerusalem, in all of Judea and Samaria, and to the ends of the earth. (GNB)

This immersion in the Holy Spirit does not just identify us with Jesus and His forgiveness (as with water baptism), but it releases opportunity for the authority, the power and the character of Jesus actually to be witnessed in us and through us. It is a time when our natural human ability comes into a new submission to supernatural, divine ability.

> John 16:14... He [the Holy Spirit] shall glorify me [Jesus]: for he shall receive of mine, and shall shew it unto you. (KJV)

Very often in the Bible, the baptism in the Holy Spirit was followed by the recipient speaking in tongues, one of the precious gifts of the Holy Spirit. However, this is not always mentioned, and should not be seen as the necessary proof of this divine impartation. In Acts 1:8 (above) we see that the primary effect of baptism in the Holy Spirit is an empowered desire and ability to be a true witness to Jesus, reflecting His presence in a way not previously possible, not least in the area of healing and deliverance. A simple picture of the meaning of this baptism is found in watching a teabag placed into hot water. The bag starts by just being in the water, but then the water fills the bag, and the full purpose of the teabag can be achieved!

Our individual walk with Jesus is, of course, very important, but it must be remembered that we are now part of His Body here on earth, *together* representing Him in bringing God's restoration to a very damaged world. It is the baptism in the Holy Spirit that enables each of us to effectively participate as gifted members of that Body.

> 1 Corinthians 12:12–13... For even as the body is one, and yet has many members, and all the members of the body, though they are many, are one body, so also is Christ. For by one Spirit we were all baptized into one body, whether Jews or Greeks, whether slaves or free, and were all made to drink of one Spirit. (NASB)

See Anointing, Fruit, Gifts of the Holy Spirit, Power, Supernatural

Barrenness (Barren) – lack of fruitfulness.

This can be a manifestation of the character of the enemy. Fruitfulness is a foundational purpose of God in the life of man (John 15:16; Genesis 1:28). It shows itself as the character of true believers becomes more like the character of God (Galatians 5:22), through the land He has given us to occupy becoming more productive (Leviticus 26:3–5), and through the procreation of children (Deuteronomy 28:4). All these are blessed through a covenant relationship with God. When our personal lives are out of line with God through sin, or where there is an inheritance of iniquity (Lamentations 5:7), the enemy has opportunity to steal fruitfulness, thus promoting his character, even in the extremely painful area of childlessness.

> Deuteronomy 28:18a... Cursed shall be the offspring of your body and the produce of your ground ... (NASB)

Through disobedience to the commands of God, the land of the Edomites was cursed with barrenness, even demonically sustained.

> Isaiah 34:10–11,14... The land [of Edom] will lie waste age after age... The LORD will make it a barren waste ... Wild animals will roam there, and demons will call to each other. The night monster will come there looking for a place to rest. (GNB)

But God redeems! When we confess our sin and the sin of our ancestors, His forgiveness removes the rights the enemy has to steal from us, and so our lives and our land can be cleansed, healed and restored to fruitfulness (Leviticus 26:40,42).

We cannot presume to know God's particular will about His giving of children, but when there is childlessness, the womb may need to be cleansed from any demonic power, such as a spirit of death. This might have been given rights to be there, for example, through generational sin such as abortion or other violent deaths. Praise God, we have seen many couples conceive a child after such prayer ministry.

See Fruitfulness, Generational Iniquity, Iniquity, Miscarriage

Behavior (Behave, Behaving) – expression of choices through words or actions.

These are affected by established beliefs and attitudes. Our behavior in any situation is the consequence of a decision of the will, but can frequently come, almost unconsciously, from the prejudice of our heart, which has been conditioned by the good and bad experiences of life, by seeing how others behave, and by the demands of our carnal nature.

As followers of Jesus, we are encouraged and enabled to respond to every situation in a completely different way from those who do not know Him. However, there will always be a conflict between the voice of the Holy Spirit and the pull of our carnality. Even Paul struggled with this battle.

> Romans 7:21... So I find this law at work: Although I want to do good, evil is right there with me. (NIV)

As we experience more wholeness and freedom, and as we let the fruit of the character of Jesus grow within us, through the work of the Holy Spirit, we can increasingly behave out of a heart that is secure in our true identity as children of God. The choice to behave in agreement with Him, rather than in agreement with the ways of the world, becomes more and more natural for us.

> Romans 12:2... Do not conform yourselves to the standards of this world, but let God transform you inwardly by a complete change of your mind. Then you will be able to know the will of God – what is good and is pleasing to him and is perfect. (GNB)

See Carnal Nature, Belief, Behavior Cycle, Mindset, Sin, Transformation

Behavior Cycle – repeated series of behaviors, typically coping mechanisms, which are triggered by a situation where we feel vulnerable, and lead to wrongful responses.

Largely driven by belief systems and mindsets which have been established since childhood, we tend to use these behaviors to seek safety and comfort, to cope with the real or imagined hostile situations of life.

Let's look at an example of a destructive behavior cycle. John has always suffered from deep rejection, since his father left home when John was five years old. One day, after problems all week at work, he experiences several people apparently ignoring or rejecting him at the Sunday morning church service and he heads home, angry and hurting. Despite pleas from his wife, he turns to alcohol and withdraws over the next couple of days, not able to work or sensibly communicate with the family, who give up trying to help, in despair over his hostility toward their attempts to intervene.

John feels increasingly lonely. He also feels angry, ashamed and even more rejected. Not until he is near breaking point, emotionally and physically, does he gradually start to return to his regular lifestyle.

Now he is carrying yet another buried measure of rejection and self-disgust.

This behavior cycle is not new to John, and both he and his family simply get used to waiting for the next time.

The good news is that God can set John free from this destructive cycle. He first needs to bring the root causes of rejection to Jesus, forgiving his father and letting the Lord bring His comfort and healing to his wounded soul and human spirit.

> Psalm 27:10... My father and mother may abandon me, but the LORD will take care of me. (GNB)

With the help of Christian friends and family, John then needs to make new choices, confessing wrong beliefs, mindsets and behaviors (2 Corinthians 10:5), particularly when he feels vulnerable. He then needs to agree with how God sees his value, rather than basing his beliefs about his value on how the world sometimes seems to treat him. The Bible says that he is unconditionally loved by the Creator of the universe, whatever today's experience might be. If he can break into the destructive behavior cycle with a choice to behave in response to God's truth, then the spiritual hold of the enemy's lies can be  severed and the downward spiral can be defeated. It may take time and determination, but Jesus truly came to set captives free.

> Galatians 5:1... It was for freedom that Christ set us free; therefore keep standing firm and do not be subject again to a yoke of slavery. (NASB)

See Acceptance, Behavior, Belief, Coping Mechanism, Defense Mechanism, Family, Mindset, Orphan Spirit

Belonging (Belong) – see Possession

Belief (Believe, Believing) – view or persuasion of the perceived truth about ourselves, other people, God and life in general.

These views are laid down through the experiences of life and can also be created through steps of faith. For example, following incidents of abuse as a small child, a person may conclude that being a victim will be the inevitable outcome of relationships throughout their life. This belief, which is at the core of their being, can mean that they increasingly face everything and everyone with a distorted attitude or mindset, expecting to be victimized.

Such core beliefs may start in the mind but they become established at a deeper level in the human spirit, and we are not always consciously aware of them. When these beliefs about ourselves, or about life, consistently disagree with the truth as God sees it, we are out of line with God and so we give the enemy a right to empower these wrong beliefs and thus hold us into his lies. Of course, the world is full of apparent solutions to humanity's quest for well-being through countless religious beliefs. For the believer in Jesus, every religious practice which denies that Jesus is the Son of God, as declared by the Bible, is a false religion based on false beliefs. What we have chosen to believe is a serious matter. C.S. Lewis wrote: *"You never know how much you really believe anything until its truth or falsehood becomes a matter of life and death to you."*[1]

Belief in Jesus is a step of faith which can become more and more established in our lives as we experience the truth of God's promises, together with the gifts and fruit of the Holy Spirit working through our lives. When we find ourselves acting out of core beliefs which have been in conflict with God, we can challenge these beliefs and replace them with choices to believe the truth of who Jesus is and the truth of what He says. For example, He says you are not destined to be a victim, but rather you are destined to be a child of God with all the significance and blessings of that amazing covenant relationship.

> Romans 8:16... The Spirit Himself testifies with our spirit that we are children of God ... (NASB)

See Attitude, Behavior, Faith, Mindset, Unbelief

Belief System – framework of linked core beliefs which determines the way we look at our lives and respond to the world around us.

God's intention is that we should receive His truth, even unconsciously, through the words and behaviors of rightful parenting, from the moment of conception. This would enable us to develop godly core beliefs to learn a plumb line of truth by which to live. The reality is that as we grow up, the example which we receive from significant people in our lives is not always consistent with God's truth. From each of these experiences, we learn a 'lesson' for life, out of which we form or reinforce certain core beliefs about ourselves and others. Out of these beliefs, we construct our personal belief systems in order to have a framework to explain the world in which we find ourselves.

> Proverbs 21:2a... Every man's way is right in his own eyes ... (NASB)

Our behaviors are often determined more by our hidden belief systems than by our conscious choices. The way we think about things comes out of past experiences which have often left hurts and wounds deep in our hearts. As a result, we have wrong beliefs about ourselves, others, and even God. For example, if our parents treated us in a way that was distant, unloving, harsh, critical or unpredictable, we can come to see ourselves as likely to be unimportant to anyone in authority.

Our beliefs are often deeply rooted and even unknown to our conscious thoughts. In other words, they are blind spots, causing us to unintentionally twist or distort the truth, using prejudice rather than reality about others or about ourselves. For example, we may think or say, *"That's just like a man!"* or *"That's just like a woman!"* or *"I'm useless, so I just won't bother"*, or *"I deserve to be punished."* These prejudices affect our ability to receive the acceptance, love, healing and security that God wants to pour into our hearts.

Unfortunately, we bring distorted beliefs such as these into our Christian life and we need the Holy Spirit to reveal them to our human spirit (1 Corinthians 2:11).

Paul encourages us to recognize and put to death all the worldly belief systems (Romans 12:2). Jesus also challenged His disciples in a similar way with a number of radical statements about how they should look at life in a completely different way, developing a new Kingdom belief system (Matthew 5:21–48).

> Matthew 5:43–44... You have heard that it was said, "YOU SHALL LOVE YOUR NEIGHBOR and hate your enemy." But I say to you, love your enemies and pray for those who persecute you ... (NASB)

See Attitude, Belief, Mindset, Truth

Believer – one who has a particular belief.

Of course, this could refer to any religious adherence, but the word is frequently used among Christians around the world (1 Timothy 4:10) to mean anyone who has declared a true belief in Jesus Christ, in accordance with the Bible.

> John 20:31... but these have been written so that you may believe that Jesus is the Christ, the Son of God; and that believing you may have life in His name. (NASB)

See Born Again, Christian, Disciple, Messianic Believer

Bereavement – loss of a friend or family member through death.

See Comfort, Death, Grief, Loss, Mourning

Bestiality – sexual intimacy with an animal.

Among those who have worked on a farm or kept pets, for example, there will be a few who have allowed their bodies to be sexually intimate with animals. Some people have got caught up in pornography involving sexual fantasy connected with animals. Such practices are contrary to the commands of God and seen in the Bible as a perverted sexual behavior.

> Leviticus 18:23... you shall not have intercourse with any animal to be defiled with it, nor shall any woman stand before an animal to mate with it; it is a perversion. (NASB)

It can be very shameful to admit such practice, but most of us have done something of a sexual nature that we regret today and would find it very hard to admit to another person. In fact, it can be the secrecy itself that the enemy uses to hold us in condemnation and gripped with a sense of shame and defilement. To tell our sin to one other person whom we trust, and to receive the Lord's complete pardon can be wonderfully liberating and healing.

> James 5:16... Therefore, confess your sins to one another, and pray for one another so that you may be healed. The effective prayer of a righteous man can accomplish much. (NASB)

Because of the defiling nature of any such relationship, it can be important to proclaim freedom from every spiritual tie with the animal, which the enemy has had the right to impose, as well as speaking out deliverance from all demonic power, including spirits of shame, and any spirits promoting characteristics of the animal. Bestiality is certainly not an unpardonable sin. Such practice will not have stopped God loving us, but He longs to cleanse us from all that has defiled His precious children in the past.

See Cleansing, Forgiveness, Sex, Sexual Sin, Shame, Soul-ties, Unclean Spirit

Betrayal (Betray) – breaking of trust in relationship.

This can cause deep wounding to the human spirit. The more we have depended on the faithfulness of another person, such as a family member, the more painful it is when their betrayal destroys that trust. The betrayal of children who have rightfully trusted an adult, particularly a parent, for protection and provision, can cause intense and lasting damage. It can be devastating when the covenant of marriage is broken by the treachery of a spouse in adultery, inevitably causing deep damage, even to the one responsible for the sin.

> Malachi 2:15b... Take heed then to your spirit, and let no one deal treacherously against the wife of your youth. (NASB)

Of course, those betrayed will be most hurt:

> Lamentations 1:2... All night long she cries; tears run down her cheeks. Of all her former friends, not one is left to comfort her. Her allies have betrayed her and are all against her now. (GNB)

Our receiving of God's healing from such wounding starts with the tough step of our forgiveness, probably repeated many times, for the one who broke the trust that we had placed in them. The comfort we need to truly repair the inner wounding of betrayal can only come from the one who knew extreme abandonment, betrayal by friends (Luke 22:48) and the injustice of undeserved crucifixion. Jesus died to bring healing to the human soul and spirit, bearing the deepest sorrows of our lives (Isaiah 53:4), so that we can come to a place of real inner peace, and find the relief of healed memories.

See Adultery, Covenant, Human Spirit, Marriage, Trust, Wound

Bible (Biblical) – compilation of writings from different human authors, so inspired by the Holy Spirit that when read under the guidance of the same Holy Spirit, it reveals the words of God for humankind.

> Psalm 119:160a… The sum of Your word is truth … (NASB)

In Paul's letter to Timothy, he confirms this truth, explaining how Scripture (at that time the Old Testament) was life-changing for those who followed the direction which God gives through His Word.

> 2 Timothy 3:16a… All Scripture is inspired by God and profitable for teaching, for reproof, for correction, for training in righteousness … (NASB)

The decision of which writings from the early church would be included in the New Testament as those deemed to be authentic, from the apostles, and truly consistent with the overall message of God's Word, was concluded by AD400. It is worth noting that the manuscript attestation for the New Testament is significantly better than for other historical works written about the same time.

God continues to speak into the lives of His children, through gifts of prophecy, knowledge and wisdom, but such revelation for today will never contradict His written word given to the Body of Christ on earth through the inspiration of the Holy Spirit. The writings of the Bible were not compiled to be a scientific manual, but to be the foundational source of truth for our spiritual and physical existence, explaining the necessity for a covenant relationship with the Creator of the universe.

The Bible remains the most widely read historical writing of all time. For the followers of Jesus, it speaks of the very meaning of life.

See Covenant, Discernment, Revelation, Truth, Word

Binding (Bind) – holding of something or someone subject to a particular spiritual control.

A policeman has the right to restrain a wrongdoer with handcuffs, provided that the policeman is acting in line with his delegated authority as an officer of the law. In a similar way, as followers of Jesus, we have been given authority to restrain the powers of darkness (Psalm 149:5–9), provided that we are acting in true obedience to Him who has already disarmed the enemy at the cross.

> Matthew 18:18… Truly I say to you, whatever you bind on earth shall have been bound in heaven; and whatever you loose on earth shall have been loosed in heaven. (NASB)

To fully expel the enemy in a particular situation, we must be able to deal with all the rights that were given to him through sin. Sometimes, where we do not have legal entitlement, this may not be an option. However, even in such cases, it will still be prudent to restrain his activity in order to bring a measure of spiritual safety. For example, many hotel rooms these days will be defiled by sexual sin, so ruling spirits will have license to put pressure and sexual temptation on those people who occupy the rooms. It is wise for Christians to speak out forgiveness to those who have been the cause of this defilement in the past and then bind any ruling spirits (to be restrained under the authority of Jesus), during the time of staying at the hotel, forbidding them to interfere with our peace.

It may also be helpful to bind particular demons and ruling spirits, as directed by the Holy Spirit, when ministering to fellow believers, while the roots and rights of the enemy's hold are being explored with the Lord. The goal is full deliverance but, in the process of finding freedom, the enemy's manifestations or interference may need to be restrained, especially where ruling demons, within or outside the person, may be directing lesser powers of darkness.

> Matthew 12:29... how can anyone enter the strong man's house and carry off his property, unless he first binds the strong man? And then he will plunder his house. (NASB)

See Authority, Loosing, Power, Powers of Darkness, a Right, Ruling Spirit, Unclean Spirit

Binding up (Bind up) – repairing what has been wounded and broken.

One consequence of the spiritual disorder in this world is brokenness in families, communities and individual lives. Binding up wounds of every kind (Luke 10:34), and restoration from brokenness into wholeness are significant aspects of the healing ministry of Jesus, not least in the heart of humankind (Isaiah 61:1, KJV).

As it was top of His list of the items of good news which Jesus brought (Luke 4:18, see KJV),[2] it should be a common prayer for those who are now the Body of Christ to heal the brokenhearted by the authority of Jesus Christ. This is the heart of God.

> Psalm 147:2–3... The LORD builds up Jerusalem; He gathers the outcasts of Israel. He heals the brokenhearted And binds up their wounds. (NASB)

See Brokenness, Fragmentation, Wholeness, Wound

Birth (Born) – emergence of a baby from life in the womb into life in the world.

The birth of a child, after the gestation period, is a hugely significant moment in a human life. It can be a physically and emotionally traumatic time if the birth is unduly prolonged or involving a sudden Caesarian section, for example. Even if the birth itself is straightforward, it can be spiritually devastating for a baby if parental approval or protection is perceived to be lacking, for any reason.

Rachel named her son *Ben-oni*, meaning *son of my sorrow*, just before she died after a difficult birth. His father, Jacob, seems to have recognized the possible effect on the baby of carrying such an identity, and so renamed him *Benjamin*, meaning the *son of my right hand* (Genesis 35:16–18).

For those who truly receive Jesus as Lord and Savior, there is a second birth, the emergence of their human spirit from darkness into spiritual light and life, through the Holy Spirit.

> John 3:6... That which is born of the flesh is flesh, and that which is born of the Spirit is spirit. (NASB)

This new birth, as a child of God, presents a wonderful opportunity for restoration from all the spiritual damage of the past, including any unresolved trauma from the time of physical birth. The starting place of healing, for the human spirit, soul and body, is to forgive those who were unwilling or unable to provide the important security which God had meant for our lives, not least at the time of our birth.

God is able to gather up every moment of our existence which has been wounded by the sin of the world, and to hold us in the absolute security of His love, so we can know restoration to abundant new life.

See Abortion, Born Again, Conception, Miscarriage, Trauma

Bisexuality (Bisexual) – desire for sexual intimacy with both men and women.

Whatever the cause of this issue in someone's life, the Bible makes it clear that this is not God's design for sexual identity, nor for the expression of that identity. That does not affect God's love for any person experiencing this type of sexual attraction, but He created men and women to desire sexual intimacy only with someone of the opposite sex, and for that intimacy to be consummated within the covenant of marriage (Matthew 19:5).

Without the plumb line of God's truth, the world has no clear concept of what is right or wrong in issues of human sexual behavior. Popular opinion says bisexuality is an alternative and valid human sexual condition. God's truth is that flawed sexual attraction is the consequence of precious lives being distorted by a fallen and sinful world (Romans 1:26–27), thus needing God's restoration rather than human endorsement.

Our identity (the answer to the question, *Who am I?*) is rooted in our human spirit. This includes our sexual identity.

> 1 Corinthians 2:11… It is only our own spirit within us that knows all about us … (GNB)

Sadly, our God-given identity is subject to distortion and brokenness, through generational iniquity, personal sin, abusive relationships and different kinds of trauma. God can heal and transform the damaged identity of those who are walking in line with Jesus, and He is ready to forgive, deliver and cleanse all who are willing to confess any sexual behavior which is contrary to divine order. However loving a sexual relationship appears to be, it can still be sinful if it breaks this divine order for sexual intimacy. God's laws and commands were established because He wants the very best for our well-being.

> Genesis 2:24… For this reason a man shall leave his father and his mother, and be joined to his wife; and they shall become one flesh. (NASB)

See Homosexuality, Human Spirit, Identity, Immorality, Intimacy, Lesbianism, Order, Purity, Sexual Sin

Bitterness (Bitter) – defiling condition of the heart which can result if unforgiveness is allowed to take hold.

> Hebrews 12:15… See to it that no one fails to obtain the grace of God; that no root of bitterness springs up and causes trouble, and through it many become defiled. (NRSV)

When we have been wounded by the sin of other people, we try to deal with the pain in various ways. Without the knowledge of the healing ministry of Jesus, many wounded people just bury the unhealed feelings, including unforgiveness, which can then act like an increasingly bitter root, feeding negative responses into today's situations.

We have all experienced barbed words which suddenly come from someone's mouth and seem to spread defilement among the listeners. Very often this happens because the situation has, for them, in some way triggered the unhealed pain and bitter feelings of the past. However well we try to hide these, they will come to the surface at some point. It is only by true forgiveness of those who have hurt us that there can be full resolution of the pain of the past and an opportunity to receive the healing balm of the Lord that takes away the bitterness.

See Attitude, Bitter Root Judgment, Forgiveness, Pain, Unforgiveness

Bitter Root Judgment – deep-rooted and defiling assumption or expectation about the character of a person or group of people.

Where there has not been true forgiveness of those who have hurt us, the bitterness can increasingly take the form of a powerful judgment on the offender, and even on all those people who are, in some way, similar (Hebrews 12:15).

For example, let's say that I was verbally abused and manipulated by my mother as a child, as she tried to meet her unhealed needs. The pain and bitterness in my heart can grow into a judgment of my mother which assumes that she has an unchangeable character in this area. This can also become my expectation of the behavior of all women, especially those in some position of authority.

Through God's law of sowing and reaping (Galatians 6:7), if I sow a judgment such as this, it can seriously affect my relationships, as I will reap the outworking of this bitter root, which seems to draw from others the very behaviors that were expected. God has called us to be men and women of discernment concerning what is sinful and spiritually bad, but we are not called to proclaim a judgment on the lives of others which denies the opportunity for God's grace. Judgment uses generalizations, such as "you always", "I never", "women are like this", "men do that".

Confessing our wrongful judgment of others and forgiving those who were the root cause of this bitterness can make a huge difference to our relationships, and remove the right of the enemy to hold us bound into reaping the consequence of such judgments. This can be a powerful opportunity for freedom.

> Luke 6:37… Do not judge, and you will not be judged. Do not condemn, and you will not be condemned. Forgive, and you will be forgiven. (NIV)

See Authority, Bitterness, Blame, Condemnation, Forgiveness, Judgment, Unforgiveness

Blame – accusation of responsibility for wrongdoing.

It is right to face the truth of who has been responsible for particular damage in our lives, because it prepares the way for either confession of our own sin or the forgiveness of others. Unfortunately, our carnal nature is usually reluctant to acknowledge personal blame for wrongdoing, being much more ready to self-justify our own actions and to point the finger at others (Isaiah 58:9). Very often, however, if we have been subject to abuse and/or struggle with issues of personal insecurity, we may feel pressure to take the blame for things that we are not responsible for, particularly when we come under pressure from others in a position of authority.

We live in a world which is unwilling to accept that *"all* have sinned and fall short of the glory of God" (Romans 3:23, NIV, my italics), a world where there is a culture of frequent blame-shifting. People are much more ready to claim entitlement than to confess sin. Of course, particular individuals may indeed have sinned against us and be wholly responsible for specific hurt in our lives. In this case, our forgiveness of them is the way through to the healing of our inner wounds.

It is certainly appropriate to consider the apportionment of responsibility in any sin issue, for truth is always a doorway to healing. However, we do not have to live with blame, because the ministry of Jesus is founded on forgiveness. His forgiveness releases each one of us from needing to carry the defiling accusations of the enemy (Revelation 12:10–11), so that we can walk as pardoned children of God, with all debts paid. It is important for us to personally pursue this healing process, step by step.

> 1 Thessalonians 5:23... Now may the God of peace Himself sanctify you entirely; and may your spirit and soul and body be preserved complete, without blame at the coming of our LORD Jesus Christ. (NASB)

See Carnal Nature, Bitter Root Judgement, Confession, Forgiveness, Guilt, a Right, Sin, Sinlessness, Truth

Blasphemy (Blaspheme, Blasphemous) – cursing words or actions that are directed against God.

Such words, though unpleasing to God, can do Him no harm. However, blasphemy gives a powerful right for the enemy to turn such curses back on the perpetrator and on those for whom he or she carries any responsibility. An adherent to Freemasonry, for example, pronounces many blasphemous statements and oaths in the progressive rituals of his membership of this false religion. Invoking the God of creation to participate in such a defiling man-made covenant is a clear license to the powers of darkness to bring curses upon the devotee and his family.

Whether uttered in frustration, in ignorance, in jest or with intent, words spoken against the person and character of the God of the Bible (especially when strengthened by ritual activity) are powerful tools for the enemy, and such words need clear renouncing, if we have sinned in this way. Mercifully, God is faithful and just to forgive and to cleanse each one of us from all such unrighteousness (1 John 1:9). His pardon, provided that we are willing to receive it, is effective for all sin and for all people.

> Mark 3:28–29... Truly I say to you, all sins shall be forgiven the sons of men, and whatever blasphemies they utter; but whoever blasphemes against the Holy Spirit never has forgiveness, but is guilty of an eternal sin ... (NASB)

However, the spiritual powers of darkness eternally oppose the Holy Spirit. For their choice of rebellion and blasphemy there is no divine forgiveness. Unlike ourselves in this life, their existence is outside time and this makes any process of redemption impossible for those living solely in the spiritual realm (Jude v.6), because it appears that confession and redemption are opportunities which are only available in the realm of time (Hebrews 9:27).

See Curse, Freemasonry, Pronouncement, Rebellion

Blessing (Bless) – pronouncement of well-being and favor, spiritually empowered when done in obedience to God's commands.

In Deuteronomy chapter 28 there is a list of the remarkable blessings for God's people that will follow their obedience to His commandments. These are not handed out by Him as a prize for good behavior; instead, they represent the inevitable consequence of being in line with the spiritual laws of His universe.

> Deuteronomy 28:1–2... If you obey the LORD your God and faithfully keep all his commands that I am giving you today, he will make you greater than any other nation on earth. Obey the LORD your God and all these blessings will be yours ... (GNB)

God's intention for His foundational laws have not changed. Jesus makes it clear (in Matthew 5:17) that He did not come to abolish the Law but to fulfill it, by His being the only human who has ever kept completely in line with the intent of God's laws and commands. It is only through belief and trust in Jesus that we can truly know the blessings of God, which now come through the covenant which He sealed for us on the cross.

We read in Genesis that in the beginning God blessed all He had made: animal life (Genesis 1:22), humankind (Genesis 1:28) and even the seventh day (Genesis 2:3). God's heart is to continually bless His creation, and we can promote that blessing toward others by our words and actions, particularly those people for whom we carry a measure of spiritual responsibility. God made a remarkable promise to Abraham:

> Genesis 22:17–18... indeed I will greatly bless you, and I will greatly multiply your seed as the stars of the heavens and as the sand which is on the seashore; and your seed shall posses the gate of their enemies. In your seed all the nations of the earth shall be blessed, because you have obeyed My voice. (NASB)

When we are rightfully walking under the anointing of the Holy Spirit we will know the goodness of God and we can speak His blessing over others. This can have a powerful effect, as when fathers speak blessing over their children. All true blessing originates from God, but we can certainly be a conduit of this divine pronouncement of well-being. We can even, and perhaps especially, speak blessing toward those who are hostile to us.

> Luke 6:28... bless those who curse you, and pray for those who mistreat you. (GNB)

See Commandment, Covenant, Curse, Pronouncement, Supernatural, Word

Blood (Bloodshed) – essential component of the human body, linked in the Bible with spiritual life.

The circulation of blood in the body sustains our physical lives, but spiritual life is strongly associated with blood in many passages of the Bible (Leviticus 17:14). The human spirit of Abel, who was murdered by his brother, reaches out to his maker, through the blood that was spilt.

> Genesis 4:10... [God] said [to Cain], "What have you done? The voice of your brother's blood is crying to Me from the ground." (NASB)

According to Scripture, when a human being is guilty of sin he or she deserves to have their own blood shed, to die (Romans 6:23). Jesus has stepped into this world and died on our behalf, shedding His own blood so that God can pardon each one of us and release us from all punishment. Blood must be shed to meet God's justice, but this is no longer through an animal offering, but rather through one particular willing human sacrifice, sufficient for all time, the sacrifice of Jesus Himself.

> Hebrews 9:22… And according to the Law, one may almost say, all things are cleansed with blood, and without shedding of blood there is no forgiveness. (NASB)

Holy Communion is an opportunity to identify with the blood of Jesus spilt at the cross, where He both sealed a New Covenant with humankind and paid all the cost of our sin.

> 1 Corinthians 11:25b… This cup is the new covenant in My blood; do this, as often as you drink it, in remembrance of Me. (NASB)

However, the enemy knows well the spiritual significance of blood and uses it to defile and bind people where there has been unrighteous exchange or shedding of blood. Through occult rituals, satanic masses, the shared syringes of drug addicts and perverted sexual intimacy, for example, powerful rights can be given to the enemy and ungodly soul-ties can become established.

It is also worth asking the Lord to bring cleansing and freedom if we have given blood or received a blood transfusion. Even if not our own sinful activity, any blood exchange can, depending on the others involved, bind people together in ways that may permit an unhealthy mixing of human spirit and personal identity never intended by God. Incidentally, our occult involvement with blood in the past can sometimes cause participation in Holy Communion to be spiritually difficult for us.

Praise God that there can be freedom through Jesus Christ. If we sense that blood has been used, shed or exchanged in wrong ways in our lives, confession and forgiveness will remove the enemy's authority. Then cleansing and deliverance can follow, along with the breaking of soul-ties and the restoring of any damage to our human spirit. Praise God that in His Kingdom mercy triumphs over judgment, because of the shed blood of Jesus. What a Savior!

See Covenant, Forgiveness, Holy Communion, Justice, Life, Soul-tie

Body (Bodies) – God's created form for a human being, made from the material of the earth and given the breath of life through His Spirit.

Sometimes the word *body* can refer to the whole of our being, including the human soul and human spirit (e.g. Romans 8:23), but more often in the healing ministry the word is used to denote the physical part of human beings. We need to remember that physical symptoms and illnesses in the body can have their roots in disorder of the soul or spirit, because the body, soul and spirit constantly interact with each other. God designed us to receive direction from Him through our human spirit, which would lead to wise choices being made by our soul and these good decisions being enacted by our body.

Unfortunately, the damage that can occur in every part of our being disrupts this right interaction. As a result, the physical condition of the body frequently reflects a condition of the heart (spirit and soul) which is not in God's order.

> Proverbs 14:30…A sound mind makes for a robust body, but runaway emotions corrode the bones. (The Message)

When we are praying for physical healing of the body, it is important to remember that the disorder may be rooted in an unseen problem which needs to be addressed first. For example, past wounding may have crushed or broken the spirit.

> Proverbs 17:22… A joyful heart is good medicine, But a broken spirit dries up the bones. (NASB)

There may also be inner spiritual bondage which needs to be untied in order that the body can be restored to health.

> Luke 13:11… And there was a woman who for eighteen years had had a sickness caused by a spirit; and she was bent double, and could not straighten up at all. (NASB)

Although we may be fully aware of the symptoms of disease in the body which we can see, it is always worth asking God what is out of line with Him in the unseen places. He can restore us to a peaceful and joyful heart; this truly is the best medicine for the whole body!

See Soul, Healing, Human Spirit, Restoration, Trauma

Body of Christ – worldwide corporate human group through which the person, authority and power of Jesus is now manifested in this world.

This Body, as with a human body, is made up of many members, people who are true followers of Jesus. Each member has a specific role, and together they can fulfill the whole purpose of God. It is the Holy Spirit who flows through this worldwide Body (1 Corinthians 12:13), enabling it to be a supernatural witness to the active presence of Jesus today.

> 1 Corinthians 12:27... Now you are Christ's body, and individually members of it. (NASB)

In the same way that the head and the hand of the human body are not equipped to perform the same function, so we need to recognize and honor the gifting and ministry of all the members of the Body, submitting to the authority and ability which the Holy Spirit distributes amongst us.

When I'm about to get in the bath, it is my hand that is well designed to test the water temperature. Then my head, with the information received, makes a decision whether to direct the whole body to get into the water or not. To avoid scalding my body, my hand has played a vital role, maybe even the most important at that moment. However, my hand does not expect to be the one directing my body, nor does my head claim the right to be thrust into the water instead of my hand. They both seem very content to submit to the unique gifting of the other, just as we should be within the Body of Christ (Ephesians 5:21).

It is important within the Body of Christ to recognize the spiritual authority that God has invested in each member and to pray that we will work in harmony, as each one of us finds healing from the wounds of the past and freedom from unresolved spiritual bondages. We may also need to forgive those who have failed to help us walk into the fullness of our place and gifting within the Body, as indeed we may have failed to do with others.

See Authority, Holy Spirit, Jesus, Gifts, Manifestation, Ministry

Body Piercing – puncturing of the skin and the underlying flesh, usually in order to insert ornamental objects, such as metal rings.

Any self-inflicted damage to the human body is a serious matter. We need to be honest about the motives and the consequences. We are encouraged to *glorify God in our body* (1 Corinthians 6:20), and this poses the question as to whether body piercing could be regarded as an unnecessary mutilation, even in a small way, of a precious creation of God.

Throughout history, body piercing has been associated with slavery, a slave owner often marking his 'possessions' by piercing the earlobe. This is also found in a biblical instruction, when a slave made a choice to renounce personal freedom and be bonded to a particular master.

> Deuteronomy 15:16–17... But your slave may not want to leave; he may love you and your family and be content to stay. Then take him to the door of your house and there pierce his ear; he will then be your slave for life. Treat your female slave in the same way. (GNB)

The practice of body piercing today is largely an issue of fashion, at least in developed nations, but it can often be associated with a measure of rebellion against rightful authority and established views of body image and beauty.

If body piercing is indeed linked to rebellion and, historically, to slavery, there are grounds for asking what spiritual authority might rule over such practice. Body piercing carried out in an act of rebellion against God, against His view of our bodies or against parental discipline may well give the enemy a right to establish some measure of spiritual enslavement in our lives. God's people belong to Him as children of a heavenly Father, not the chattels of a slave driver.

We may also need to ask if there were problems of self-worth or identity in our lives that could have led us to feel the need for associating ourselves with others through body piercing. If we become convicted

that sinful motives such as rebellion were part of the reason for our actions, then the solution will be confession, repentance and seeking God for His cleansing through deliverance from any controlling spirit. There may be soul-ties to break with others involved, particularly those who have pierced our bodies (inevitably releasing blood), especially when it was related to some form of occult practice.

See Body, Foothold, Rebellion, Slavery, Soul-tie

Bond (Bonding, Bound) – emotional or spiritual attachment between two or more people.

Related to the word *bind*, a bond between people usually refers to a good attachment, a godly soul-tie, between family members or friends, founded in a rightful, loving relationship, where there is no ungodly control.

> Colossians 3:14... Beyond all these things put on love, which is the perfect bond of unity. (NASB)

A healthy bonding between a mother and child in the early months of a child's life is particularly important for the nurture and strengthening of the child's human spirit. Weak or absent parental bonding can cause ongoing issues of deep anxiety and emptiness in a person's life. However, as we invite Jesus into the innermost part of our personhood (Revelation 3:20), He will fill this deepest of voids with His loving, accepting presence.

As adult believers, we are described in the Bible as *bondslaves* of Jesus (Colossians 4:12), meaning that we have chosen to surrender our lives in a loving relationship to Him, something which brings so much blessing into our lives.

However, we can be wrongly bound to another person, resulting in an ungodly soul-tie and in spiritual bondage. This was the situation between Jacob and his son Benjamin. Their lives were tied up with each other in an unhealthy dependence, which meant that Jacob could not live without the presence of his favorite son.

> Genesis 44:30–31a... Now, therefore, when I come to your servant my father [Jacob], and the lad [Benjamin] is not with us, since his life

BONDAGE

is bound up with the lad's life, when he sees that the lad is not with us, he will die. (NASB)

A similar situation today could be resolved by the son or daughter forgiving the parent for such wrong dependence, and asking the Lord to release the unhealthy bond. Hopefully the parent would also see the need to repent and find freedom.

See Bind, Dependence, Family, Love, Relationship, Soul-tie

Bondage – wrongful spiritual hold on our lives.

When Philip was in Samaria, he encountered a powerful magician called Simon, who believed in Jesus when he heard Philip's preaching. However, it became clear that Simon was not yet free from the holds that the enemy had had on his life. He offered money to the visiting apostles, Peter and John, in return for the Holy Spirit power which he saw manifested through their ministry, and Peter's response was very strong.

> Acts 8:22–23... repent of this wickedness of yours, and pray the LORD that, if possible, the intention of your heart may be forgiven you. For I see that you are in the gall of bitterness and in the bondage of iniquity. (NASB)

Out of our wounding and through our sinful responses, wrong attitudes of heart and wrong relationships can frequently become a place of bondage in our lives. To be free from such bondage we will need God's freedom and cleansing. This can even apply to our relationship with God Himself, when it is founded in legalism.

Thankfully, when we bring any sinful part of our lives before the Lord in confession, God's forgiveness removes any authority the enemy has to keep us in bondage. Any unclean empowering spirit can then be evicted, so that we can be truly free from any defiling bondage. Unfortunately, it seems that Simon the magician was not willing to get right with God in personal repentance.

> Acts 8:24... But Simon answered and said, "Pray to the LORD for me yourselves, so that nothing of what you have said may come upon me." (NASB)

See Deliverance, Dependence, Freedom, Power, Relationship, Soul-tie

Born – See Birth

Born Again – vitalized new condition of the human spirit, the result of receiving Jesus as the Lord of our lives.

At physical birth, our body comes into the physical light and life of this world. But Jesus says that a further birth is required if we are to know true spiritual life. Our human spirit needs to be born, through the enabling of the Holy Spirit, so that we can come from spiritual darkness to spiritual light.

> John 3:6–7... That which is born of the flesh is flesh, and that which is born of the Spirit is spirit. Do not be amazed that I said to you, "You must be born again." (NASB)

The human spirit is imparted into our physical being at conception, so we all have a human spirit at our physical birth. If we later accept Jesus as Lord and Savior, our human spirit is then born into spiritual light, so allowing revelation of our true identity and destiny. At this rebirth we bring into our new existence all the good and bad experiences of our past lives and, even when born again, we are not immune to future trouble in this world. But Jesus knows all about us and is ready to restore us through the atoning work of the cross, into the abundant life of His Kingdom, for which we were created, and that includes the restoration of damage to our human spirit.

> Matthew 5:3... Blessed are the poor in spirit, for theirs is the kingdom of heaven. (NASB)

In being born again we are sealed by the Holy Spirit as children of God through Christ Jesus (Ephesians 1:13, John 1:12). However, to be able to powerfully witness to the one who rules our lives, each believer should seek baptism in the Holy Spirit (Acts 1:5,8)

See Anointing, Baptism in the Holy Spirit, Cross, Holy Spirit, Human Spirit, Identity

Bound – See Binding, Bondage

Boundary (Boundaries) – extent of intimacy in a relationship, or limit of delegated authority.

When we give authority to someone, it is very important that the extent of that authority is clearly defined. We see the significance of this principle in God's delegation of authority to the man in the Garden of Eden, before the Fall.

> Genesis 2:15–17... Then the LORD God took the man and put him into the garden of Eden to cultivate it and keep it. The LORD commanded the man, saying, "From any tree in the garden you may eat freely; but from the tree of the knowledge of good and evil you shall not eat, for in the day that you eat from it you will surely die." (NASB)

Even today, within the Body of Christ, if we do not respect God-given boundaries of authority, this can be a serious issue and may indeed give opportunity for the enemy to usurp the very authority that has been delegated to the various members of the Body. In a military analogy, no battleship can operate successfully if the various members of the crew overstep their boundaries of authority. Even the captain needs to keep to his role of giving overall direction and refrain from dangerous meddling in the complexities of the engine room, the oversight of which has been delegated to others who have been fully equipped for the job.

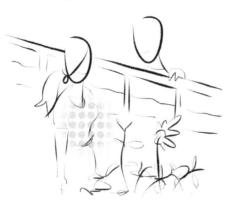

How about right boundaries of intimacy in our relationships generally? How much of our personal lives should we share with one another (Proverbs 4:23)? Our understanding of these issues was intended by God to be learned from our parents as we watched them and listened to them during childhood years. Unfortunately, when parenting has been abusive or dysfunctional, we can enter adult life very unable to establish our own rightful boundaries, especially when in childhood we were not allowed to say 'no' to abusive overstepping of our own boundaries by others. In adulthood we will then be very unclear about how to respect the boundaries of others. As we inadvertently overstep these lines of intimacy and thereby offend others, we inevitably find ourselves rejected and confused.

Jesus demonstrated perfect levels of intimacy with all of those with whom He related, and we can learn from Him. As we forgive those who should have given us a better understanding, and as we acknowledge the mistakes that we have made, we can receive the wisdom of God, through the Holy Spirit, into these difficult issues of relationship, and be restored from the damage caused by ourselves and by others through wrongful trespassing over the rightful boundary lines between the personal territories of human lives.

See Authority, Co-Dependence, Intimacy, Relationship, Respect

Brokenness (Broken, Break) – loss of wholeness.

This is a major cause of dysfunction in people's lives. Many things get broken by sinful actions, particularly through lack of rightful protection or poor spiritual covering (Ezekiel 34:2–5): property, friendships, marriages, families, nations and, not least, people's hearts. Jesus made it clear that dealing with broken hearts was to be a significant part of His mission on earth.

> Luke 4:18... The Spirit of the LORD is upon me, because he hath anointed me to preach the gospel to the poor; he hath sent me to heal the brokenhearted, to preach deliverance to the captives, and recovering of sight to the blind, to set at liberty them that are bruised ... (KJV)

Brokenness in our lives is not God's order, except, of course, for the contrite heart that has become rightfully broken and yielded to God from a place of hardness (Psalm 51:17). However, most brokenness is harmful – for example, the division which has torn apart relationships – and it gives rights to the enemy.

A particularly harmful type of brokenness is that which has fragmented the precious inner wholeness of a person, separating a part of our being from full relationship with ourselves and with God. This can be caused through emotional trauma or a violent shock to the body, including through drugs, and is discussed in more detail under the headings Partial Fragmentation and Full Fragmentation.

Such inner brokenness can also be deliberately induced through intentional trauma to the body. One example is Electro Convulsive Therapy (ECT), which is used sometimes for emergency psychiatric treatment, to shut away distressing feelings or memories. Some occult or satanic practices also use trauma and the resulting brokenness to produce, and demonically control, fragmented parts of people's lives. Such vulnerability can even occur in the lives of candidates going through traumatizing rituals, including those used in Freemasonry.

No brokenness is beyond God's covenant promise to restore and heal when we come to Him and seek His ways of truth and forgiveness.

> Psalm 147:2–3... The LORD builds up Jerusalem; He gathers the outcasts of Israel. He heals the brokenhearted and binds up their wounds. (NASB)

See Accident, Full and Partial Fragmentation, Dissociation, Wholeness.

Bullying (Bully) – oppression of the weak.

See Abuse, Control, Oppression

Burnout (Burnt Out) – condition when chronic inner stress has reached a level which causes deep exhaustion, particularly in the human spirit, resulting in emotional and physical dysfunction.

We are designed to deal with stress in our human spirit, soul and body, but not solely in our own strength. The burdens of life which we carry need to be under the authority and direction of Jesus, in order to avoid becoming overstressed and vulnerable to inner breakdown (Proverbs 18:14), which can then affect the whole body.

> Matthew 11:28–30... Come unto me, all ye that labour and are heavy laden, and I will give you rest. Take my yoke upon you, and learn of me; for I am meek and lowly in heart: and ye shall find rest unto your souls. For my yoke is easy, and my burden is light. (KJV)

Many people carry false responsibilities or inappropriate burdens which are not what God intended for us. Holding on to worry about family, work or the state of the world does not solve the issues.

CARNAL NATURE

Anxiously or wrongly trying to control situations or people, however good our intentions, is not God's way.

> Proverbs 12:25a... Anxiety in a man's heart weighs it down ... (NASB)

The Kingdom solution is to bring every persistent anxiety to the Lord in prayer, petition and thanksgiving (Philippians 4:6). It can be very helpful to list on paper all the burdens that we are carrying and take the time to hand over and release every one of them to Jesus in prayer, asking Him if we have any particular role in their resolution, and to heal us from the wrongful distress and dysfunction which these heavy weights have caused in every part of our being.

See Anxiety, Brokenness, Control, Human Spirit, Stress, Soulishness

Calling – See Destiny

Captivity – See Bondage

Carnal Nature (Carnality) – sinful tendency in every human being, resulting from the Fall.

Before the Fall, there was no carnality in God's creation of human beings, but there was free will, and therefore the possibility of choosing to sin. When Adam and Eve made the choice to agree with Satan and disobey God, there was an immediate loss of innocence and the impartation of a defiling knowledge of good and evil, whereas previously they had only been aware of God's goodness. A doorway to darkness was opened in humankind, bringing a desire to act according to their own reason, spiritually contaminating the life of every man and woman. Even as Christians, we walk with a carnal nature, which is a tendency to sin.

For those who have received Jesus into their lives, thankfully there is an opposing power, the work of the Holy Spirit, which enables us to refuse to allow our carnal nature to direct our lives. But it will always be a battle. The wounding of life and the bondages of the enemy tend to promote behaviors which are in line with the carnal nature rather than those in line with the Spirit of God. We need to be active in challenging these sinful responses, because we can become so familiar with these coping mechanisms that they become almost unconscious reactions.

At the same time, we need to seek the Lord's healing and deliverance for those root issues which fuel the sinful patterns of behavior. But we must never see our need for healing as an excuse for tolerating carnality. Like dealing with a parasitic plant which entwines itself around a beautiful tree, we need to keep battling with our carnal nature. We must not allow it any opportunity to grow and further defile our lives or to give rights to the enemy.

> Romans 8:5... Those who live as their human [carnal] nature tells them to, have their minds controlled by what human [carnal] nature wants. Those who live as the Spirit tells them to, have their minds controlled by what the Spirit wants. (GNB)

See Behavior, Choice, Coping Mechanism, Fall, Iniquity, Sin

Celibacy (Celibate) – resolution to abstain from sexual intercourse.

See Singleness, Virginity

Character – inner qualities expressed through a person's behavior.

God has created us all with an individual identity and a unique personality. When we become followers of Jesus, and we are open to the work of the Holy Spirit in our lives, God grows within us a new character which increasingly has the image of Jesus. This is the fruit of the Holy Spirit, and is the primary evidence that Jesus is truly Lord of our lives. There is a fundamental spiritual law which can be expressed like this: *we progressively take on the character of whomever or whatever we worship*. God created this law so that we might together express His character on earth as we worship Him through Jesus Christ. This is a supernatural work of the Holy Spirit.

> 2 Corinthians 3:18... And we all, with unveiled face, beholding the glory of the LORD, are being changed into his likeness from one degree of glory to another; for this comes from the LORD who is the Spirit. (RSV)

Conversely, this same law also results in people expressing the enemy's character through demonic activity when they walk in rebellion and idolatry.

> Psalm 115:8... Those that make them [idols] will become like them, Everyone who trusts in them. (NASB)

God's true healing and sanctifying process in our lives will always bring a change in our character, which will glorify Jesus. We simply need to be willing for that change to occur.

> John 16:14... He [the Holy Spirit] will glorify Me [Jesus], for He will take of Mine and will disclose it to you. (NASB)

See Behavior, Fruit, Idolatry, Image, Personality, Sanctification

Charm – specific procedure, object or words used to invoke occult power.

Verbal charms are sometimes called *spells*, when associated with magic, or *hexes*, in malevolent witchcraft. They may be used for seeking personal well-being, for divining the future, for cursing or control of others, or for control of events. Whatever the purpose, they are inviting the involvement of occult power which is not under the authority of Jesus. This gives a right to the enemy to defile the people, places and relationships involved, as well as demonically inhabiting any objects involved in the practice. Even though we may not knowingly be using objects as charms, it is worth seeking the Lord for understanding about any gifts, possibly inherited, which we have received and which may have been used as charms in the past.

> Deuteronomy 18:10b–11... don't let your people practice divination or look for omens or use spells or charms, and don't let them consult the spirits of the dead. (GNB)

When we confess to the Lord any occult practice in which we have had involvement, He is ready to forgive and cleanse us from all that has cursed us or defiled us through the enemy's grip.

See Control, Cursing, Deliverance, Divination, Foothold, Occult, Power, Superstition, Witchcraft

Childlessness – See Barrenness

Choice (Choose, Chose) – ability to decide what to believe, what to speak or how to behave.

In particular, God has given us the ability to choose to walk in obedience or disobedience to Him. Every choice that we make has consequences (Jeremiah 21:8) and God has made clear to us that our choices have a profound effect not only on our own lives but also on friends, family and descendants, for whom we carry a measure of responsibility. Every choice which agrees with God establishes more of His authority and blessing over our lives. Every choice which agrees with the enemy gives more license to him to control a part of our lives. Joshua boldly spoke out his personal choice to the Children of Israel:

> Joshua 24:15... If it is disagreeable in your sight to serve the LORD, choose for yourselves today whom you will serve: whether the gods which your fathers served which were beyond the River, or the gods of the Amorites in whose land you are living; but as for me and my house, we will serve the LORD. (NASB)

See Agreement, Behavior, Disobedience, Free Will, Soul, Will

Christ – The Anointed One of God.

This description of Jesus as the *Christ* (from a Greek word) has the same meaning as *Messiah* (from a Hebrew word), and they both translate as the *Anointed One*. This truth about Jesus was powerfully declared by the disciple Peter.

CHRISTIAN

> Matthew 16:16–17... Simon Peter answered, "You are the Christ, the Son of the living God." And Jesus said to him, "Blessed are you, Simon Barjona, because flesh and blood did not reveal this to you, but My Father who is in heaven." (NASB)

For every follower of Jesus, this same God-given revelation is the foundation of our faith. Throughout the Old Testament, there is the promise of someone who would come, anointed, marked out and empowered by God to bring salvation to His people. This promised person was known as the Messiah or Christ (meaning *Anointed One*). At the start of His ministry on earth, at the synagogue in Nazareth, Jesus states that *He* is the Anointed One (Luke 4:18–21), fulfilling the words of Isaiah (Isaiah 61:1).

We have a choice today to believe that statement or not. Peter did believe and later discovered, as today's disciples do, the essential anointing which God also imparts to every follower of Jesus.

See Anointing, Christian, Jesus, Resurrection, Revelation, Son of God, Son of Man

Christian (Christianity) – follower of Christ.

Apparently it was a term first used when Peter and Paul were together with other believers in Antioch (Acts 11:26). However, being called a Christian or using the name of Jesus Christ in prayer is no guarantee of a true relationship with Him (Matthew 7:22–23).

It is our simple obedience to His commands which allows the Holy Spirit to grow the fruit of His character in our lives as He dwells within us. Only then does the world see a true reflection of what it means to be a Christian, a believer in the true Messiah, as opposed to the tragically distorted image presented by so many within the church down through history.

> John 13:34–35... A new commandment I give to you, that you love one another ... By this all men will know that you are My disciples, if you have love for one another. (NASB)

See Believer, Body of Christ, Born Again, Christ, Church, Messianic Believer

CHURCH

Church – congregation of those who follow Jesus Christ, called by God to be separated from the ways of the world.

As believers in Jesus, the church is primarily *who we are, what we belong to,* rather than *where we go* at particular times of the week. It is important to be part of a fellowship of believers for our personal well-being, and also to enable the church to be effective in its corporate destiny. Together we make up the Body of Christ, and His healing in this dysfunctional world comes through the gifting distributed by the Holy Spirit to each of us for the common good (1 Corinthians 12:7). A body only functions successfully when the members of that body are working in close harmony with each other.

When we are meeting as a church, we can walk together, experiencing teaching, leadership, discipline and the shared sacraments, such as Holy Communion. However challenging it can sometimes be to work in true unity with others in the church, it is never right to isolate ourselves for any length of time from this corporate manifestation of the one who is the author and finisher of our faith (Hebrews 12:2). Unfortunately, the worldwide church has become more denominational than relational. It is not the church's size that is the problem, but its health, and there will no doubt be much cleansing necessary within the church in these strategic end days.

Thankfully, God does not ask humans to build His church, but He simply challenges us to be humble witnesses to the foundational revelation given to the church that Jesus is the Christ, the Messiah, the Son of God (Ephesians 5:25b). The powers of darkness cannot destroy the community of believers who are secure in this truth.

> Matthew 16:16–18… Simon Peter answered, "You are the Christ, the Son of the living God." And Jesus said to him, "Blessed are you, Simon Barjona, because flesh and blood did not reveal this to you, but My Father who is in heaven. I also say to you that you are Peter, and upon this rock I will build My church; and the gates of Hades will not overpower it." (NASB)

See Body of Christ, Christian, Kingdom, Manifestation, Ministry, Witness

Cleansing (Cleanse) – removal of spiritual defilement that is caused by sin.

The wonderful fact of the redeeming work of Jesus on the cross is that not only is there now the forgiveness of God available for every sinner, but there is also opportunity for cleansing from everything that has become defiled through our being out of line with God.

> 1 John 1:9... If we confess our sins, he is faithful and just to forgive us our sins, and to cleanse us from all unrighteousness. (KJV)

Cleansing will involve the restoration of God's order, the removal of unrighteousness or iniquity and the expelling of any demons which are seeking to hold us captive to the lies of the enemy. The more our lives bear the good fruit of the character of Jesus, the more His purity will be displayed in our behavior (2 Tim 2:21).

C.S. Lewis perceives God challenging us with these words: *"'Make no mistake,' He says, 'if you let Me, I will make you perfect. The moment you put yourself in My hands, that is what you are in for.'"*[3]

See Forgiveness, Defilement, Deliverance, Iniquity, Righteousness, Sin

Codependence (Codependent) – unhealthy relationship in which the participants seek to find and fulfill something of their identity through the other person.

This type of relationship is not a place of freedom. We become wrongly bound to the other person, seemingly unable to find emotional or spiritual fulfillment *without* them, but also unable to find the fullness of our true identity *with* them, as we become entrapped in a wrongful joining of each other's lives.

Codependent relationships can be found anywhere, for example, between a parent and child (especially where the parent's marriage is dysfunctional), between siblings (especially twins) or between a husband and wife. In all of these there will be a root of wrong emotional reliance, usually because of a lack of personal affirmation and security.

We see an extreme example of codependence in the Bible in the controlling relationship between Ahab and Jezebel. Ahab seems pathetically reliant on the scheming ways of his wife to fulfill his kingly role, while Jezebel finds significance in exhibiting the spiritual governance which her husband lacks. There is an ungodly mutual dependence feeding on Jezebel's witchcraft and Ahab's abdication of responsibility.

> 1 Kings 21:7... Jezebel [Ahab's] wife said to him, "Do you now reign over Israel? Arise, eat bread, and let your heart be joyful; I will give you the vineyard of Naboth the Jezreelite." (NASB)

It is very easy to be blind to codependent relationships which affect our own lives, and it can sometimes seem a fearful prospect to live without this deeply entrenched emotional support, however unhealthy it might have been. However, God wants us to discover the fullness of who we are in our dependence on Him, as He brings increasing wholeness and freedom.

There will be strong ungodly soul-ties to deal with, as we confess our part in this type of wrong relationship and as we forgive the other person who has controlled our lives, and taken something of our God-given identity and destiny.

See Boundary, Control, Dependence, Identity, Relationship, Soul-tie

Comfort (Comforting) – relief from pain or distress.

God has designed us to need comfort when we have been hurt. All true comfort originates from God, enabled through the work of the Holy Spirit.

> John 14:16... And I will pray the Father, and he shall give you another Comforter, that he may abide with you for ever ... (KJV)

God uses human beings as an instrument of comfort, not least through parents responding rightfully to the needs of their children. When this essential comfort is not available, it causes deep distress to the human spirit and soul, and this will be physically reflected in the body.

> Lamentations 1:16b... This is why I weep and my eyes overflow with tears.
>
> No one is near to comfort me, no one to restore my spirit. (NIV)

Without someone to provide for this need, or an understanding of God's desire to comfort us when we have felt the pain of wounding, we will likely try to comfort ourselves, through self-pity, self-protection and wrongful behavior connected with eating, drinking, sexual activity or drug misuse, for example. The carnal nature of humanity and the enemy's lies are always ready with a counterfeit answer to our needs, but they have the inevitable end result of more pain, and they sometimes lead to the bondage of addictive dependence. We can easily settle for a place of false comfort, from which it is very hard to move.

It is never too late to come to God, to seek Him for the true comfort that He has always wanted to provide, although it may seem a very vulnerable step at first. However, as we forgive those who did not meet our needs as God had intended, and as we confess the coping mechanisms by which we have tried to wrongfully self-comfort, the Holy Spirit can do His wonderful work of bringing true and lasting relief to the pain of the past.

> Isaiah 40:1... "Comfort, O comfort My people," says your God. (NASB)

See Carnal Nature, Coping Mechanism, Kindness, Pain, Selfishness, Self-pity

Commandment (Command) – God's instruction to ensure that we stay in line with His spiritual laws.

The law of gravity keeps our feet on the ground as we go about our daily work. It is a God-created physical law, designed to benefit our lives. However, if we carelessly walk over the edge of a cliff, we will discover that the same law of gravity can do us great harm. Very often along the edge of a cliff there will be clear notices instructing us to beware of danger and to go no further. These commands, placed by the local authorities, are not written to spoil our fun, but to save us from disaster.

It is exactly the same principle with God's commands. Like warning notices, His commands are there to turn us back from danger (Ezekiel

33:11). Under the Old Covenant, God instructed His people concerning His foundational spiritual laws (which are unchangeable, like the law of gravity), in particular through the Ten Commandments (Deuteronomy 4:13). For example, He instructs them to honor father and mother (Exodus 20:12) because His foundational divine law has determined that this prolongs life. However, just like the law of gravity, it has a downside when the rightful instructions of the one in authority are ignored: continued dishonoring of our parents can bring a curse upon our lives.

These commands formed the basis of the covenant which God made with the Children of Israel (Leviticus 26:15). Unfortunately, they did not obey the commands and so reaped the consequence (Deuteronomy 31:16–18). Now God has chosen to relate, not only to Israel but to all humankind, through a New Covenant, sealed at the cross with the blood of Jesus. However, just like the law of gravity, God's foundational spiritual laws will not change until the end of time. The coming of Jesus on earth was not to abolish these laws (Matthew 5:17) but to show to humankind God's heart intention for His laws, and to provide someone (Jesus) who would follow God's instructions and keep wholly right with the spirit of His laws. In this way, the Son of Man obeyed God perfectly on our behalf, so that God's covenant with humanity could be renewed. We are now able to benefit from all God's unchanging spiritual laws (Romans 8:1–2) by obeying a new commandment:

> 1 John 3:23–24a... This is [God's] commandment, that we believe in the name of His Son Jesus Christ, and love one another, just as He commanded us. The one who keeps His commandments abides in Him, and He in him. (NASB)

It is as if God has overwritten new commands on a noticeboard at the top of a spiritual cliff. Under the Old Covenant He spelled out Ten Commandments for the well-being of His people, but now He tells us that our spiritual safety, indeed our very salvation, depends on complete surrender to His Son Jesus Christ, because He alone has fully obeyed all of God's instructions on our behalf.

See Choice, Covenant, Disobedience, Law, Rebellion, Righteousness

Committal – affirming, at death, the return of a person's physical and spiritual being back to where they came from.

The rightful process at death is that our physical being returns to the dust of the ground and our spiritual being returns to God.

> Ecclesiastes 12:7... then the dust will return to the earth as it was, and the spirit will return to God who gave it. (NASB)

It is wise to affirm this as God's rightful order when we are involved with the death of a family member or friend. Even Jesus considered it important to declare such words.

> Luke 23:46... And Jesus, crying out with a loud voice, said, "Father, INTO YOUR HANDS I COMMIT MY SPIRIT." Having said this, He breathed His last. (NASB)

Words committing the person's spirit to God are traditionally spoken out at Christian funerals, and we can always personally endorse these words today if we are unsure of what was spoken out in the past. This can be particularly helpful in prayer ministry related to abortions or miscarriage. It does not take away our precious remembrance of those who have died, but it is a way of ensuring that we have fully given them into the hands of God. This is the place of spiritual safety at the point of separation through death, whatever has occurred in a person's life.

Death is a spiritually significant time, and the enemy will seek to hold any place of control given to him by human disobedience to God but, thankfully, when we are under the authority of Jesus, the enemy is rendered powerless over death (Hebrews 2:14).

See Abortion, Death, Human Spirit, Miscarriage, Mourning

Compassion (Compassionate) – deep sympathy for those who are suffering.

This will be in the heart of every true follower of Jesus, because it was at the heart of His ministry to those He encountered as He walked the earth.

> Matthew 9:36... Seeing the people, [Jesus] had compassion for them, because they were distressed and dispirited like sheep without a shepherd. (NASB)

Compassion founded in Jesus does not overlook wrongdoing but seeks the true well-being of others, through lovingly helping them to face the reality of sins and wounds, and so find God's unending grace for the troubled heart. In fact, compassion is an important part of all human relationships. Receiving genuine compassion in times of trouble nurtures our human spirit.

True compassion demands no recompense from those who receive kindness, and is never motivated by a need to be needed. Importantly, compassion for others will never fully resolve the deep wounds in our own lives, but it can be a powerful motivator to move away from personal self-centeredness and self-pity.

See Comfort, Kindness, Loving-kindness, Nurture, Pity, Self-pity

Complementary Medicine – see Alternative Medicine

Compulsion (Compulsive, Compel) – drivenness in behavior fueled by emotional or spiritual control.

This may be the result of wrongful control by one person over another (1 Peter 5:2), but the compulsion we are considering here comes from within ourselves. In every moment of our lives, we have God-given free will as to how we respond to the circumstances around us. Sometimes, however, people can feel compelled to respond in wrongful ways that are irrational and seem almost outside their ability to choose. The feelings are so strong that there appears to be only one possible course of action, similar to the desperate 'need' for another cigarette, for someone who is addicted to smoking.

Compulsive and ritualistic behaviors, such as irrational counting, repeated checking or hand-washing, are a desperate response to obsessive thoughts which are themselves frequently the result of unhealed inner wounds and distorted core beliefs in the human spirit. For example, a deep belief that "I am a dirty person", the result perhaps of sexual abuse, could lead to compulsive washing rituals.

The journey of restoration will include bringing these inner disorders to the Lord for His healing, forgiving those who have been the cause of distress to the soul and spirit. We will also need to confess our past soulish ways of trying to comfort or protect ourselves, for these have probably added to the problem, and very often contributed to the compulsions.

We all battle with a carnal nature, the tendency to please and fix ourselves rather than to please God and let Him fix us! He has designed our lives such that every decision we make in agreement with His commands gives the Holy Spirit opportunity to touch our deep places of wounding, and to strengthen our good choices, so that we walk more fully in His ways and in our personal destiny. The apostle Paul even felt compelled by the Holy Spirit toward good choices:

> 1 Corinthians 9:16... For if I preach the gospel, I have nothing to boast of, for I am under compulsion; for woe is me if I do not preach the gospel. (NASB)

As the character of Jesus fills our lives more and more, we discover that we want to think and act like Him. However, the more we walk in agreement with our carnal nature, the more rights are given to the enemy to empower the formation of *his* character in us. If we find comfort in a pornographic website, for example, there will be a growing compulsion to return to this activity, a compulsion that is likely to be driven by unclean spirits. We still have an ability to choose, but we will seem to have less and less freedom to make a choice in agreement with God.

As with all wrong dependence, facing the reality of compulsive or addictive behavior is the first step to freedom. Sometimes obsessive thoughts can have partial roots in the sins of our ancestors, so it may be important to deal with generational iniquity. Then, as we agree with God and receive His forgiveness for the wrong choices we have personally made, the enemy's right to compel us to repeat those choices is removed and the powers of darkness can be expelled. It is a time when the help of mature and understanding Christian friends is invaluable.

See Addiction, Choice, Control, Dependence, Distress, Free Will, Obsession, Unclean Spirit

Conception (Conceive) – moment when God initiates a physical human life.

As sperm and egg fuse together, a unique human spirit, imparted by God, gives life to a new and precious human being.

> Zechariah 12:1b... Thus declares the LORD who stretches out the heavens, lays the foundation of the earth, and forms the spirit of a man within him ... (NASB)

Sadly, this new life may end quickly if there are physical difficulties for the human cells so that they are unable to implant in the womb. This may be either through biological dysfunction or through a particular chosen method for contraception. Where the method of contraception, such as the coil, disrupts implantation of a fertilized egg, this is a form of abortion. Of course, the child growing in the womb may also never reach the point of birth if later abortion or miscarriage takes place. God alone fully sees these hidden months of our lives.

> Psalm 139:13... You made all the delicate, inner parts of my body and knit me together in my mother's womb. (NLT)

At the time of conception, even though so little development of soul and body has occurred, the human spirit is well aware of the spiritual environment surrounding this miraculous time. Spiritual trauma from a conception involving lust or rape, for example, can leave lasting damage in the human spirit of the child. Praise God that He can truly renew the early moments of our lives when we seek His healing and deliverance from all that was not His order for the start of our earthly existence.

> Psalm 103:2,5... Bless the LORD, O my soul, And forget none of His benefits ... Who satisfies your years with good things, So that your youth is renewed like the eagle. (NASB)

See Abortion, Birth, Contraception, Human Spirit, Life, Miscarriage

Condemnation (Condemn, Condemning) – judgment of guilt that leaves no room for grace.

Even the woman caught in the act of adultery was not condemned by Jesus (John 8:11). The enemy was very ready to accuse her through the scribes and Pharisees who brought her before Jesus. However, they were forced to leave when they recognized the authority of His judgment of the situation, providing an opportunity for His forgiveness and her release. It's clear from the Bible that the conviction of God binds us to truth, whereas the condemnation of the enemy binds us to punishment.

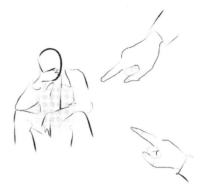

God is ready to convict us of our sinful ways, but His solution to our unrighteousness is not condemnation but rather grace and freedom. When we feel condemned it can seem that there is no light at the end of the tunnel, but with God's conviction there is always light as He leads us to specific confession.

It is the Holy Spirit's job to convict people of sin (John 16:8). When helping others who need to address sin issues in order to find healing, we must be careful that we don't become instruments of the enemy's condemnation, but rather of the Holy Spirit's loving conviction.

See Confession, Conviction, False Religion, Freedom, Grace, Guilt, Judgment

Confession (Confess) – agreement with God concerning sin.

This can be one of the most powerful steps that we take in the process of finding more wholeness and freedom in our lives. God is fully aware of all that we have done in the past, both good and bad. His forgiveness is always available for our wrongdoing, but our agreement with Him, and our turning away from sin, is essential for His grace and His cleansing to be applied.

> 1 John 1:9... If we confess our sins, He is faithful and righteous to forgive us our sins and to cleanse us from all unrighteousness. (NASB)

Many times I have found myself sitting with someone who has just shared a complicated and painful past, and is now looking for God's healing. Often my response has been, "Let's start with confession, agreeing with God about the sin issues in this story." For all of us there are times when much forgiveness of others may be necessary and much restoration is needed in our wounded heart, but somehow an agreement with God about our own sinful responses to life can often open the first door to His precious healing. We can, of course, confess privately with God, but there is undoubtedly something very powerful and healing about confessing to other trusted believers, and being in agreement with them.

> James 5:16... Therefore, confess your sins to one another, and pray for one another so that you may be healed. The effective prayer of a righteous man can accomplish much. (NASB)

Confession of sin should never be the result of another person's persuasion, but only through the sharing of truth and the conviction of the Holy Spirit. Jesus promised that He would lead us into all truth (John 16:13), and He will never leave us feeling condemned, as the enemy is likely to do. Confession and repentance seem old-fashioned concepts to many people, but they are an extraordinary key to God's grace.

See Agreement, Condemnation, Conviction, Forgiveness, Repentance

Confidence – See Self-confidence

Confrontation (Confront) – facing someone with the truth.

In our walk together within the Body of Christ, there are times when we are very aware of the sin in someone else's life and we can see that they are unaware of the issue or maybe just reluctant to bring it into the light. It may be that we have been personally wronged by the person or we are simply aware of the damage that is being caused to themselves and to others.

Confrontation is a necessary part of Christian life, but we need to be as willing to be challenged as we are to challenge others. The Bible warns us about the hypocrisy of confronting sin in the life of another person when we are not willing to face the truth of our own sin.

> Luke 6:41... Why do you look at the speck that is in your brother's eye, but do not notice the log that is in your own eye? (NASB)

However, our relationships within the Body of Christ should be such that we can lovingly, and without condemnation, help our brother or sister to see the truth of their lives, not least in regard to sin issues. It should never be the consequence of our continuing to carry an offense against them, nor an opportunity to prove ourselves right. Both the timing and the purpose should simply be to help one another to see what God says is right.

For godly confrontation to be effective, there needs to be much maturity, humility and trust shown by both people involved. Jesus saw the issue of hidden sin as sufficiently important that He gives a procedure for leaders to confront a person who is unwilling to face the truth, a process which may even result in their separation from the church (Matthew 18:15–17). May the Lord give each of us His grace to confront lovingly and a willingness to be confronted ourselves when it is the right time.

See Condemnation, Conviction, Grace, Offense, Truth

Conscience – God-given inner arbiter of morality, rooted in the human spirit.

This instinctive indicator of right and wrong is in the heart of every human being (Romans 2:14–15), but it is very vulnerable to damage, deception and defilement.

> 1 Corinthians 8:4,7… Therefore concerning the eating of things sacrificed to idols, we know that there is no such thing as an idol in the world, and that there is no God but one. … However not all men have this knowledge; but some, being accustomed to the idol until now, eat food as if it were sacrificed to an idol; and their conscience being weak is defiled. (NASB)

Without new spiritual birth in the Holy Spirit, this innate moral compass can only be calibrated by our spiritual inheritance, or by what we have learned from others during our lives. Unfortunately the function of our conscience is continually challenged by the pressure of our carnal nature, and further defiled by iniquity, both generational and from the sin which we have experienced throughout our lives (Titus 1:15).

For true followers of Jesus, there is a new and powerful arbiter of morality, and a purifier of conscience, as the Holy Spirit reveals the righteousness of Christ within us. Of course, we have a free will choice

CONTRACEPTION

as to how to respond to His conviction about the iniquity residing in our lives and, sadly, some are not willing to pursue the grace and purifying of conscience that comes from Jesus.

> 1 Timothy 4:1–2... The Spirit says clearly that some people will abandon the faith in later times; they will obey lying spirits and follow the teachings of demons. Such teachings are spread by deceitful liars, whose consciences are dead, as if burnt with a hot iron. (GNB)

See Carnal Nature, Conviction, Human Spirit, Righteousness, Truth

Contraception – behavioral, mechanical or chemical means for stopping conception taking place.

Conception is the beginning of human life through the fertilization of a human egg by sperm, together with the impartation of the human spirit from God. This embryo of human life then needs to become embedded in the womb of the mother in order for a viable pregnancy to begin.

True contraception (contra-conception), such as a *condom*, inhibits the mixing of the sperm with an egg and hence no human life can start. However, there are a number of techniques that do not stop conception but do deny a pregnancy by stopping the formed human embryo from embedding in the womb. These methods, such as the *coil*, are in effect forms of abortion and therefore carry particular spiritual consequences. Once human life has started, our taking of that life through abortion can give authority to the enemy to hold the womb as a place of future defilement and death. There may, therefore, be a need for God's forgiveness and deliverance.

It is important to seek the Lord over every method of contraception being considered, but it may be necessary to confess any method used already that has taken life. When we come to Him, acknowledging the truth, He is always there with unending grace.

> 1 John 1:9... If we confess our sins, He is faithful and righteous to forgive us our sins and to cleanse us from all unrighteousness. (NASB)

See Abortion, Conception, Human Spirit, Life, Miscarriage, Safe Sex

Contrition (Contrite) – deep sorrow as a result of conviction of personal sin.

See Conviction, Forgiveness, Repentance, Sin

Control (Controlling) – use of authority and power to direct people's choices and behavior.

Depending on whose authority is in place and how it is being used, control can be bad or good for us.

> Galatians 5:25... The Spirit has given us life; he must also control our lives. (GNB)

Control is harmful when someone applies physical, emotional or spiritual pressure to govern the will choices of another person, without giving them a true freedom to resist. Except in the careful discipline of children, the constraint of lawless and damaging behavior or the safeguarding of particularly vulnerable adults, we should not personally override the free will of another person. Such control is soulish, is not under godly authority, and can give the enemy a right of access.

The pilot of an airplane is under the authority of the airline company, and he has the power to fly the plane from one airport to another. He is in control of the flight and the passengers are very happy to let him take that responsible position. They have freely chosen to submit to

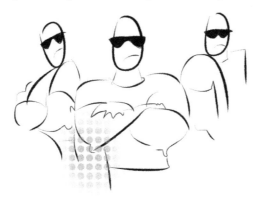

his authority. If, however, a hijacker takes charge of the flight using the power of a weapon, he is very likely to gain control, but not with legitimate authority.

In the same way, all ungodly control, however justified it may seem as a means to a helpful end result, defiles the rightful flow of divine authority which God has delegated to humanity. We see through the example of Jesus that in God's Kingdom there is no coercion, but rather freedom to make our own decision about whether we will choose to operate within God's order. The Bible pictures wrongful control as being like a damaging yoke on the backs of those affected, which can even be reflected in the shape of our bodies.

> Leviticus 26:13... I am the LORD your God, who brought you out of the land of Egypt so that you would not be their slaves, and I broke the bars of your yoke and made you walk erect. (NASB)

We control, or come under wrong control, through domination, manipulation, emotional blackmail, intimidation, humiliation, disapproval, seduction, threats, anger, condemnation, use of money, religious behavior and even through the withholding of love. This can all lead to significant damage in the human spirit, soul and body, causing anxiety and frequently physical infirmity.

The roots of wrong control are in the sinful choices which we have made to self-protect when we have experienced wounding or insecurity. By controlling our relationships, our environment and even our own lives through various coping mechanisms, we believe that we can avoid further inner pain, as well as achieving a place of emotional security and peace. It is not true! The solution to wrongful control is to acknowledge how it has affected our lives, to confess and repent of our own wrong behaviors in controlling others or controlling ourselves, to seek God's healing for the root places of wounding and to forgive those who have controlled us.

We may also need to evict the enemy's power which has strengthened the control. Queen Jezebel was clearly seen to be operating in witchcraft alongside her controlling lifestyle (2 Kings 9:22). The same ungodly spirit can affect people today. It will also be important to deal with the ungodly soul-ties which have been established through any controlling relationships, and to recognize that there is often a robbing of personal identity through enforced dependence on another person. When we have come under a wrong yoke of control, the Lord is able to release us from this slavery so that we can walk freely as sons and daughters of a loving heavenly Father.

See Authority, Fear, Freedom, Free Will, Intimidation, Jezebel, Power, Self-control, Soul-tie, Witchcraft

Conviction (Convict) – acknowledgment of sin issues in our lives, which comes through revelation given by the Holy Spirit.

Because of our carnality, we are naturally very blind to the reality of sin. We need the truth revealed in God's Word, together with conviction of sin by the Holy Spirit, to make it possible for us to be fully aware of what is truly right or wrong in our lives, and to understand how it is possible for God's mercy to triumph over judgment.

> John 16:8... And [the Holy Spirit], when He comes, will convict the world concerning sin and righteousness and judgment ... (NASB)

Confession without conviction can be superficial and ineffective. When we are receiving prayer ministry from another person, it is important that we are allowed the time to come to a conclusion about the sin issues in our life through God's gentle conviction and not by human well-meaning persuasion. It is good for others to sometimes hold up a plumb line of truth from God's Word, but we need to come to a personal place of conviction that our lives are out of line with Him in some particular place. Then our confession, our agreement with God, can bring the fullness of His forgiveness and cleansing.

See Agreement, Condemnation, Confession, Forgiveness, Grace, Holy Spirit, Sin, Truth

Coping Mechanism – process of thinking and behavior to minimize inner pain, where we rely on our own methods.

When we have suffered wounding from others, it is painful and we necessarily seek comfort or escape. Where we have not had a willingness or, more often, the understanding of how to bring the issues to God, most of us have found our own ways of handling inner distress and providing self-comfort.

> Jeremiah 2:13... for my people have committed two sins: they have turned away from me, the spring of fresh water, and they have dug cisterns, cracked cisterns that can hold no water at all. (GNB)

Coping mechanisms frequently become behavior cycles, which are repeated patterns of activity often arising from unconscious choices we make in response to pain, but which never end in true peace. Because our coping mechanisms prevent us from finding the true comfort of God, they can become compulsive behaviors, in which the enemy drives the process and keeps us in bondage to the root issues.

Examples of ungodly coping mechanisms are denial of pain, escape through alcohol or drugs, embracing unreality or fantasy, dissociation, escape through excessive work or religious practice, compulsive exercise or dieting, eating disorders, self-harming, promiscuity, pornography, inappropriate anger, joking or tears, sexual sin, and even inappropriate compulsion to help other hurting people in an attempt to mask our own pain.

Actually we need to be aware that these behaviors are all forms of ungodly self-control, as we seek to fix our own hurts (Job 36:21). Sometimes we can cause ourselves more inner damage through these ungodly responses to emotional pain than we received from the original wounding. Ungodly coping mechanisms are sin and need to be confessed, when we recognize the truth of how we have behaved.

> Isaiah 30:1... "Woe to the rebellious children," declares the LORD, "Who execute a plan, but not Mine, And make an alliance, but not of My Spirit, In order to add sin to sin ..." (NASB)

God not only forgives us, but He wants to be the one who truly comforts us in our pain and heals our wounds. Just as drug dependence inevitably distorts the chemical systems of the body, so all ungodly coping mechanisms distort the emotional and spiritual systems within the body, and their interaction. We need to tell the enemy that he is no longer wanted as a false comforter and, as we acknowledge the ungodly behavior patterns, we need to clearly speak and act in the opposite way, in agreement with God's commands.

Deliverance may be needed from the powers of darkness which have been given rights to wrongly control the way the God-created systems of the body respond to distress.

See Behavior Cycle, Comfort, Defense Mechanism, Denial, Pain, Self-control, Self-pity

Core Belief – belief which is strongly established deep in the heart.

Such beliefs may be about our identity, our value, about God, about our destiny and so on. For example, "I will always have to look after myself. No one else cares for me." These beliefs can become established, even from the moment of our conception, as a result of the hostile experiences we have in life. They are frequently opposed to God's truth about our lives, and they seriously affect the ways we think and act.

See Attitude, Badness, Belief, Belief System, Identity, Mindset, Truth, Value

Counseling (Counsel) – advice to help someone overcome disorder in their life.

Such advice may be given for the purpose of helping someone reflect on the difficult issues in their lives, or may be more directive in helping them to change certain behaviors. The only perfect counselor is the Holy Spirit, because He knows everything of how God made us, all that has happened to us, and all that is required to bring restoration. He comes to counsel those for whom Jesus is Lord.

> Isaiah 9:6… And the government will rest on His shoulders; And His name will be called Wonderful Counselor … (NASB)

Within the Body of Christ, and under the anointing of the Holy Spirit, we can help to bring revelation of the disorder and healing process in one another's lives, but we need to be cautious not to promote our own wisdom when only divine wisdom will bring true resolution.

Prayer ministry for healing and deliverance may well need to include the sharing of foundational and powerful Kingdom truths, but only the Holy Spirit knows precisely which of these truths, the *rhema* word of God, together with people's right choices, will undermine the enemy's hold at any particular moment.

> Ephesians 6:17... the sword of the Spirit, which is the word of God. (NASB)

Secular counseling can be helpful in finding doorways to understanding the underlying issues in someone's life, but only Jesus holds the keys to true wholeness and freedom. He has passed on to His disciples, that's you and me, the responsibility to proclaim these precious healing keys. For example, when a person has repented, Jesus encourages us to affirm the truth of God's forgiveness, when directed by the Holy Spirit.

> John 20:22–23... And when [Jesus] had said this, He breathed on [the disciples] and said to them, "Receive the Holy Spirit. If you forgive the sins of any, their sins have been forgiven them; if you retain the sins of any, they have been retained." (NASB)

See Freedom, Holy Spirit, Ministry, Prayer, Prayer-ministry, Revelation

Counterfeit – something which is false but has the appearance of truth.

Fishermen are very familiar with this type of deception, especially when choosing a man-made fly to catch a trout or salmon. To the fish it looks like good food, but it is actually a death trap.

In our search for good spiritual food, in a world ruled by the devil, the father of lies (John 8:44), it is inevitable that he will seek to deceive us with counterfeits of the bread of life. This can include false manifestations of power seeming to come from the Holy Spirit, and done in Jesus' name, but actually coming from another power. This is false healing and false deliverance (Matthew 7:21–23). Jesus calls such healing "lawless", meaning that it is not done under God's authority.

The problem is that when we embrace a counterfeit, we give the enemy spiritual authority over that area of our lives, which not only leads to bondage, but can block the true wholeness and freedom which God has planned for us.

In these end days there will be an increase in counterfeit manifestations of power by the ruler of the world, signs and wonders which are perhaps impressive to witness but are not fully consistent with biblical truth, and which are lacking in establishing the fruit of the character of Jesus. It is, therefore, very important that believers continue to earnestly desire the gift of discernment given by the Holy Spirit (1 Corinthians 12:10).

Actually, all counterfeits are best exposed by our increasing familiarity with the truth (John 8:31–32) and it is often said that those employed to spot counterfeit money are best trained by handling large quantities of genuine money, so that the false will be easily identified. It is important that the followers of Jesus are alert to the ways of the enemy, particularly in these end times, and that we submit only to the Good Shepherd. We become more certain of His voice through the work of the Holy Spirit in our lives.

> John 10:5... When [the shepherd] puts forth all his own, he goes ahead of them, and the sheep follow him because they know his voice. A stranger they simply will not follow, but will flee from him, because they do not know the voice of strangers. (NASB)

If we have embraced counterfeit spiritual food or power, it is important to confess and receive the Lord's forgiveness and His release from all that is false and harmful to us. We do not need to walk in fear or condemnation. The trout may not get a second chance but, by God's grace, we do!

See Deception, Discernment, False Fruit, Lie, Manifestation, Satan, Truth

Covenant (Covenantal) – everlasting, spiritually binding, and life-changing agreement between participants.

In a contract, people agree to exchange goods or services on certain terms and conditions. In a covenant, people exchange a commitment concerning their lives.

Importantly, the Bible encourages us to uphold marriage as a covenant, because of the deep intimacy and permanency of relationship that God intended (Malachi 2:14). Breaking a marriage covenant inevitably leads to deep spiritual damage.

> Malachi 2:15... Therefore take heed to your spirit, And let none deal treacherously with the wife of his youth. (NKJV)

God has made covenants with humanity, which are always unbreakable from His side. His covenants are expressions of His faithful loving-kindness toward us. He wants His children to understand His promises and His commandments, and so to experience the blessings, rather than the curses, of His divine laws. He has repeatedly expressed His limitless compassion toward all His covenant children, even to those who proved to be unfaithful.

> Ezekiel 16:8... "Then I passed by you and saw you, and behold, you were at the time for love; so I spread My skirt over you and covered your nakedness. I also swore to you and entered into a covenant with you so that you became Mine," declares the LORD God. (NASB)

A covenant agreement in the Bible was usually sealed in a ritual involving sacrifice, which expressed the binding nature of the promises made, even to the point of shedding blood, and it frequently involved a representative from each of the parties to the agreement (1 Samuel 20:16,42). When God confirmed that His everlasting promises to Abraham and his descendants, which included the provision of land and nationhood (Genesis 17:1–8), were to be founded in a covenant, animals were cut in half, and the presence of God in fire passed through the middle (Genesis 15:17–18). In recent history we have been privileged to see God's faithfulness to these early covenant promises, in the amazing restoration of the nation of Israel in 1948.

Many centuries after Abraham, God declared, through Moses, a covenant in which the blessings for the Children of Israel would be conditional upon their obeying Him, specifically the Ten Commandments (Deuteronomy 4:13). The covenant also provided a remedy for the consequence of sin through their repentant obedience to God's commands in the sacrificing of animals. Then through Jeremiah, God foretold of a New Covenant with His people, the blessings of which would be dependent not on written commandments, but on a new heart relationship with Him (Jeremiah 31:31–33).

This covenant, though rooted in God's promises to the Jewish people, was also extended beyond them to all Gentiles who would choose to be followers of Jesus, and so they would become spiritual descendants of Abraham (Galatians 3:29), grafted into the olive tree of Israel (Romans 11:17–24). This allows us all to be beneficiaries of an amazing divine commitment to our well-being. It was achieved through the sacrifice of Jesus on the cross. There He represented both sides to this New Covenant, being both Son of God and Son of Man. So now there is this final expression of God's covenant with humanity, with a new commandment (1 John 3:23) based entirely on relationship, out of which a new remedy for sin, healing and deliverance can flow for those who respond to Jesus as Lord of their lives.

> Luke 13:16... And this woman, a daughter of Abraham as she is, whom Satan has bound for eighteen long years, should she not have been released from this bond on the Sabbath day? (NASB)

Just like this woman who had been bent over double for so many years, believers today are covenant children of God (John 1:12) and have a right to the covering and healing which is available to all who truly walk as disciples of Jesus. Despite the enemy's authority being given license through the hostile voices in the synagogue that day, this woman simply surrendered to Jesus and she discovered the wonderful restoration which can come through God's faithful covenant with humankind.

Unfortunately, it is also important to mention that ungodly covenants throughout history have had powerful and damaging consequences. God apparently endorsed the demand that the Gibeonites made to King David for the death of seven of Saul's descendants (2 Samuel 21:1–14). That was because Saul had broken a covenant made between God's people and the Gibeonites in the time of Joshua. God still required the terms of the covenant to be kept, even though the covenant itself had been a wrong one. No wonder the Bible warns us not to make oaths (James 5:12).

The effects of ungodly covenants are still experienced today, for example in the destructive consequences on families of the vows, rituals and oaths of Freemasonry, and in the endless bloodshed which can result from spiritually empowered religious declarations, such as that made by the Protestant community of Ireland in the Ulster Covenant of 1912.

Thankfully, Jesus has now paid the death penalty for false and broken covenants so that we can receive forgiveness, freedom and healing once we have acknowledged the truth of the wonderful New Covenant which was painfully, but lovingly, sealed by Him at the cross.

See Agreement, Blessing, Blood, Commandment, Covering, Freemasonry, Loving-kindness, Marriage, Relationship, Right, Ritual, Soul-tie, Vow

Covering (Cover) – spiritual protection over our lives which God provides through our relationship with Him, and with each other, in order to keep us safe from the hostility of the enemy.

From the moment of the Fall in the Garden of Eden, humanity has been aware of their vulnerability to the spiritual powers of darkness, which were given rights over humankind through our rebellion against God. Adam quickly found that trying to fix it with his own covering of leaves was useless.

> Genesis 3:10… He answered, "I heard you in the garden; I was afraid and hid from you, because I was naked." (GNB)

Throughout the Bible, there are many references to the importance of God's covering. In fact, the Hebrew word that is translated atonement actually means *cover*. The Old Testament *Day of Atonement* (Leviticus 16) was God's way of annually restoring His covering over a rebellious people, forgiving and cleansing them from all the defilement which had occurred. The clearest biblical explanation of what it means to be under God's covering is given to us in Psalm 91.

> Psalm 91:1–3… Whoever goes to the LORD for safety, whoever remains under the protection of the Almighty, can say to him, "You are my defender and protector. You are my God; in you I trust." He will keep you safe from all hidden dangers and from all deadly diseases. (GNB)

So how do we lose this protection? Throughout our lives, our spiritual safety has been dependent upon our personal response to God, but also upon the godliness of those who have carried a responsibility for our well-being, including parents, teachers, leaders, pastors and even our ancestors (Ezekiel 34:4-5, Lamentations 5:7). Even the conduct of the ruler of a nation will affect all those who work under him.

> Proverbs 29:12... If a ruler pays attention to falsehood, All his ministers become wicked. (NASB)

In a similar way, when we were young, our earthly father was entrusted by God to hold His protective umbrella over the whole family, including ourselves.

> Proverbs 14:26... Reverence for God gives a man deep strength; his children have a place of refuge and security. (TLB)

In reality, many of us have experienced a very leaky umbrella, as a result of parental sin, carelessness or even absence. This was not God's order for our lives, and for some of us it has resulted in significant spiritual damage, with an added opportunity for the enemy to get a foothold in our lives.

Thankfully, through the death of Jesus at the cross, God is now able restore the spiritual covering over any and every moment of our lives. We simply need to bring these vulnerable times to Him, through acknowledgment and confession of our own sin (often, how we tried to self-protect), and through forgiveness of those whose sin was the cause of our becoming exposed. God has always wanted to restore His precious people through His covering, His covenant and His cleansing.

> Ezekiel 16:8–9... "Then I passed by you and saw you, and behold, you were at the time for love; so I spread My skirt over you and covered your nakedness. I also swore to you and entered into a covenant with you so that you became Mine," declares the LORD

CREATION

God. "Then I bathed you with water, washed off your blood from you and anointed you with oil." (NASB)

See Atonement, Covenant, Defense Mechanism, Enemy, Father Heart, Generational Iniquity, Protection, Self-protection

Creation (Create) – act by which God has brought everything into existence.

A belief that the universe, and in particular human beings, exist by the creation of God, rather than simply through the chance mutation of cells, significantly affects how we view our relationship with Him. The Bible says that each one of us is individually known, created and loved by God, no matter what the circumstances of our conception may have been.

> Psalm 139:13... You created every part of me; you put me together in my mother's womb. (GNB)

Humankind, created in God's image (Genesis 1:26), is very different from the animal world, each created after their own kind (Genesis 1:25). It is not just the size of our brain that makes us human, nor our ability to speak and empathize with one another, but it is our human spirit and our conscious awareness of life and death, good and bad, justice and injustice, all imparted by God uniquely to human beings, however distorted these concepts have become through sin (Psalm 8:4-5, Romans 1:19).

The universe has been created to operate by God's physical and spiritual laws. The disorder which we see in and around our lives is the result of humankind's rebellion against the Creator and not the consequence of chaotic chance (Genesis 3:17-19). Healing is the restoration of God's order, for all His creation (Romans 8:21).

In the story of Jesus creating wine out of water at a wedding party (John 2:1–11), the head waiter is surprised at the quality. Had he scientifically analyzed the wine, no doubt he would have been able to accurately discover its history going back to a particular vineyard, but his understanding of the true origins of the wine would have been wrong. The servants who witnessed the miracle were the only ones apart from Jesus who knew for certain that this apparently mature wine had been created just minutes before. It is just the same with this extraordinary universe. Scientific analysis may indicate a history going back countless numbers of years, but the Bible gives us God's revelation of miraculous creation.

In a simple challenge to those who doubt God's creation and His care of this universe, Jesus suggests that we take a look at the beauty of wild lilies.

> Matthew 6:28–30... Observe how the lilies of the field grow; they do not toil nor do they spin, yet I say to you that not even Solomon in all his glory clothed himself like one of these. But if God so clothes the grass of the field ... will He not much more clothe you? ... (NASB)

See Belief, Bible, Creativity, God, Human Spirit, Miracle, Value

Creativity (Creative) – activity which reflects the nature of God in bringing things into being.

We are made in God's image and, since He is creative, we must therefore be creative in a significant way, whether we feel like it or not. Creative ability is imparted by God and rooted in the human spirit.

> Exodus 31:2–3... See, I have called by name Bezalel, the son of Uri, the son of Hur, of the tribe of Judah. I have filled him with the Spirit of God in wisdom, in understanding, in knowledge, and in all kinds of craftsmanship ... (NASB)

Unfortunately, the deep brokenness in many of our lives often means that this gift has been crushed, robbed, hidden or lost. Sometimes people have experienced strong criticism of their creative experiments as young children which has caused them to shut down on that part of their lives. When we make a choice to rediscover this God-given aspect of our identity, it may expose painful feelings, but it can give us a wonderful opportunity to find the truth and the freedom to be more fully the person God made us to be.

Although the finished result of a creative endeavor may be rewarding, it is the activity itself which God often uses to progress the healing journey in our lives. A childlike response to creativity is the best way to bring restoration to the human spirit, not searching for perfection, but content to allow free expression, experimentation and even mistakes!

We have discovered that encouraging people into creative activities can be one of the most effective ways of seeing them receive revelation and healing, as God is given an opportunity to touch gently into the wounded heart.

See Healing, Human Spirit, Identity, Image, Truth

(the) Cross – place of crucifixion of the Son of God.

The death of Jesus on the cross was through His choice (John 10:17–18), because of His love for you and me. His resurrection was inevitable because death cannot hold someone who has not sinned (Acts 2:24; Romans 6:23). In the hours of agony on the cross, Jesus paid with His life the cost of humanity's sin for all time. He also carried in His body the iniquity that results from all our sin (Isaiah 53:6). Because of these facts there is a healing ministry through, and for, followers of Jesus today.

This work of the cross was foreshadowed in the Old Covenant by the sacrifice of one goat and the sending away of another goat (the scapegoat) on the Day of Atonement, the special day each year when God's people were restored into His spiritual covering (Leviticus 16).

Along with this atonement for humanity's sin, Jesus acted as the representative of both humankind and God in sealing the New Covenant through the shedding of His blood. If we are truly followers of Jesus, then He specifically represented us at the cross and we become entitled to all the blessings of this renewed divine covenant, including reconciliation with God, His healing and His deliverance.

Colossians 1:19–20... For it was the Father's good pleasure for all the fullness to dwell in Him, and through Him to reconcile all things to Himself, having made peace through the blood of His cross; through Him, I say, whether things on earth or things in heaven. (NASB)

See Atonement, Covenant, Forgiveness, Reconciliation, Resurrection, Son of God

Cult (Cultish) – group of people strongly bound to each other, and subject to a specific spiritual belief system and to practices not consistent with true biblical Christianity.

Although cults are just a form of false religion, they are often characterized by idolatry of a particular leader, and the teaching tends toward legalism, ritual, secrecy, exclusivity, indoctrination, isolation and strong control.

When helping people to get free from the hold of a cult, it will be necessary to recognize that for those involved, loyalty to the group will often be more important than facing the reality of the false beliefs. Commitment to vows or pledges within the group will result in strong, often demonic, bondages. There will be ungodly soul-ties between the members of the group and especially with the leader. Despite there sometimes being a Christian label over the movement, cults will always display clear discrepancies with biblical truth, most noticeably with the doctrine of the Trinity and the divinity of Jesus.

In Christian Science, for example, through the biblical interpretation and writings of Mary Baker Eddy, Christ is described as the *idea of God* and the Holy Spirit is described as *divine science*. She dismisses the biblical Trinity of Father, Son and Holy Spirit as false, replacing this concept with a *tri-unity of life, truth and love*. The beliefs of most cults are easily accessed on the internet. We do not need to become experts, but it will be necessary when helping someone to walk free for us to hold up a clear plumb line of biblical truth in the areas of false teaching, in order to lead them toward repentance.

We need to show those caught up in cults that God unconditionally accepts him or her as a person, and that there is precious healing available in a relationship with Jesus as He is truly described within the pages of the Bible. The apparent security, the fellowship and the rituals of a cult can be very attractive to those with a troubled past who are looking for acceptance and the security of an ordered routine. Paul, the apostle, knew all too well the dangers of cults.

> 2 Corinthians 11:3–4... I am afraid that your minds will be corrupted and that you will abandon your full and pure devotion to Christ – in the same way that Eve was deceived by the snake's clever lies. For you gladly tolerate anyone who comes to you and preaches a different Jesus, not the one we preached; and you accept a spirit and a gospel completely different from the Spirit and the gospel you received from us! (GNB)

See Acceptance, Bible, Bondage, Control, Discernment, Deception, False Religion, Jesus, Trinity, Truth

Cure – absence of sickness or method of achieving this.

People have looked for a cure for their diseases ever since the Fall. The word has been applied to sound medical treatments, to occult folk medicine and, in the Bible, to the true healing that comes through Jesus. Curates in the Anglican Church were so named because of their part in bringing a divine cure to troubled souls. Wherever we go to find a cure for the disorders in our lives, it is best to seek the Lord for what is His way forward, to ensure both spiritual and physical safety.

> Luke 9:11b... and welcoming them, [Jesus] began speaking to them about the kingdom of God and curing those who had need of healing. (NASB)

See Alternative Medicine, Healing, Medicine, Occult, Quackery

Curse (Cursing) – spiritually empowered and damaging pronouncement.

God's plan from the beginning was to bless all of His creation, but this was always dependent on humankind remaining in line with His spiritual laws (Deuteronomy 11:26–28). When humanity is disobedient to God's commandments, breaking covenant with Him, we reap an inevitable and damaging consequence from these laws.

> Deuteronomy 28:15... However, if you do not obey the LORD your God and do not carefully follow all his commands and decrees I am giving you today, all these curses will come on you and overtake you ... (NIV)

This curse on creation began at the Fall. The result was fear for humanity (Genesis 3:10) and a curse upon land (Genesis 3:17). When we are disobedient to God, our words and actions can be an instrument of cursing toward both things and people, especially those for whom we carry a measure of spiritual responsibility. For example, the cursing words of a father toward one of his children will carry particular power, because this undermines the relationship of protection which God intends there to be within families.

Through the principle of generational iniquity, sinful practices by our ancestors, such as in Freemasonry, can bring curses into our lives through a defiled spiritual inheritance. We can open our own lives to curses through sinful activity and ungodly self-pronouncements. We have prayed for many people who, at some time in their lives, have spoken out in despair words like, "I'd be better off dead!" Such a statement agrees with the enemy and not with God, and can therefore bring a curse of untimely death upon their lives.

> Proverbs 18:21... The tongue has the power of life and death ... (NIV)

Some witchcraft practices are specifically directed at bringing harm to other people through spells, pronouncements, rituals and even sacrifice. Whenever Satan is given spiritual authority through human disobedience, he can empower that authority through demonic spirits which will promote any curses which have been voiced. However, the enemy must have a clear right to bring a curse into effect in someone's life. This right could be through the sinful words of someone with a position of authority over the person, or through the sin of the person themselves.

> Proverbs 26:2... Like a sparrow in its flitting, like a swallow in its flying, So a curse without cause does not alight. (NASB)

As we follow Jesus and His instructions for our lives, we can walk in the blessings of the New Covenant. At the cross, Jesus took into His body all the spiritual consequence of sin, including all the curses which have affected our lives through our own unrighteous words and actions, or those of other people. Through confession of our own sin, together with the forgiveness and blessing (Luke 6:28) of those who have been a means of curse upon our lives, the effect of all curses which have harmed us can be disabled.

> Galatians 3:13... Christ redeemed us from the curse of the Law, having become a curse for us – for it is written, "CURSED IS EVERYONE WHO HANGS ON A TREE" ... (NASB)

See Blessing, Deliverance, Generational Iniquity, Occult, Power, Pronouncement, Witchcraft, Word

Darkness (Dark) – spiritual environment which affects the world, as a result of humanity's rebellion against God.

From the moment of the Fall, this world has suffered from the spiritual rule and hostility of the Evil One. Thankfully, through obedience to Jesus Christ and His commands, we can walk in spiritual safety, despite the Ruler of the World.

> Acts 26:18a... that they may turn from darkness to light and from the dominion of Satan to God ... (NASB)

> Ephesians 6:12... For our struggle is not against flesh and blood, but against the rulers, against the powers, against the world forces of this darkness ... (NASB)

> John 8:12... Then Jesus again spoke to them, saying, "I am the Light
> of the world; he who follows Me will not walk in darkness, but will
> have the Light of life." (NASB)

See Deliverance, Light, Powers of Darkness, Ruler of the World, Spiritual

Death (Dead, Die) – physical or spiritual lifelessness.

Death, as described in the Bible, is about separation from relationship
(whether human or divine) rather than annihilation (Genesis 3:2–7).
The life source for the human body is the human spirit (James 2:26a),
given, sustained and enlightened by the Holy Spirit.

At the Fall, humankind disobeyed the commands of God and found
themselves separated from His divine life source, suffering spiritual
death. This led to our eventual physical death. At this physical death,
the human spirit is separated from the physical matter of the body and
from those people remaining on earth.

> Ecclesiastes 12:7... then the dust will return to the earth as it was,
> and the spirit will return to God who gave it. (NASB)

However, God has made a way for us to be released from permanent
spiritual death (eternal separation from God) through a covenant
relationship with Him, sealed by the blood of Jesus at the cross. Death
could not hold Jesus, because He had never sinned (Acts 2:24). Every
true believer has their name written in God's book of life, and this is
available now and into eternity, beyond physical death.

> Revelation 20:14–15... Then death and Hades were thrown into the
> lake of fire. This is the second death, the lake of fire. And if anyone's
> name was not found written in the book of life, he was thrown into
> the lake of fire. (NASB)

Satan, the spiritual ruler of this disobedient world, looks for opportunity
to control the life of human beings. Without the saving work of Jesus,
Satan has power over the spiritual and physical death of humanity, but
we can remove both this power and the fear of death by surrendering
every part of our lives to the authority of Jesus.

> Hebrews 2:14–15... Since the children [that's us] have flesh and blood, he too [Jesus] shared in their humanity so that by his death he might break the power of him who holds the power of death – that is, the devil – and free those who all their lives were held in slavery by their fear of death. (NIV)

At some point in life, we will experience a disorder in the body which will result in physical death. It is good today to give Jesus lordship over that time which is still to come.

Until that day we have a destiny to fulfill. We need sufficient strength and enough days to complete all that God has planned for us, just as Jesus spoke over Lazarus (John 11:4). Without fear or condemnation, it is a good idea to seek the Lord about any potential hold that the enemy might have on our lives which would make us vulnerable to untimely death. Such holds could come through false covenants (such as Freemasonry) and other sinful actions or pronouncements which were effectively inviting death. They may have been said or done by ourselves, by those carrying responsibility for our lives, or by our ancestors. Examples include wishing for death, attempted suicide or speaking words which invite death.

A declaration of God's authority over our life and death can be a powerful way of claiming for ourselves the benefits of what Jesus did when He defeated the one that He calls a *murderer* (John 8:44). We have found the following scripture very significant for those who have, for example, had thoughts of suicide in the past.

> Psalm 118:17–18... I will not die, but live, And tell of the works of the LORD. The LORD has disciplined me severely, but He has not given me over to death. (NASB)

See Abortion, Committal, Generational Iniquity, Human Spirit, Miscarriage, Mourning, Necromancy, Pronouncement, Resurrection, Suicide

Debt – payment owed.

This, of course, can refer to money which needs to be paid for some reason. However, there is a much more serious debt due when a person has sinned against God's laws. According to the Bible, from that person will be due the payment of their very life (Romans 6:23). That debt is essentially a spiritual issue but it has a lasting, defiling and destructive effect on the whole of their being.

Any debt can be forgiven by the one who has the relevant authority. God has ordained that forgiving the debt due as a result of sin is only possible through appropriate bloodshed. It is that serious.

> Hebrews 9:22... In fact, the law requires that nearly everything be cleansed with blood, and without the shedding of blood there is no forgiveness. (NIV)

Rather than the repeated sacrifice of animals under the Old Covenant, Jesus has now made a once-and-for-all payment with His life on the Cross (Hebrews 10:12). In this New Covenant between God and humanity, the debt due from every human being as a result of their sin is fully paid in advance. No further contribution whatsoever is needed from any of us, no matter how serious the wrongdoing.

> Colossians 2:14... having canceled out the certificate of debt consisting of decrees against us, which was hostile to us; and He has taken it out of the way, having nailed it to the cross. (NASB)

How do we receive this divine pardon and cleansing into our personal lives? We need to be truthful about our sin (1 John 1:8), acknowledge Jesus as the one who has paid the debt for God's children (John 1:12) and, by obedience to Him (which includes forgiving others the debt which they owe us for their sin), demonstrate that we are sincerely choosing to repent and walk in the New Covenant relationship with God.

> Matthew 6:12... And forgive us our debts, as we also have forgiven our debtors. (NASB)

See Blood, the Cross, Forgiveness, Punishment, Repentance, Sin

Deception (Deceive, Deceit, Deceiving) – lie which is hidden and appears to be truth.

Jesus calls Satan the *father of lies* (John 8:44). This implies that Satan has an opportunity for spiritual patronage wherever the whole truth is lacking in our lives. Sadly, we use deception in many of our relationships with one another, which gives a foothold to the father of lies. Even more importantly, Jesus tells us that deception will be a particular aspect of these last days, and even followers of Jesus will be led astray.

> Matthew 24:24... For false Christs and false prophets will arise and will show great signs and wonders, so as to mislead, if possible, even the elect. (NASB)

There will be miracles, healing, prophecy, teaching and deliverance which will have an appearance of coming from God but will actually be false, or at least defiled by the enemy (2 Corinthians 11:14). These manifestations of spiritual power will not be by the authority of Jesus.

We should remember that deception, by definition, is not obvious. In fact, it looks good.

It can be compared with a deadly hook concealed in a juicy worm cast into a river to catch an unsuspecting fish: a large amount of truth hiding a devastating lie!

The good news is that God has given us clear ways to avoid deception and to be able, when we come into contact with spiritual power, to check whether it is the work of the Holy Spirit or a counterfeit. This is particularly important in these days when many alternative and false ways of supernatural healing are being offered, sometimes with a Christian label.

Here are some checks that God has given us:

1. If we have taken time to know the true voice of Jesus, He says that false healers will seem like strangers to us (John 10:5).

2. If we earnestly desire the Lord to gift the Body of Christ with the ability to discern spirits, the Holy Spirit will empower us to know what is false (1 Corinthians 12:10–11).

3. Without bringing condemnation, is sinful behavior clearly addressed in the teaching and ministry? (1 John 1:8–9)

4. Is the divine order and balance between Father God, Jesus Christ and the Holy Spirit clearly acknowledged in the teaching and ministry? (1 John 2:22, John 16:13-15)

5. Is the character of Jesus, the fruit of Holy Spirit, His grace and truth, seen to be growing in those ministering and receiving, however impressive the power displayed? (Matthew 7:20)

We need to be careful not to be fooled by 'colorful' displays of spiritual power (Matthew 24:4). Some while ago, an impressive flowering tree caught my attention in a garden. It was covered in attractive blossom and stood out from the rest of the trees all around. For some reason I felt the need to take a closer look, and I was shocked to find that the flowers did not belong to the tree at all, but to a creeping shrub. As I looked underneath, I could see that there was a mountain ash tree also in flower, although with more subtle coloring, but this was being completely smothered by the entanglement of the creeping plant, growing from a hidden root.

If we discover that we have been personally involved in deceit, it is important to come to the Lord for His forgiveness, freedom and cleansing, so that His true character and healing can be established in our hearts (Psalm 32:1-2).

See Authority, Counterfeit, Falsehood, Fruit, Lie, Miracle, Power, Trinity, Truth

Decision (Decide) – see Choice

Dedication (Dedicate) – setting apart, in order to be devoted to a cause, a person or a spiritual being.

We may, of course, choose to dedicate ourselves to Jesus Christ, so declaring His lordship over our lives, and receiving all the covenant blessing of such a choice. However, dedication is used in many religious practices to submit or link someone, often a newborn baby, to perhaps a particular historical person, angelic being or deity. This is sometimes done with vows and rituals, seeking to invoke prosperity or protection from the one to whom dedication has been made.

Surrendering our life to a false protector in this way can have unhealthy spiritual, and even physical, consequences. Jesus commands us to follow Him alone as Master and Savior, not to be bound through dedication to anyone else, however good or powerful they might have been.

As Jesus is invited to direct our lives, God's desire is that increasingly we will take on the likeness and character of Jesus. If we have been dedicated to human individuals or false gods, the enemy has rights to promote aspects of their unrighteous character in and through our lives. In this case, it will be important to forgive those who carried out the dedication (if we were a child, for example), renounce the false protection, claim release from any ungodly soul-ties and seek the Lord for cleansing from all defilement and disorder in our human spirit, soul and body. Sometimes in dedication there is a specific naming after the one being revered. It will be helpful to renounce any ungodly association through such names that we have been given. We have a unique identity before God, and He wants us to walk in spiritual freedom as His children, surrendered only to Him, and to the destiny which He has prepared for us.

> Romans 12:1... So then, my friends, because of God's great mercy to us I appeal to you: Offer yourselves as a living sacrifice to God, dedicated to his service and pleasing to him. This is the true worship that you should offer. (GNB)

See Anointing, Control, Destiny, False Religion, Identity, Protection, Soul-tie

Defense Mechanism – self-protection of places of unresolved inner pain and insecurity, in a way which is in line with our carnal nature.

The soul and particularly the human spirit are easily hurt by the sinful behavior of others, and the trespassing of the enemy into our lives. If there is no rightful guard ruling over our spirits, we can feel extremely vulnerable.

> Proverbs 25:28... Like a city that is broken into and without walls Is a man who has no control over his spirit. (NASB)

The verse above might seem to imply that we should protect ourselves, but that is not what God tells us in His Word. Instead, He offers to be that strong wall around our spirit. If we let Him, God wants to have that loving control over our hearts and to defend the painful places for us, but we so easily turn to our own means of security.

> Proverbs 18:10–11... The name of the LORD is a strong tower; The righteous runs into it and is safe. A rich man's wealth is his strong city, And like a high wall in his own imagination. (NASB)

Walls around our hearts are very good if God is the one constructing them, but our own self-made defenses will simply isolate the hurting places from God's healing touch. We conceal pain in many different ways, even with laughter.

> Proverbs 14:13... Laughter may hide sadness. When happiness is gone, sorrow is always there. (GNB)

Defense mechanisms are the choices and behavior patterns which we follow, often unconsciously, in an attempt to avoid further inner pain. They are sinful decisions of the soul, overruling and often crushing the quiet voice of the human spirit. As with all iniquity, wrongful self-protection significantly affects our relationships with other people and more particularly with God (Isaiah 59:2, Hebrews 3:15).

Such behaviors include rebellion, cynicism, criticism, sarcasm, ungodly use of anger, arrogance, hatred, pride, ridicule, control, religious practices, manipulation, inappropriate joking and laughter, wearing a mask, fantasy, emotional shut down, independence, denial and dissociation. We have seen that defense mechanisms are like building our own walls around the city of our heart. There is an interesting picture in Isaiah of how very destructive God sees humanity's self-protection to be, simply adding to the inner damage.

> Isaiah 22:9–11... And you saw that the breaches In the wall of the city of David were many ... Then you counted the houses of Jerusalem And tore down houses to fortify the wall. ... But you did not depend on Him who made it, Nor did you take into consideration Him who planned it long ago. (NASB)

God is best able to defend us and fight for us. As we choose to confess and dismantle all our own defensive behaviors and receive His forgiveness, then His righteousness can bring true peace to the places of need.

> Isaiah 32:17–18... And the work of righteousness will be peace, and the service of righteousness, quietness and confidence forever. Then

my people will live in a peaceful habitation, and in secure dwellings and in undisturbed resting places ... (NASB)

See Carnal Nature, Coping Mechanism, Dissociation, Mask, Righteousness, Self-control, Self-protection, Rebellion

Defilement (Defile, Defiling) – spiritual and physical impurity resulting from sin.

When we sin, we give opportunity for the enemy to govern that part of our lives and display something of his unclean nature, rather than the purity of Jesus.

> Leviticus 18:24... Do not defile yourselves in any of these ways [with the sins of the Canaanites], because this is how the nations that I am going to drive out before you became defiled. (NIV)

Defilement through sin will not only affect our own lives, but also those for whom we carry responsibility. A father caught up in online pornography, for example, will defile not just himself but the whole of his family. The father is, in effect, misusing his priestly role in the family, through the personal idolatry of pornography.

> Ezekiel 44:12... "Because they [the Levites] ministered to them before their idols and caused the house of Israel to fall into iniquity, therefore I have raised My hand in an oath against them," says the LORD God, "that they shall bear their iniquity." (NKJV)

Interestingly, another verse in Leviticus 18 goes on to explain that land itself also gets defiled.

> Leviticus 18:25... For the land has become defiled, therefore I have brought its punishment [iniquity] upon it, so the land has spewed out its inhabitants. (NASB)

This happens because of rights given to the enemy through the sin of those who own or occupy that land. Unclean spirits can occupy land as well as affecting people (Zechariah 13:2).

The father involved in pornography defiles even the dwelling place of his family. The iniquity or unrighteousness brought into his household can allow impurity and dysfunction to "spew out" over every member of

the family, even though they may have no awareness of the root issue, which is the father's sin. The wonderful answer to all such defilement is clear from Scripture:

> 1 John 1:9... If we confess our sins, He is faithful and righteous to forgive us our sins and to cleanse us from all unrighteousness. (NASB)

Amazingly, God can and will cleanse even the land and homes that we occupy, if we come to him in humility and confession.

> 2 Chronicles 7:14... If my people, who are called by my name, will humble themselves and pray and seek my face and turn from their wicked ways, then I will hear from heaven, and I will forgive their sin and will heal their land. (NIV)

Jesus walked this earth in perfect purity. He has made it possible for us to also walk in that purity as we increasingly let Him reign within us.

See Confession, Cleansing, Deliverance, Forgiveness, Iniquity, Pornography, Reclaim Ground, Righteousness, Sexual Sin, Sin

Deliverance (Deliver) – release from hostile spiritual control.

For a Christian, deliverance is encountered not just in the wonderful process of being born again – the precious transfer from the spiritual darkness of the enemy's domain to the light of the Kingdom of God (Colossians 1:13) – but also in the ongoing, and very necessary, cleansing of our lives. This can be pictured if we consider the saving of a seabird

DELIVERANCE

from a deathly oil spill. The bird first needs to be removed from the oil. Then the oil must also be carefully removed from the body of the bird, if it is to be fully restored.

> Ephesians 5:8... for you were formerly darkness, but now you are Light in the LORD; walk as children of Light ... (NASB)

Spiritual control is a combination of authority and power. When spiritual authority over some aspect of our lives is handed over to the enemy through ongoing sin, he can gain a measure of spiritual control over us. Sin gives him authority, and he empowers that authority through the use of unclean spirits, which then seek to drive a person's choices, in order to maintain the place of sin. Jesus saw deliverance as part of the normal needs of a believer, when He taught His disciples the essentials of prayer.

> Matthew 6:13... And lead us not into temptation, but deliver us from the evil one. (NIV)

True deliverance comes as follows: First of all, the full reality of sin is acknowledged through revelation by the Holy Spirit (John 16:8, John 14:17). This may be our own sin, for which we need to repent, or it may be the sin of those who have misused some responsibility they had for our lives. This sin of others needs to be forgiven. Jesus calls the devil *the father of lies* (John 8:44), but the enemy's work is exposed when truth is fully revealed.

For a follower of Jesus, the forgiveness of those who have sinned against us and the receiving of God's forgiveness for our own sin completely removes the spiritual authority (right, entitlement, foothold, license, upper hand or advantage) formerly held by the powers of darkness (2 Corinthians 2:10–11). The final part of the process will often be to evict any unclean spirits (Luke 4:35) through the power of the Holy Spirit (Matthew 12:28), which results in real freedom, and indeed the furthering of the authority of the Kingdom of God in our lives. It is like throwing out backseat drivers who have previously been allowed to clamber into the vehicle of our lives, and who have constantly been trying to press us to go down wrong and harmful roads. Deliverance for a Christian has been well described as removing the power of cancelled sin.

See Authority, Control, Darkness, Foothold, Freedom, Holy Spirit, Kingdom, Manifestation, Power, Powers of Darkness, Right, Truth, Unclean Spirit

Delusion (Delude, Deluding) – extreme condition of self-deception.

Delusional behavior may result from chemical imbalance in the body, but there can be a spiritual root as a consequence of persistent isolation, independence or rebellion, with ultimately tragic results for some who are unwilling to receive truth.

> 2 Thessalonians 2:10–11... they did not receive the love of the truth so as to be saved. For this reason God will send upon them a deluding influence so that they will believe what is false ... (NASB)

God's way for us to remain in the safe place of His truth is for us to be in rightful submission to Him and to His distribution of gifting within the Body of Christ.

> Ephesians 5:21... be subject to one another in the fear of Christ. (NASB)

God has conferred gifts on each one in the Body of Christ for the benefit of all the members. As we work in mutual submission to the ministry of the Holy Spirit through one another, some discerning, some leading, some healing, some teaching, some prophesying, for example, we will remain safe from deception. Rightful dependence on the Word of God and our seeking of truth *together* steers us away from the lies of the enemy and from the spiritual authority he craves in our lives. His aim is to drive us into destructive pathways of human-centered wisdom.

> James 3:15... This wisdom is not that which comes down from above, but is earthly, natural, demonic. (NASB)

We can help those suffering from delusion by encouraging them to walk a path of clear accountability (rightful submission) to God and to mature members of the Body of Christ, who are able to confront false beliefs and sinful behaviors with truth and grace, gradually robbing the enemy of all his rights to maintain the defiling grip of delusion.

See Authority, Coping Mechanism, Deception, Discernment, Lie, Rebellion, Truth, Unreality

Demon (Demonize, Demonic) – See Unclean Spirit

Denial (Deny) – choice not to acknowledge the truth.

This can be a response to a fearful situation as when Peter denied knowing Jesus (Luke 22:34), or a way of trying to deal with our own sin or inner wounding.

The issues of life often cause deep pain, shame or fear, so we try to minimize the discomfort in various ways, including the defense mechanism of denial. It can seem beneficial to disconnect from the reality of a wounded heart by convincing myself that the damage was nothing, *it didn't hurt, it hasn't affected me, it's forgotten and it doesn't need God's healing.* We can also do something similar with sinful choices and guilty feelings from the past, justifying or denying the fact of wrongdoing.

> Jeremiah 2:35... you say, "I am innocent; surely the LORD is no longer angry with me." But I, the LORD, will punish you because you deny that you have sinned. (GNB)

You can put cheese into a kitchen cupboard, close the door and pretend it's not there. Such denial may be successful for a few weeks or even months, but eventually, and inevitably, the cheese will make itself known by the smell around the house. It is the same with the denial of sin or pain. The odor of the past will eventually pollute our lives today.

There are also many dysfunctional behaviors, such as eating disorders and addictions, usually rooted in inner distress, where the people concerned are particularly prone to denial because of shame. Many an alcoholic has convinced themselves for years that they do not have a problem, until some trauma occurs which means that the truth eventually has to be faced.

At the extreme, we can even deny the truth of our relationship with Jesus, like Peter did through his fear of persecution.

DEPENDENCE

Denial never calms nor heals the hurting heart. It simply hides the painful issues in the dark and allows spiritual mold to grow, fed by the *father of lies*. In contrast, allowing Jesus, the Way, the Truth and the Life, to pay for the cost of our sin and carry the weight of unhealed pain is the true route to lasting peace. It could well be the right time today for some of us to get real about some 'cheese' in the cupboard, and let God's truth and grace clear the air!

> Psalm 24:3–4… Who may ascend into the hill of the LORD? And who may stand in His holy place? He who has clean hands and a pure heart, Who has not lifted up his soul to falsehood And has not sworn deceitfully. (NASB)

See Coping Mechanism, Defense Mechanism, Dissociation, Lie, Truth, Unreality

Dependence (Depend) – reliance on someone or something.

Such reliance can be healthy or unhealthy. There is a rightful interdependence between all those who are part of the Body of Christ (Ephesians 5:21), taking advantage of the gifts distributed by the Holy Spirit for the common good (1 Corinthians 12:7). We are dependent on food to sustain physical life and on shelter for our protection, but an unhealthy and controlling dependence on certain substances or behaviors is actually an addiction and can be very harmful to our lives. Similarly, we can be wrongly dependent on other people, seeking to find something of our identity through a relationship with them, while actually putting ourselves into the controlling bondage of codependence.

There can sometimes be an unhealthy dependence on a person who has been instrumental in our healing process. This is a consequence of wounding that makes us look for inner security from a particular relationship even when such support is no longer needed, and could even be harmful. Healthy relationships are very important to our well-being. Sometimes in the midst of particular distress we can find ourselves very dependent on other people. This is not necessarily wrong, but ultimately it is only our dependence on God that will truly sustain us through the challenges of life. A lifeboat is wonderful for helping to rescue us from a sinking ship, but we need to quickly get onto solid ground to be fully restored to abundant life.

In the process of ministering to one another in the Body of Christ, we need to be careful to avoid prolonged dependence on one another to the detriment of our reliance on Jesus. In the acute needs of dynamic prayer ministry, God's wisdom, comfort and healing can come through the gifting of a particular person, but it is very important that Jesus is seen as the foundational answer to every need, rather than any human-centered solution, or any individual, however compassionate they may be.

> Isaiah 22:11... And you made a reservoir between the two walls For the waters of the old pool. But you did not depend on Him who made it, Nor did you take into consideration Him who planned it long ago. (NASB)

See Addiction, Codependence, Comfort, Control, Interdependence, Soul-tie

Depression (Depressed) – deep, persistent and debilitating despair.

Everybody has days when life seems particularly hard or unhappy, but the issue that we are considering here, sometimes called *clinical* depression, is far more serious. It can last for weeks or months and is one of the biggest health issues of our day, with symptoms which include a profound and persistent absence of positive emotions, loss of interest in activities, fatigue, low self-confidence, hopelessness, disrupted sleep patterns and sometimes thoughts of suicide. The Bible reminds us that just encouraging a sufferer to *snap out of it* or just trying to cheer them up can be worse than useless.

> Proverbs 25:20... Singing to a person who is depressed is like taking off a person's clothes on a cold day or like rubbing salt in a wound. (GNB)

Along with various talking therapies, the medical profession prescribes substantial quantities of antidepressant drugs worldwide, and we praise God that medication can indeed help to alleviate the serious and miserable symptoms experienced by the sufferers. However, in Christ, we have a wonderful opportunity to go further in bringing help to one another by acknowledging the deep spiritual heaviness which is frequently the underlying issue, whatever today's trigger might be:

> Isaiah 61:3a... [The LORD has sent Me] To console those who mourn in Zion, To give them beauty for ashes, The oil of joy for mourning, The garment of praise for the spirit of heaviness ... (NKJV)

Short bouts of depression can be caused by issues such as a recent trauma or hormonal imbalance. However, from a Christian perspective, the root cause for persistent depression is likely to be found in unresolved disorder deep within the human soul and human spirit (Psalm 69:20 KJV). Especially when we have experienced times of a serious deficit in spiritual protection during childhood, our human spirit can be left carrying deep anxiety and hopelessness, often made worse by our own ways of trying to hide or overcome the problem. For example, suppression of deep anger from particular injustice experienced as a child can place a severe burden on our human spirit, which may eventually manifest in symptoms of depression.

> Jonah 4:9... I'm so angry I wish I were dead. (NIV)

Whilst we are not pretending to provide a quick fix, followers of Jesus do have very good news for those suffering with this painful disorder, namely that Jesus has come to take away the heaviness of the human heart (Matthew 11:28). He has come to bring life to the wounded spirit. God wants us to call on Him even from the deepest pit of our lives (Lamentations 3:55–57).

As those suffering depression manage to forgive the people who have deeply wounded them in the past, they can seek and receive God's comfort and healing for inner brokenness. They can also receive His forgiveness for their own damaging behaviors in trying to resolve the problems, which may include having suppressed rightful emotions, such as anger. As they do this one step at a time, it opens the way for God to completely transform the condition of their hearts. Every choice that we make in agreement with Jesus gives the Holy Spirit a powerful opportunity to bring increasing and true peace, a living hope and a lasting joy deep into our human spirit (1 Peter 1:3, Romans 15:13).

See Anger, Burnout, Grief, Hopelessness, Human Spirit, Joy, Soulishness, Suicide, Trauma

Desire (Desirable) – passionate longing for something or someone.

There is nothing wrong with desire if it is driven by God. It is a motivator for the rightful fulfillment of vision and destiny. We are created to have passion for the abundant life which God has purposed. Indeed, He loves to respond to the desires of a heart which is in line with His plans.

> Psalm 37:4... Delight yourself in the LORD; And He will give you the desires of your heart. (NASB)

However, desire can also be driven by our carnal nature, and is sometimes empowered by an unclean spirit. Desires frequently control our choices of behavior, so it is important that we recognize who is governing the process. Walking in the desires which spring from the Holy Spirit will bring immense satisfaction. Following the lusts of our sinful nature will eventually lead to destruction (Romans 8:6).

God is not a killjoy. Jesus showed considerable passion in His calling to this world, and He experienced deep joy in seeing the progress of His Kingdom happening through precious friends.

> Luke 10:21a... At that very time He rejoiced greatly in the Holy Spirit ... (NASB)

The wellspring of godly desire is the human spirit. This happens when our spirit is fed by the pure water of the Holy Spirit, as God intended (John 7:38). Unfortunately, the brokenness of our lives can often result in soulish and distorted desires, where we are seeking to meet our own needs of temporary comfort rather than following God's perfect plan and thus receiving God's permanent comfort. Let's allow Him to bring further healing and let's seek Him, asking Him to give us increasing spiritual maturity so that we will know and follow the longings of a heart which agrees with Him.

C.S. Lewis wrote: *"Human will becomes truly creative and truly our own when it is wholly God's, and this is one of the many senses in which he that loses his soul shall find it."*[4]

See Carnal Nature, Destiny, Lust, Soulishness, Vision, Will

Despair (Desperation) – See Hopelessness

Despising (Despise) – strong contempt for someone with regard to their value or ability.

It is right for us to despise those things which are contrary to God's purposes in our lives, as Jesus did in despising the shame that the world wanted to dump on Him at the cross (Hebrews 12:2). However, here we are talking about the despising of people. This despising may come as a response to those who have wronged us in some way, or perhaps from learned attitudes toward particular people or groups of people. For example, a despising of men can be handed down from mother to daughter if the parent still holds the offense of particular abuse in her past. Despising is a fruit of deep-rooted judgment against others and it is very harmful (2 Samuel 6:16–23). It can only be cleansed by giving and receiving forgiveness, in order to disempower the defiled mindset.

Being the victim of a despising attitude from someone can be deeply wounding. Again, it is important that we reach a place of true forgiveness and find release and healing from the controlling soul-tie that will have become established, where we have come under the power of a person's judgment. Jesus knows well the pain of being personally despised, and He is ready to bring us His wonderful healing and deliverance.

> Isaiah 53:3–4... He was despised and forsaken of men, A man of sorrows and acquainted with grief; And like one from whom men hide their face He was despised, and we did not esteem Him. Surely our griefs He Himself bore, And our sorrows He carried ... (NASB)

See Affirmation, Approval, Bitter Root Judgment, Judgment, Rejection, Value

Destiny – calling and purposes of God for each one of us in this life.

It is the answer to the question, *What am I doing here?* Within the corporate destiny for the whole Body of Christ, God has given each one of us a unique personal identity and a unique personal destiny. Identity answers the question, *Who am I?* This is not the same as destiny, although they are closely related. Our sense of identity needs to be first discovered through the revelation of the Holy Spirit. If we are followers of Jesus, the Holy Spirit seals into our human spirit the

truth that we are God's own children, with whom God has a special love relationship.

> Romans 8:16… God's Spirit joins himself to our spirits to declare that we are God's children. (GNB)

As God's children, we grow into the likeness of Jesus, but each of us has a unique personality.

Our heavenly Father leads us into His purpose for us as part of the worldwide Body of Christ. As we follow Him day by day, we gradually discover the good works that He has created us to fulfill, the things that he prepared for us in advance (Ephesians 2:10). The precise gifts and callings will be different for each person, but these will serve a greater purpose for which God has created humankind, and for which we have now been chosen by Jesus.

> John 15:16… You did not choose me; I chose you and appointed you to go and bear much fruit, the kind of fruit that endures. And so the Father will give you whatever you ask of him in my name. (GNB)

The overriding call on the life of every believer is to *bear fruit*. It was the very first command of God at the moment of the creation of man and woman (Genesis 1:28) and, as we see in the verse above, it is the key destiny of every disciple of Jesus. If we are obedient to the commands of God, walking under the anointing of the Holy Spirit, we will do amazing things, but the essential purpose is to be fruitful.

This means we will corporately display the image, character and qualities of God. He gifts us, enables us and empowers us to do this as He grows this amazing fruit in us through the Holy Spirit (Galatians

5:22–23). The disciple Peter needed to become firmly established in his true identity, found in an honest love relationship with Jesus, before he could be commissioned into his particular destiny of being a shepherd of God's people. It was painful for him to realize how much change was necessary in his life in order that he could fully move into his God-given destiny. It's likely to be the same for each of us, but the result will be extraordinary fulfillment.

> John 21:17... A third time Jesus said, "Simon son of John, do you love me?" Peter became sad because Jesus asked him the third time, "Do you love me?" and so he said to him, "LORD, you know everything; you know that I love you!" Jesus said to him, "Take care of my sheep." (GNB)

See Anointing, Disobedience, Fruit, Gifts of the Holy Spirit, Identity

Disappointment – loss of something hoped for.

We should not underestimate the effect that disappointment can have on a person's life. From the seemingly small issue of a father regularly failing to fulfill a promise to read a child's bedtime story, to the overwhelming disappointment of a failed marriage, such wounding events can often be the seed for strong responses of judgment, cynicism, rejection, unbelief, hopelessness, despair or rebellion in the heart of those affected.

> Proverbs 13:12... Hope deferred makes the heart sick, But desire fulfilled is a tree of life. (NASB)

Disappointment can eat away at our hearts if it is not resolved. God wants us to discover His faithfulness through walking in fellowship with the Holy Spirit, whose counsel will always be good for us. We will need to own the wrongful heart attitudes that have become part of our lives, and we will need to forgive those who have caused the disappointments. Many people in this world will promise much and deliver very little, often causing us pain and a deep sense of betrayal. We can bring to God every one of these hurts, whether big or small, and know a deep comfort and an absolute certainty of His trustworthiness.

> Romans 5:2,5... we exult in hope of the glory of God. ... and [this] hope does not disappoint, because the love of God has been poured

out within our hearts through the Holy Spirit who was given to us. (NASB)

See Betrayal, Faith, Hope, Hopelessness, Loss, Trust

Disapproval (Disapprove, Disapproving) – judgmental rejection of someone's worth or ability.

God does not disapprove of us. He will never condone our sin, but He rejoices over each one of his children with shouts of joy, even while we are on our journey of cleansing and restoration (Zephaniah 3:17).

Constant disapproval crushes the human spirit. Maybe you know someone literally bent over with the weight of relentless disapproval, perhaps from a spouse or a parent. A father, particularly, is called by God to be a significant source of affirmation for his children in their identity and destiny. Even Jesus heard the affirming words of His Father declaring God's pleasure as His Son came out of the water of baptism.

> Luke 3:22... the Holy Spirit descended upon Him in bodily form like a dove, and a voice came out of heaven, "You are My beloved Son, in You I am well-pleased." (NASB)

When we have experienced the wounding of disapproval, we will need to forgive those who have crushed rather than strengthened our hearts, particularly as we grew from childhood to adulthood. Very often those needing our forgiveness will include one or both parents. Then the Lord is ready and willing to give us revelation of His unconditional love and approval, which we so need, in order to feed the hunger of our human spirit.

> Psalm 27:10... For my father and my mother have forsaken me, But the LORD will take me up. (NASB)

See Affirmation, Approval, Father, Rejection, Value

Discernment (Discern) – ability to know what spiritual authority is operating in any particular situation.

Jesus wants to be Lord of every aspect of our lives and to empower our walk and ministry with Him, through the Holy Spirit. However,

there is a ruler of the world who seeks to gain spiritual authority over the lives of Christians by deceiving them into mistakenly embracing his defiling power rather than the life-giving power of the Holy Spirit (2 Corinthians 11:14). Discernment is one of the gifts of the Holy Spirit (1 Corinthians 12:10), and it is particularly important in these end times when deception will become much more intense, according to Jesus (Matthew 24:24).

Have a look in this book under the heading 'Deception' for five checks that God gives us in the Bible to help us avoid the enemy's counterfeits. We should earnestly desire the Holy Spirit's gifts (1 Corinthians 14:1), not least discernment, which is an ability to distinguish the true source of all spiritual manifestations. God's leading through this gift will always be consistent with the other very important test given to us by Jesus to help us discern whether we are experiencing His authority or the authority of the enemy: He tells us to carefully assess the fruit (Matthew 7:16). The key question in any such circumstance is this: Are we seeing the character of Jesus growing over time, or are we seeing something more akin to the character of the enemy (Colossians 2:8 GNB)?

A spiritual source is always eventually revealed in the character displayed, because the enemy can counterfeit a measure of God's power, but he can never sustain God's grace and truth. We truly need to grow in discernment in these challenging days.

> Hebrews 5:14... solid food is for the mature, who because of practice have their senses trained to discern good and evil. (NASB)

See Bible, Counterfeit, Deception, Fruit, Gifts of the Holy Spirit, Lie, Manifestation, Power, Word

Disciple (Discipleship) – one called and willing to follow the teaching of Jesus.

Of course, people can be disciples of any teacher, but Christians have made a choice to believe that Jesus is the only person who has ever walked this earth teaching nothing but absolute truth. His disciples desire to live in accordance with the teaching and example of Jesus (John 13:14–15),

DISCIPLE

and so discover more and more truth about themselves and about God (John 8:31–32). They believe that following Him is the way to abundant life now and into eternity, because Jesus is the only way to really know God, and He alone has saved humankind from the effect of sin, by His death on the cross.

Jesus initially called twelve disciples to follow Him, and He gave them instructions (Luke 9:1–2) to proclaim the kingdom of God and heal diseases by His authority and power. He then appointed seventy others to do the same (Luke 10:1–9). Finally, as He was about to return to His Father, He instructed the first disciples to continue to make more disciples, who in turn would make others who would do the same work until His return in the last days.

> Matthew 28:19–20… Go, then, to all peoples everywhere and make them my disciples: baptize them in the name of the Father, the Son, and the Holy Spirit, and teach them to obey everything I have commanded you. And I will be with you always, to the end of the age. (GNB)

While having this amazing promise of His constant presence in our lives, we must face the fact that it is not easy to be a disciple of Jesus (Luke 9:57-62). When we follow Him we put ourselves severely at odds with the ways of the world, and this is very likely to mean sacrifice, pain and may even, for some, end in martyrdom. However, we can be assured that Jesus asks His disciples to go only where He has gone before.

> Mark 8:34… Whoever wants to be my disciple must deny themselves and take up their cross and follow me. (NIV)

True disciples of Jesus will be recognized primarily not by their powerful ministry, not by their eloquent words, not by their place in the church, but by their demonstrating, through the presence of the Holy Spirit, the gracious and loving character of Jesus, in ways that will surprise and challenge the world around them.

> John 13:34… And now I give you a new commandment: love one another. As I have loved you, so you must love one another. If you have love for one another, then everyone will know that you are my disciples. (GNB)

See Believer, Body of Christ, Christian, Commandment, Jesus, Messianic Believer, Teaching

Discipline – teaching and training to bring us in line with what is right.

Discipline is necessary both for the children of an earthly family, and for those belonging to God's family.

> Hebrews 12:9... Furthermore, we had earthly fathers to discipline us, and we respected them; shall we not much rather be subject to the Father of spirits, and live? (NASB)

The first disciples of Jesus followed His teaching. The discipline they received was often challenging, but never controlling nor crushing. Through the Bible and through the Holy Spirit, this same teaching continues for followers of Jesus today, helping us to see what is right, or wrong, in our lives.

> John 16:8... And [the Holy Spirit], when He comes, will convict the world concerning sin and righteousness and judgment ... (NASB)

Unfortunately, many of us have received harsh discipline in our homes, in school or in church, perhaps, often condemning us rather than convicting us of the precious truth and the boundless grace of God. As we forgive those who have used discipline to try to make us conform to their own wisdom rather than imparting the wisdom of God, we can find healing, and so we will find it easier to surrender to the vital discipline which Jesus brings to us through the Holy Spirit. This may be too difficult for some, but it is life-giving for those who persevere.

> John 6:66–68... As a result of this [challenging teaching] many of His disciples withdrew and were not walking with Him anymore. So Jesus said to the twelve, "You do not want to go away also, do you?" Simon Peter answered Him, "LORD, to whom shall we go? You have the words of eternal life." (NASB)

See Commandment, Control, Disciple, Free Will, Holy Spirit, Teaching, Truth

Disease – see Sickness

Dishonor – treating something or someone with a lack of respect.

See Honor

Disobedience (Disobey) – acting in opposition to God's commands or to human authority.

The commands of God are not given to spoil our lives but rather to instruct us, so we can keep in line with the spiritual laws of the universe and so enjoy the abundant life for which we were created.

People usually find obedience acceptable when they believe it to be a matter of life and death. We tend to obey the red flag at a beach that warns us not to swim in dangerous seas, but we frequently disobey God's warnings, which are even more serious. This is a spiritually hostile world ruled by an unseen but ruthless fallen angel called Satan.

To disobey God is to step away from the place where we are safe under His loving protection and to enter enemy territory, where theft, destruction and death prevail (John 10:10).

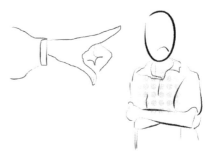

For our safety, God has designed structures of authority and relationship within families and within the Body of Christ, where the various members are equipped by the Holy Spirit for the benefit of the whole group; some in teaching and some in leading, for example. Recognizing the authority which God has invested in all the different members is essential if the group is to move forward safely in the plans and purposes of God.

Mutiny on board a fighting ship on which men have chosen to serve is destructive to all the crew. It is equally destructive in families, churches etc. We need to help one another to walk faithfully under the particular anointing that God has placed upon our lives, recognizing that we are all imperfect vessels, on a journey of healing. God is very able to cover our genuine mistakes, but He cannot cover rebellion until we are willing to acknowledge our sin and receive His pardon (Psalm 37:23–24; 1 Samuel 15:23a).

In these end days, the world is generally being encouraged to pursue entitlement rather than value obedience. We are told that the declaration of rights is now the way to justice rather than the conviction of sin. Obedience to God's commands is increasingly regarded as an irrelevant concept, but the Word of God says it is the only route to true wholeness and freedom.

> 1 John 3:23... This is His commandment, that we believe in the name of His Son Jesus Christ, and love one another, just as He commanded us. (NASB)

See Authority, Choice, Commandment, Covering, Law, Protection, Rebellion

Disorder – condition of being out of line with God's created order.

God gives clear commands to us in the Bible about how to come into line with the spiritual order of His creation, through a covenant relationship with Him. He also makes it clear that rejecting His order is truly harmful to humanity.

> Romans 1:32... [People] who, knowing the righteous order of God, that those practicing such things [rebellion and immorality] are worthy of death, not only do them, but also approve those practicing them. (LITV)

God's perfect order is shown in right authority, loving obedience and spiritual wholeness. However, disorder has affected all of our lives, in some measure, as we experience wrongful control, rebellion, brokenness and bondage, both in individuals and throughout society. The world reaps the consequences of spiritual disorder, for example, with anarchy, terrorism, drug abuse, pornography and family breakdown, despite all the intellectual and scientific advances of humankind.

William Pitt, the British prime minister at the time of the French Revolution, commented that the anarchical events in France had *trampled on the divine order of nations.* Many would say that the world is suffering a no less serious condition today, through its rejection of God's truth and commands. It would be easy, like Job, to despair of the future!

> Job 10:22... The land of utter gloom as darkness itself, Of deep shadow without order, And which shines as the darkness ... (NASB)

Someone commented to me recently how they felt that that the world was simply *not as it was meant to be*. However, God is truly the Redeemer. Spiritual rebirth and the healing ministry of Jesus are wonderful steps in the process of God restoring His order in the lives of His children, both individually and corporately. This happens by means of forgiveness and cleansing, made possible through the death of Jesus on the cross. The world *can* change if He is recognized as Lord.

See Authority, Dysfunction, Eating Disorder, Healing, Iniquity, Order, Rebellion

Disrespect – not showing the respect that is due to another person.

See Abuse, Despising, Honor, Neglect, Value

Dissociation (Dissociate, Dissociative) – an expression used in a particular way by Ellel Ministries to describe self-abandonment of a core part of ourselves in an attempt to cope with major inner distress.

We are not talking about the helpful 'switching off' that everyone engages in from time to time during recreational pastimes, such as reading or painting. Nor are we referring to the kind of denial that many people use to cope with difficult situations, by saying things like, "It wasn't that bad!" or "It didn't really affect me." The significant disengagement that we are considering here is a longstanding disconnection from part of our God-given identity. It is a coping mechanism which requires us to self-construct an alternative outer identity in order to present an acceptable and adequate image of ourselves to other people, and to compensate for something we don't like or want in ourselves.

> Proverbs 18:14... The spirit of a man can endure his sickness, But as for a broken spirit who can bear it? (NASB)

Dissociation is a decision, often subconscious, which we make to cope with inner pain from deep distress. Such distress may include brokenness, such as full or partial fragmentation. Dissociation is a way of trying to deal with, and negate, an overwhelming sense of inadequacy, badness, guilt or shame, for example, which we feel deep down, and wanting to reinvent ourselves in a better light.

For example, the outer image we create and present to people may be responsible and capable, thus denying the truth of the hurting and trapped, and possibly despised, inner self who feels inadequate and shameful. This is like a crumbling building being hidden by a newly constructed façade, giving the impression of solidity throughout, but actually masking the shattered places inside. Dissociation of this kind is remarkably common, at some level.

In a similar way, another person may choose to disconnect from, and mask, an inner place of strength and capability, in order to present to the world an outer image of wounding and neediness, thus appearing to be someone who constantly requires the attention of others to meet their needs. What they are doing is disconnecting from the core of their personhood, where God intends them to take rightful personal responsibility and thus grow, mature and blossom in life. Or a person may choose to appear slightly incompetent to cover a fear of failure, disconnecting from their true inner self, which actually has a real, God-given need to take responsibility and to be allowed to grow through making mistakes in life.

For those operating in dissociation, there is considerable fear that the true state of the inner place will be discovered. The outer façade that we have constructed is not the full truth of all that we are but, instead of accepting who we really are, we present what we consider to be a more acceptable image (Isaiah 28:15b). When, for example, this is an image of a strong person, we will often be exaggerating our God-given abilities, in order to compensate for the turmoil inside us.

Dissociation soon becomes a lifestyle choice, as it is our preferred way of coping. The inner, abandoned identity is still there and remains in turmoil. From this core place, a dissociated person will seek relief in ungodly ways which cause more distress and which increase the wounding and reinforce the lies we believe about the unacceptability of our true self. Our carnal nature drives the wrong behaviors of both the inner and outer places. This gives opportunity for the enemy to demonically empower both the separation from our true self and the sinful behaviors. Such ways of trying to self-protect through dissociation are actually very self-destructive, denying God the opportunity to bring His answer to our needs. This is not

DISTRESS

unlike the picture that Isaiah gives us when he refers to the destructive fortification of Jerusalem.

> Isaiah 22:9–11… you saw that the breaches In the wall of the city of David were many … Then you counted the houses of Jerusalem And tore down houses to fortify the wall. … But you did not depend on Him who made it, Nor did you take into consideration Him who planned it long ago. (NASB)

God's desire for our lives is wholeness, so the choice to separate from and abandon part of our personhood and create an unreal and incomplete outer identity will be very damaging to the functioning of our body, soul and human spirit, distorting both our gifting and our destiny. The key issue is the soulish control used to maintain the acceptable image, which then inevitably crushes our human spirit. Because God cannot heal the falsehood of an unreal human-created identity, true restoration will only come when we choose to live in the reality of who we are, however damaged and inadequate that may feel. We need to let Jesus be the one who heals and delivers the broken, crushed, trapped and abandoned places inside us. Our part is to acknowledge and repent of abandoning this part of ourselves. We need to respond in godly ways to the truth of the damage that has happened during our lives, forgiving those who have wounded us and receiving God's forgiveness and cleansing for our unrighteous ways of trying to fix the pain by ourselves. Then we can pour out the pain of our hearts to our loving God and receive His healing.

> Psalm 86:11… Teach me Your way, O LORD; I will walk in Your truth; Unite my heart to fear Your name. (NASB)

See Brokenness, Carnal Nature, Coping Mechanism, Defense Mechanism, Full and Partial Fragmentation, Identity, Self-protection, Unreality

Distress – condition of painful overload in the body, soul or human spirit.

See Burnout, Stress

Distrust – lack of trust.

See Faith, Trust

Disunity – division between people, with regard to belief and purpose.

See Agreement, Unity

Divination (Divining) – pursuit of supernatural knowledge obtained from the powers of darkness.

> Acts 16:16… Now it happened, as we went to prayer, that a certain slave girl possessed with a spirit of divination met us, who brought her masters much profit by fortune-telling. (NKJV)

People tend to think that such activity is confined to history and primitive cultures, but it is still quite widespread. We have prayed with people who have used divining rods to find underground water, and seen them delivered from an unclean spirit which had been given a right to operate in the person's life through the pursuit of this supernatural, but ungodly, power. There are many types of divination, such as the use of pendulums, mediums, palm reading etc. God has made it very clear that any form of divination is not a permitted or safe practice for those who are in covenant with Him.

> Deuteronomy 18:14… Then Moses said, "In the land you are about to occupy, people follow the advice of those who practice divination and look for omens, but the LORD your God does not allow you to do this." (GNB)

See Deception, Deliverance, Occult, Powers of Darkness, Supernatural, Unclean Spirit

Divorce – legally recognized dissolution of a marriage relationship.

Biblical marriage is not just a special relationship, but a covenant agreement between a man and a woman, presided over by God.

DIVORCE

> Malachi 2:14... the Lord has been a witness between you and the wife of your youth, against whom you have dealt treacherously, though she is your companion and your wife by covenant. (NASB)

When He has been witness to this important union, God hates to see any breaking of the covenant through sinful separation, deceit or betrayal, and He warns of the deep damage which such behavior can cause.

> Malachi 2:16... "For I hate divorce," says the LORD, the God of Israel, "and him who covers his garment with wrong," says the LORD of hosts. "So take heed to your spirit, that you do not deal treacherously." (NASB)

Human laws may permit divorce under particular circumstances, but when God presides over a marriage covenant, He sees that divine joining as remaining an effective bond unless *His* justice is truly met for release (Matthew 19:8–9), irrespective of human assessment.

> Matthew 19:6... So they are no longer two, but one flesh. What therefore God has joined together, let no man separate. (NASB)

The Bible explains that sexual infidelity by a marriage partner (which could include persistent use of pornography – Matthew 5:28) inevitably breaks the terms of the marriage covenant, because such activity is tantamount to giving oneself into an alternative and conflicting covenant relationship. God would always most desire forgiveness and reconciliation, but if there is divorce due to infidelity (Jeremiah 3:8), it is consistent with God's justice in releasing the aggrieved partner from the marriage bond.

> Matthew 19:9... And I say to you, whoever divorces his wife, except for immorality, and marries another woman commits adultery. (NASB)

Other major sin issues within a marriage, such as cruelty, neglect, intimidation, ridicule, deceit and desertion, clearly cause huge damage and defilement to the covenant agreement and to God's purpose for marriage. He understands the distress many of us experience from these broken relationships, so we can always come to the Lord to seek a just solution for dealing with a covenant bond which has been grossly dishonored by a marriage partner, with no willingness by them to truly repent.

All divorce brings painful emotional and spiritual consequences. For the children, it is often the subsequent confusion of loyalty to parents that does the most damage. But when there is divorce which ignores God's view of justice, this will also have ongoing and defiling spiritual consequences. However, such divorce is not an unpardonable sin, and anyone who truly humbles themselves before God to seek His full resolution can receive His forgiveness and cleansing from all spiritual bondage.

In every troubled area of our lives, not least with the issues of marriage and divorce, God requires us to depend on His wisdom rather than our own. We will find His wisdom when we are truly seeking His ways, His grace and His cleansing.

See Adultery, Betrayal, Covenant, Justice, Marriage, Sexual Sin

Domination (Dominate) – overt control (mastering) of someone's will.

See Control, Fear, Jezebel

Dominion (Domain) – spiritual or physical realm of rule.

See Authority, Darkness, Kingdom, Light, Power, Ruling Spirit, Satan

Doubt (Doubting) – uncertainty as to the truth.

The Bible records for us the story of a famous doubter by the name of Thomas.

> John 20:25... The other disciples were saying to [Thomas], "We have seen the LORD!" But he said to them, "Unless I see in His hands the imprint of the nails, and put my finger into the place of the nails, and put my hand into His side, I will not believe." (NASB)

Thomas had heard the words of other disciples but he decided that he needed a very personal encounter with Jesus in order to truly believe in what they had said. We may not be able to have quite the same tangible experience of Jesus today as Thomas experienced, but we can ask the Lord to bring His confidence into our hearts for whatever He is revealing to us. Jesus did not rebuke Thomas for voicing a doubt, but rather He was concerned about the defilement which the continuation of doubt, and a mindset of unbelief, can cause. This can block God's essential gift of faith, the Holy Spirit power which permits us to perceive as real what has not yet been seen in fact.

Honest questioning can give space for essential discernment, but surrendering to a place of unbelief in God's true word can drive us into cynicism and rebellion. When we find ourselves doubting the truth of words spoken to us about the Lord, we can always come to Him to seek His gift of discernment (1 Corinthians 12:10).

If we find that unbelief and cynicism toward God have taken root, seeded by negative experiences in our lives, we can confess this to the Lord and receive His cleansing and the precious impartation of faith in the truth of His Word. Jesus will always be there to reach out to those who are troubled with doubt.

> Matthew 14:31... Immediately Jesus stretched out His hand and took hold of [Peter], and said to him, "You of little faith, why did you doubt?" (NASB)

See Discernment, Faith, Truth, Unbelief, Revelation

Drug Abuse (Drugs, Drug Misuse) – use of substances, usually outside of medical prescription, in order to find pleasure, to seek experience, or to dull inner pain.

For thousands of years, the effect of certain substances, such as opium and alcohol, have been known and used as an analgesic or a means of escape from reality. God created human beings to need comfort when there is inner pain, but He wants to be the foundational source of that comfort, not least through godly parenting when we were growing up. Unfortunately for many of us, the experiences of life have convinced us that deep personal comfort will only be found through our own effort. However, this is the way of the world and not the truth of God.

> 2 Corinthians 1:3... Blessed be the God and Father of our LORD Jesus Christ, the Father of mercies and God of all comfort ... (NASB)

When we give over the emotional and spiritual needs of the body to a chemical substance rather than to God, we give the enemy a right to spiritually control that aspect of our being. The hold of drug abuse on people's lives will be a combination of chemical dependence, emotional dependence and spiritual bondage, and all these areas will need to be dealt with for there to be true freedom. With hallucinatory drugs there will be an added and often lasting problem of a damaging break to the emotional and spiritual unity of the person, sometimes referred to, during drug use, as *a trip*.

Governments find it difficult to know whether to tackle drug abuse by legislation or treatment. Is it a moral or a medical problem? They are unsure whether to give priority to challenging people's wrong choices through the law or to managing the addictive behavior through chemical intervention, such as a methadone prescription to replace heroin. Both routes are well-meaning and have a place in trying to tackle this hugely destructive issue, made worse these days by the proliferation of recreational drugs. But all these procedures are a management of the problem and not a true healing of broken and bound lives.

However, there is an answer through Jesus. If we open our hearts to Him, He will not only convict us to walk in repentance from the wrong choices that we have made, but He will also bring true healing to the root places of insecurity and pain in the soul and human spirit. The process of healing and deliverance may take time, but if we believe that God is the true answer for the comfort of the wounded heart, there can be complete freedom from all the holds and damage of drug abuse, including the brokenness, shame, deception, and all the bondages of relationships which have been instrumental in the addictive lifestyle.

See Addiction, Alcoholism, Brokenness, Comfort, Coping Mechanism, Freedom, Dependence, Shame, Soul-tie

Dysfunction (Dysfunctional) – condition of disorder when God's creation is not operating as He intended.

The word is applied to individuals, families and even nations. Dysfunction is a result of human sin and the wounding caused by it. God intended the whole of His creation to operate in covenant with Him and according to His order. Jesus has come to redeem everything back into right order and right function.

See Disorder, Healing, Order

Eating Disorder – unhealthy behavior and routines with food.

Anorexia nervosa (starving), bulimia nervosa (overeating and purging) and binge eating (overeating without purging) are some of the labels given to food-related behaviors which have become compulsive, controlling, and often include secret routines, in the lives of those who suffer from such disorders. Sadly, there has been a rapid rise in these issues among young people in recent years.

Eating is foundational to our well-being, a God-given pleasure we can share, but food intake should not become an area in which we exert wrongful control, either over ourselves or over others. When any bodily need is not subject to God's order and authority, the enemy is given rights to strengthen the ungodly control of that need in a destructive way.

> 1 Corinthians 6:12–13... All things are lawful for me, but not all things are profitable. All things are lawful for me, but I will not be mastered by anything. Food is for the stomach and the stomach is for food, but God will do away with both of them. ... (NASB)

Although eating routines which can become a form of ritual are very damaging, for some people they can seem indispensable in the search for inner comfort or for an acceptable self-image. Anorexic activity, for example, can release endorphins which subdue inner pain, as well as controlling the body shape to fit perceptions of image. There can be deep anxiety and a sense of self-betrayal whenever the person challenges self-imposed routines of eating, not eating, or purging (through the use of an emetic or laxative). A person's very life can seem to depend on a behavior which is, in fact, destroying them.

The roots of eating disorders can be in trauma, abuse, rejection, bereavement, ungodly control in parenting or family pressure around childhood meal times. These can result in low self-esteem, unmet needs for love and affirmation, or helpless feelings of disempowerment. Often triggered by peer pressure, it can seem natural to use eating behaviors to achieve inner comfort, an acceptable image, or even control over those who are close to us.

Recovery from an established eating disorder is unlikely to be easy, but with the truth and grace of God, complete freedom is possible. It is obviously different from other substance addictions in that it is impossible to avoid all food. Those suffering this disorder need unconditional acceptance, while being lovingly challenged in their choices. The healing process starts with acknowledgment of the sometimes secret behaviors and the very real damage that has occurred to themselves and to others.

Those who are helping need to encourage belief that God's view of a person's identity is the truth, rather than that person's own distorted view. They will need to receive God's healing into the root issues of wounding, and to confess the spiritual control which has been handed over to the enemy. Most addictions and compulsive behaviors are a combination of physical, emotional and spiritual holds, but when Jesus is given complete lordship, every need of freedom and comfort can be fully met.

> John 6:35... Jesus said to them, "I am the bread of life, he who comes to Me will not hunger and he who believes in Me will never thirst." (NASB)

See Affirmation, Addiction, Anxiety, Behavior Cycle, Compulsion, Control, Coping Mechanism, Dependence, Image, Order, Rejection, Wounding

Emotion (Emotional) – expression of feelings in response to the circumstances of life.

Anger, fear, elation, sadness, joy, grief, amazement, despair and many more human emotions are given by God to motivate us into an appropriate response to the situations we face, such as injustice, danger, friendship and loss.

Jesus knew all the human emotions. He wept with grief at the death of a friend (John 11:35), He knew joy in the walk with His disciples (Luke 10:21) and He was deeply troubled by the impending betrayal by a friend whom He had trusted (John 13:21). His response to these feelings was to express them openly to His disciples and more particularly to His Father.

> John 12:27–28... "Now My soul has become troubled; and what shall I say, 'Father, save Me from this hour'? But for this purpose I came to this hour. Father, glorify Your name." ... (NASB)

God wants us to be able to do the same as Jesus, because rightful expression of emotions brings God's order in our lives whenever we find ourselves facing demanding issues (Psalm 62:8). It strengthens relationships as we share how we are feeling with friends and family. It is not God's will for the sun to go down on our anger (Ephesians 4:26-27), nor indeed any other painful emotion, and so allow it to become trapped, unresolved and even empowered by the enemy.

Unfortunately, the truth for most of us is that especially in our childhood, such emotions could not always be expressed as God intended, which has left us with a painful store of 'emotional magma' ready to erupt like a volcano, often at inappropriate times. We can hold emotions down in many ways, using the British 'stiff upper lip', keeping our lives too busy to connect with the pain, or even covering the negative feelings with a mask of laughter.

> Proverbs 14:13... Even in laughter the heart may be in pain, And the end of joy may be grief. (NASB)

God led Joseph, after some thirteen years of abuse by family and friends, to a point of reconciliation with his brothers. All the stored pain from the hurt and injustice of his lonely journey of captivity could at last be expressed and an inner peace restored.

> Genesis 45:1–2... Then Joseph could not control himself before all those who stood by him, and he cried, "Have everyone go out from me." So there was no man with him when Joseph made himself

known to his brothers. He wept so loudly that the Egyptians heard it, and the household of Pharaoh heard of it. (NASB)

As we forgive those who have hurt us and give Jesus lordship over all the emotional pain of the past, we can know a restoring of His order and a new place of peace in our body, soul and human spirit, even if full reconciliation, as Joseph was able to experience, is not always possible.

See Anger, Coping Mechanism, Denial, Fear, Feeling, Guilt, Joy, Mask, Pain, Shame, Soul

Empowerment (Empower, Empowering) – application of power to something or someone.

When our choices are in agreement with the teaching and commands of Jesus, the Holy Spirit empowers our lives to be more effective in our activity and to be more like Jesus in our character.

> Acts 1:8… But you will receive power when the Holy Spirit comes on you; and you will be my witnesses in Jerusalem, and in all Judea and Samaria, and to the ends of the earth. (NIV)

When we walk in disobedience to God, we give authority to the enemy and we allow him to empower sinful (or idolatrous) activity with the power of unclean spirits, which will inevitably cause us to reflect, in some measure, the character of their master, Satan.

> Psalm 115:8… Those who make [idols] will become like them, Everyone who trusts them. (NASB)

So spiritual empowerment in our lives can come from either God or the enemy; through the Holy Spirit or through unclean spirits. It strengthens the consequence of the choices that we make, and in an unseen way, it promotes and drives the beliefs and behaviors relevant to those choices.

See Authority, Foothold, Holy Spirit, Power, Powers of Darkness, Unclean Spirit

Enemy (Enemies) – one of the names which Jesus uses to refer to Satan and his realm of spiritual darkness.

> Luke 10:19... Behold, I have given you authority to tread on serpents and scorpions, and over all the power of the enemy, and nothing will injure you. (NASB)

See Authority, Powers of Darkness, Satan, Unclean Spirit

Enlightenment (Enlighten) – attainment of spiritual or intellectual revelation.

Divine Light, which overcomes spiritual darkness, came into the world in a unique way when Jesus was born. He is the only one ever to have walked the earth speaking absolute truth. Unfortunately, most people do not recognize this true enlightenment, but it is revelation, from the Holy Spirit, which can transform the human heart (Ephesians 1:18–19) if we choose to believe in the one who is light.

> John 1:9–10... There was the true Light which, coming into the world, enlightens every man. He was in the world, and the world was made through Him, and the world did not know Him. (NASB)

By nature, human beings choose to search for enlightenment mostly through their own religious practices (Isaiah 50:10–11), ability and reason.

During the 17th and 18th centuries in Europe, many people became increasingly disillusioned with the tyranny and corruption of much of the church.

There was a search for new ways of interpreting the mysteries of life, and a burning desire for progress. Many people rejected biblical understanding as being false, because those who were advocating it

were so often corrupt. Historians have called it the *Age of Enlightenment* or the *Age of Reason;* a time of remarkable scientific progress, spiritual contention and political upheaval.

God has given humanity an extraordinary brain, capable of vast exploration and innovation. However, if we believe that human virtue can be attained simply by human reason (the basis of humanism), we are in danger of inviting the powers of darkness to be our source of understanding. Equally, there have been countless false religions, from Buddhism to Freemasonry, which have promised enlightenment for the heart of humanity. The Bible warns us of the danger of human-centered wisdom.

> James 3:15... This wisdom is not that which comes down from above, but is earthly, natural, demonic. (NASB)

Jesus has come to us with a claim which the world ignores at its peril. Millions of people have discovered this claim to be absolutely true and wonderfully healing.

> John 8:12... Then Jesus again spoke to them, saying, "I am the Light of the world; he who follows Me will not walk in the darkness, but will have the Light of life." (NASB)

See Born Again, Darkness, False Religion, Freemasonry, Light, Reason, Revelation, Wisdom

Enslave (Enslaving) – See Slavery

Entitlement (Entitle) – See a Right

Entrust – trust a person to carry out a duty or to care for and protect something.

See Trust

Envy – See Jealousy

Eternity (Eternal) – timeless and endless existence.

The foundational name that God has given Himself is *I AM*. He exists in an ever-present spiritual realm of His own creation. He chose also to create, and interact with, another realm which is temporal (existing in time) and physical, where humanity experiences conception, birth and death.

C.S. Lewis wrote: *"If I find in myself a desire which no experience in this world can satisfy, the most probable explanation is that I was made for another world."*[5]

During our time on earth, and only during this lifespan, we have the opportunity to choose to become part of God's eternal spiritual family (John 1:12) and citizens of the Kingdom of God (Colossians 1:13), through receiving the Son of God as the Lord of our lives. This critical choice, confined by time, determines the condition of our eternal existence beyond physical death, both in our relationship with God and in the degree of fruitfulness of our eternal lives.

> John 15:16… You did not choose Me but I chose you, and appointed you that you would go and bear fruit, and that your fruit would remain, so that whatever you ask of the Father in My name He may give to you. (NASB)

Sowing and reaping, cause and effect, can only progress in a situation where time exists. Eternity will be the continual reaping of what has been sown in this precious life, the period of time which God has given for the Body of Christ to be prepared and cleansed as the eternal bride for the Bridegroom of heaven, the King of kings, Jesus Christ. Let's not waste this precious opportunity which God has given us to get right with Him and to bear much fruit, both in the present and for eternity.

Matthew 6:12–13… forgive us our debts, as we also have forgiven our debtors. And do not lead us into temptation, but deliver us from evil. For Yours is the kingdom and the power and the glory forever. Amen. (NASB)

See Death, Fruit, God, Heaven, Hell, Kingdom of God, Life, Spirit, Temporal

Evangelism (Evangelize, Evangelist) – act of proclamation of the good news of Jesus.

The original Latin word for *evangelist* refers to the one who speedily carried and proclaimed to the Roman people the good news of (say) a military victory. Christians bear witness to Jesus in many different ways, especially by our lifestyle, our love for neighbors and our love for one another (John 13:35). However, true Christian evangelism specifically involves carrying and speaking out the gospel message of how men and women can have victory over spiritual death through receiving Jesus Christ into their hearts. Ploughing the ground with our love for others is important, but there can be no harvest if no seed is sown in evangelism.

For the effective healing and deliverance ministry of Jesus in the life of someone who is seeking His healing touch, the starting place must be the person's acceptance of the lordship of Jesus. The ministry of evangelism and the ministry of healing should always go hand in hand within the Body of Christ. This is because the fullness of salvation requires both removing the believer from darkness (Colossians 1:13) and removing darkness from the believer (Ephesians 5:11; Philippians 2:12). We need the transferring of our spiritual location followed by the transforming of our spiritual condition. The success of our evangelism is not measured by numbers, but by our obedience to proclaim the message.

Mark 16:15… And He said to them, "Go into all the world and preach the gospel to all creation." (NASB)

See the Cross, Gospel, Ministry, Salvation, Witness, Word

Evil – condition of a defiling rebellion against God.

EVIL ONE

Evil shows itself in a display of character utterly opposed to that of God.

C.S. Lewis said this: *"There is but one good; that is God. Everything else is good when it looks to Him and bad when it turns from Him."* 6

It is a hard truth, but there is no righteousness in this world except that which truly reflects the goodness of God. According to the Bible, the whole world lies under the power of the Evil One.

> 1 John 5:19... We know that we are of God, and that the whole world lies in the power of the evil one. (NASB)

Satan has this ability to promote evil on the earth because of humanity's rebellion against God. It is only when Jesus reigns in the heart of humankind that evil can truly be replaced with good.

Most people are well-meaning in some measure but, without an antidote to the carnal nature through the power of the Holy Spirit, evil will contaminate every thought, word and deed of our lives. Jesus considered the hold of evil in His first disciples to be such an important issue that He made sure He taught them, and indeed us, the life-changing words which He left for us to pray to the Father.

> Matthew 6:12–13... And forgive us our debts, as we also have forgiven our debtors. And do not lead us into temptation, but deliver us from evil. ... (NASB)

When we have received His forgiveness for our sinful ways, through repentance and surrender to the lordship of Jesus in our lives, we can ask the Father to set us free from the stain of evil and the grip of the Evil One. What an amazing opportunity, at any time, to deal with this defilement of evil where it has had a place in our lives.

See Badness, Defilement, Goodness, Iniquity, Righteousness, Evil One

Evil One – one of the names used in the Bible to refer to Satan.

In fact the Greek word often translated evil in the Lord's Prayer is best translated the *Evil One.*

> Matthew 6:13... Do not bring us to hard testing, but keep us safe from the Evil One. (GNB)

See Enemy, Satan

138

Evil Spirit – See Unclean Spirit

Exercise – physical movement, especially to bring well-being to the body.

There is no doubt that regular and appropriate exercise is good for you! However, a problem occurs if it becomes a persistent means of escape from facing inner distress, or becomes an obsessive need to meet a perceived demand of body image, or it embraces spiritual practices such as Tai Chi Chuan, a martial art from Southeast Asia, now hugely popular around the world.

Simple exercise such as walking, swimming or cycling can indeed nurture the human spirit, but healing of our spiritual dysfunction will never come from exercise alone. It will only come by responding to the truth given to us by the one who made us.

> 1 Timothy 4:8... for bodily discipline is only of little profit, but godliness is profitable for all things, since it holds promise for the present life and also for the life to come. (NASB)

We need to be aware that, at their roots, exercise regimes such as Tai Chi Chuan and yoga seek to make the body receptive through specific postures and routines, to a flow of energy from the spiritual realms. Any such submission of our bodies can be an invitation to the powers of darkness, because the spiritual authority which is being given license over our lives is unclear, at the least. However well-intentioned we may be, we are participating in the occult, and therefore in potentially unsafe practices.

As children of God, our image (body, soul and spirit) needs to be shaped by Him, rather than by what the world says (Romans 12:2). If we have been using exercise as a way of trying to meet, by ourselves, needs that Jesus wants to meet, we may feel it right to confess that to Him. Having said that, of course walking, running or cycling with Him might sometimes be the very thing we need as another part of our getting fit for His return!

> 1 Thessalonians 5:23... May God himself, the God who makes everything holy and whole, make you holy and whole, put you together – spirit, soul, and body – and keep you fit for the coming of our Master, Jesus Christ. (The Message)

See Alternative Medicine, Body, Coping Mechanism, New Age, Obsession, Yoga

Failure (Fail) – not meeting a standard, whether in appearance, ability or behavior.

The question of success or failure in our lives is very dependent on who is setting the standard. The criteria for success are very different in God's Kingdom as compared with those in the world. Income, appearance, celebrity, intellect, status, title, property and power are daily promoted in the media as important factors for a successful life. Jesus stepped into the world presenting a radically different measure of success found in a divine Kingdom which can be entered now. Success in the world demands that I promote my strengths and hide my weaknesses. Success in God's Kingdom asks that I surrender all my strengths and weaknesses to the service of the King of kings.

One day this King met a woman at a well. She was an inferior person by all the standards of Jewish society at the time: a Samaritan, unmarried but living with a man, carrying a very dubious history of relationships and, not least, a *woman* rather than a *man*! The disciples were astonished that Jesus would spend quality time with such a person.

> John 4:27... At this point His disciples came, and they were amazed that He had been speaking with a woman, yet no one said, "What do You seek?" or, Why do You speak with her?" (NASB)

However, she had opened her heart to Jesus and He had shown her complete acceptance. He had explained to her, possibly more fully than to any of His other followers, some of the profound ways of His Kingdom, and how, in this Kingdom, her truthful response to Him made her valuable and successful.

As we learn the ways of Jesus, the mistakes of the past do not need to define us as a failure. A toddler only learns to walk

through many falls. Peter, the disciple, found that despite many mistakes (he even denied association with Jesus), success could be restored as he responded to the love, the truth and the grace of Jesus when they spoke on the shore of the Sea of Galilee.

> John 21: 15... So when they had finished breakfast, Jesus said to Simon Peter, "Simon, son of John, do you love Me more than these?" He said to Him, "Yes, LORD; You know that I love You." Jesus said to him, "Tend My lambs." (NASB)

In the same way, Jesus is always ready to release us from the mistakes, sins and failures of the past, which have often been made worse by the condemning hold of the enemy, and He is able to bring us into a precious new security of being truly successful citizens in His wonderful Kingdom.

See Affirmation, Forgiveness, Identity, Restoration, Sin, Success, Value

Faith – reliance on something or someone out of a deep personal assurance of the truth, even before the result of our trust is necessarily seen as fact.

Christian faith is primarily a condition of the human spirit, as God imparts a deep assurance about certain things that we may also hope for in our soul. As we place our trust and faith in the truth of God and His Word, it activates the promises of God into our lives and enables the will of God to be done on earth in that particular area.

Human reason alone, without faith, simply empowers human sinful nature, and strengthens the grip of humanism, which seeks the improvement of humanity through our own capability. God asks us to reason *with* Him and so find a faith in Him and His Word, which is life-transforming.

> Isaiah 1:18... "Come now, and let us reason together," Says the LORD, "Though your sins are as scarlet, They will be as white as snow; Though they are red like crimson, They will be like wool." (NASB)

Faith in Jesus brings true change to human hearts. The scientific age in which we live wars against such ideas, because faith, we are told in the

Bible, perceives God's Word as real even if it is not yet fully revealed in our lives, and a rational world sees this as foolish.

> Hebrews 11:1... Now faith is the assurance of things hoped for, the conviction of things not seen. (NASB)

Indeed the Bible tells us that faith is essential in our walk as believers. Faith shields us from the enemy (Ephesians 6:16), enables God to accomplish His work in us and through us (Matthew 8:5–10), and it grows as we respond to God's truth with our words and actions (Ephesians 4:15). It is a gift of the Holy Spirit (1 Corinthians 12:9) and without it we cannot please God (Hebrews 11:6).

Faith for spiritual healing must be centered on Jesus and not simply on an unknown power to heal. Countless faith healers throughout history have offered restoration through unseen spiritual forces. However well-meaning these may be, it is only when the sin of humankind is resolved that true healing can come to the whole of our being. God alone has life-giving and restoring water for each of us. It is belief in Jesus Christ, by faith, that causes this spiritual water to flow through our lives.

> John 7:38... He who believes in Me, as the Scripture said, "From his innermost being will flow rivers of living water." (NASB)

See Belief, Doubt, Gifts of the Holy Spirit, Reason, Trust, Unbelief

Faithfulness (Faithful) – trustworthiness and loyalty to the extent that it causes others to have faith in that person, and in what that person says and does.

God alone is utterly faithful and will be loyal to all His covenant promises. He will protect and provide for all His children. Faith in, and dependence on, the Faithful One is the foundation of all security, something so desperately needed in our human spirit.

> Psalm 36:5... Your lovingkindness, O LORD, extends to the heavens, Your faithfulness reaches to the skies. (NASB)

God also wants to grow His character of faithfulness in all believers. It is part of the fruit of the Holy Spirit which grows within us as we surrender our lives to Jesus (Galatians 5:22–23). Many people have experienced betrayal in the past, and God wants those who have been damaged by this deep wounding to find healing as they discover His perfect faithfulness, demonstrated through the Body of Christ on earth. The world is sadly lacking in this much-needed aspect of human relationship.

See Betrayal, Covenant, Faith, Fruit, Loyalty, Marriage, Trust

the Fall (Fallen) – moment when humanity's first rebellion against God, in the Garden of Eden, caused separation from divine spiritual life.

Before the Fall, there was an intimate relationship between God and humanity. Through this relationship came all the wisdom, authority and power needed for human beings to fulfill their destiny of fruitfulness, and to rule over the earth.

> Genesis 1:28... God blessed them; and God said to them, "Be fruitful and multiply, and fill the earth, and subdue it; and rule over the fish of the sea and over the birds of the sky and over every living thing that moves on the earth." (NASB)

As soon as Adam and Eve followed the instruction of Satan, the serpent, by eating the forbidden fruit, the enemy was given the right to intervene as the spiritual authority over the life of humankind. Humanity effectively handed over to Satan the spiritual rule of the earth, resulting in a very destructive governance, bringing sickness and death as an inevitable outcome for all people.

FALSEHOOD

Satan even boasted of this handover when he was seeking to tempt Jesus to also come under his spiritual authority.

> Luke 4:6... And the devil said to [Jesus], "I will give You all this domain and its glory; for it has been handed over to me, and I give it to whomever I wish." (NASB)

God continued to love His human creation, but humanity's choice meant a devastating fall from spiritual intimacy with their Creator and all the abundance of life that God had intended. This spiritual contamination of human existence established a carnal nature in everyone, resulting in a destructive *tendency* to sin rather than just the *choice* whether to do so, which had existed before the Fall. Today, Jesus offers the opportunity for every fallen aspect of our lives to be 'lifted up' to His place of personal relationship with His Father. This is a place where we can be seated with Him even today, above every hold and defilement of the enemy, empowered to resist the carnal nature and to be reconciled to the precious intimacy with God which He had planned for us from the beginning of creation.

> Ephesians 2:5–6... even when we were dead in our transgressions, [He] made us alive together with Christ (by grace you have been saved), and raised us up with Him, and seated us with Him in the heavenly places in Christ Jesus ... (NASB)

See Authority, Carnal Nature, Creation, Death, Power, Rebellion, Sickness, Sin

Falsehood (False) – anything not consistent with God's truth.

Unless we take particular care, falsehood can defile many parts of our spiritual journey with the Lord. This happens through the enemy's deceptions, such as false religion (Acts 17:22), false healing (Matthew 7:22–23), false guilt, false comfort (Matthew 16:22–23), false wonders (Matthew 24:24), false Christs (Matthew 24:5), false apostles (2 Corinthians 11:4), false testimony (Matthew 26:59), false brethren (Galatians 2:4) and false prophecy (Matthew 7:22–23). Our carnal nature tends to draw us into what we see as natural, palatable or fascinating, rather than following the challenging wisdom of God.

Isaiah 28:15b... For we have made falsehood our refuge and we have concealed ourselves with deception. ... (NASB)

Whenever humans depend on their own understanding, they will be vulnerable to following what is false, which brings bondage, rather than following what is true, which brings freedom. If not alert, we can even be drawn into the enemy's traps of distorted responses to sins and wounds, such as carrying false guilt when the wrongdoing actually belongs to others. As the father of lies (John 8:44), the enemy has the right to empower and strengthen whatever is false in our lives, because falsehood is his domain. He is always ready to tempt us into seeking solutions to our needs which may have an appearance of being right (2 Corinthians 11:14), but are actually human wisdom (James 3:15) rather than God's wisdom.

In desperation to alleviate pain, many have turned to holistic treatments which apparently offer spiritual and physical restoration, but these can be spiritually dangerous without the safeguard of the authority of Jesus. Many such treatments are false healing, perhaps changing symptoms but frequently bringing further spiritual bondage, and indeed blocking God's true healing. God has given us the ways and the gifting to discern what is truly of Him. Thank God for the one who is never false, the one who is the *Way*, the *Truth* and the *Life*.

1 Peter 2:22... [Jesus] WHO COMMITTED NO SIN, NOR WAS ANY DECEIT FOUND IN HIS MOUTH ... (NASB)

See Alternative Healing, Coping Mechanism, Deception, Delusion, Discernment, False Religion, Lie, Satan, Truth

False Comfort – coping with inner pain outside of God's ways.

See Comfort, Coping Mechanism, Pain

False Guilt – feelings of guilt, even affecting our identity, which are not the consequences of our own sin.

See Guilt, Shame

False Healing – See Falsehood

False Memory – unreal, self-created recollection of a past event.

Sometimes, pressed by our carnality, we can unconsciously construct a memory that seems to explain the symptoms of unresolved inner pain. Of course, we can all be mistaken in how we remember painful issues from the past, but it is very important, if we are to receive healing from the Lord, that we earnestly pursue the truth when seeking the root causes of today's distress. God can only bring restoration to our lives within an atmosphere of reality (John 4:17; John 8:32).

The seed of a false memory can come from reading about other people's healing journey, or from susceptibility to suggestions made by those trying to help. For this reason, when ministering to others we must be extremely careful not to casually suggest possible past causes of their problem, for example, sexual abuse, without very clear evidence. Hurting people can sometimes be very quick to 'buy into' anything that seems to make sense of their pain, even to the point of unconsciously forming (or adjusting) a memory to fit the assumed root issue. It can soon become an all-consuming focus in the person's search for healing, confusing the true pathway which God has for them.

Of course, it is also very important for those who have truly suffered severe wounding from others to be believed when they find the courage to share their story. With the help of the Holy Spirit, by walking carefully into a determination of the truth, and by verifying all the facts as far as is possible, we should be able to avoid either encouraging unreality or denying the truth.

Jesus describes Satan as the father of lies; anything false is in Satan's domain. For this reason, false memories, especially when endorsed by careless agreement, can become a breeding ground for demonic activity, confusion and further damage to the one in search of healing. Helping someone step away from the bondage of a false memory will require time, trust and grace. They will need courage to let go of what had seemed to be the answer to their distress in order to take hold of what the Lord is saying, which will always be the truth. Thank God that He has promised to guide us as we wait on Him.

> John 16:13... But when He, the Spirit of truth, comes, He will guide you into all the truth... (NASB)

See Coping Mechanism, Deception, Discernment, Holy Spirit, Lie, Memory, Prayer Ministry, Truth, Unreality

False Religion – spiritual belief system held by a group of adherents, which does not in any way depend on submission to the lordship of Jesus Christ.

Many of the Jews who were listening to Jesus' teaching, including His disciples, were earnestly seeking their heavenly Father, but Jesus tells them that the only way by which they could truly find the Father was through Him.

> John 14:6... Jesus said to him, "I am the way, and the truth, and the life; no one comes to the Father but through Me." (NASB)

For Christians to say that the only true way to fully know the God who created us is through submission to Jesus Christ, has often been regarded as exhibiting intolerance and discrimination toward other religions. However, these are the words of the Bible. In fact, they are the words of Jesus, and it is clear when studying other religions that their adherents do not serve the Father God to whom Jesus refers. We can respect the genuine sincerity of those following the practices of Islam, Hinduism or Buddhism, for example, but we have to be honest and say that for a follower of Jesus Christ, every other spiritual pathway is, according to the Bible, a false religion.

The Bible tells us that although the love and mercy of God are freely available for every human being, it is only our surrendered response to Him, through Jesus Christ, that can now save us and restore us into the covenant relationship which He has purposed between Himself and humankind. False religion promotes living and worshipping in accordance with certain rules and rituals (however well-meaning) as opposed to walking in true relationship with Jesus.

It is also important to recognize that false religious practice can exist within any Christian organization or denomination where, in some measure, dependence on the doctrines, traditions, rituals and works of human beings have taken the place of dependence on the grace and truth of God, which can only be received through Jesus Christ (Colossians 2:20–23).

Such a Christian organization is best not labeled as a false religion, which necessarily implies that all adherents are unsaved, but is better described as an organization defiled by false religious practices and likely to put many into spiritual bondage.

For those who have come to a knowledge of Jesus out of a background in false religion, there will be a need for them to clearly renounce the worship of false gods, false beliefs and the associated rituals, taking back all the spiritual authority that has been given to the enemy. Religious spirits can blind us to the real truth of Jesus, defile the precious gifts of the Holy Spirit, promote legalism and steal the treasure of God's grace in our lives.

I remember hearing the testimony of a man whose father and grandfather had both been members of the Orange Order, a religious organization particularly for men, most usually associated with Northern Ireland. It was not until this man had dealt with the effects on his life of the religious bondage in his family background that he was able to move in the gifts of the Holy Spirit. Although he had been a Christian for many years, he described the extraordinary change that took place in his life when he renounced, and was delivered from, the effects of the false religion, vows and rituals of his forebears.

See Antichrist, Covenant, the Cross, Cult, False, False Religious Practice, Freemasonry, Generational Iniquity, Legalism, Religion, Ritual, Trinity

False Religious Practice – dependence on human doctrines which have, even within a Christian organization, replaced or added to dependence on the grace and truth of God through Jesus Christ.

> Colossians 2:20–22... You have died with Christ and are set free from the ruling spirits of the universe. Why, then, do you live as though you belonged to this world? Why do you obey such rules as "Don't handle this," "Don't taste that," "Don't touch the other"? All

these refer to things which become useless once they are used; they are only human rules and teachings. (GNB)

A Christian organization exhibiting false religious practices (which is not uncommon) should not be labeled as a false religion, implying that all adherents are unsaved, but is better described as an organization defiled by beliefs, rules and rituals which may harm or even deny a true relationship with Jesus. All false religious practice will lead to condemnation and bondage for those involved, rather than conviction and freedom, and such practice is very likely to attract the powers of darkness.

> Galatians 4:8–10... In the past you did not know God, and so you were slaves of beings who are not gods. But now that you know God – or, I should say, now that God knows you – how is it that you want to turn back to those weak and pitiful ruling spirits? Why do you want to become their slaves all over again? You pay special attention to certain days, months, seasons, and years. (GNB)

See Condemnation, False Religion, Grace, Jesus, Legalism, Religion, Religious Spirit

False Worship – See Worship

Family (Families) – group of people (often descendants of a common ancestor) in close relationship for the purpose of protection and provision, both physically and spiritually.

The essentials of belonging and care are needed by everyone, but particularly by the young and the elderly. God's plan for humankind was that the foundational family unit would be led by a father and mother, covenanted together in marriage. In fact, the Greek word used for *family* in the New Testament (Ephesians 3:14–15) literally implies a group of people who are being rightfully fathered. Of course, wider concepts of family and various types of leadership exist in extended households, tribes and even nations, giving protection for larger groups of people who are not necessarily linked by blood ties.

Unfortunately, we live in a world which has become distorted through sin. Family life is very often broken and dysfunctional, and instead of it being a place of spiritual safety and well-being, for many it has been a place of distress and wounding. But God is a redeemer. He planned for the Body of Christ to be a worldwide family under the headship of Jesus, restored to a heavenly Father, with all of His children identified and secured through the anointing of the Holy Spirit. Each one of us who has chosen to follow Jesus is entitled to be part of this eternal family.

> John 1:12... But as many as received Him, to them He gave the right to become children of God, even to those who believe in His name ... (NASB)

Jesus knew the pain of being separated from His Father at the cross. He knows the history of our personal family lives, both the good and the bad. He knows that even as adults we need the spiritual protection and nurture of a heavenly Father. He also knows that we need restoration from the damage of the past, so He has made a promise to all His disciples, including to you and me:

> John 14:18... I will not leave you as orphans; I will come to you. (NASB)

As we forgive those who did not provide the family life that God intended, the Holy Spirit can come to comfort and heal, restoring us into a deep place of security in being a treasured member of the family of God.

> Psalm 27:10... For my father and my mother have forsaken me, But the LORD will take me up. (NASB)

See Body of Christ, Covenant, Covering, Father, Headship, Identity, Marriage, Mother, Protection, Relationship

Fantasy (Fantasize) – unreal experience devised by humankind, often to avoid difficult reality.

There's nothing wrong with enjoying a good adventure story or romantic novel, even if these are just fiction. The problem comes when we persistently enter this fictional world in order to find comfort for inner needs that should be met through relationship with God.

One of our most important needs is to discover our true identity in God. However, when this search becomes defiled through, say, fantasy games or pornography, there is a serious risk of identity distortion and demonic intrusion.

I remember our praying, alongside his parents, for a young man who was deeply caught up in a fantasy game which involved powerful mythical creatures. We became aware of his need to be delivered from demonic spirits, each of which manifested their grotesque nature from the game. He had become so identified with each of the characters as the intensity of the game progressed, that the fantasy world which he persistently entered became almost real to him, and the enemy had seen an opportunity to distort his thinking and his personality.

The young man admitted that it had been a "useful" escape from difficult situations at school, but as he invited Jesus to be his source of reality and comfort, the Lord brought wonderful cleansing from the defilement of the enemy. Satan is not just the father of lies, but also the ruler of the world of seductive fantasy (John 8:44).

> Ecclesiastes 5:7... But against all illusion and fantasy and empty talk There's always this rock foundation: Fear God! (The Message)

See Comfort, Coping Mechanism, Denial, Lie, Pornography, Truth, Unreality

Fascination (Fascinating) – unhealthy attraction to something or someone, so distorting reality.

Jesus was passionate about His ministry to this broken world, but He was not drawn to concentrate on one particular aspect of healing, or a particular people-group, or some technique of spiritual warfare at the expense of the fullness of His calling. He was determined and uncompromising in His desire to fulfill the instructions of His Father, but never fascinated by His own authority and power.

We can easily be drawn into the ways of the world which feed fascination by pursuing, for example, celebrity, scandal, gossip, sex, disaster, horror or the occult. But these pursuits will never nurture the human spirit; rather, they add to its defilement (2 Corinthians 7:1). Any continued unhealthy attraction can soon become an obsession or an addictive behavior, eventually handing over to the enemy some control in part of our lives.

Even within Christian work, we need to be on our guard. For example, deliverance and prophecy are essential ministries within the Body of Christ, but fascination in these areas can be unhelpful and even dangerous. The authority and power which Jesus has delegated to His disciples to challenge the enemy are remarkable, but a prayerful study of the person of the Holy Spirit will be much more edifying than a fascinating study of the behavior of demons. A measure of understanding is very important in all aspects of the spiritual battle in which we are involved, but when the primary focus of our lives is diverted from our dependence on a relationship with Jesus, a door to deception can be opened which may be surprisingly enticing.

> Luke 10:19–20... Behold, I have given you authority to tread on serpents and scorpions, and over all the power of the enemy, and nothing will injure you. Nevertheless do not rejoice in this, that the spirits are subject to you, but rejoice that your names are recorded in heaven. (NASB)

God is always willing to forgive us for pursuing unwise fascination, and to cleanse us from any of the enemy's defilement. Jesus should always be the main attraction!

See Addiction, Deception, Dependence, Obsession, Power, Truth

Fast (Fasting) – choice not to eat, undertaken as an aid to serving God.

The Bible sometimes uses the word *fast* to refer to abstention from various normal routines in order to better serve the Lord (Isaiah 58:3–7; Daniel 10:3), but mostly it relates to not eating. Food satisfies hunger and gives nourishment to the physical body. It is good for us, when taken in the right amount and at the right times. God has also made us to know spiritual hunger in the heart, which needs to be met with spiritual food.

There can be strategic occasions when it is particularly important in the challenges of life for us to seek the Lord for this spiritual food of His wisdom. At these times fasting may be helpful, as the Lord directs, to give perseverance in our seeking for God's answers, when food in the stomach might dull the hunger of the heart. Fasting is not a technique to get noticed by God or to twist His arm for an answer to our needs, but a useful aid to prayer which deepens our dialogue with God in the midst of spiritual battles.

> Mark 9:29... And he said unto them, This kind can come forth by nothing, but by prayer and fasting. (KJV)

Fasting should never become a religious formula, an opportunity for pride, nor a means of self-imposed suffering (Matthew 6:16). It is simply a biblical principle of significant value in focusing our hearts on the search for further revelation from God.

> Acts 13:2... While they were ministering to the LORD and fasting, the Holy Spirit said, "Set apart for Me Barnabas and Saul for the work to which I have called them." (NASB)

See Eating Disorder, Intercession, Prayer, Religion, Suffering

Fatalism (Fatalistic) – belief that what happens is predetermined, irrespective of our decisions.

Such a belief can result in a person leading a passive and pointless way of life, existing simply as a pawn to be moved from place to place in some divine chess game.

Jesus taught His disciples a very different way. He made it clear that our day-to-day choices have a significant effect on the course of both the physical and the spiritual realms. As we choose to walk in agreement with His instructions, we can see the Kingdom of Heaven become a reality on earth, displacing the rule of the enemy, just as the seventy disciples discovered when they were obedient to the commands of Jesus.

FATHER

> Luke 10:17... The seventy returned with joy, saying, "LORD, even the demons are subject to us in Your name." (NASB)

God has clearly chosen to involve the Body of Christ on earth in the restoration of His creation (Matthew 28:17–20). Jesus has disarmed the enemy at the cross, but it is ourselves, as His followers under the direction of the Holy Spirit, who can now challenge the rights previously handed to the powers of darkness to control human life (2 Timothy 2:24–26).

If our religious or cultural roots or the experience of frequent disappointments have sown within us an attitude of fatalism, we need to confess this wrong belief, and seek the Lord for a change of heart and a disempowering of the enemy, in order that we can take an active and decisive part within the purposes of the Body of Christ.

> Hebrews 12:1... Therefore, since we have so great a cloud of witnesses surrounding us, let us also lay aside every encumbrance and the sin which so easily entangles us, and let us run with endurance the race that is set before us ... (NASB)

See Belief System, Choice, False Religion, Free Will, Generational Iniquity, Passivity

Father (Fathering) – male parent.

We have all had a human father. For some people, this relationship has been a source of emotional, spiritual and sometimes physical damage. Our concept of how God intended a father to behave can be very distorted by the experiences of life. To find God's healing for the damage of poor parenting we need to look to the example of Jesus to understand the true role of a father.

He explains to His disciples that He is the Son of Father God, empowered in His humanity on earth by the Holy Spirit. The significance of this Father-Son relationship is clearly shown as the Father affirms His pleasure in the innate value and unique identity of His Son (Luke 3:22), and in the times when Jesus simply cries out to His Father for fellowship and spiritual protection (John 12:27).

The key role of an earthly father toward his young son or daughter is for him to be the means of God's spiritual covering and to make known the God-given value and identity of his children, safely affirming their masculinity or femininity, their destiny and their gifting. When, through a father's neglect or abuse, this has not been our experience, there is frequently damage to our human spirit, often distorting our sense of self-worth, our sense of security and the understanding of our sexuality. Such neglect can be, for example, a root in the development of homosexual attraction. But God has an answer: redemption from all that has wounded us as a result of inadequate fathering.

> Psalm 28:10... For my father and mother have forsaken me, But the LORD will take me up. (NASB)

When we acknowledge the reality of imperfect parenting, forgiving our earthly father for his sin against us, we can discover in Christ today, through His perfect relationship with His Father, all the protection and provision which our human spirit was made to enjoy. We can discover the Father-heart of God (Jeremiah 31:9).

See Covering, Father-heart, Identity, Parent, Sexuality

Father God – one of the persons of the Holy Trinity.

See God, Trinity

Father-heart (of God) – nature of God which particularly expresses His deep love for His children.

God is often presented more as an instrument of harsh divine judgment than a loving merciful Father. But this is a distortion of His true character and can bring condemnation in our hearts, rather than security and comfort (Deuteronomy 1: 30–31). Alongside His need for justice, God is a loving father. We were created by Him to receive both truth and grace. Jesus, exactly representing His Father (Hebrews 1:3), came to earth perfectly demonstrating these two qualities (John 1:17).

It is so important for us to understand that although God's law does indeed demand the meeting of His justice where there is sin, it was always His plan, because of His endless love for His children, to fulfill all that is necessary for that justice by the sacrifice of His Son on the cross.

If we agree with Him about our sin, Jesus pays all the spiritual debt that is due, and we can go free. What an amazing divine deal! We are so personally valuable to God that Jesus has given His life for our restoration. If we seek the true nature of God, we will discover not just His absolute truth and justice, but also His Father-heart of unending forgiveness, love and grace. And we will find a peace and a confidence for our own hearts beyond all that we thought possible.

> Isaiah 63:16… For You are our Father, though Abraham does not know us And Israel does not recognize us. You, O LORD, are our Father, Our Redeemer from of old is Your name. (NASB)

See Father, Forgiveness, Grace, Justice, Love, Loving-kindness, Truth

Fear (Fearful, Fearfulness) – God-created emotion in response to perceived danger, intended to motivate us to look for God's means of protection.

When situations threaten to separate us from the spiritual and physical protection which God has intended for our lives, we experience an agitation or troubling within our bodies, warning us of danger and heightening our urgency to find a place of safety. Fear can be caused by any impending danger, and can also originate from our personal sin, from insecurity in our relationship with God, or from the carelessness of those who are meant to guard us.

Jesus felt troubled (by a fear that cautions) as He came nearer to the time of His death on the cross, through the hostility and betrayal of those around Him. Such fear is not sinful.

FEAR

> John 12:27–28a... Now My soul has become troubled; and what shall I say, "Father, save Me from this hour"? But for this purpose I came to this hour. Father, glorify Your name. (NASB)

His response to the troubling, the warning of danger, was to look to His Father for all that would be needed to find true safety. Unfortunately, instead of looking for God's covering, many of us seek to self-protect, just as Adam and Eve did when they felt so exposed as a result of disobeying God.

> Genesis 3:9–10... Then the LORD God called to the man, and said to him, "Where are you?" He said, "I heard the sound of You in the garden, and I was afraid because I was naked; so I hid myself." (NASB)

When we try to self-protect, such as hiding behind a brave face, without knowing or seeking God's help, the anxiety and fear can remain unresolved, with a grip on our lives today. It often controls us and even causes physical dysfunction long after the original danger has passed. Three times, cursing and swearing, Peter denied knowing Jesus because of fears that gripped his heart. But God had a special plan to bring Peter back into his true destiny. Together again with Jesus on the beach at Galilee, Peter faced both the truth of his fears and the most profound question of his life. Jesus asked him, "... do you love Me...?" (John 21:15).

It is the same question for us today. What will motivate or control our decisions each day? Will it be fear of man, fear of failure, fear of rejection, fear of violence, fear of sickness, fear of death and so on, or will it be our love for Jesus? Healing from unresolved past fears comes by forgiving those who have endangered us, repenting of our ways of self-protection, pouring out our feelings to the Lord, and by inviting the Lord to spiritually cover those fearful places in the safety of a perfect loving relationship with Him. It is also important to drive out the enemy's grip of fear, held through any unclean spirits.

> 1 John 4:18... There is no fear in love; perfect love drives out all fear. So then, love has not been made perfect in anyone who is afraid, because fear has to do with punishment. (GNB)

See Anxiety, Control, Covering, Emotion, Protection, Security

Fear of God – deep sense of safe surrender to the absolute authority and awesome power of God.

It is not a fear of God's punishment. Being afraid of what He might *do* to us will just cause us to withdraw from Him, and that's the last thing He wants. Rather, He calls us to fear and respect *Him*. He is awesome and great. The rightful fear of God is not a place of vulnerability, but a place of mercy and protection.

> Isaiah 8:13–14… It is the LORD of hosts whom you should regard as holy. And He shall be your fear, And He shall be your dread. Then He shall become a sanctuary … (NASB)

God has given us understanding of the consequence of sin, but He wants us to be obedient to Him because we recognize His awesome majesty and because we freely choose, for example, to respond to Him in heartfelt love. Actually, the Bible tells us that fear of God is the beginning of knowledge (Proverbs 1:7), the beginning of wisdom (Proverbs 9:10), the fountain of life (Proverbs 14:27), the way to keep from evil (Proverbs 16:6).

When there is a sustained place of fear in our lives, it is in effect a place of submission to something or someone. The enemy would want us to fear him or to fear what he might do to us. For him this would be the same as worship, but Jesus encourages us not to let this happen, even in the most challenging of situations, because God alone eventually determines the outcome of our lives.

> Matthew 10:28… Do not be afraid of those who kill the body but cannot kill the soul; rather be afraid of God, who can destroy both body and soul in hell. (GNB)

These words may not sound very comforting, but they powerfully remind us that it is only the rightful fear of God that should be given a permanent place in our hearts, if we truly want to know personal safety. No other fear should be allowed to become an established master, but simply our temporary servant (warning us of any current danger).

See Authority, Covenant, Covering, Disobedience, Fear, Honor, Love, Power, Respect, Worship

Feeling (Feel) – physical or emotional sensation in the body.

At every moment of our conscious lives (and even at times during sleep) we are experiencing certain feelings within: contentment, sadness, tiredness, unease, hunger and so on. Some of these feelings are a consequence of the present circumstances of our lives, and some linger from the unresolved issues of the past. At times, a feeling such as an inner disquiet can develop into a stronger emotion, like despair, as the mind and body start to respond to and express what is being experienced and felt (Psalm 137:1).

God has given us feelings not to rule us, but to help us make choices in the day-to-day journey of life – to look for food when we feel hungry, to find help when we are troubled; these are important for our well-being. However, our feelings and the associated emotions should not be the only guide to our decision-making. The world may say, "If it feels right, just do it", but the Bible tells us to surrender all our feelings to God so that He can be the ultimate guide, just as Jesus did when he felt deeply troubled by his impending death (John 12:27–28).

There are times when we may feel worthless and even suicidal, but the choice that needs to be made is clearly not to seek death, but to seek God for the reason why we are carrying such a distressed heart. Jesus died that we might resolve the issues and troubled feelings of our past and so find His promised abundant life.

> Psalm 40:1–3... I waited patiently for the LORD's help; then he listened to me and heard my cry. He pulled me out of a dangerous pit, out of the deadly quicksand. He set me safely on a rock and made me secure. He taught me to sing a new song, a song of praise to our God. Many who see this will take warning and will put their trust in the LORD. (GNB)

See Choice, Distress, Emotion, Soul, Will

Femininity – female identity.

God created all women with natural beauty and loveliness. His intention is that each woman would embrace that beautiful feminine aspect of herself. God intended that during puberty, a girl would develop increased confidence in her femininity as she hears safe but genuine affirmation of this, particularly from her father. She needs to hear from him that he sees her as a beautiful young woman. Such rightful encouragement and affirmation from him is extremely important to her.

If her father abuses the trust she rightly places in him, and makes any sexual advances toward her, this can be truly devastating to a girl, as it is a direct attack on her identity and personhood. Not only does she suffer the destructive effects of the abuse itself, but she will often also lose the rightful affirmation of her femininity, because it is defiled by his lust and no longer feels safe for her to accept it. Many girls in this situation will reject their true femininity because it seems to bring them nothing but pain.

Or suppose a girl's father persistently makes negative comments about her appearance, then she is likely to grow up believing that she is intrinsically unattractive and may find it difficult to accept her femininity. If a girl's father is not abusive but is just absent, or simply says nothing to affirm her femininity, she may grow up with uncertainty about herself in this area, constantly wondering, "Am I good enough? Do I look all right?"

A girl's attitude to her femininity can be affected in other ways also. For example, if her parents wanted a boy and were disappointed at her birth, she may subconsciously try to be the boy they desired and reject her own femininity. In doing so, she is rejecting who she really is, the unique and lovely person God wanted and created.

> Genesis 1:27,31... So God created mankind in his own image, in the image of God he created them; male and female he created them. ... God saw all that he had made, and it was very good. ... (NIV)

See Abuse, Affirmation, Identity, Lesbianism, Masculinity, Parenting, Sexuality

Feminism (Feminist) – belief in and promotion of women's perceived rights, as opposed to God's true order between men and women.

The carnality of both men and women has constantly undermined what God intended for the relationship between the sexes, not least in marriage. As a result of the wrong attitudes and behaviors of men toward women in despising, controlling or abdicating rightful responsibility, many women have responded to such abuse by aggressively claiming a right to equality and independence, rather than seeking God for His answer to distorted relationships.

Particularly within marriage, God has explained in the Bible that there is an important order of relationship between a man and a woman which He has ordained to bring safety and peace. There can be no doubt that in God's view, a woman has absolutely equal significance to a man (Galatians 3:28), but when they join together in a covenant of marriage, it is necessary that one of them is given the lead, particularly when there are differing opinions. God has asked the woman to give that lead to the man (Ephesians 5:22).

However, many men, through their woundedness and carnality, have exercised this role toward women with crushing dominance, humiliating contempt or, conversely, with frustrating weakness. Hence the attraction of feminism, which has often encouraged rejection and even despising of the God-planned position of men. As we seek God for personal healing from the wounding and bondage of the past, we become more able to take our rightful place in all relationships, especially the challenging interdependence required in the covenant of marriage.

In God's Kingdom, dysfunctional relationships can be restored, not by claiming some humanistic rights for men or women, but by confession and forgiveness of our sinful ways, where we have been out of line with God's truth and His order. This certainly does not mean that He asks women to live as second-class citizens in His Kingdom, but rather He calls them to delight in their God-given identity and destiny.

> Proverbs 31: 10–11,30... An excellent wife, who can find? For her worth is far above jewels. The heart of her husband trusts in her, And he will have no lack of gain. Charm is deceitful and beauty is vain, But a woman who fears the LORD, she shall be praised. (NASB)

See Control, Femininity, Headship, Honor, Marriage, Order, Sexuality

Fidelity – See Faithfulness

FIRE OF GOD

Fire of God – supernatural manifestation of God's holiness.

The fire of God appears throughout the Bible to declare His awesome presence (Exodus 13:21, 19:18), sometimes burning sacrificial offerings (Leviticus 9:24), sometimes confirming His unique holiness (Exodus 3:2–5), but most often it comes to destroy all that is incompatible with that holiness (Numbers 16:35).

> Deuteronomy 4:24... For the LORD your God is a consuming fire, a jealous God. (NASB)

We need to be aware that though full of grace and truth, Jesus came also to bring this same challenging aspect of God's holy purpose for humankind.

> Luke 12:49... I have come to cast fire upon the earth; and how I wish it were already kindled! (NASB)

God's desire for our lives is fruitfulness, a reflection of His holy character here on earth (John 15:16). Any branches of a tree that consistently bear bad fruit are cut away and burnt, to avoid perpetuating the condition. So it must be, Jesus says, for our individual lives (John 15:6).

We are pleased to hear that Jesus has come to baptize His followers in the Holy Spirit, but we often fail to recognize that John the Baptist warned that this experience would also come with God's fire to burn up the chaff, the unfruitful characteristics of our lives (Matthew 3:11–12). This warning of a consuming fire is not to threaten us, but rather to ensure that we are fully aware that God's judgment inevitably comes to us all at some point. The good news is that judgment has been overruled by divine mercy, provided that we truly acknowledge the saving and cleansing work of Jesus.

We read in the Bible of the presence of the Holy Spirit on the day of Pentecost being like *tongues of fire*, the writer giving us a picture of this remarkable phenomenon (Acts 2:3). We may sometimes experience an intense and revelatory passion of God burning in our hearts, just as the disciples did on the road to Emmaus (Luke 24:32). However, these are not manifestations of the consuming fire of God that John the Baptist mentioned. We should be careful in calling for this fire to come, for its likely purpose will not be to just give us an exciting experience, but to test and purify our hearts, preparing us to be part of the holy bride of Christ.

FOOTHOLD

1 Corinthians 3:13… each man's work will become evident; for the day will show it because it is to be revealed with fire, and the fire itself will test the quality of each man's work. (NASB)

See Baptism in the Holy Spirit, Cleansing, Justice, Manifestation, Testing

Foothold – place in our lives where the enemy has been given the right to establish his grip of authority and power.

The enemy has always had spiritual muscle (power) but he lost the right (authority) conferred by God to use that power, because of his rebellion (Revelation 12:7–9). God gave authority over the earth to mankind (Genesis 1:28). Satan desired to regain authority in order to use his power, so he had to deceive people into handing their authority over the earth to him. If you obey someone, you are giving them authority (Romans 6:16).

So from the Fall, Satan has sought the right to rule in the life of humanity through enticing people to hand over a measure of authority to him. They do this through sin (Genesis 1:28; Romans 6:12-16). Satan even tried this, unsuccessfully, with Jesus (Luke 4:5–8). Every time we walk in disobedience to God's ways and follow the ways of this world, we give the enemy a license to rule in and through some aspect of our lives.

Ephesians 4:26–27… And "don't sin by letting anger control you." Don't let the sun go down while you are still angry, for anger gives a foothold to the devil. (NLT)

The word *foothold* in this verse means a place in our lives where the enemy can get a grip. When, through sin, we give him authority over any part of our lives, he can then use the power of unclean spirits to control us (2 Peter 2:19b). Thankfully, Satan has never had any control over the Son of God (John 14:30), so when we choose to join with Jesus, by repenting from our own sin and forgiving others, we can receive God's pardon and be lifted out of the enemy's control.

2 Corinthians 2:10–11… When you forgive people for what they have done, I forgive them too. For when I forgive – if, indeed, I need to forgive anything – I do it in Christ's presence because of you, in

FORGIVENESS

> order to keep Satan from getting the upper hand [control] over us;
> for we know what his plans are. (GNB)

Think for a moment of a picture of each believer being like a vintage Rolls-Royce car, an imaginary vehicle which can make choices for itself! It is now being driven by an invited new and loving owner, Jesus, along beautiful roads. It belongs to Him. Unfortunately, from the time of the previous careless owner, the car is still carrying some unpleasant unseen passengers who had been allowed to have a seat in the back, with names such as fear, unforgiveness, pride, occult, lust, rejection or unbelief, for example. Every now and then one of these back-seat drivers reaches forward, grabs the wheel and tries to pull the car off-course down one of the dark roads of the past. The new owner is very willing to throw them out, but He says that it is first necessary for this special car to make it very clear that the passengers are no longer welcome to the seats (the footholds) which they have been occupying.

We need to ask ourselves and God this question: "Even though I now fully belong to God, has any sinful belief or behavior been given the opportunity to take control of some part of my life (2 Timothy 2:26)?" As we confess to Jesus the wrong things done by ourselves and others which let unwanted passengers have a back seat in our lives, He will give us the strength to kick them out!

> 1 John 3:8b... The Son of God appeared for this very reason, to
> destroy what the Devil had done. (GNB)

See Authority, Deliverance, Forgiveness, Power, a Right, Sin, Unclean Spirit

Forgiveness (Forgive, Forgiving) – decision, by someone who has been wronged, to release the offender from all debt that is due.

God's justice has ruled that there is a serious cost to humans when they sin.

> Romans 6:23... For the wages of sin is death ... (NIV)

However, at the cross Jesus paid all the debt which is due to humankind, providing forgiveness for all those who choose to receive Him as Savior (Colossians 2:13-14).

No amount of self-righteousness, religious rituals, superstitious practice or paying penance will be able to meet the debt (Colossians 2:23). It is only possible by genuine confession and repentance of sinful ways, and then we can receive the forgiveness of God.

However, unless we actually participate in this forgiveness, even though it is freely given by God, the enemy has a right to demand payment (Matthew 18:34-35; 2 Corinthians 2:10–11). To receive that forgiveness, we need to show that our lives are truly surrendered to the instructions of the one who has saved us. Jesus clearly tells His followers to forgive all those who have wronged them. He does not ask us to say that any sin committed did not matter, but He encourages us to fully abide by the terms of this New Covenant system of divine justice – which are that we forgive others for their sin against us, we repent for our sin, Jesus pays the full cost of all sin, and God sets us free with His forgiveness. It's a remarkable deal!

> Matthew 6:14–15... For if you forgive others for their transgressions, your heavenly Father will also forgive you. But if you do not forgive others, then your Father will not forgive your transgressions. (NASB)

Forgiveness is the most powerful key to the healing and deliverance ministry of Jesus. Seeking truth exposes the works of the enemy, while receiving God's pardon removes the rights that the powers of darkness have to press for our punishment. I remember watching a man being healed from deafness simply by receiving God's forgiveness for a shameful thing for which he had carried hidden guilt over many years. In receiving God's

forgiveness, it is equally important that we forgive ourselves and do not continue to blame or punish ourselves. C.S. Lewis once wrote: *"if God forgives us we must forgive ourselves. Otherwise it is almost like setting up ourselves as a higher tribunal than Him."* [7]

This extraordinary principle of healing might be expressed like this: the cost of all the sin and defilement of our past can be fully charged to God's account, as long as we no longer demand payment from those who have wronged us.

Philemon 1:18... But if he has wronged you in any way or owes you anything, charge that to my account ... (NASB)

See Confession, Debt, Foothold, Judgment, Justice, Mercy, Punishment, Repentance, Sin, Unforgiveness

Fornication (Fornicate) – sexual activity outside of rightful intimacy within the covenant of marriage.

This is rather an old-fashioned word, but certainly not a redundant biblical issue.

Hebrews 13:4... Marriage is to be held in honor among all, and the marriage bed is to be undefiled; for fornicators and adulterers God will judge. (NASB)

Sexual intercourse between a man and woman before marriage is unfortunately seen as a normal and acceptable practice by the world, and also by some Christians today. The Bible sees this as contrary to God's laws for our spiritual well-being, and with the added potential for emotional and physical harm. There are more than thirty forms of sexually transmitted disease, some causing serious health issues, some causing infertility and some which, contrary to popular belief, are not necessarily prevented by the use of condoms. A world which operated by God's laws, free from fornication, would be both right with Him and free of the associated diseases, while we would still have God's endorsement of sexual intimacy, through His plan of marriage. Analysis of marriages in the USA has shown that they fail at a higher rate when there has been premarital sexual intercourse by the couples.[8]

For restoration of God's order, any sexual activity which has been contrary to God's laws should be confessed, preferably with another trusted person, also forgiving sexual partners who have exercised any persuasion or control. It will be important to seek freedom from soul-ties, restoration of lost sexual identity, and expulsion of any powers of darkness that have had license to bring control and defilement of our bodies.

See Comfort, Covenant, Homosexuality, Intimacy, Lesbianism, Marriage, Sexual sin, Soul-tie

Fragmentation – see Full Fragmentation and Partial Fragmentation.

Freedom (Free) – release from physical, mental, emotional or spiritual bondage.

People mostly regard freedom as an innate right to pursue life unrestrained by what they consider to be unreasonable control by other people or by restrictive laws. Actually, humankind knows that society can only operate if we all surrender some of this desired freedom for the common good. The Bible says something even more radical: we can become a bond-servant of Jesus (Titus 1:1–3) and find the true and lasting freedom for which we were all made. God sees freedom as primarily the removal of the spiritual grip of the enemy, who has been given a right to bring bondage because of human sin. Only God can reveal the true roots of this bondage and the true solution, which is through Jesus Christ.

> John 8:36… So if the Son makes you free, you will be free indeed. (NASB)

Many people are also looking for freedom from specific disorders in their lives. Secular treatments for addictive or psychological bondage bring much relief, but the medication or therapy is usually designed more to manage symptoms than to eradicate the root issue. The healing and deliverance ministry of Jesus is very different. Only He sees into our hearts. He alone knows what truly lies beneath the presenting problem. One day He met a woman in a synagogue. She was physically disabled in her spine, but Jesus knew that the underlying issue was a spiritual bondage established over eighteen years (Luke 13:16). He called her to come forward and He began the healing process by proclaiming freedom for her from the enemy's long-standing grip.

> Luke 13:11–12… there was a woman who for eighteen years had had a sickness caused by a spirit; and she was bent double, and could not straighten up at all. When Jesus saw her, He called her over and said to her, "Woman, you are freed from your sickness." (NASB)

Once the woman in the synagogue had been spiritually untied by Jesus from the issues of the past, her physical body could reflect this new liberty, in the straightening of her back.

> Luke 13:13... And He laid His hands on her; and immediately she was made erect again and began glorifying God. (NASB)

We don't know whether this bondage was, perhaps, from wrong dependency or a wrong relationship, but the authority of Jesus alone is able to overcome the powers of darkness because as He walked the earth, He never surrendered to the tempting advice of the Evil One. It is very important to understand that Satan can never take away our freedom to make a will choice to walk in obedience to God. Jesus tells His disciples that the journey to freedom must begin with a revelation of truth, which comes from obeying the words that He speaks to us.

> John 8:31–32... So Jesus was saying to those Jews who had believed Him, "If you continue in My word, then you are truly disciples of Mine; and you will know the truth, and the truth will make you free." (NASB)

The essence of Christian healing can be summarized as the restoration of lives that have been broken by a sinful world, and held spiritually captive by a hostile enemy (Isaiah 61:1; Luke 4:18). Followers of Jesus can look beyond simply managing their problems to an increasing freedom, which is God's promise to all His children.

See Authority, Bondage, Control, Deliverance, Perfectionism, Power, Soul-tie

Freemasonry – international organization, primarily for men, requiring adherence to specific vows and rituals for both the initiation and the progression of membership.

Although these are not understood by most Freemasons, the ceremonial steps or degrees by which they participate in the lodges (meeting places) are clearly religious in nature and they form a covenant. The members are required to make vows of allegiance and oaths invoking spiritual powers, combined with personal enactments or rituals which are intended to demonstrate the importance of the promises being made, as well as signifying strong penalties for breaking the covenant.

The vows and rituals are not in any way consistent with biblical Christianity. In fact, the rituals and proclamations use a confused mixture of religious and occult symbolism, implying progress on a pathway of enlightenment for the candidate, a process which categorically denies the true light and salvation of Jesus Christ.

As an example, candidates for the first degree, or step, of Freemasonry allow themselves to be humiliated, and spiritually controlled, through wearing scanty clothing, having a rope placed around the neck, a blindfold placed over their eyes and a sharp instrument held against their chest. Paul warns us against such practice.

> Romans 6:13a... do not go on presenting the members of your body
> to sin as instruments of unrighteousness ... (NASB)

All this intimidating ritual takes place while the candidate recites vows and oaths, which initiate him into the organization, and he confirms agreement to severe bodily punishment if the vows are broken. This false covenant plays into the hands of the enemy and can give him serious rights to promote spiritual, mental and physical disorder within the body of the participant.

> Matthew 5:34–37... But I tell you, do not swear an oath at all: either
> by heaven, for it is God's throne; or by the earth, for it is his footstool
> ... All you need to say is simply "Yes" or "No"; anything beyond this
> comes from the evil one. (NIV)

A number of cults, brotherhoods and other organizations have been birthed out of Freemasonry or have clear similarities, such as Mormonism and the Orange Order. Because of the covenantal aspect of such practices, there is a strong influence on families down the generational line. Men entering these organizations are making vows not just for themselves but on behalf of their descendants. This is the essence of covenant, be it good or bad, that those participating

FREE WILL

are representing the wider family for whom they carry responsibility, whether they are aware of this or not (1 Samuel 18:3, and 20:42).

Because of the systematic pronouncements made during the various degrees and rituals in the process of finding freedom, the person will need to renounce vows and associated curses in a more detailed way than in normal prayer ministry. We see an indication of this process with the disciple Peter. When he was restored by Jesus (John 21) from the harmful effects of his three denials of knowing the Lord, strongly spoken with cursing and swearing (Matthew 26:72), Jesus encouraged Peter to make a clear declaration of his love for Him three times, in order to fully counteract the three defiling pronouncements he had previously made.

However, we need to be cautious not to be challenging religious powers of darkness with religious prayer ministry, for we are in danger of giving license to the enemy if we miss out just one small part of a set of legalistic prayers (James 2:10). It is only the Lord who breaks someone free from the covenant bondages of Freemasonry, not the length of our prayers. We should always seek Him for wisdom on how detailed the renunciation of vows and oaths needs to be.

When we humbly face the truth of how damaging these organizations can be to both individuals and families, we can then find the amazing grace, healing and deliverance of God as the rights of the enemy are removed through our giving and receiving of forgiveness for the wrongful ways of life entered into by our ancestors or ourselves.

> 1 Peter 1:18–19... For you know what was paid to set you free from the worthless manner of life handed down by your ancestors. It was not something that can be destroyed, such as silver or gold; it was the costly sacrifice of Christ, who was like a lamb without defect or flaw. (GNB)

See Covenant, Curse, False Religion, Generational Iniquity, Ritual, Vow

Free Will – freedom to choose my personal response to God, to other people and to life's circumstances, without physical, emotional or spiritual pressure.

Throughout history there has been much argument about the issue of free will. Some Christians have said that everything is predetermined by

FREE WILL

God, irrespective of our apparent choices, and therefore they embrace a form of fatalism. Some philosophers and scientists have said that everything which happens in our lives, including our decisions, is simply determined by the history of interaction of the countless particles of the universe since the Big Bang. However, the Bible tells us that God requires us to exercise responsibility and so, even though God remains sovereign, He has given humanity a precious gift of free will. This is the ability always to choose our response to Him, even when we are struggling with difficult issues such as inherited traits or addiction, for example. God made this principle of free-will choice very clear to His covenant people, the Jews.

> Deuteronomy 30:15–16... Today I am giving you a choice between good and evil, between life and death. If you obey the commands of the LORD your God, which I give you today, if you love him, obey him, and keep all his laws, then you will prosper and become a nation of many people. The LORD your God will bless you in the land that you are about to occupy. (GNB)

God has never coerced His children into loving Him or obeying Him. For our love of God to be real, we must have the ability to say *no* to Him. He has always instructed (or commanded) us how to keep right with His laws, telling us that it is truly a matter of life and death, but even the first followers of Jesus had the freedom to walk away, and many did.

> John 6:66... As a result of this many of His disciples withdrew and were not walking with Him anymore. (NASB)

A forced relationship is rarely life-giving. Jesus was modeling how things operate in His Kingdom, and He expects us to behave in a similar way. As C.S. Lewis wrote: *"free will, though it makes evil possible, is also the only thing that makes possible any love or goodness or joy worth having."*[9] Respecting the free will of one another is essential in all our relationships. This is a principle that can only be overridden if we have been given legitimate and conditional control over part of someone's life, for example, a policeman, or the parent of a young child. Even then, there are biblical warnings to be careful of unjust discipline.

> Ephesians 6:4... Fathers, do not provoke your children to anger, but bring them up in the discipline and instruction of the LORD. (NASB)

FRUIT

The wrongful denial of another's free will is abusive and damaging to the person's soul and human spirit. We need to forgive those who have done this with our lives, so that we might know God's healing and the freedom to exercise choices in a rightful way.

It is important also to note that in these days of increasing persecution, however much pressure others may put on Christians, what can never be taken from us is our freedom to choose to obey or disobey the foundational commandment of the New Covenant, which of course, for some, has led to martyrdom.

> 1 John 3:23... This is His commandment, that we believe in the name of His Son Jesus Christ, and love one another, just as He commanded us. (NASB)

See Choice, Commandment, Control, Disobedience, Fatalism, Freedom

Fruit (Fruitful, Fruitfulness) – evidence which we can see, confirming the nature and character of an unseen source.

In the Bible, the concept of good fruit, or fruitfulness, most commonly refers to the revealing of God's character in the life of humanity. For His children today, the fruit of the Holy Spirit *in* our lives is evidence of the authority of Jesus *over* our lives. In the book of Galatians, we see a list of some of the precious aspects of the character of God which He grows within us as we surrender our lives more and more to Jesus.

> Galatians 5:22–23... But the fruit of the Spirit is love, joy, peace, patience, kindness, goodness, faithfulness, gentleness, self-control; against such things there is no law. (NASB)

Fruitfulness is very important to God. At the moment of the creation, He commanded humankind to be fruitful, or to bear fruit. This was not just an instruction to have many children, but a command to display the character and qualities of God by His Spirit operating in and through the heart of human beings. Jesus picks up this essential purpose of God when He explains that He has chosen each one of us to be His followers in order that we can bear fruit that will last.

> John 15:16... You did not choose Me but I chose you, and appointed you that you would go and bear fruit, and that your fruit would remain ... (NASB)

In fact, Jesus tells us in this same chapter that we are like branches of a vine which will require frequent pruning and must be fully connected into Him, the vine, if we are to produce the precious fruit which is His primary purpose within us. An interesting aspect of fruit is that seeds will be the only part of a tree that endures when that tree eventually dies. And so it is with us. Our works may have been significant but it is the fruit, or the image and character of God, growing within us during our walk on earth, which will be the enduring witness of relationship with Him into eternity. It has been said that God is cultivating us to maximize return on His investment!

Jesus also tells us that in these end times when there will be much deception, good fruit in people's lives will be the primary test as to whether they are operating under His spiritual authority or under the counterfeit dominion of the ruler of the world.

> Matthew 7:16–17... You will know them by their fruits. Grapes are not gathered from thorn bushes nor figs from thistles, are they? So every good tree bears good fruit, but the bad tree bears fruit. (NASB)

The enemy can reasonably counterfeit the power of God (2 Thessalonians 2:9), but he cannot sustain God's true character. Good fruit in our lives can only come from a good 'tree', because it is a foundational principle of God's creation that we increasingly take on the image and character of whatever or whoever we worship. We are warned that those who make or worship idols become like them (Psalm 115:8). But those who are surrendered to Jesus and are willing to be pruned or cleansed by Him, will inevitably show more and more good fruit, manifesting His precious character. This fruit will last for ever.

See Character, Deception, Destiny, Holy Spirit, Image, Pruning

Full Fragmentation – An expression used in Ellel Ministries to describe a complete fracture in the human soul and spirit caused by an overwhelming trauma.

Just as bones can be fully broken when there are traumas to the body, so our inner being can be deeply broken by a sudden and serious impact, whether the blow is physical or emotional. Full fragmentation can result, for example, from a major accident, from suffocation, torture or other extreme abuse. Such a deep fracture affects not only our emotions but also our human spirit, which is the primary place of our identity, and so the damage leaves a real part of us disconnected from the person that we are today. It is as if part of us is frozen into the spiritual darkness and emotional distress of the time of the trauma. It is helpful to call this part of us a 'person-part' because it is a real part of the person, with identity, soul and spirit. It is locked into time, unchanged from the age that the person was at the time of the trauma.

The remaining person continues through life, but with severe consequences to their personhood, frequently requiring psychiatric help to function adequately.

> Proverbs 18:14…The spirit of a man will sustain him in sickness, But who can bear a broken spirit? (NKJV)

Because full fragmentation is not God's order for human existence, the enemy can take advantage of such brokenness, reinforcing the fracture and defiling the parts of our lives that are affected.

> Psalm 143:3–4… For the enemy has persecuted my soul; He has crushed my life to the ground; He has made me dwell in dark places, like those who have long been dead. Therefore my spirit is overwhelmed within me; My heart is appalled within me. (NASB)

Think of a fine porcelain plate which not only looks beautiful but makes a vibrant ringing note when tapped. One day it is dropped on the floor. It cracks and loses a sizeable piece, which gets trapped under a heavy kitchen dresser. The remaining plate is still just useable, but the wholeness is lost and the note that it now makes is dull and lifeless. We may not find the broken piece until we do some thorough spring cleaning! In fact, it may be years before it is discovered, carefully cleaned and glued back in place to restore the plate to its whole condition.

Thankfully, God sees any broken condition of our heart, and He is ready and willing to restore the wholeness and vibrancy of His beautiful creation as we walk with Jesus.

Full fragmentation can cause a deep sense of insecurity and even terror which is experienced by the person concerned, often without their knowing the source of the distress. The sense of insecurity, fear and vulnerability can be so severe that the individual may well have unconsciously abandoned, or dissociated from, this unwanted aspect of their identity and sought to live out of a manufactured identity which seems to enable them to cope better with life.

A fully fragmented person will normally have neither memory of the trauma nor awareness of the broken part, or parts. They may experience symptoms such as time loss, unexplained blackouts, sleepwalking, phobias, likes and dislikes in food and drink that repeatedly and markedly change from one hour to another, memory loss relating to that earlier period of their lives, deep and irrational mood swings, panic attacks and depression, together with compensatory behaviors such as addictions and compulsions. However, it is important not to assume full fragmentation until God has made it very clear that this is truly an issue to be healed. Full fragmentation is not nearly as common as partial fragmentation.

Although operating in an adult body, broken person-parts can express themselves through the subconscious of the adult person in a way that is entirely consistent with the age and condition of the person at the time of the trauma. For example, on occasions they may exhibit very immature behavior, chronic insecurity, fear, panic or suicidal urges, which makes ordinary living extremely distressing.

In prayer ministry situations, it is possible that under the leading of the Holy Spirit, the traumatized person-part may fully surface and take over the consciousness of the adult, in which case the adult would have little or no memory later of what was said or expressed. From the symptoms mentioned above, we see that it is also possible for this to happen when the person is alone and, if so, they may experience time loss, because the adult will have no recollection of what happened while the person-part was on the surface. It can also happen if the adult person chooses not to take responsibility in difficult situations and allows the person-part to surface in order to protect the adult from distressing feelings, or if the adult's level of consciousness is diminished, for example, when briefly waking from sleep during the night.

The healing process can take time, especially where the fragmentation happened in childhood in the context of chronic neglect and abuse. During this time of healing, it is important for the person-part to respond to the adult person more and more, as both accept the reality of the person's history, the damage caused by breaking away from those memories and associated feelings, and the need for God's restoration. The adult's earnest desire to walk under the lordship of Jesus is key to providing the spiritual covering that is necessary for the inner healing and growth of the person-part(s). As we seek the Holy Spirit, He will guide the process of healing and cleansing. At the right time He will heal the traumatized person-part(s) and, when the adult is willing to accept it, will bring the parts of the person into unity in one identity through the redeeming work of Jesus at the cross.

> Luke 4:18... The Spirit of the LORD is upon me, because he hath anointed me to preach the gospel to the poor; he hath sent me to heal the brokenhearted, to preach deliverance to the captives, and recovering of sight to the blind, to set at liberty them that are bruised ... (KJV)

See Abuse, Accident, Brokenness, Dissociation, Memory, Partial Fragmentation, Trauma

Gambling (Gamble) – spending money or other resources to produce more, in a way that essentially depends on chance.

The possibility of winning money, particularly a large sum, by spending a small amount, is clearly very attractive. Some would even say that market trading in stocks and shares can simply be a form of gambling. The risk, the sport, the potential win, the euphoria, even the associated fear can all create a strong draw that excites those involved, as well as being a way to subdue some of the distressing realities of life.

If gambling of any kind has become a regular means of my seeking comfort, hope, escape or some quick answers to my needs, I have, in effect, handed over a part of my life, emotionally and spiritually, not to the one who has promised to give me my daily bread, but to the ruler of the world, who seeks only to rob, kill and destroy (1 John 5:19; John 10:10).

As with many other addictions, the damage caused by gambling frequently extends to the wider family, bringing despair, shame and sometimes financial ruin. The solution comes by facing the truth of sinful behavior, both with God and with trusted friends or relatives. It is important also to look at the underlying issues which have made gambling an attractive coping mechanism to deal with unresolved inner healing needs. God is a true comforter and provider, as we walk in His truth and grace.

When faith in God and in His provision is believed and declared, in opposition to a destructive dependence on 'Lady Luck', then the rights which the enemy has had to empower the gambling addiction can be removed, and God's order can be restored.

See Addiction, Compulsion, Coping Mechanism, Dependence, Shame, Unreality

Generational Iniquity – damaging spiritual condition inherited from our ancestors as a result of their sin.

The Bible tells us that this inheritance can affect family lines, each sinful idolatrous practice reaching its full effect after three or four generations.

> Exodus 20:5... You shall not worship [idols] or serve them; for I, the LORD your God, am a jealous God, visiting the iniquity of the fathers on the children, on the third and the fourth generations of those who hate Me, but showing lovingkindness to thousands, to those who love Me and keep My commandments. (NASB)

God intended His pathway of spiritual inheritance to be something that brings a blessing into our lives (Deuteronomy 7:9) but as with so many other areas of God's creation, sin has distorted what God meant for our good (Isaiah 65:6–7).

Generational iniquity causes us to be out of line with God from the very start of our lives, walking in a cursed rather than a blessed inheritance (Daniel 9:8 and 18), which can leave us particularly vulnerable to sin issues in the same areas which troubled our ancestors, as well as being liable to inherited disorders such as infirmity or distorted identity. We are particularly vulnerable to the consequence of the vows and actions of our ancestors in false religions or wrong covenants (2 Samuel 21:1–2). The effect is like a flow of contaminated spiritual water coming

GIFTS OF THE HOLY SPIRIT

down the family line and into our lives, spiritual water which God had intended to be pure.

Release from the effects of generational iniquity is available for followers of Jesus because He carried all the iniquity of humankind in His body on the cross. As we forgive our ancestors for their sinful behaviors which have affected us, particularly idolatry and wrong covenants, and also confess our own wrongful participation in any similar practices (Leviticus 26:40–45; Nehemiah 9:2), we can take hold of the freedom that Jesus has provided for us.

A pathway of generational iniquity is spiritually dark territory and gives the powers of darkness a right to hold our lives bound to inherited curses. When we actively appropriate God's redemption and cleansing from this inherited iniquity, these rights are removed and all demonic power can be evicted.

> 1 Peter 1:18–19... you were not redeemed with perishable things like silver or gold from your futile way of life inherited from your forefathers, but with precious blood, as of a lamb unblemished and spotless, the blood of Christ. (NASB)

It is not the pathway of spiritual inheritance that is harmful, but the iniquitous content which defiles our lives. This scripture reminds us that Jesus has cleaned up this spiritual water not by some financial deal with humankind, but through His being both the sacrifice to pay for sin and the scapegoat to carry iniquity, on the cross, all on our behalf (Leviticus 16:10,15,22).

See   Covenant, Covering, Curse, Freemasonry, Inheritance, Iniquity, Sin

Gifts of the Holy Spirit (Gift, Gifting) – supernatural empowering for the Body of Christ distributed by the Holy Spirit to and through each one of us.

To bring true restoration to this broken and spiritually captive world, the Body of Christ needs both the delegated authority of God *and* His power, just as Jesus equipped His first disciples.

> Luke 9:1... And He called the twelve together, and gave them power and authority over all the demons and to heal diseases. (NASB)

The *authority* of Jesus is evident in us if we walk in obedience to His instructions, and so display the fruit of the Holy Spirit, which is His character working through us (Galatians 5:22–23).

The *power* of God is released through the gifts of the Holy Spirit as He reveals truth and distributes, to and through each of us, exactly what is needed to enable the Body of Christ to fulfill God's purposes in bringing change to this troubled world. Gifts are a means to an end, and are not the end purpose. Fruit, in the image of Christ, is the end purpose for our lives (John 15:16).

As well as divine authority, different members of the Body of Christ are, at certain times, gifted by God with supernatural ability (power): sometimes to speak words that help us to see things as God sees them; sometimes to have specific understanding of situations that does not come from our own intellect; sometimes to exhibit extraordinary faith in the promises of God; sometimes to impart God's healing through words or touch; sometimes to exercise miraculous authority and power over the enemy; sometimes to speak convicting revelation out of the heart of God; sometimes to clearly distinguish between what comes from the Spirit of God and what comes from the spirit of this world; sometimes to dialogue with God in a language that engages the human spirit rather than just the mind; sometimes to be able to interpret this language, for public edification (1 Corinthians 12:4–11).

There can be no effective Christian ministry of healing and deliverance without these gifts being corporately manifested through the followers of Jesus. Indeed, we are encouraged to seek this empowerment whilst recognizing that the use of gifts (Greek word – *charisma*) does not necessarily equate with Christian maturity, which is rather displayed through a heart transformed by love. It has rightly been said that *charisma* without character is no good to God!

GLORY

> 1 Corinthians 14:1... Pursue love, yet desire earnestly spiritual gifts ... (NASB)

See Fruit, Holy Spirit, Power, Prayer Ministry, Supernatural

Glory (Glorious, Glorify) – honor and splendor.

Only God fully deserves to be spoken about with such words, for His magnificence is perfect and eternal.

> Matthew 6:13b... For Yours is the kingdom and the power and the glory forever. (NASB)

His created world was also completely glorious before the Fall, but it has been contaminated by humanity's sin. However, God is in the process of redeeming and restoring the whole of creation to be glorious once again, as we let Him transform our lives and cause us to become true witnesses of His character into the world.

> 2 Corinthians 3:18... But we all, with unveiled face, beholding as in a mirror the glory of the LORD, are being transformed into the same image from glory to glory, just as from the LORD, the Spirit. (NASB)

See Character, Honor, Transformation, Value

God (Godhead) – Creator of the universe, declaring Himself in the Bible to be *I AM*, existing in the Trinity of Father, Son and Holy Spirit.

God is revealed throughout the Bible as the Father of His people.

> Deuteronomy 32:6b... Is not He your Father who has bought you? He has made you and established you. (NASB)

Jesus, the Son of God, has demonstrated to us the nature of God as He walked the earth, full of truth and grace (John 1:14), and He declared that there is only one way to find Father God.

> John 14:6... Jesus said to him, "I am the way, and the truth, and the life; no one comes to the Father but through Me." (NASB)

The Holy Spirit is the one who today reveals God's truth into human hearts.

> John 16:13… But when He, the Spirit of truth, comes, He will guide you into all the truth … (NASB)

See Christ, Father, Holy Spirit, Jesus, Son of God, Son of Man, Trinity

Godliness (Godly) – righteous lifestyle reflecting God's nature.

> 2 Peter 1:3–4… His divine power has granted to us everything pertaining to life and godliness, through the true knowledge of Him who called us by His own glory and excellence. For by these He has granted to us His precious and magnificent promises, so that by them you may become partakers of the divine nature … (NASB)

See Character, Fruit, Righteousness

God's Order – see Order

God's Word – The whole Bible.

The eternal truth of God (Psalm 119:160).

See Bible, Jesus, Word

Goodness (Good) – reflection of the perfect nature and character of God.

> Matthew 19:17… And [Jesus] said to him, "Why are you asking Me about what is good? There is only One who is good: but if you wish to enter into life, keep the commandments." (NASB)

God has always desired good for His children (Micah 6:8), but it is only when Jesus dwells within us, by the Holy Spirit, that true goodness can be manifested through our lives and be seen by the world around us (Galatians 5:22–23). Obeying the commands of Jesus brings us into the special covenant relationship which God has established with humankind through His Son, allowing His goodness to grow in us.

Humanism says that human goodness can be achieved by human reason alone; the Bible says that this is utterly impossible (Jeremiah 17:9; Romans 3:12).

See Character, Fruit, God, Holiness, Righteousness

Gospel – good news about the truth of Jesus.

Jesus makes very clear the essence of this good news when He stands up in the synagogue at the beginning of His ministry on earth. It was to be as Isaiah had prophesied (Isaiah 61:1), the restoring of broken and spiritually captive lives, a ministry of healing into a world devastated by sin.

> Luke 4:18... The Spirit of the LORD is upon Me, Because He has anointed Me To preach the gospel to the poor; He has sent Me to heal the brokenhearted, To proclaim liberty to the captives And recovery of sight to the blind, To set at liberty those who are oppressed ... (NKJV)

This good news is as relevant and effective today as it was when Jesus spoke these words and we, the Body of Christ on earth, are now the ones who are entrusted to carry and impart this wonderful message. Unfortunately, these days some preach a gospel comprising simply of pursuing good works, but true believers must not distort the full and powerful good news of Jesus, that He died for our sins, was buried and rose victorious from death (1 Corinthians 15:1–4), and that only in Him can humankind know abundant life.

See the Cross, Evangelism, Forgiveness, Freedom, Healing, Restoration

Grace (Gracious, Graceful) – undeserved kindness and mercy of God.

God passionately invites us to receive from Him all that He knows we need to save us and to sustain us, not because of our merit, but because of His love (John 3:16).

This invitation includes His undeserved forgiveness, undeserved generosity, undeserved protection, undeserved provision, undeserved comfort, undeserved restoration and His unending love. It cannot be earned, it cannot be contained and it cannot stop. This grace of God has defeated all the condemnation of the world and its ruler, because each one of us is so loved by the one who made us.

However, in God's Kingdom we cannot receive the fullness of His grace without acknowledging His truth, including His justice. It is this combination of truth and grace that is the essence of God's nature and was so clearly manifested by Jesus as He walked the earth.

> John 1:14... The Word [Jesus] became flesh and made his dwelling among us. We have seen his glory, the glory of the one and only Son, who came from the Father, full of grace and truth. (NIV)

God cannot ignore divine justice nor compromise absolute truth, but His heart was to redeem even the very worst of the consequences of humanity's rebellion against Him. His way of doing this was to send His Son to pay the ultimate cost of justice on behalf of humankind, so that then His forgiveness and His mercy could be fully shown to all those who are willing to accept Jesus as the only source of true salvation and true grace (John 1:17).

See Condemnation, Forgiveness, Guilt, Kindness, Loving-kindness, Mercy, Religion, Truth

Gratitude – See Thankfulness

Greed – unhealthy desire for something beyond what is truly needed.

Greed is an outworking of our carnal nature, and it will be challenged by the voice of the Holy Spirit as we give Him increasing access to our lives through the lordship of Jesus. God knows our true needs, and we are encouraged to trust Him for all our necessary provision. It does not mean advocating idleness, but it does mean freedom from anxiety.

> Matthew 6:31,33... Do not worry then, saying, "What will we eat?" or "What will we drink?" or "What will we wear for clothing?" ... But seek first His kingdom and His righteousness, and all these things will be added to you. (NASB)

For some people who have been deprived of godly provision and nurture, especially while growing up, there can be a distorted view of the true needs of the body, whether physical or emotional, and this can sometimes lead to areas of greed in an attempt to somehow make certain of a sufficiency. It will never result in peace, because we can never be sure that we have taken hold of enough. When God is given the opportunity to meet the hunger of our heart, through our forgiveness of those who caused us to be deprived in the past, through confession of our ungodly coping mechanisms in trying to compensate and through pouring out our fears to Him in prayer, a new place of security can be found. We can then trust Him to provide enough, as and when we need it, rather than as and when we want it.

> Philippians 4:19... And my God will supply all your needs according to His riches in glory in Christ Jesus. (NASB)

See Carnal Nature, Coping Mechanism, Eating Disorder, Lust, Security

Grief (Grieve, Grieving) – painful emotion linked to loss.

Grief is one of the most painful feelings we experience. After any significant loss, grief is actually a normal and right response. It is important for our well-being, including the well-being of our physical body, for us to have opportunity to express the painful feelings that result from any kind of loss, just as Jesus did (John 11:35). This may be loss through the death of a person or the death of significant hopes and dreams. The process of mourning any loss must include the rightful expression of grief if the body and emotions are to fully recover.

God intended that we should be able to fully express grief in words and actions at the time of the loss. Tears are a very important part of God's plan to release emotional, and even chemical, distress within the body. Our heavenly Father knows every cause of grief in our lives, and He wants us to give Him all the pain that wells up from inside.

> Psalm 56:8… You have taken account of my wanderings; Put my tears in Your bottle. Are they not in Your book? (NASB)

If we were unable to express grief and distress at the time of a loss, the pain can become trapped inside and sometimes gives the enemy an opportunity to hold ground in our lives. However long ago the loss was, it is always possible to bring the hurting places to God today. If others have wrongly restrained our expression of emotions in the past, forgiving them will help to set us free. We may also need to confess our own ungodly self-control, where at the time this seemed our only way of coping. Jesus knows the grief and is able to carry the full weight of it with us as we bring it to Him.

> Isaiah 53:3… He was despised and forsaken of men, A man of sorrows and acquainted with grief; And like one from whom men hide their face He was despised, and we did not esteem Him. (NASB)

See   Death, Emotion, Loss, Mourning, Pain, Self-control

Guilt (Guilty) – recognition of sin and awareness that payment is due.

True guilt is a God-given emotion and is necessary to bring conviction of wrongdoing and a desire for resolution. Our confession, or agreement with God, together with repentance, provides the opportunity for us to receive His forgiveness. This means that we fully accept that He has paid everything that is due. We are declaring that we did sin but we no longer have to pay any spiritual cost. The enemy seeks to hold us in condemnation, but once we have received the pardon of God, through the intervention of Jesus, the enemy's accusation and his demand for our punishment has to cease. We are truly free from all the destructive spiritual bondage resulting from our sin (Colossians 2:14–15).

This is exactly what happened for the woman caught in adultery.

> John 8:10–11... Straightening up, Jesus said to her, "Woman, where are they [the accusers]? Did no one condemn you?" She said, "No one, LORD." And Jesus said, "I do not condemn you, either. Go. From now on sin no more." (NASB)

Guilt cannot be truly lifted if we fail to receive God's forgiveness for our own sin. This may happen if we believe that we must suffer the punishment along with Jesus, if we believe that something of our identity is always to be a scapegoat or martyr, if we believe that God's forgiveness comes through our religious works rather than His undeserved grace, or if we deal with past sin by trying to forget it rather than choosing to confess it.

False guilt can also be a problem if we have carried blame for the sin of others. Sometimes it's hard for those who have experienced gross injustice in their lives, harsh discipline or control, to realize that they do not have to carry the blame for all that has gone wrong in their past. Once we have recognized and repented of what was truly our responsibility, God's forgiveness is there to set us free. One perfect sacrifice has paid the price. We need to be careful not to give the enemy any opportunity to hold us in a place of guilt by still seeking to resolve the sin of the past by our own efforts. Jesus has fully carried the guilty verdict on your behalf.

> Hebrews 10:2... If the people worshiping God had really been purified from their sins, they would not feel guilty of sin any more, and all sacrifices would stop. (GNB)

See Blame, Condemnation, Conviction, Debt, Forgiveness, Freedom, Shame, Sin

Habit – repeated behavior which can be good but, if unhealthy, might be a form of addiction.

See Addiction, Behavior, Compulsion, Coping Mechanism, Obsession

Headship (Head) – God's order for authority within the Trinity of heaven and within the families of earth, including the Body of Christ.

> 1 Corinthians 11:3... But I want you to understand that Christ is the head of every man, and the man is the head of a woman, and God is the head of Christ. (NASB)

Within any group, there needs to be a clear structure of authority for following God's direction, so He has ordained that one person needs to be given the ultimate lead. This is how God planned it to be for the operation of every family, even between Father God and His Son, Jesus.

> Philippians 2:6–7... although [Jesus] existed in the form of God, [He] did not regard equality with God a thing to be grasped, but emptied Himself, taking the form of a bond-servant, and being made in the likeness of men. (NASB)

> John 17:4... I [Jesus] glorified You [Father] on the earth, having accomplished the work which You have given Me to do. (NASB)

We can choose not to agree with God's plan for headship as, for example, in some of the tenets of feminism, but this is likely to lead to disorder in marriage and family life. A battleship is directed by a *captain* who carefully listens to the expertise of the crew, not by a *committee* that votes on the best course to take. The head in a marriage, in a household or in a wider family, is not of more value before God than any other member of the family, and headship is not a license for domination, but it is a role through which God brings protection and provision to all those who walk in accordance with this godly principle.

We may need to forgive those who have not followed God's way of headship, whether in wrong control or careless abdication, and seek His cleansing from any effect that this has had on our lives.

See Authority, Covering, Family, Feminism, Marriage, Trinity

Healing (Heal, Health) – restoration of God's created order.

This simple definition is more significant than it at first seems. Without our knowing a 'normal' condition for humanity, healing is an uncertain pursuit. For example, there is much confusion in our secular society over issues such as sexual attraction, personal integrity, family relationships and moral boundaries. Unless there is some measure of what is right for human life, how can we know what restoration of health truly means?

HEALING

> 1 Thessalonians 5:23... May God himself, the God who makes everything holy and whole, make you holy and whole, put you together – spirit, soul and body – and keep you fit for the coming of our Master, Jesus Christ. (The Message)

The Bible sees healing as essentially a recovery from both spiritual defilement and inner brokenness or wounding, human conditions which are contrary to God's order. Because the physical body reflects the condition of the heart, physical healing will often follow spiritual cleansing and inner healing, as in the story of the paralyzed man lowered through the roof. First he received from Jesus a pardon to free the paralysis of his guilty heart, and then received the healing of his body (Luke 5:17–25). This is an important biblical principle.

> Proverbs 14:30... A heart at peace gives life to the body ... (NIV)

There is much disorder and dysfunction in people's beliefs, attitudes and behaviors. There is much anxiety where there should be peace, much distortion of identity and sexuality, much bondage where there should be freedom, much insecurity where there should be confidence in our right to be children of God (John 1:12). His healing is a restoration of His order in and around our lives, when we pursue the truth of His Word. Healing is part of the ministry for which the Body of Christ has been given power through the Holy Spirit.

The process and extent of God's healing in this fallen and spiritually hostile world, where physical deterioration and death are inevitable facts of human life, will always be something of a mystery, but we can be absolutely certain that we serve a God who has a heart to redeem and restore our lives so that we can be fruitful (John 15:16) in the destiny to which He has called each one of us.

> Psalm 103:1–5... Bless the LORD, O my soul, and all that is within me, bless His holy name. Bless the LORD, O my soul, and forget none of His benefits; Who pardons all your iniquities, Who heals all your

diseases; Who redeems your life from the pit, Who crowns you with lovingkindness and compassion; Who satisfies your years with good things, So that your youth is renewed like the eagle. (NASB)

God's overall purpose for our lives is that He should build character in us, to be progressively transformed into the image of Christ (2 Corinthians 3:18). There is not a short cut to such transformation, but it is always good to ask Him what truth, freedom and healing He wants us to pursue next in our lives, in order that we might truly bear much fruit.

See Brokenness, Deliverance, Freedom, Order, Restoration, Sickness, Sin, Transformation, Unanswered Prayer, Wholeness

Heart – unseen core being of a person, revealed through the interaction of the human soul and human spirit.

Of course, we have a physical heart which is essential to our well-being, but there is an inner part of us which cannot be seen by people but is very much seen by God.

1 Samuel 16:7… But the LORD said to him, "Pay no attention to how tall and handsome he is. I have rejected him, because I do not judge as people judge. They look at the outward appearance, but I look at the heart." (GNB)

The heart is revealed in both the soul, where our thoughts, emotions and decisions are active in the daily walk of life, and the human spirit, where our identity and core beliefs reside, not bound by time.

The human heart was defiled and separated from God at the Fall, and His desire for each one of us today is that by fully receiving Jesus within our being, we will rediscover purity and the true relationship with God for which we were created. As well as the impurity of heart with which we were all born (and which we continue to add to through sin), there is wounding and brokenness through life's events and through the wrong choices that we make. Thankfully, God not only sees our hearts but He is able to cleanse and repair all the damage that has resulted from human sin, including our own. In fact, Jesus declares this to be a primary reason for His time on earth.

Luke 4:18... The Spirit of the LORD is upon me, because he hath anointed me to preach the gospel to the poor; he hath sent me to heal the brokenhearted, to preach deliverance to the captives, and recovering of sight to the blind, to set at liberty them that are bruised ... (KJV)

We do not truly know, nor can we repair, our own hearts. God alone is able to cleanse and restore. As by His Word He reveals the condition deep in our hearts (the interaction of soul and spirit) we can agree with Him about our need for forgiveness, healing and deliverance.

Hebrews 4:12... For the word of God is living and active and sharper than any two-edged sword, and piercing as far as the division of soul and spirit, of both joints and marrow, and able to judge the thoughts and intentions of the heart. (NASB)

See Brokenness, Carnal Nature, Healing, Human Soul, Human Spirit, Idolatry, Wounding

Heaven (Heavenly) – eternal dwelling place of God and of those who walk in obedience to Him.

This highest spiritual realm and all realms below, both spiritual and physical, are subject to Jesus, by the appointment of His Father.

Matthew 28:18... And Jesus came up and spoke to them, saying, "All authority has been given to Me in heaven and on earth." (NASB)

He is both the King of heaven and the King of an extended Kingdom that covers all that is surrendered to Him. We may not yet be in heaven itself but we can, on earth today, experience and participate in the Kingdom that is centered in heaven.

See Angel, Eternity, Hell, Kingdom of Heaven, Spirit

Hell – place of eternal separation from the life-giving presence of God.

Jesus wants us to follow Him, not because of fear of eternal punishment, but because we have chosen to love Him (John 21:15). However, He does not want us to be ignorant of the serious consequences of the choices that we make in this lifetime (Matthew 5:22). Beyond this physical life we all have a spiritual existence, and the condition of that existence depends on our relationship with Jesus now. The choice is whether we let the ways of humanity, and the ruler of this world, control our lives, or we submit to the ways of God. Jesus expresses it very clearly to His disciples as they prepare to take on the challenge of serving Him in the world.

> Matthew 10:28… Do not fear those who kill the body but are unable to kill the soul; but rather fear Him who is able to destroy both soul and body in hell. (NASB)

Hard words indeed, but Jesus loves us too much to soften the truth. The encouragement to *fear* God throughout the Bible is not about being afraid of His wrath but about a deep recognition of His limitless love and awesome power. God has already paid the full cost of the sin of humankind. He has taken the punishment. There is no need for anyone to accompany the powers of darkness into the lake of fire (Matthew 25:41; Revelation 20:10). We are pardoned! There is nothing for us to pay!

But unfortunately most people in this world have rejected this divine forgiveness and, as one of our friends recently said, "Hell will be full of sinners, pardoned at the cross, who never accepted Jesus and His offer of salvation." The enemy does not want this world to take seriously the truth of hell. Even within the Body of Christ there is confusion and deception. Jesus is not telling us to live in fear of hell, but to take very seriously His loving offer of a safe eternal dwelling with Him.

See Darkness, Death, Disobedience, Eternity, Fear, Heaven, Justice, Punishment

Herbal Medicine – medication ingested or applied to the body, produced directly from plant material.

God has given us many plants which can be effective in alleviating disorders of the body and in assisting the normal physical healing process. The problem comes when there is an expectation in a particular therapy that the plant material itself provides some form of spiritual restoration.

Whenever taking a herbal remedy, we need to check the beliefs of those supplying or administering the remedy (whether labeled Christian or not). Some will be operating out of a foundational belief that there is an unseen spiritual energy or power at work, for example with the Yin and Yang of Traditional Chinese Medicine or with those administering a Bach Flower Remedy. Since the beginning of human existence, people have sought their own ways to find health and well-being. Just because a therapy is old, it does not mean that it is necessarily spiritually safe.

> Proverbs 14:12... There is a way which seems right to a man, But its end is the way of death. (NASB)

When practitioners are invoking an unspecific power to heal through any plant material, then we need to be very careful about submitting to that spiritual authority over our lives. If, however, they and we truly believe that the herbal treatment is only causing a quantifiable and repeatable chemical response to take place in the body, with no spiritual power involved, then we are simply taking advantage of the therapeutic chemicals which God has provided in nature.

Any spiritual disorder which needs to be addressed in our lives should only be pursued under the clear instructions of Jesus; that is, through confession and forgiveness of sin. If we have received herbal treatment which in retrospect we now consider spiritually unsafe, we can bring these issues to the Lord for cleansing and for His true healing, as well as asking Him to untie us from any spiritual holds (soul-ties) relating to the practitioner.

See Alternative Medicine, Deliverance, Healing, Soul-tie

Holiness (Holy) – spiritual purity which grows as we surrender our whole inner being to Jesus.

He is the only person who has walked the earth in complete holiness and He offers the opportunity to each one of us to become like Him, through His Spirit dwelling in our hearts.

To walk in holiness can sound a bit religious, a bit dry, a bit restrictive, a bit joyless, but these words could never describe the life of Jesus. He was the most dynamic, the most vibrant man ever to live on earth. It is

the desire of God that we might become holy like Him, for in holiness there is peace, confidence and liberty.

> 1 Corinthians 1:30... God has brought you into union with Christ Jesus, and God has made Christ to be our wisdom. By him we are put right with God; we become God's holy people and are set free. (GNB)

The writer to the Thessalonians prayed for this holiness to grow and be sustained in the believers in that city.

> 1 Thessalonians 5:23... May God himself, the God who makes everything holy and whole, make you holy and whole, put you together – spirit, soul and body – and keep you fit for the coming of our Master, Jesus Christ. (The Message)

God alone can make the human heart holy and whole. Our part is to allow the Holy Spirit to reveal the unholy and broken aspects of our lives and to agree with Him about the need for change. What an amazing adventure, to increasingly display the holiness of Jesus through His daily renewing of our minds. Holiness cannot be achieved by human beings and it will never share a place with pride. It starts in the heart and, from there, gradually changes our thinking and our actions.

> Romans 12:2... do not be conformed to this world, but be transformed by the renewing of your mind, so that you may prove what the will of God is, that which is good and acceptable and perfect. (NASB)

See Cleansing, Fruit, Holy Spirit, Lordship, Love, Purity, Sin, Religion

HOLISTIC HEALING

Holistic Healing – medication or therapy intended to bring restoration to the entire body, recognizing the inter-relationship between body, mind and human spirit.

There is, of course, truth in the need for us to be aware of our spiritual as well as physical condition, but unless the biblical concepts of sin and forgiveness are seen as the foundation, there can be significant dangers when people are seeking to heal the spiritual needs of human beings. Most so-called holistic healing is founded in New Age philosophy, and therefore linked to various false religions and to the occult.

In these numerous therapies, there is often reference to the need for spiritual balance, energy transfer, energy blockage and spiritual harmony, for example, but never a requirement to deal with sin. We need the true restoration of God's order in our lives, not some vague spiritual rebalance, and it is very important to be on guard against the enemy's counterfeits.

God desires His order in the whole of our being through submission to Jesus, confessing how we have been out of line with God, and letting Him bring spiritual, emotional and physical healing as we walk under the direction of the Holy Spirit. Paul prays for this true holistic well-being for the believers in Thessalonica, and we can seek the same today.

> 1 Thessalonians 5:23... May God himself, the God who makes everything holy and whole, make you holy and whole, put you together – spirit, soul and body – and keep you fit for the coming of our Master, Jesus Christ. (The Message)

See Alternative Medicine, Counterfeit, Deception, Healing, Human Spirit, New Age Movement, Restoration

Holy Communion – specific practice of eating bread and drinking wine, instructed by Jesus to draw His followers into a powerful remembrance and proclamation of His sacrificial death.

This significant act of remembrance is also called the Lord's Supper, the Messianic Supper or the Eucharist. It was initiated at the strategic Passover meal that Jesus shared with His disciples just before His death. Jesus told His first disciples to provide a regular opportunity for the shared eating of bread and the drinking of wine, for the purpose of corporately identifying with His broken body and His shed blood on the cross.

Paul explained the practice:

> 1 Corinthians 11:23–26… For I received from the LORD that which I also delivered to you, that the LORD Jesus in the night in which He was betrayed took bread; and when He had given thanks, He broke it and said, "This is My body, which is for you; do this in remembrance of Me." In the same way He took the cup also after supper, saying, "This cup is the new covenant in My blood; do this, as often as you drink it, in remembrance of Me." For as often as you eat this bread and drink the cup, you proclaim the LORD's death until He comes. (NASB)

In this special act of obedience, all disciples of Jesus can now also visibly proclaim their belief in the one (the perfect Passover lamb) who was sacrificed to reconcile them to God in a New Covenant. This covenant is one of forgiveness, healing and deliverance. When Jesus explained to His followers that to truly receive Him was to feed on Him, as if they were eating His body and drinking His blood, many walked away in protest at the extreme demands of His teaching (John 6:52–66).

Identifying so strongly with the body and blood of Jesus, as happens in Holy Communion, directly challenges the authority and power of the enemy. It can be a very effective step in bringing wholeness and freedom to damaged and spiritually captive lives by declaring, through words and actions, the power of God's forgiveness and cleansing for repentant hearts.

See Atonement, Blood, Covenant, the Cross, Deliverance, Forgiveness

Holy Spirit – third Person of the Trinity of God, along with the Father and the Son.

Jesus refers to Him as the Spirit of Truth (John 14:17), the Helper (John 16:7) and the Holy Spirit (Acts 1:8). There is order within the Trinity, such that the Holy Spirit will always point us toward Jesus.

> John 16:14… He [the Holy Spirit] will glorify Me [Jesus], for He will take of Mine and will disclose it to you. (NASB)

A primary role of the Holy Spirit is to bring truth into the human heart (John 16:13). He brings conviction of what is right and wrong, what is true about God, and true about our own God-given identity (Romans 8:16). This truth comes as revelation in our lives through our being born again of the Spirit (John 3:6) and through baptism in the Holy Spirit (Acts 1:8; Acts 11:16). What Jesus made *possible* at the cross, the Holy Spirit makes *actual* in our lives.

> Acts 2:33... Therefore having been exalted to the right hand of God, and having received from the Father the promise of the Holy Spirit, [Jesus] has poured forth this which you both see and hear. (NASB)

The Holy Spirit came upon particular people in the Old Testament (1 Samuel 10:10), He was the instrument of anointing on Jesus as He walked the earth (Acts 10:38), He inspired the writers of Scripture (2 Peter 1:20–21), He indwells our lives (1 Corinthians 2:16), He is the pledge of our eternal relationship with God (2 Corinthians 1:22), He intercedes for us according to the will of God (Romans 8:26– 27), He distributes gifts of power to the Body of Christ (1 Corinthians 12:11), He changes us to become like Jesus, so we bear the fruit of God's character (Galatians 5:22–23).

The human spirit is the wellspring through which God irrigates the thirsty land of our lives. The water of the Holy Spirit flows into and out from this deep place within us, bringing life to dry places, when we ask Jesus to meet our thirst (John 7:37–38). Water from this precious spring needs open watercourses so it can flow into the ground of our soul and body.

> Proverbs 4:23... Watch over your heart with all diligence, For from it flow the springs of life. (NASB)

As we first open ourselves to this powerful flow, it can make a dramatic difference to lifeless ground in us, bringing immediate revelation and color to our lives. The Bible calls this, under the New Covenant, the baptism in the Holy Spirit. However, blockages in the irrigation channels can be a problem. Blockages such as fear, pride and unbelief will leave parts of our lives unproductive and even in enemy hands. When the Holy Spirit meets any such resistance, He is very willing to show us the truth so that we can agree with Him about what needs changing. He will not force a way, but waits for us to surrender further ground to the lordship of Jesus, so we can receive His living water.

We should try not to resist, grieve or quench the Holy Spirit, and we should certainly never direct Him. We should let Him direct and comfort us, and go on filling us with His wonderful presence (Ephesians 5:18).

See Anointing, Baptism in the Holy Spirit, Antichrist, Counterfeit, Fruit, Gifts of the Holy Spirit, Trinity, Truth

Homosexuality (Homosexual) – ongoing desire for sexual intimacy with someone else of the same gender.

God truly loves all those who experience homosexual attraction, but He does not love our bodies being used in sexually intimate ways for which they were not designed (Leviticus 18:22; 20:13). The Bible very clearly explains that such a desire is a *degrading* condition and out of line with God's created order, and furthermore, it says that to condone or express such a desire through an intimate relationship between two men or between two women is an *indecent* and therefore sinful choice.

> Romans 1:26–27... For this reason God gave them over to degrading passions; for their women exchanged the natural function for that which is unnatural, and in the same way also the men abandoned the natural function of the woman and burned in their desire toward one another, men with men committing indecent acts and receiving in their own persons the due penalty of their error. (NASB)

Studies have shown that social and environmental factors play a larger part in the development of homosexual attraction than genetic factors do. If one of two identical twins (with the same DNA) has this attraction, there is only a 20 to 30 per cent chance of the other being the same. That figure would be close to 100 per cent if sexual orientation was entirely genetic.[10] We do carry certain spiritually inherited tendencies, for the Bible tells us that we are all born carrying generational iniquity (Psalm 51:5), but it is during our lives that wounding most often occurs. To understand the problem and the solution, we need to separate the inner attraction of homosexuality from the sinful choices of certain beliefs and behaviors.

The Fall resulted in each one of us being continually pressed by a sinful nature, this being further defiled and strengthened by the sin of our ancestors, our parents, those carrying responsibility for our lives, and not least by ourselves. Our life, including our sexual identity, is wounded and distorted by both our spiritual inheritance and by the iniquity that surrounds us from the moment of conception. This is particularly significant where there has been any form of sexual abuse, or where there has been poor bonding between a boy and his father in childhood.

All distorted inner desires, whether they are feelings of self-hatred, addictive tendencies, promiscuity, pedophilia, transgender leanings or homosexual attraction, can each be given or denied license by the choices that we make. The world increasingly encourages us to condone some of these as an acceptable and indeed a wholesome aspect of our identity. The Bible disagrees and tells us that the more license we give to the sinful desires of our defiled heart, the more of a hold that sin will have on our lives.

> John 8:34... Jesus said to them, "I am telling you the truth: everyone who sins is a slave of sin." (GNB)

The biggest issue for a Christian who is attracted to, or involved in, a homosexual or lesbian lifestyle, is to decide whether he or she agrees with the words of the Bible that such desires are degrading and that such a lifestyle is indecent and sinful. Seeking to change a homosexual attraction is strongly opposed by many in the world, not least because if this is truly possible in an individual, it would seem to threaten those who do not wish to change. However, if a person is convicted that their homosexuality is essentially a distorted sexual identity, which has been strengthened by life's wrong choices, then healing is possible. It starts with forgiving ancestors, who have sown generational iniquity, and also forgiving those who have abused or neglected us, particularly fathers, who did not provide the protection and affirmation of the true person and identity that was God's purpose for their lives, or a mother who wished for a child of the opposite sex.[11]

There will need to be confession and repentance of sinful beliefs, relationships and sexual practices. There will be strong ungodly soul-ties to sexual partners, to spiritually defiled locations and to the homosexual community, which will all need to be broken by the Lord. Changing friends and lifestyle are not easy and will need support and understanding. Deliverance will probably be necessary to evict the powers of darkness which have been given license to promote the distorted beliefs and

HONOR

behaviors. The Bible does not regard homosexuality as a God-ordained sexual identity or practice, but it is no worse than countless other areas of sexual sin. It is the consequence of a wounded heart and sinful choices, which God can truly redeem.

After listing many areas of human sin, including homosexual activity, Paul affirms to the believers in Corinth the truth that full restoration is always possible if we earnestly seek God's cleansing.

> 1 Corinthians 6:9–11... Do not be deceived: Neither the sexually immoral nor idolaters nor adulterers nor men who have sex with men nor thieves nor the greedy nor drunkards nor slanderers nor swindlers will inherit the kingdom of God. And that is what some of you were. But you were washed, you were sanctified, you were justified in the name of the LORD Jesus Christ and by the Spirit of our God. (NIV)

See Father, Generational Iniquity, Identity, Lesbianism, Masculinity, Order, Orientation, Redemption, Rejection, Sexual Sin

Honor (Honoring) – heartfelt expression of respect for something or someone.

God deserves the greatest honor for He alone is the eternal King (1 Timothy 1:17).

However, we are also encouraged to honor particular institutions such as marriage (Hebrews 13:4); certain people within our lives, because of the significance of our relationship to them; those who procreated our lives (Ephesians 6:2), those whom God has ordained to give direction to our lives (Ephesians 5:33, Romans 13:7, 1 Timothy 5:17; 6:1), and, not least, those with whom we have a close and interdependent relationship, within marriage (1 Peter 3:7) and within the Body of Christ (Romans 12:10).

Whilst not at all condoning another person's sinful ways, we should honor their innate value, made in the image of God (Genesis 1:26); we should honor what is good in character, especially as we see the changes that God is bringing (Proverbs 22:1); and finally we should honor the abilities and achievements with which God has gifted them for the benefit of the Body of Christ. And indeed it is important to consider ourselves worthy of the same honor and not to dishonor our bodies with self-hatred, or with impure thoughts and actions (Romans 1:24).

> 1 Thessalonians 4:3-5... Keep yourselves from sexual promiscuity. Learn to appreciate and give dignity to your body, not abusing it, as is so common among those who know nothing of God. (The Message)

We should dwell more on the good in one another rather than the bad, seeking to avoid criticizing, exposing of weakness, fault-finding and disrespect. In fact, dishonor can be a serious issue, for example, when children dishonor parents (Deuteronomy 27:16). Jesus experienced dishonor from those who wrongly accused Him (John 8:49), and He is always there to bring healing to us, when we too have suffered similar pain.

We earn the respect of others by increasingly walking in the character of Christ and the enabling of the Holy Spirit. We soon lose the respect of others by displaying selfishness and lack of integrity. The giving and receiving of due honor is an essential ingredient for healthy relationships and a healthy life.

> Exodus 20:12... Honor your father and your mother, that your days may be prolonged in the land which the LORD your God gives you. (NASB)

See Affirmation, Approval, Character, Despising, Relationship, Respect, Value

Hope (Hopeful) – expectation of a future positive event.

The Bible encourages us to have hope in all that God has promised for our well-being in Him. The Holy Spirit transforms such hope, which is primarily a decision of the soul, into a gift of faith, which becomes settled in the human spirit.

Galatians 5:5... For through the Spirit we eagerly await by faith the righteousness for which we hope. (NIV)

Many of us have hoped for things promised by leaders, friends, family, or even things which we have expected from God, and we have felt the pain of disappointment when such hope has been dashed.

Proverbs 13:12... Hope deferred makes the heart sick, But desire fulfilled is a tree of life. (NASB)

The Lord is ready to comfort us and show His absolute faithfulness when we forgive those who have let us down and acknowledge that God truly knows what is best for us. Hope in God will never prove to be a mistake. It is the antidote to depression, a life-saver for the suicidal, and it transforms the downhearted.

Psalm 71:5... For You are my hope; O LORD God, You are my confidence from my youth. (NASB)

See Depression, Disappointment, Faith, Hopelessness

Hopelessness (Hopeless) – condition of despair about the future.

Unresolved grief, illness, disappointment, betrayal, rejection or failure, for example, can lead to a response of hopelessness becoming established in the heart. The enemy will always try to reinforce such an attitude, seeking to steal our destiny in God, but we need to stand against the powers of darkness (James 4:7)!

We can choose to agree with God's viewpoint of our lives, for He has shown us that we have immense value and that we are chosen for a purpose. He has planned a destiny for us and He calls us to repent of hopelessness, and to follow Him into the future with confidence, whatever the current circumstances. Here's a good verse for covenant children of God to challenge the enemy's jibes:

Jeremiah 29:11... "For I know the plans that I have for you," declares the LORD, "plans for welfare and not for calamity to give you a future and a hope." (NASB)

See Depression, Disappointment, Failure, Hope, Loss, Rejection, Suicide

Humanism (Humanist) – belief that human virtue can be achieved through human intellect and reason, without the need for belief in God.

In 2002, a declaration was made by *The International Humanist and Ethical Union* at a conference in Amsterdam:

> *Humanism is a democratic and ethical life stance, which affirms that human beings have the right and responsibility to give meaning and shape to their own lives. It stands for the building of a more humane society through ethics based on human and other natural values, in the spirit of reason and free inquiry through human capabilities. It is not theistic and does not accept supernatural views of reality.*[12]

Humanism as a philosophical pursuit in particular developed during the period of the Enlightenment, or the Age of Reason, during the eighteenth century, partly in response to corruption and tyranny in much of the Christian church. There was at that time very little evidence that the teaching and witness of the church provided a basis for true justice and peace for this world. A significant moment came in 1789 when the *Declaration of the Rights of Man* in France effectively denied the validity of the commandments of God as a basis for seeking a just society. Although well-meaning in trying to use human reasoning to understand the world, humanism is centered on human wisdom rather than the wisdom of God. The Bible tells us that this is a dangerous way of life.

> James 3:15... This wisdom is not that which comes down from above, but is earthly, natural, demonic. (NASB)

God certainly wants human beings to use their powers of reason for tackling the questions of life, but He wants us to do that *with* Him not *instead* of Him. We may need to confess that our quest for answers has been too often only through human endeavor and with the desire to avoid the issue of sin.

> Isaiah 1:18... "Come now, let us reason together," Says the LORD, "Though your sins are as scarlet, They will be as white as snow; Though they are red as crimson, They will be like wool." (NASB)

See Enlightenment, Reason, a Right, Unbelief, Wisdom

Human Soul – unseen part of a human being which includes our mind, will and emotions.

The soul is where thoughts, decisions and feelings reside. The human soul operates in the temporal realm, expressing our life today. Contrast this with our human spirit, which operates in the eternal realm. The soul may be said to be an interface between the human spirit and the physical body. The workings of the soul and spirit are not easily understood, but increasing revelation comes through seeking God. A passage in Hebrews explains how the soul expresses life, similar to the articulation of joints in a human body, whereas the human spirit, like the hidden marrow in our bones, is a source and sustainer of life itself.

> Hebrews 4:12... For the word of God is living and active and sharper than any two-edged sword, and piercing as far as the division of soul and spirit, of both joints and marrow, and able to judge the thoughts and intentions of the heart. (NASB)

God's design is that we should be led by our human spirit, itself inspired by the Holy Spirit (Galatians 5:16). The soul is designed to respond to the direction of the human spirit. For example in Psalm 42, the psalmist's spirit encourages his soul:

> Psalm 42:5...Why are you downcast, O my soul? Why so disturbed within me? Put your hope in God, for I will yet praise him, my Savior and my God. (NIV)

However, before we are born again, or even after, the broken, crushed and defiled condition of the human heart can result in the soul taking charge and directing the body in line with the ways of the world, and according to the ruler of the world (Ephesians 2:2). The carnal nature of humankind is ever ready to steer us away from the Spirit of God into soulish behavior, driven by human reason, searching for a sense of identity by comparing ourselves with those around us.

When the mind, will and emotions have been distressed and damaged by the sinful actions of others or by the wrong choices which we have made in trying to fix our needs, we desperately need divine help. Jesus offers that divine solution through His restorative rule over our lives.

> Matthew 11:28–29... Come to Me, all who are weary and heavy-laden, and I will give you rest. Take My yoke upon you and learn

from Me, for I am gentle and humble in heart, and YOU WILL FIND REST FOR YOUR SOULS. (NASB)

Jesus speaks here about His yoke. A yoke on animals brings them under the authority and direction of their owner. When that owner has a kind attitude toward the animals, the yoke results in right order, well-being and fulfillment of purpose. So it is also for the human soul of those who are surrendered to Jesus.

See Choice, Emotion, Heart, Human Spirit, Mind, Mindset, Reason, Soulishness, Will, Yoke

Human Spirit – that part of a human being which is eternal and created by God to be the life-sustainer of the body.

It is imparted into our physical being at conception. When we accept Jesus as Lord and Savior, our spirit is born again into spiritual light, giving revelation of our true identity and destiny. The Bible tells us, however, that this part of us can be damaged by being crushed, overwhelmed, grieved, broken or defiled by the events of life (Psalm 142:3; 2 Corinthians 7:1; Isaiah 54:6a; Job 17:1). The human spirit is the place within us that carries a deep awareness of our identity, the answer to the question *Who am I?*, but sadly this is an identity which is often much distorted by the effects of a sinful world.

> 1 Corinthians 2:11... It is only our own spirit within us that knows all about us ... (GNB)

When we are born again of the Spirit of God (John 3:3–6), we bring into this new existence all the experiences of our past, and we will not be immune to future trouble in this world. The wounding experiences of life can damage the human spirit and so affect every part of us, distorting our relationship with God and with other people, defiling our identity, our sexuality, our conscience, our creativity, and even sapping our physical strength.

> Proverbs 18:14... The human spirit can endure in sickness, but a crushed spirit who can bear? (NIV)

The physical body will reflect the condition of the heart (Proverbs 14:30), so when the human spirit is crushed by abuse or defiled through betrayal, for example, if this damage is left unresolved, then the whole body can become weakened and trapped by the enemy in the disorder. Very often the soul tries to protect and compensate for the wounding of the spirit, but this just brings further damage. This is what happens, for example, in the issue of dissociation.

Thankfully Jesus knows all about the condition of our human spirit. He sees the deep damage that has been caused in people's lives and so He came into this world and declared, "I've come to bind up the brokenhearted" (see Luke 4:18), and "Blessed are the poor in spirit, for theirs is the kingdom of heaven" (Matthew 5:3, NIV).

The human spirit, in rightful relationship with God, is intended to be the life source (James 2:26a) and sustainer for our bodies, a wellspring overflowing with the water of the Holy Spirit (John 7:38). It is designed to be the primary place of our fellowship with Him (John 4:24) and the means by which we come to an assurance of our foundational God-given identity, namely that we are His covenant children.

> Romans 8:16... The Spirit Himself testifies with our spirit that we are children of God ... (NASB)

Healing for the human spirit is a precious work of God's grace available for all believers, as we allow Him to show us the true condition of our hearts, the deep wounding caused by others and the need for us to extend forgiveness. Betrayal, a broken marriage covenant, abuse, shame, disapproval, control, neglect, grief, shock and trauma can all have a profound effect on the human spirit, far deeper than just emotional distress, actually crushing and even defiling the person whom God meant us to be.

> Malachi 2:15b... Take heed then to your spirit, and let no one deal treacherously against the wife of your youth. (NASB)

If we are open to Him, God will also convict us of our sinful behaviors, soulish protection, self-comfort, and the distorted beliefs about our identity which have further damaged our spirit. As we respond to God, simply as His children, fully dependent on the Father's love, He brings wonderful restoration to this part of our being which, under the direction of the Holy Spirit, is the true sustainer of abundant life.

See Betrayal, Born Again, Brokenness, Conscience, Dissociation, Full Fragmentation, Holy Spirit, Human Soul, Identity, Shame, Soulishness

Humility (Humble) – absence of pride and self-promotion.

When there is inner security in our God-given identity and value, the focus of our lives no longer needs to be in promoting our own significance or our abilities. God has declared our personal value by giving the life of Jesus as a ransom for our release from spiritual captivity.

All that we now are, and all the gifting that we express, becomes centered on the one who makes us life-changers in this broken and defiled world, through the authority and power that He gives us. We are each of immense significance in the Body of Christ, but we no longer have any need to persuade others of this fact. Walking under the daily direction of Jesus will cause us not only to be enabled by Him, but also to become like Him, not least in His true humility.

> Matthew 11:29… Take My yoke upon you and learn from Me, for I am gentle and humble in heart, and YOU WILL FIND REST FOR YOUR SOULS. (NASB)

See Identity, Power, Pride, Security, Significance, Value

Humiliation (Humiliate) – public degrading of a person's significance and perceived value.

This can cause deep inner wounding, whether it is a consequence of our own sin or the abuse of others.

Particularly as children we are vulnerable to the humiliating words and actions of those in authority over our lives, not least parents and teachers. Such words crush the human spirit, defile identity and drive us to build defensive walls of, for example, withdrawal, rebellion or unreality.

In contrast, every interaction with Jesus nurtures our innate significance, unless we actively oppose His lordship and expose our own sinfulness.

> Luke 13:16–17... "And this woman, a daughter of Abraham as she is, whom Satan has bound for eighteen long years, should she not have been released from this bond on the Sabbath day?" As He said this, all His opponents were being humiliated; and the entire crowd was rejoicing over all the glorious things being done by Him. (NASB)

The start of healing from the wounding of humiliation is to recognize our defense mechanisms and allow God to touch the places of pain. We will need to forgive those who exposed us, especially if they should have been the very people God had put in place to guard us. Jesus surely knows the pain of humiliation and has taken upon Himself at the cross all that has hurt us.

> Luke 23:11... And having humiliated Him with his soldiery, and mocking Him by putting around Him luxurious clothing, Herod sent Him back to Pilate. (LITV)

See Abuse, Failure, Humility, Shame, Significance, Value, Wounding

Hurt (Hurting, Hurtful) – see Pain

Identity – concept and declaration of individuality.

It is the answer to the question, *Who am I?* It is what makes me – me. Personal identity is discovered through relationship with others, not least with God, and is closely linked with what we have been called, or what we have called ourselves. Throughout our lives there have been names, spoken and unspoken, which have expressed views of our identity. Even Jesus faced this (Matthew 16:13–14). Such names have very often opposed the true identity that God seeks to establish within us. He wants us to rediscover, and walk in, the truth of who God made us each to be, just as He spoke over the corporate identity of the city and people of Jerusalem:

> Isaiah 62:2,4... Jerusalem, the nations will see you victorious! All their kings will see your glory. You will be called by a new name, A name given by the LORD himself ... No longer will you be called "Forsaken," Or your land be called "The Deserted Wife." Your new name will be "God Is Pleased with Her". ... (GNB)

Our identity, including our sexual identity, is rooted within our human spirit. The cells of our physical bodies are completely replaced many times throughout our lives but the human spirit within us holds the unchanging reality of who God made us to be, even though this is distorted by what we have inherited from our ancestors and from the issues of life.

> 1 Corinthians 2:11a... It is only our own spirit within us that knows all about us ... (GNB)

Sometimes codependent or other wrongly dependent relationships can result in a confusion of identity, where one person's identity is unhealthily linked with another person. I wonder what the effect was on Jacob's youngest son to be called by his dying mother, at the moment of his birth, Ben-oni, *son of my sorrow*. His father, in this moment of desperate loss, declared another name, Benjamin, *son of my right hand* (Genesis 35:18). Interestingly, we find later that Jacob is, to some extent, wrongly living his life through Benjamin, seemingly unable to fully exist without this son (Genesis 44:30). God wants us to walk in the identity that He alone has given us. It is closely connected with the destiny that He has purposed for each one of us. It is only in Christ Jesus that we can discover the truth of who we are.

> Acts 17:28... For in him we live, and move, and have our being ... (KJV)

God intended that our true foundational identity would be revealed and sealed in our human spirit through the witness of the Holy Spirit, as we walk in covenant with God as followers of Jesus. The Holy Spirit says that you are a child of God, valuable and loved.

> Romans 8:16... God's Spirit joins himself to our spirits to declare that we are God's children. (GNB)

IDENTITY

We are indeed now children of God's family and citizens of the Kingdom of God (Colossians 1:13), but unfortunately, the experiences of life have brought many other distorting messages from the world deep into our hearts, very often causing us to believe that our identity is very far from what God has apparently declared. When people have consistently treated us badly, especially when we were children, we naturally conclude that their attitude toward us must surely define something of who we are. Mephibosheth, crippled as a child due to family strife, displays a false and very degrading self-image when he is brought before David, even though he has just become an adopted and honored son of the king.

> 2 Samuel 9:8... Again he prostrated himself and said, "What is your servant, that you should regard a dead dog like me?" (NASB)

I'm a victim, I'm a nobody, I'm an outsider, I'm a mistake, I'm useless, I'm inadequate, I'm the wrong sex, I'm just bad. These and many other false identities affect the lives of countless people, driving their attitudes and behaviors. They are frequently strengthened by the enemy's power as we agree with his lies. Even as Christians, we may try to deal with these painful notions of our identity by pushing them away, almost abandoning part of ourselves in order to present an acceptable Christian image to those around us. Unfortunately, this dissociation literally just tears us apart on the inside!

The transformation for our identity back into God's order starts by our recognizing the wounding that has happened in our lives and forgiving those who have hurt us, so that we can find God's true comfort. We also need to renounce agreement with all the distorted labels of identity which have become entwined with our lives, acknowledging that the wounding may have been true, but only God holds the absolute truth of the identity that He has given us. According to His Word, we are made in God's image, we are engraved on the palms of His hands, we are chosen in Christ before the creation of the world, we are summoned by name before God, we are His covenant children and therefore able to be fully confident in His love, His protection and His provision. God delights in the identity which He has imparted to each one of us, even while He understands the damage that can occur to us in this sinful world.

209

See Codependence, Creativity, Destiny, Dissociation, Human Spirit, Image, Sexuality, Transformation, Transgender

Idolatry (Idol, Idolatrous) – making something an object of worship.

It has been said that you find out the idols in a person's life when you see a strong reaction to those things being taken away from them. This may not be entirely fair when thinking of loved ones or certain essentials of life, but it makes the point that there can be many things which we have come to rely on more than God. Such idols can be people, possessions, image, status, healing needs, routines, rights, rituals, religious practices, and even strongly held Christian beliefs which have taken wrongful precedence over a surrendered relationship with Jesus.

> 1 John 2:15... Do not love the world nor the things in the world. If anyone loves the world, the love of the Father is not in him. (NASB)

The Bible explains a very important principle concerning idols. Whatever or whoever we surrender to gains spiritual authority over us and increasingly we become like the object of this worship. If we give ourselves to Jesus, the Holy Spirit indwells our lives and gradually changes us to become like Him. If, however, we have made idols of other gods, other people, or other practices, the enemy is given the right to rule these areas of our lives and demonically promote aspects of his defiling character through our beliefs and behavior.

> Psalm 115:8... Those who make [idols] will become like them, Everyone who trusts in them. (NASB)

It's a tough question, but dare we ask God, "Who or what do I rely on more than You?" His answer will never condemn us, but it may convict us of where idolatry is damaging our lives. False worship or idolatry of worthless things will always eventually lead to our experiencing a sense of personal worthlessness.

> 2 Kings 17:15... They worshiped worthless idols and became worthless themselves ... (GNB)

See Authority, False Religion, Fruit, Image, Power, Value, Worship

Image – how we appear to ourselves and to others.

It is the presentation of our identity and personality. The book of Genesis tells us that human beings are made in the image of God, whereas animals are created after their own kind (Genesis 1:24–27).

Due to the spiritual blindness caused by the Fall, we exist in a world that is very focused on human image, how we look, how we dress, how we live, all encouraged through the media, and pursued through following fashion leaders, celebrities and other human role models. But God, through our spiritual rebirth, wants to shape our true identity by our becoming more and more conformed to the image of Jesus Christ, not by losing our unique personality, but rather through finding the fullness of the person that God has created us to be.

God delights in our knowing His given image in our human spirit and in our having the confidence to express the full truth of that image to the world around us. This is a work of the Holy Spirit as we look into the divine mirror which God has provided, through the person of Jesus (2 Corinthians 3:17–18).

C.S. Lewis wrote: *"Your real, new self ... will not come as long as you are looking for it. It will come when you are looking for Him."*[13] We will never find the security of a true image by simply copying another human being, however attractive that person might be. To surrender to God's changing of our hearts, to become increasingly like Jesus, is actually the purpose of our being and the answer to the deepest of our inner needs.

> Romans 12:2... And do not be conformed to this world, but be transformed by the renewing of your mind, so that you may prove what the will of God is, that which is good and acceptable and perfect. (NASB)

See Creation, Character, Fruit, Identity, Personality, Transformation

Inadequacy (Inadequate) – condition of not meeting the perceived standards or expectations of others.

Humankind is created in the image of God, unlike animals which are created in the image of their own kind (Genesis 1:24). However, without new birth of our human spirit and the revelation of our true identity, we are vulnerable to the deceptive demands of others in this world, namely that we should conform to their requirements of ability, intellect, enjoying or owning certain things, our body shape, masculinity, femininity and so on.

Wrongful messages about adequacy can also be given by parents during a person's childhood, whether intentionally or not. This could happen, for example, where the child was not the gender they had wanted, or where, because of their own unmet needs, the parents were unable to give affirmation and love in the way God intended. This can leave the child wondering, deep down, why they are apparently so unlovable, and with a growing sense of inadequacy, as he or she feels that they are failing to meet all the expectations of their parents.

Such lies concerning our adequacy are an opportunity for the evil ruler of the world to promote within us the false belief that we are never going to be good enough for those around us. In sharp contrast, God's view of our adequacy in His family is simply measured by our willingness to be surrendered to Jesus. Amazingly, He has met every necessary standard on our behalf.

> 2 Corinthians 3:5... Not that we are adequate in ourselves to consider anything as coming from ourselves, but our adequacy is from God ... (NASB)

He is wonderfully able to be our adequacy in all things, restoring our confidence and transforming our lives more and more into the true image for which we were created, being shaped by the Holy Spirit rather than the lying spirit of this world (Ephesians 2:1-2).

Maybe it is time for us to forgive those, however well-meaning, who have put pressure on us to meet their own expectations, rather than helping us to embrace the true image and gifting which God has given us through Jesus Christ. Where parents have not been able to bond with us or to show us the unconditional love that we needed, forgiving them from our hearts will open a door for God's healing to begin in us.

Where we have agreed with the enemy by disliking and rejecting ourselves, we will need to confess this and ask God, who made us, to help us accept ourselves, even with all our inadequacies and vulnerabilities. Maybe it is also time to confess and repent of our own strivings to conform to this world (Romans 12:2).

Let us make a decision that we will now begin to fully rest in the real joy and the huge significance of being a child of God, knowing that amazingly we are being changed by Him from one degree of glory to another (2 Corinthians 3:18).

See Acceptance, Affirmation, Failure, Identity, Perfectionism, Rejection, Sexuality, Significance, Value

Independence (Independent) – choice of separation from rightful relationship and authority.

When authority figures have been uncaring, harsh or wrongly controlling, independence can seem to be a good solution. We may have decided deep inside to pursue our lives without rightful dependence on others, especially those in authority. We choose to do without their help or direction, because it seems that this will stop us getting hurt. But God never intended us to live emotionally or spiritually isolated lives. He designed us for interdependency within families, within communities and as part of the Body of Christ, where there should be rightful authority and safety.

Independence is a form of rebellion, and it can give the enemy rights to use demonic power to strengthen the choice of separation that we have made, bringing division and dysfunction in all our relationships. To overcome this, we need to walk in mutual submission to one another and to the gifting that God has distributed among the Body of Christ, so that we can live in spiritual safety, guarded from isolation and deception. Perhaps we need to forgive some authority figures today and confess that independence has been a wrong way of trying to deal with the pain of disapproval or rejection. God longs to welcome us back into full participation in His precious family, so that together we can become the pure bride of Christ.

> Ephesians 5:21... be subject to one another in the fear of Christ. (NASB)

See Authority, Covering, Dependence, Headship, Interdependence, Rebellion

Infirmity – See Disease

Inheritance (Inherit) – anything passed down through families to the living, from those who have died.

We may or may not be pleased with what has been handed down to us through family inheritance, but more importantly, we need to be aware of the spiritual significance of what has come from our ancestors, and what we hand down to our children.

Occasionally objects passed down can be a curse rather than a blessing, particularly items intended by our ancestors, even unconsciously, to exercise some form of control over our lives (such as jewelry with unhelpful inscriptions), or things linked to occult or religious practices (such as the regalia of Freemasonry). We will need God's revelation regarding objects which might need to be discarded because of spiritual impurity.

Whether or not there are physical items, the Bible tells us that we are also subject to a spiritual inheritance which is affected by the righteousness or otherwise of our ancestors. God intended there to be significant blessing for us resulting from their godliness (Deuteronomy 7:9) but, where this is a defiled and destructive inheritance (generational iniquity) due to the way of life of those who have gone before us, our own lives can be affected by that also (Lamentations 5:7). Thankfully, through the shedding of His blood at the cross, Jesus has provided for the full redemption of lives damaged by wrong inheritance.

> 1 Peter 1:18–19... you were not redeemed with perishable things like silver or gold from your futile way of life inherited from your forefathers, but with precious blood, as of a lamb unblemished and spotless, the blood of Christ. (NASB)

As we forgive our ancestors for all that has come from them which is not right with God, we can know His wonderful cleansing and healing, as those who have now become heirs to His covenant promises. This is the wonderful inheritance that God has planned for all of His children.

> Galatians 3:29... And if you belong to Christ, then you are Abraham's descendants, heirs according to promise. (NASB)

See Blessing, Covenant, Curse, Generational Iniquity

Iniquity (Iniquitous) – spiritual condition which is out of line with God.

We can be in this condition through our own sin or the sin of other people who have misused their responsibility for our lives, such as our parents, or even our ancestors, who have defiled the inheritance with generational iniquity. Iniquity distorts our lives, taking us out from God's covering, and it leaves us vulnerable to dysfunction in the body, soul and human spirit. Isaiah pictures humanity's iniquity as being like a wall with a bulge. Any masonry wall that is not vertical and straight (right) is vulnerable to further damage and even collapse when under pressure.

> Isaiah 30:13... Therefore this iniquity will be to you Like a breach about to fall, A bulge in a high wall, Whose collapse comes suddenly in an instant ... (NASB)

The Hebrew word for *iniquity*, used in the Old Testament, is *avon*, which means *crooked* or *bent*, the opposite of right or straight. This idea of sin leading to distortion of our lives is recognized in common language; for example, in England, there is a slang expression, *a bent copper*, which refers to a dishonest policeman. God's desire for all of us is that we will get right or straight with His plumb line of truth, and so find His restoration (Isaiah 6:7, NASB). This is now made possible because Jesus took all our iniquity in His body on the cross, and we can get right with God today when we truly follow Him and receive His forgiveness.

> Isaiah 53:6... All of us like sheep have gone astray, Each of us has turned to his own way; But the LORD has caused the iniquity of us all To fall on Him. (NASB)

Interestingly, places as well as people can have a condition of iniquity, as a result of the sin of those carrying responsibility for the land. Iniquity, whether in individuals, land or buildings, creates spiritual darkness and an opportunity for the enemy to hold authority and bring his defilement. God's people were warned of the hostile condition of the Promised Land due to the sin of the previous occupants.

> Leviticus 18:24–25... Do not defile yourself with all these, for with all these the nations have been defiled, which I am casting out before you; and the land is defiled, and I will visit its iniquity on it; and the land is vomiting out its inhabitants ... (LITV)

See Darkness, Defilement, Forgiveness, Generational Iniquity, Iniquity, Reclaiming Ground, Righteousness, Ruling Spirit, Sin

Injustice (Unjust) – disregard of what is right in human or divine law.

Whether believers or not, we are made by God to have some instinctive understanding of what is just or what is unjust, both in our own lives and in the world around us (Romans 2:15), even though such awareness of injustice can be much distorted by our carnal nature, the attitudes of society and the wounding of life.

A primary God-given response to injustice is the emotion of anger, which is intended to motivate a search for (His) justice. For many of us, the reality of our lives is that we have, at times, experienced deep injustice, and that these painful issues remain unresolved, together with the associated angry feelings which couldn't be fully expressed at the time. From the earliest moments of our lives, there may have been unfair punishment, unwarranted criticism or denial of freedom to develop as God intended, all of which robbed us of being able to know our true personhood.

This deep wounding of the human spirit commonly leads to soulish responses, encouraged by our carnality, where we bury the unresolved injustice under sinful attitudes and behaviors. The anger which rightly came from the injustice becomes trapped and defiled with rebellion, bitterness, jealousy, feelings of revenge, blaming others or self-blame. It is not easy to forgive those who have been the cause of serious injustice against us, but when we do forgive, there is a precious opportunity to receive our healing from all the hurt that they caused.

Jesus has stepped into this world of injustice with a radical solution. He has established a new covenant relationship between humanity and God. When we confess and turn away from sin, giving forgiveness to others and receiving the forgiveness of God, divine justice is fully met by all that Jesus did at the cross. Here, He dealt not only with sin but carried, on our behalf, all the struggle and pain of the injustice that we have experienced. This means that we cannot only be free from all the guilt and damage of our own sinful responses, but we can also be restored from the deep wounding that injustice causes. The cross is where true healing of the human spirit begins. Sadly, most of the world continues to ignore this wonderful provision.

Now, as part of God's family, we are called to be instruments of true justice rather than those who provoke others to anger, not least in parenting our children.

> Ephesians 6:4... Fathers, do not provoke your children to anger, but bring them up in the discipline and instruction of the LORD. (NASB)

Unfortunately, the world is increasingly trying to achieve justice by declaring the (assumed) rights of humanity, in line with humanism, rather than bringing themselves into line with the Bible and resolving the underlying problem, which is the sin of humanity, and ignoring the heart intent of God's laws. When we ignore God's ways, we simply open a door to more injustice, just creating a contest of the perceived entitlements of those in conflict with each other. Praise God that whether we have received injustice or given license to injustice, the mercy of God triumphs over judgment (James 2:13).

See Anger, Grace, Humanism, Jealousy, Judgment, Law, Mercy, Punishment, Revenge, Right, Truth

Inner Healing – God's healing for the heart of a human being (which is the soul and the human spirit).

The damage can be in the mind, will and emotions, or it can be in the core of our identity, through brokenness or defilement of the human spirit. Such inner disorder will also be an opportunity for the enemy to move in to seek to control where possible. For example, if we bury anger, however understandable that may be, it is contrary to God's order in our bodies and can therefore give spiritual authority to the enemy.

> Ephesians 4:26–27... BE ANGRY, AND yet DO NOT SIN; do not let the sun go down on your anger, and do not give the devil and opportunity. (NASB)

Inner damage occurs as a result of the sinful activity of others against us, and also (and often more significantly) as a result of our attempts to deal with the wounding issues ourselves without God's help. God's people, individually and corporately, have consistently tried to find their own solution to distressing situations, but eventually it just leaves them more exposed.

> Isaiah 30:1–3... "Woe to the rebellious children," declares the LORD, "Who execute a plan, but not Mine, And make an alliance, but not of My Spirit, In order to add sin to sin; Who proceed down to Egypt Without consulting Me, To take refuge in the safety of Pharaoh And to seek shelter in the shadow of Egypt! Therefore the safety of Pharaoh will be your shame And the shelter in the shadow of Egypt, your humiliation." (NASB)

It is the same in our personal lives. Abuse by a family member, for example, can cause immense inner damage, but choosing to cope with the pain by trying to find refuge in pushing it out of our memory will only exacerbate the problem. Shutting moldy cheese in a cupboard of your house will never solve the ongoing issue of distressing odors!

A priority for Jesus, as He fulfilled the prophecy of Isaiah, was to bind up the brokenhearted and to comfort all who were in mourning (Isaiah 61:1–2). He clearly brought inner restoration to many people, including men like Peter the disciple, for his issues of inadequacy, fear and unreality. The mission of Jesus, now through the Body of Christ, has not changed. Inner healing is desperately needed by countless people, as Jesus witnessed (Matthew 9:36).

Because the physical body reflects the condition of the heart, much physical healing is seen as God brings restoration to the soul and spirit.

> Proverbs 14:30a... A tranquil heart is life to the body ... (NASB)

See Abuse, Brokenness, Coping Mechanism, Disorder, Distress, Forgiveness, Human Soul, Human Spirit, Pain, Restoration, Wounding

Insecurity (Insecure) – see Security

Integrity – oneness or wholeness of the human spirit, soul and body.

This means that a person of integrity will not say one thing, and be thinking another. They will not hide behind masks or a false identity, they will not conceal wrongful motives or sinful attitudes, or seek to be covered by self-righteousness. Jesus was a man of perfect integrity. We can let God's oneness fill and transform our lives, both as an individual and as a part of the Body of Christ.

> Psalm 86:11... Teach me Your way, O LORD; I will walk in Your truth; Unite my heart to fear Your name. (NKJV)

> John 17:22... The glory which You have given Me I have given to them, that they may be one, just as We are one ... (NASB)

See Dissociation, Brokenness, Mask, Righteousness, Truth, Wholeness

Intercession (Intercede, Intercessory) – acting and speaking, in prayer and proclamation, in agreement with God concerning His will for particular people and situations.

Agreement with God undermines the authority of the enemy. Intercession advances the Kingdom of God on earth and brings about His purposes in human lives (Matthew 6:10).

Intercession differs from the type of spiritual warfare in which the enemy is being addressed directly and his power is being specifically confronted. While undoubtedly that may be important at certain times, we should remember that before we command the powers of darkness, we need to be sure of our authority in Christ for the particular issue being challenged. This authority will only come through confession and forgiveness of relevant sin, so removing the rights of the enemy to hold on to his spiritual position.

Without this divine authority, we can have no empowering by the Holy Spirit and may even find ourselves overwhelmed by the strength of the enemy (Acts 19:13–16).

Intercession, however, is essentially a dialogue with God, and not with the powers of darkness. It means standing in agreement with God on behalf of those who may not yet see clearly the spiritual battle over their lives, for example, by parents in petition for their children. Interestingly, the psalmist urges intercession by God's people for the peace of Jerusalem (Psalm 122:6–9), which is surely very relevant in these troubled days. Entered with humility, it is always safe, effective and pleasing to God, unless, of course, He has specifically (although rarely) commanded us not to pray (Jeremiah 7:16). He is indeed saddened when there is a lack of intercessors who will agree with Him in prayer, and so stand in any breach in the protective wall around God's people. This is what Moses did for the Children of Israel (Psalm 106:23).

> Ezekiel 22:30… I searched for a man among them who would build up the wall and stand in the gap before Me for the land, so that I would not destroy it; but I found no one. (NASB)

In Ellel Ministries, we have found it to be very effective when a group of intercessors is set aside to seek the Lord during significant times of teaching or prayer ministry. Such agreement within the group, and with God, often brings extraordinary spiritual light and breakthrough in otherwise dark situations, undermining the strongholds of the enemy when he is seeking to promote deception and confusion.

> Matthew 18:19… Again I say to you, that if two of you agree on earth about anything that they may ask, it shall be done for them by My Father who is in heaven. (NASB)

See Agreement, Prayer, Prayer Ministry, Spiritual Warfare

Interdependence (Interdependent) – healthy relationship between people in which the gifting of each of the participants is acknowledged and used for the good of all involved.

Interdependent people are able to rely on one another in a right way. This type of relationship is what God has intended for all groups of people, not least in marriage and families. The different attributes and giftings of a husband and wife can truly complement one another, and bring the fullness of God's protection and provision for the whole family.

Beyond individual families, the Body of Christ is intended to operate as a living body, with each member acting under the authority and direction of the Holy Spirit for the common good (1 Corinthians 12:7). All parts of the Body are expected to rightfully submit to the godly gifting in others, and through this inspired interdependence, carry out the extraordinary works of God here on earth.

> Ephesians 5:21... be subject to one another in the fear of Christ. (NASB)

A body gets damaged when its members act in independence of or rebellion to one another. Many believers get deeply hurt in churches when the principle of rightful interdependence is neither understood nor followed. Another damaging alternative to interdependence is codependence.

See Authority, Body of Christ, Codependence, Gifts of the Holy Spirit, Independence

Intimacy (Intimate) – closeness in a relationship and emotional openness.

How much should I know about others? How much should they know about me? If I have experienced neglect or abuse, affecting and distorting the deep place of my identity in my human spirit, it can be hard to know the right boundaries of intimacy in my relationships with others, and even with God. Many people struggle with these issues, some being too guarded, some too intense and some even promiscuous.

Jesus permitted different levels of human intimacy with His followers while He walked the earth. This is also God's order for our own lives. It appears that John, the beloved, was closest to Jesus, then Peter and James (Matthew 17:1), then the rest of the twelve, and then some sixty other disciples. Through the Holy Spirit today, God offers a deep intimacy of relationship with Himself through our human spirit, for all those who have received Jesus as Lord of their lives.

> John 14:17... that is the Spirit of truth, whom the world cannot receive, because it does not see Him or know Him, but you know Him because He abides with you and will be in you. (NASB)

In all significant human relationships, there is a revealing of ourselves, a touching of human spirit to human spirit in some measure, but it would not be right for us to share all our deepest thoughts with everybody. For married people, the deepest sharing should just be with our spouse, the one to whom we have chosen to give most fully of ourselves, even in sexual intimacy, in the safety of a covenant relationship. The older translations of the Bible sometimes use the word *knowing* to describe sexual intercourse, and this draws attention to the particular emotional and spiritual intimacy intended between marriage partners.

Beyond this closest of relationships, there should be others whom we have found trustworthy to share the hopes and fears of our lives, knowing that they will bring loving encouragement or correction when needed. In order to walk in rightful intimacy with others, we may need the Lord's help, first admitting that we have not always understood the importance of clear boundaries due to the wounding of the past. As we pour out our emotions to God and find healing for the damage of wrong relationships, we will discover the precious and safe intimacy that God desires with each one of us. As we find this healing, and learn to acknowledge and accept who we really are, we can have a new confidence and clarity about the level of godly intimacy in all our human relationships.

> Proverbs 3:32... For the devious are an abomination to the LORD; But He is intimate with the upright. (NASB)

See Covenant, Human Spirit, Marriage, Openness, Relationship, Sexuality, Sexual Sin, Trust

Intimidation (Intimidate) – control through fear.

See Control, Fear

Isolation (Isolate) – separation from human or divine fellowship.

Sometimes people can experience a very deep sense of isolation, perhaps triggered by today's circumstances, but actually rooted in unresolved painful experiences from the past. A newborn baby placed in an incubator, a child separated from parents during a hospital stay, a serious accident, a child experiencing traumatic loss of mother or father due to death or family breakdown; all these can damage the security and integrity of the human spirit, leaving an unhealed and isolated place needing the restoration of heartfelt acceptance and belonging which only the Lord can fully provide.

> Isaiah 49:15–16... Can a woman forget her nursing child and have no compassion on the son of her womb? Even these may forget, but I will not forget you. Behold, I have inscribed you on the palms of My hands ... (NASB)

As we forgive those who have abandoned us in the past, for whatever reason, the place of isolation which is in the human spirit can be embraced by the Holy Spirit, expelling any painful grip of the enemy. God wants us to have a deep confidence in the intimacy and certainty of our eternal relationship with Him.

See Abuse, Acceptance, Depression, Human Spirit, Intimacy, Neglect, Rejection, Relationship

Jealousy (Jealous) – intense desire or concern for things or people, even to the extent of envy toward perceived rivals.

God created humankind for Himself and He is jealous for the covenant relationship which He purposed with each one of us, an intimacy lost through humanity's sin (Exodus 34:14–15). His jealousy over our inherited separation from Him has a serious consequence for our lives.

> Exodus 20:5... You shall not worship [idols] or serve them; for I, the LORD your God, am a jealous God, visiting the iniquity of the fathers on the children ... (NASB)

However, He has determined that through Jesus, there is rescue for us from the false friendship of the ruler of the world, and He has made a way back into His family, just as a bridegroom would be rightfully jealous of his bride being seduced by another, and would fight to win her back. This is the same godly jealousy which Paul felt for those whom he had brought to Christ (2 Corinthians 11:2).

Unfortunately, most human jealousy is in the form of envy, which is the result of our carnality, claiming an entitlement to what we see others possess. God has called each of His children to be content with His provision for our lives, for He alone truly knows our needs. He does not condone the poverty which society has allowed through sin, nor does He condemn those who seek to better their standard of living, but this needs to be done with eyes fixed on Him and not focused on the apparent advantages enjoyed by our neighbor.

> Exodus 20:17a... You shall not covet your neighbor's house ... (NASB)

There is no peace in wrongful jealousy, which is covetousness or envy. In fact, unresolved envy can be deeply damaging to the whole body.

> Proverbs 14:30... A heart at peace gives life to the body, but envy rots the bones. (NIV)

God wants us to be free from these negative passions, although Paul says that God will even use the jealousy of the Jews toward Gentile believers to bring the Children of Israel back into true relationship with Him (Romans 11:11). By our confessing unrighteous envy and through receiving God's forgiveness, we can know His healing and be content in the abundance of life which has been promised by Jesus (John 10:10).

See Desire, Entitlement, Faith, Trust

Jesus – Son of God and the Savior of the world.

Jesus, or *Yeshua* in Hebrew, is the name that God has given to the one within the divine Trinity who came to earth in human form to pay the full cost of humanity's sin and to permanently re-establish God's new covenant with humankind. An angel of the Lord instructed Joseph in a dream how to name the child that was to be born.

> Matthew 1:20–21... Joseph, son of David, do not be afraid to take Mary as your wife; for the Child who has been conceived in her is of the Holy Spirit. She will bear a Son; and you shall call His name Jesus, for He will save His people from their sins. (NASB)

The Hebrew name means *God who saves* and He has indeed saved us from unending spiritual death, the consequence of our sin, through giving us individually the choice to receive a new right to life in God's family by accepting Jesus as the Lord of everything that we are and everything we do.

> John 1:12... But as many as received Him, to them He gave the right to become children of God, even to those who believe in His name ... (NASB)

Acknowledging the divinity and Lordship (2 Peter 1:1-2) of Jesus is the starting place for all true spiritual healing, including all the restoration that flows from God's covenant promises. His motivation for this amazing act of grace is simply that He loves each one of us so much that He does not want anyone to be lost in spiritual death (John 3:16).

Sadly, throughout history, the name *Jesus* (a false Jesus) has been used by human imposters claiming to be Him at His second coming (Matthew 24:24), cursing tongues by using His name as a swear word, and by counterfeit spirits performing false miracles through the wrong invoking of His name (Matthew 7:22). We need to be careful not to give rights to the enemy in any deceptions by assuming that we are witnessing the presence of the true Jesus when, despite His name being used, in fact, the fruit of His character is clearly not evident. The fruit on the branch always confirms the variety of the tree (Matthew 7:16).

Jesus will always point us to His Father in His walk with us, and He Himself will be revealed by the increasing fruit of the Holy Spirit evidenced in the lives of those under His spiritual authority. The enemy is able to counterfeit the power of God in some measure but he cannot sustain a manifestation of the true character of Jesus of Nazareth, the Messiah, the Son of God who came in flesh to save the world. How amazing to be so loved by this servant-hearted King of kings.

See Christ, the Cross, God, Salvation, Son of God, Son of Man, Trinity

Jezebel (Jezebellic) – name given to a particular demonic power showing the strong controlling characteristics evident in Ahab's wife of this name.

In His challenge to the members of the church at Thyatira, Jesus refers to a woman, whom He pointedly calls *Jezebel*, because He was exposing the spiritual entity which was operating through her. He rebuked the church for not confronting this destructive power.

> Revelation 2:20… But I have this against you, that you tolerate the woman Jezebel, who calls herself a prophetess, and she teaches and leads My bond-servants astray so that they commit acts of immorality and eat things sacrificed to idols. (NASB)

The character of this spirit can be discerned from both Old and New Testament references: it is manipulative, seductive, religious, contemptuous of true leadership, intimidating and is given license by human sin where godly authority is ineffectual, defiled or undermined through rebellious behavior. It was Ahab's false worship and his abdication of rightful leadership that opened a door to his queen seeking sinful control within the royal family and wrongful personal allegiance from the community of false prophets. The Jezebel spirit looks for allies in promoting manipulation of rightful authority.

> 1 Kings 18:19… Now then send and gather to me all Israel at Mount Carmel, together with 450 prophets of Baal and 400 prophets of Asherah, who eat at Jezebel's table. (NASB)

This demonic spirit needs to be confronted in a godly way whenever the telltale characteristics appear within any fellowship of believers in Jesus Christ. It can manifest through wounded men and women, often resulting from their struggles with ungodly authority. Confrontation of those affected must come with a huge measure of grace, hating the grip of the enemy but loving the person. Any one of us can be vulnerable to this spirit if we join in undermining God's rightful order and authority within the Body of Christ. The Bible even describes this enemy activity as witchcraft, when allowed sufficient license in someone's life.

> 2 Kings 9:22... When Joram saw Jehu, he said, "Is it peace, Jehu?" And he answered, "What peace, so long as the harlotries of your mother Jezebel and her witchcrafts are so many?" (NASB)

But remember, whatever intimidating hold this spirit might have gained, it is expelled by confession, repentance and the precious forgiveness of God.

See Authority, Control, Headship, Manipulation, Rebellion, Religion, Ruling Spirit, Seduction, Unclean Spirit

Joy (Joyful, Joyfulness) – deep and intense well-being.

Joy is more a condition of the human spirit than just an emotion in the soul. Happiness in life is something that everyone seeks, but it will be transient if not founded in something eternal. St Augustine wrote: *"Do not let your happiness depend on something that you may lose."*[14] Happiness is an emotion which can come from many of life's experiences but true joy is a fruit of the Holy Spirit, as He imparts the character of Jesus into our hearts.

> Galatians 5:22–23... But the fruit of the Spirit is love, joy, peace, patience, kindness, goodness, faithfulness, gentleness, self-control ... (NASB)

However, it is not unusual for Christians to carry deep sadness, even despair, in their hearts, from the wounding issues of life. Thankfully, we can bring these to Jesus, by forgiving those who have been the cause of deep sorrow, and we can choose to give the burden of sadness to Jesus. This removes the enemy's destructive grip on our hearts and opens the door for a radical change.

> Isaiah 53:4... Surely our griefs He Himself bore, And our sorrows He carried; Yet we ourselves esteemed Him stricken, Smitten of God, and afflicted. (NASB)

The Holy Spirit can supernaturally transform the condition of our human spirit, sowing in the joy of Christ, which is God's covenant promise for every one of His children. This joy is not dependent upon our circumstances but upon His presence.

> Isaiah 61:3... To console those who mourn in Zion, To give them beauty for ashes, The oil of joy for mourning, The garment of praise for the spirit of heaviness; That they may be called trees of righteousness, The planting of the LORD, that He may be glorified. (NKJV)

See Grief, Human Spirit, Loss, Pain, Wounding

Judgment (Judge, Judgmental) – decision about what is right according to law.

This decision can relate to an individual, when guilt and punishment need to be determined, or it can be the result of our seeking direction from the Holy Spirit about particular situations, as when James made a judgment on behalf of the disciples at the council at Jerusalem.

> Acts 15:19... Therefore it is my judgment that we do not trouble those who are turning to God from among the Gentiles. (NASB)

God called judges in the Old Testament for this same purpose of discerning His laws on behalf of the people. However, judgment can also be the outworking of unhealed lives and carnality, as we make assumptions and decisions about people which deny the truth and grace of God. Such prejudice can hold people to the enemy's condemnation rather than convicting them with the truth which leads to freedom.

JUSTICE

> Matthew 7:1… Do not judge so that you will not be judged. (NASB)

We need to be cautious that our judgments are truly seeking the ways of God rather than making our own condemning assessment (Titus 1:12), when there actually needs to be forgiveness and healing. God alone is the final judge of human hearts and actions.

> James 2:13… For God will not show mercy when he judges the person who has not been merciful; but mercy triumphs over judgment. (GNB)

See Belief, Bitter Root Judgment, Blame, Condemnation, Discernment, Forgiveness, Grace, Law

Justice (Just) – adhering to human or divine law, without bias.

There is a God-given awareness in our hearts of the need for true justice in the life of human beings. We most often encounter this issue when confronted with the pain and anger which results from experiencing *injustice*.

The search for an answer to the question "What is justice?" has challenged philosophers throughout history. Unfortunately, most have rejected God's laws as the foundation of what is right, choosing instead to define justice in terms of unclear notions of personal freedom, as well as equality of opportunity, benefit and risk.

Justice and morality are commonly measured these days not by what God says through the Bible, but by man-made ethical frameworks, which are well-meaning but can lead to contradictory viewpoints; for example, saying that justice is simply that activity which results in the greatest good (or happiness) for the greatest number of people (known by philosophers as *utilitarianism*). Unfortunately, if you ask ten people what makes them happy, you will probably get ten different answers!

International law increasingly promotes the establishing of justice or fairness through the concept of certain innate human entitlements or rights, rather than tackling the real underlying cause of injustice, which is sin, the breaking of God's commandments. In effect, God says in the Bible, "Ask me what is right, just and fair, for I made you and I know best what will meet the cry of your heart for justice" (see Isaiah 1:16–20).

Jesus has come to restore true justice in this world. True justice is to be fully right with God's laws, both now through His followers, and in complete fulfillment at His return to earth.

> Isaiah 16:5... Then one of David's descendants will be king, and he will rule the people with faithfulness and love. He will be quick to do what is right, and he will see that justice is done. ... (GNB)

See Anger, Debt, Injustice, Law, Right, a Right, Righteousness, Sin

Justification (Justify) – perceived legitimacy for release from any accusation.

When we are challenged about ungodly behavior, our carnal nature will invariably tend toward self-justification, seeking to absolve ourselves from any blame, along with pride, accusation of others, excuses or denial. Jesus gave stern warning about such activity:

> Luke 16:15... And He said to them, "You are those who justify yourselves in the sight of men, but God knows your hearts; for that which is highly esteemed among men is detestable in the sight of God." (NASB)

However, if our behavior is sinful, there is only one way, in the sight of God, for true justification which will leave us free from the spiritual consequences of our actions. We need to confess our wrongdoing, receive God's pardon, and let the Lord Jesus carry all the accusation and punishment on our behalf.

> Isaiah 53:11... After he has suffered, he will see the light of life and be satisfied; by his knowledge my righteous servant will justify many, and he will bear their iniquities. (NIV)

It sounds almost too good to be true, but this is the wonderful gospel of salvation. Praise God!

See Blame, Confession, Debt, Forgiveness, Grace, Guilt, Salvation, Sin

Kindness (Kind) – goodness, love, warm-hearted care, compassion, gentleness and grace in relationship.

I remember my elderly mother in the last few months of her life being asked what she most wanted from those caring for her, in order to be at peace each day. "Just kindness," she said. Receiving kindness is a basic need of the human spirit. Walking in truth is an essential pathway to freedom from emotional and spiritual bondage, but without kindness, truth can be too hard to bear. Kindness to one another is a command of Jesus.

> Luke 10:36–37... And Jesus concluded, "In your opinion, which one of these three acted like a neighbor toward the man attacked by the robbers?" The teacher of the Law answered, "The one who was kind to him." Jesus replied, "You go, then, and do the same." (GNB)

Kindness is not weak, it is not a compromise, it is not false, it is not foolish; in fact, it is an essential aspect of God's character, which He shows to every human being, whether they choose to receive it or not.

> Luke 6:35... But love your enemies, and do good, and lend, expecting nothing in return; and your reward will be great, and you will be sons of the Most High; for He Himself is kind to ungrateful and evil men. (NASB)

As we walk in obedience to Jesus, become healed from the past, and grow more into His likeness (2 Corinthians 3:18), kindness will become a way of life for us in every relationship, even when confronting difficult issues. God is always ready to heal any inner wounding from unkindness that we have experienced from others in our lives, as we speak out forgiveness for their behavior and let God's precious and covenantal loving-kindness restore our hurting places.

> 1 Kings 8:23... He said, "O LORD, the God of Israel, there is no God like You in heaven above or on earth beneath, keeping covenant and showing lovingkindness to Your servants who walk before You with all their heart ... " (NASB)

See Acceptance, Compassion, Fruit, Grace, Love, Loving-kindness

Kingdom of God (Kingdom of Heaven) – spiritual realm that is centered on heaven and covers all on earth that is surrendered to Jesus.

We become citizens of this Kingdom when we choose to walk in accordance with the will of God, trusting Jesus and following His commands (Colossians 1:13). God's desire to establish His people in a divine kingdom was clearly declared when He spoke to Moses on Sinai about the fledging nation of Israel (Exodus 19:6). Later, in the time of Samuel, the Children of Israel rejected God as their king, demanding a human king like other nations. God told them that this demand would inevitably lead to a rule of injustice (1 Samuel 8:7–18).

Now Jesus has come to re-establish this divine kingdom under His just kingship, for both Jew and Gentile, for all those who choose to receive Him as the King of their lives. The growing of God's Kingdom is not only about an increasing number of believers, but is also about an increasing obedience of those who are in the Kingdom.

The ways of God's Kingdom are radically different from the ways of this world, and the character of this world's spiritual ruler, Satan, who promotes deception, condemnation, brokenness and bondage. In God's Kingdom there is absolute truth, unending grace, eternal salvation, together with divine healing and deliverance in this present life. We can experience the dynamic of the Kingdom of Heaven whenever the power of the Holy Spirit overrules the powers of darkness.

In fact, there is extension of God's kingdom on earth when spiritual ground is taken from the enemy, through establishing the authority or kingship of Jesus.

> Matthew 12:28... But if I cast out demons by the Spirit of God, then the kingdom of God has come upon you. (NASB)

> 1 John 3:8b... The reason the Son of God appeared was to destroy the devil's work. (NIV)

Indeed, Jesus encourages His disciples to pray for and proclaim the progress of His Kingdom and His will through the lives of believers on earth.

> Matthew 6:10... Your kingdom come. Your will be done On earth as it is in heaven. (NKJV)

Jesus spent much of His time on earth teaching about the ways, or culture, of the Kingdom of Heaven (Luke 9:11). He told many parables to explain the mysteries of the unseen realms, where wonderful treasures are to be found by those walking in righteousness, but where eternal separation from God awaits those walking in rebellion. The religious and political leaders were challenged and threatened by all His teaching of a new Kingdom, but He responded at His trial by telling them that although He was truly a King, His Kingdom was elsewhere, rather than of this world's power conflicts.

> John 18:36... Jesus answered, "My Kingdom is not an earthly kingdom. If it were, my followers would fight to keep me from being handed over to the Jewish leaders. But my Kingdom is not of this world." (NLT)

See Commandment, Heaven, Jesus, Ruler of the World, Spiritual

Law (Lawful, Legal) – divine or human rules set in place to define or regulate how people and things are meant to operate.

National governments devise laws in a desire to bring justice and order in society, and these human laws have sometimes been based on God's laws from the Bible, such as the Ten Commandments. Legal statutes explain the laws and the consequence of breaking them: murder someone and you will go to prison! However, there are some laws which are more basic, more foundational, than the laws made by governments. These foundational laws can be physical (e.g. the law of gravity) or they can be moral/spiritual laws.

If I hold up a plumb line, the physical law of gravity has an effect on the line, causing it to hang exactly vertical. When God told Amos that He intended to hold a plumb line up in the midst of His people (Amos 7:8), He was wanting to show how sin among His people had distorted their lives, so they were not straight when they were compared to His plumb line of what is right.

LAW

The distorted condition of the people's lives was the result of the working of a divine law; namely, that the activity of sin leads to the condition of iniquity, which is being out of line with God. Sin leads to iniquity – this is a divine law, just like the law of gravity. Another foundational law is that of sowing and reaping (Galatians 6:7) – if you sow something, good or bad, that is what you will reap. All such physical and spiritual laws of the universe come from God, and humankind stands at the interface between these two realms.

To maintain order in His creation, God has put in place both physical and spiritual laws to be of benefit to humankind. However, if you neglect or abuse these laws, you will inevitably do yourself harm. If you walk off the top of a high cliff, the law of gravity may lead to your physical death. If you walk in continual sin, the law of sowing and reaping applies, and this can lead to your spiritual death, which is separation from God.

In the same way as there may be strongly worded warning notices at the top of a dangerous cliff, so God has given strong commandments in the Bible, intended to keep us from reaping the harmful consequences of abusing His foundational moral laws (Leviticus 26:3,6).

> Exodus 20:5... You shall not worship [idols] or serve them ... [a divine commandment] for I, the LORD your God, am a jealous God, visiting the iniquity of the fathers on the children, on the third and fourth generations of those who hate Me ... [a foundational divine law] (NASB)

God's foundational laws for the Children of Israel, known to the Jews as the Torah, were written down in the first five books of the Bible. The Torah explained how the chosen nation of Israel was to operate under the Old Covenant for the well-being of the people, in accordance with the ways of God. The coming of Jesus has not changed the intent and spirit of these laws, for those seeking the Kingdom of God on earth (Matthew 5:17–18). He came to explain and demonstrate with grace and truth every intention of God's laws. He was heralding a New Covenant, a time when these laws would be written not simply on paper but on human hearts, through the work of the Holy Spirit (Jeremiah 31:33). Although God's foundational laws have not changed, the commandments of God, which tell us how to keep right with His foundational laws, have been stated in a significantly new form under this New Covenant, which puts a surrendered relationship with Jesus at the center (1 John 3:23).

The good news of Jesus is that even if we have rebelled against God's laws, neglecting His commandments, we can receive a divine pardon, provided we confess the truth of our sin and recognize Jesus as Savior. That is the wonderful message of the New Covenant.

> John 1:17... For the Law was given through Moses; grace and truth were realized through Jesus Christ. (NASB)

See Blessing, Curse, Commandment, Covenant, Forgiveness, Grace, Iniquity, Justice, Order, Plumb Line, Rebellion, Repentance, Right

Lawlessness (Lawless) – rebellion against divine or human law.

See Commandment, Disobedience, Law, Rebellion, Satan

Lay Hands (Laying on of Hands) – particular relational activity among God's people, enabling the work of the Holy Spirit.

Besides rightful spiritual impartation (Numbers 27:18–20), laying hands on someone can also be an occult practice or even an act of hostility (Acts 5:18, NASB). Here, however, we are looking at how God empowers His Body of believers on earth to receive His gifts, both for revelation and restoration (Acts 19:6). He gives these to bring about the progress of His Kingdom. These manifestations of the power of the Holy Spirit are imparted to believers, sometimes directly by God and sometimes via others, through our interdependent relationships within the Body of Christ.

> Ephesians 5:21... be subject to one another in the fear of Christ. (NASB)

Allowing others within the Body to lay hands on me, to receive (say) God's healing, demonstrates rightful submission to the authority of Jesus, which He has distributed among us, and it opens my life to whatever the Holy Spirit chooses to impart. The spiritual safety of this activity is wholly dependent on Jesus having authority over the heart attitudes of both those laying hands and those receiving. Without being fearful, we need to be aware of the enemy's ability to pervert what God intends for our good, when beliefs and behaviors are out of line with Him. The Bible warns us to take care that we do not join with others in what can be sinful practice, and furthermore we need to be aware that in such circumstances it is possible for unclean spirits to be imparted, because sinful motives give rights to the enemy.

> 1 Timothy 5:22... Do not lay hands upon anyone too hastily and thereby share responsibility for the sins of others; keep yourself free from sin. (NASB)

It is very important that laying hands on someone is done at appropriate times and in appropriate ways. It should always be done with the consent of the one receiving. It should never be used as a means of manipulative control. It may not be at all appropriate to lay hands on someone who is working through issues of physical or sexual abuse. Particular care should be taken where both men and women are participating.

Jesus laid hands on people to impart the power of the Holy Spirit, particularly in healing (Luke 13:13). As the Body of Christ now operating on earth, we are called to do the same things that Jesus did, together yielding to the enabling work of the Holy Spirit, laying hands on Christian brothers or sisters for healing, gifting or baptism in the Holy Spirit (e.g. Acts 9:17).

If we sense that there has ever been a wrongful laying of hands on our bodies, we should forgive those involved and seek the Lord's freedom from any controlling soul-ties or powers of darkness. Discernment, not fear, will be the best guard for believers in the use of this important activity within the Body.

See Anointing, Body of Christ, Control, Discernment, Gifts of the Holy Spirit, Healing, Holy Spirit, Manifestation, Occult, Power

Legalism (Legalistic) – Christian teaching and lifestyle which demands adherence to perceived instructions from God's Word whilst failing to fully understand God's grace.

The commandment of God under the New Covenant is centered on our relationship with Jesus and with each other, not on following rules.

> 1 John 3:23... This is His commandment, that we believe in the name of His Son Jesus Christ, and love one another, just as He commanded us. (NASB)

Keeping right with God cannot be achieved simply by legalistic or religious behavior, however well we keep to a set of rules.

It is only true surrender to Jesus which brings us into a covenant relationship with Father God, and the consequence of following Jesus will always be increasingly righteous behavior.

The reality of the struggles which we continue to have in certain areas of our lives becomes an opportunity for discovering the truth. We find where we need to confess sin, know healing for the inner wounds, and allow Jesus to bring a further change of heart in the journey of becoming more like Him. As we follow Jesus, we must choose to walk in obedience to His instructions. This agreement with Him brings supernatural ability, through the Holy Spirit, to deny the Evil One and to grow the fruit of Jesus' character in our lives.

God's foundational laws and commandments in the Bible show us what He says *is* right. Jesus has now made it possible for us to *get* right with Him, by letting His perfect presence gradually fill our lives. Legalism tends to turn us into restless slaves of ruling spirits rather than restful sons of the Living God.

> Galatians 4:8–10... In the past you did not know God, and so you were slaves of beings who are not gods. But now that you know God – or, I should say, now that God knows you – how is it that you want to turn back to those weak and pitiful ruling spirits? Why do you want to become their slaves all over again? You pay special attention to certain days, months, seasons, and years. (GNB)

See Commandment, Grace, Law, Religion, False Religious Practice, Ritual

Lesbianism (Lesbian) – ongoing attraction or relationship between women, involving sexual intimacy.

The Bible clearly says that sexual attraction between women is not His created order for our lives. It is a consequence of the damaged condition of the heart, which itself is rooted in humankind's idolatry. As with any wrongful attitude or behavior, however, God is seeking not to condemn us but rather to lovingly restore us.

> Romans 1:25–27... For they exchanged the truth of God for a lie, and worshiped and served the creature rather than the Creator ... For this reason God gave them over to degrading passions; for their women exchanged the natural function for that which is unnatural, and in the same way also men abandoned the natural function of the woman and burned in their desire toward one another ... (NASB)

This is an issue of identity, and identity is rooted in our human spirit. The attraction of lesbianism is not something with which God created women, but it comes from a wounded human spirit. However, a choice to walk in this desire, and enter into an intimate relationship with another woman is sinful behavior, which will inevitably bring further emotional and spiritual damage. The call of Jesus is to a transformation and purification of our sense of identity, not least in the area of our sexuality. This is deeply demanding but fully possible, through Him.

God truly loves every woman caught up in lesbianism. He knows all about the inherited spiritual damage, the lifetime issues of wounding, and the personal sin that have all led to today's beliefs and behaviors. However, His desire is for a revelation of truth rather than the condoning of sin, the healing of inner wounds rather than the promotion of any dysfunction. To accept lesbianism as His created order for our bodies (an increasing trend in much of the Christian world today), when God has declared it as dis-order, is to give the enemy a powerful right to strengthen any distorted attitudes of the heart. This is especially dangerous for young people seeking to understand their immature sexual identity in teenage years.

Identity distortion may arise from generational iniquity, from a wrong relationship with mother, from abusive experiences from father or from other men, or for other reasons. There are many possible roots for a heart attraction to lesbianism. Thankfully, these inner places of disorder can be restored. We need to forgive those who have damaged us, and our own sinful choices to walk in sexual impurity need our confession and repentance. Where the enemy has gained a hold over our sexual identity, the powers of darkness will need to be expelled.

Jesus came to heal and deliver, not to condemn, and His followers need to be instruments of His liberating truth and His unending grace, not least in the issues of sexual disorientation.

See Choice, Feminism, Homosexuality, Human Spirit, Identity, Intimacy, Order, Sexual Orientation, Sexual Sin

Liberty (Liberate) – See Freedom

License – See a Right

Lie (Lying, Liar) – absence of truth.

Jesus said of Himself that He is the Way, the Truth, the Life (John 14:6), and He called Satan the father of lies.

> John 8:44... You are of your father the devil, and you want to do the desires of your father. He was a murderer from the beginning, and does not stand in the truth because there is no truth in him. Whenever he speaks a lie, he speaks from his own nature, for he is a liar and the father of lies. (NASB)

In accordance with his character, Satan and his domain operate in the darkness of unreality, deception, masks and pretense. He is the originator (Genesis 3:4) and the father of lies, and everything that is not truth is spiritually ruled by him. We give rights to the enemy to have a hold over our lives whenever we reflect his nature as a liar. Jesus has come full of grace and truth (John 1:14) and He offers us a place in His Kingdom of light, if we let His truth fill our hearts.

> John 8:31–32... So Jesus was saying to those Jews who had believed Him, "If you continue in My word, then you are truly disciples of Mine; and you will know the truth, and the truth will make you free." (NASB)

Dealing with every lie in our lives is our doorway to the freedom and the abundant life which Jesus has brought. As we follow His teaching and progressively come into agreement with God concerning the sinfulness

LIFE

of our lives, His forgiveness and cleansing can transform the whole of our being. A lie is stressful to sustain, but is unfortunately the tendency of our carnal nature when we feel insecure or in pain. Suppressing the truth of wounds and sin is exhausting, destructive and it causes spiritual darkness that gives license to the enemy.

Determinedly seeking God for revelation about ourselves and about Himself will take us on a remarkable journey from lies to truth, from darkness to light, which will be, step by step, utterly life-changing.

See Carnal Nature, Darkness, Deception, Discernment, Revelation, Truth, Unreality

Life (Live, Living) – God-given vital existence.

God has given us human life, in order to be fruitful in expressing His character here in this world which He has created (John 15:16). Jesus came to make it possible for life to be not just endurable, but active and abundant (John 10:10).

At conception, the human spirit fuses with physical matter (Zechariah 12:1) and a new human life on earth begins. From then on, we begin to have rudimentary physical and spiritual awareness of our surroundings (Luke 1:41). Interactive physical life, in direct relationship with other people, effectively starts at our physical birth. Interactive spiritual life with God effectively starts at the re-birth of our human spirit (John 3:6). The essence of each person's life and of their identity resides in their spirit. God loves the whole of our being, but He has determined that the truth of our God-given identity should be revealed and sealed in the human spirit.

> Romans 8:16... The Spirit Himself testifies with our spirit that we are children of God ... (NASB)

At the point of physical death, our body returns to the dust of the ground and our human spirit departs (Ecclesiastes 12:7). Our spirit continues to exist, but it will be without joyful eternal life if no relationship with God has been established while we walked the earth.

It is so important to value the life which God has given us. We need to seek Him for restoration from inner wounds, and find freedom from any past bondages which have compromised our spiritual life. For example, those who seek healing from past addictions may well need to ask the Lord for restoration of their spiritual integrity where the sharing of needles has exchanged blood, and therefore something of spiritual life with other addicts. In the Bible, the life of the human spirit is strongly identified with blood.

> Genesis 4:10... He said, "What have you done? The voice of your brother's blood is crying to Me from the ground." (NASB)

For those who have contemplated suicide in the past, there is powerful healing in clearly choosing life today. It is important to take away any rights which we have given to the enemy, whom Jesus pointedly calls a murderer (John 8:44). We can remove those rights by declaring a new choice in line with God's Word.

> Psalm 118:17... I will not die, but live, And tell of the works of the LORD. (NASB)

See Birth, Blood, Conception, Death, Fruit, Human Spirit, Soul-tie, Suicide

Light – spiritual environment resulting from obedience to God.

The apostle Paul was told very clearly on the Damascus road that God's call on his life was to help bring people's lives from darkness to light, and what these words referred to was explained to him. The followers of Jesus today must surely continue in this same calling.

> Acts 26:18... to open their eyes [Jews and Gentiles] so that they may turn from darkness to light and from the dominion of Satan to God, that they may receive forgiveness of sins and an inheritance among those who have been sanctified by faith in Me [Jesus]. (NASB)

True spiritual light is the atmosphere of the Kingdom of God, as opposed to the realm of darkness which is under the authority of Satan (Colossians 1:12–13). Where light prevails there is truth rather than lies, grace rather than condemnation, the Holy Spirit rather than evil spirits, abundant life rather than spiritual death, righteousness rather than iniquity.

> Ephesians 5:9... (for the fruit of the Light consists in all goodness and righteousness and truth) ... (NASB)

Light is actually the inevitable consequence of the presence of Jesus, because He *is* true Light.

> John 1:9... There was the true Light which, coming into the world, enlightens every man. (NASB)

But we need to be discerning of false light (2 Corinthians 11:14), coming in the form of false religions, false miracles, and false teachers. Because God made humankind to live in the light, people have consistently searched for some form of enlightenment, most often through their own reasoning and wisdom. This is dangerous territory, giving the enemy license to promote false religious practice.

> Isaiah 50:11... But now, all you who light fires and provide yourselves with flaming torches, go, walk in the light of your fires and of the torches you have set ablaze. This is what you shall receive from my hand: You will lie down in torment. (NIV)

See Darkness, Enlightenment, Grace, Kingdom of God, Spiritual, Truth

Logos – See Word

Loneliness (Lonely) – painful condition of the heart, when deeply in need of fellowship.

God made us for relationship, both with Him and with people.

The circumstances of life can cut us off from genuine relationships. Sometimes even our own bad behavior, resulting from the wounds of the past, can cause others to avoid contact with us. Hospitalization, old age, bereavement or relocation, for example, can all lead to loneliness. However, the Holy Spirit, the Comforter, is at hand to meet our needs. The starting place for resolving this issue is to know with certainty God's faithful concern and care for each of His covenant children, especially those who lack important relationships.

> Psalm 68:5–6... A father to the fatherless, a defender of widows, is God in his holy dwelling. God sets the lonely in families, he leads out the prisoners with singing ... (NIV)

From this place of inner security, where we know God's loving care for us, we can seek the conviction of the Holy Spirit for anything which may need changing in our hearts or in our behavior, for example, unforgiveness, judgments, cynicism, self-protection or self-pity.

Finally, we need to discover, with the help of trusted brothers and sisters, our particular place within the Body of Christ. Truly moving under the anointing of the Holy Spirit in our personal areas of His gifting will bring us into rewarding fellowship and rightful significance. This may entail our taking the initiative, reaching out to others, both inside and outside the Body of Christ, rather than simply waiting for their contact with us. Even though we may not in any way be responsible for the loneliness that we are experiencing, it is a divine principle that rightful giving always opens a door to rightful receiving.

> 2 Corinthians 9:6... Whoever sows sparingly will also reap sparingly, and whoever sows generously will also reap generously. (NIV)

Reaching out to others can feel scary, and we need to be courageous and risk rejection, but it is the way to overcome loneliness. What selfless fellowship can I give to someone else today?

See Bereavement, Comfort, Isolation, Openness, Pain, Rejection, Relationship, Self-protection, Significance

Loosing (Loose) – freeing someone or something from the hold of a hostile spiritual authority.

The enemy seeks authority to operate in this world. He gets this authority through the rights that people give him when they walk in sin. When this spiritual authority in a person's life becomes empowered by unclean spirits, the hold on that part of someone's life can be strong and destructive.

LORDSHIP

Through confession of sin and receiving God's forgiveness, we can be released from both the enemy's authority and power. This is called deliverance. It not only releases us from the hold of the powers of darkness, but it restores our lives to the rightful authority of Jesus. It is like being released from a dark prison into daylight through the absolute pardon of a judge. Or it is like loosing a rope that was holding an animal in a harmful place (Luke 13:15–16).

On the cross, Jesus won the victory over the enemy's control in the life of humankind. And Jesus has delegated authority to His disciples, to bring into practical effect on earth today that victory of the cross. This authority is ours through our obedience to His commands.

> Matthew 18:18... Truly I say to you, whatever you bind on earth shall have been bound in heaven; and whatever you loose on earth shall have been loosed in heaven. (NASB)

As we walk under the guidance of the Holy Spirit, in obedience, truth and forgiveness, we can see lives, and even land or buildings, loosed from the grip and defilement of the powers of darkness.

See Authority, Binding, Bondage, Deliverance, Forgiveness, Freedom, Power, Reclaim Ground

Lordship (Lord) – spiritual rule over human lives.

God's order is that our ruler would be His Son, Jesus Christ. However, there is an evil ruler of the world (John 14:30) who seeks to be lord over any area of our lives which we give to him, by our disobeying the commands of God and agreeing with the ways of the world. Satan even tried this with Jesus.

> Luke 4:5–7... And he [Satan] led Him [Jesus] up and showed Him all the kingdoms of the world in a moment of time. And the devil said to Him, "I will give You all this domain and its glory: for it has been handed over to me, and I give it to whomever I wish. Therefore if You worship before me, it shall all be Yours." (NASB)

Thankfully Jesus replied with a *no*! The lordship of Jesus is important for our spiritual safety in this world. It is a lifelong journey of surrender to Him in every belief, attitude, behavior, concern, need and plan. There's a prayer at the end of this section which we often use in Ellel Ministries to give God opportunity to challenge us about the extent to which Jesus is really Lord in our lives, and to convict us of any heart changes which He still needs to bring.

> Romans 10:9... If you confess with your mouth Jesus as LORD, and believe in your heart that God raised Him from the dead, you will be saved ... (NASB)

He will never condemn us for the condition of our lives, but God's view of His lordship over our body, soul and spirit will always be very different to ours. Today is a good opportunity for all of us to take another step nearer to His ideal.

A Lordship Prayer:

Lord Jesus, I acknowledge my need of You and accept You as my Savior, my Deliverer and my Lord. I invite You now to be Lord over the whole of my life.

Lord of my human spirit and all my spiritual awareness and worship

Lord of my mind, my attitudes, my thinking, my beliefs and my imagination

Lord of my feelings and emotions

Lord of my will and all of my decisions

Lord of my body, my physical health, my exercise, my diet, my rest and my appearance

Lord of my sexuality and its expression

Lord of my family and all my relationships

Lord of my secular work and my service as a believer

Lord of my material goods and my perceived needs

Lord of my finances

Lord of my plans, my ambitions and my future

Lord of the timing and manner of my death

Thank you that Your blood was shed that I might be free from the defilement of sin and that my name is written in the Book of Life.

Amen.

See Authority, Commandment, Confession, Disobedience, Jesus, Kingdom

Loss – taking away of people and things that have been of value and significance to us.

Loss is very often unexpected, suddenly taking away a person, a vision, a hope, a possession or a place of security on which we have come to depend. It can cause huge distress in our lives, especially when there is loss of hope for (say) companionship, health, provision or protection.

> Proverbs 13:12... Hope deferred makes the heart sick, But desire fulfilled is a tree of life. (NASB)

God wants us to bring to Him all the pain of our loss, whether that loss is current or in the past. There is a rightful grieving process, especially with the death of a loved one, and although grief can feel overwhelmingly painful, it is actually healthy for us to go through this pain and not to block it off. Jesus knows our weakness and is close to us in all our suffering, even when our emotions are too wounded to feel Him.

However, in due time, He wants us to find the fullness of comfort and security in Him. This will come as we forgive those who may have been the cause of loss, and as we confess any wrong ways in which we have tried to deal with it by ourselves. Jesus will never belittle the pain of our loss, but He does come with a remarkable solution which can bring true peace to all those mourning loss.

> Isaiah 61:1–2... The Spirit of the LORD GOD is upon me, Because the LORD has anointed me To bring good news to the afflicted; He has sent me to bind up the brokenhearted, To proclaim liberty to captives And freedom to prisoners; To proclaim the favorable year of the LORD And the day of vengeance of our God; To comfort all who mourn ... (NASB)

See Comfort, Death, Disappointment, Grief, Hope, Mourning, Wound

Love (Loving) – affectionate and caring heart attitude, which God desires should be the active bond in all relationships.

The kind of love that God has for us, and which He is determined to grow in the life of His children, is a giving, sacrificial love (Greek word – *agape*). This depth of love is not so much a feeling but a choice, which can only be sustained by the presence of the Holy Spirit. It is not commonly seen in the world, except perhaps in motherhood, but it is at the very center of God's own being.

> 1 John 4:8... he who is not loving did not know God, because God is love. (YLT)

> John 3:16... For God so loved the world, that He gave His only begotten Son, that whoever believes in Him shall not perish, but have eternal life. (NASB)

It is rightly said that sinful humanity has been relentlessly pursued by the love of God. C.S. Lewis wrote: *"God ... loved us not because we were lovable, but because He is love ... He certainly loved all to the death."*[15] God created us to give and receive love, this being the essence of Christian living and the most important need for nurturing of the human heart. The command to love encapsulates all the instructions of Jesus to His disciples.

> John 13:34... A new commandment I give to you, that you love one another, even as I have loved you, that you also love one another. (NASB)

This kind of love is expressed not just through thoughts and words but also actions. Love pervades the character of God (1 John 4:16). It is the essential test of the true lordship of Jesus in our lives (John 13:35), it is the overriding fruit of the Holy Spirit (Galatians 5:22) and the only real means of unity in the Body of Christ (Colossians 3:14).

The apostle Paul describes the extraordinary nature of true love as patient, kind, not jealous, not bragging, not arrogant, not acting unbecomingly, not self-seeking, not provoked, not taking into account wrongs suffered, not rejoicing in unrighteousness, and never failing (1 Corinthians 13:4–7). In fact, he says that without this kind of love, all my apparent gifting and generosity are of no value whatsoever (1 Corinthians 13:1–3).

Unfortunately the word *love* can mean many different things to different people, depending on what they have experienced in their lives. For some, God's true purpose in love has become defiled with negative concepts such as lust, control, disappointment, indulgence, selfishness or greed. There may be many people whom we need to forgive for the way they have given us an abusive or distorted version of love.

God's love for us, and the love He desires for us to have for one another, is both unconditional and pure. He is the source of all real love and He wants to restore the true meaning of love and the true effect of love in the hearts of His children. When we confess to Him all the distorted beliefs that we have had about love, and the wrong ways in which we have tried to meet the love-hungry place within, and ask Him to reveal His love to us, He can come and fully answer the cry of our human spirit: to be loved without condition and without end.

See Acceptance, Attitude, Character, Commandment, Fruit, Human Spirit, Kindness, Lust, Relationship

Loving-kindness – merciful compassion of God which is at the heart of His covenant with His children.

The Hebrew word *khesed* means loving-kindness. It is a word which appears many times in the Old Testament, and it describes one of the foundational attributes of God.

> Psalm 23:6… Surely goodness and loving-kindness will follow me all the days of my life, And I will dwell in the house of the LORD forever. (NASB)

See Covenant, God, Kindness, Love, Mercy

Loyalty (Loyal) – faithful support of a person or a cause.

Faithfulness is a precious aspect of the character of God. He will never leave us or forsake us. He is always faithful to His promises and completely trustworthy at all times. We are encouraged to develop the same faithfulness and dependability in our own lives as part of the growing fruit of the Holy Spirit.

However, loyalty can sometimes be contrary to the purposes of God, if it inhibits the revealing of truth. False religions and cults, for example, will have a powerful hold on people's lives, not least through misplaced and sometimes very strong issues of loyalty.

I remember a dear lady asking for prayer related to terrible abuse which had continued for years in her home as a child, never brought to the attention of anyone outside because they had been taught as children that loyalty to the family was always more important than telling the truth. The Bible disagrees with this, provided that truth is always accompanied by grace and love (Ephesians 4:15). Rightful loyalty is commendable, but it should never be made the reason for wrongful secrecy, as this can be enemy territory. Jesus is completely faithful and completely truthful with all who follow Him.

> Matthew 28:19–20... Go therefore and make disciples ... teaching them to observe all that I commanded you; and lo, I am with you always, even to the end of the age. (NASB)

See Betrayal, Cult, Faithfulness, Secrecy, Truth

Lust (Lustful) – passionate desire for particular things or people, driven by our carnal nature rather than the nature of God.

Lust is often associated with an ungodly sexual attraction which has been given license through our ignoring God's instructions for His way of pure love in all relationships.

> Matthew 5:28... I say to you that everyone who looks at a woman with lust for her has already committed adultery with her in his heart. (NASB)

God designed us to express intimately our sexual identity and sexual desire only within the safety of the marriage covenant. Unfortunately this world encourages early awakening of sexual desire in young people, promoting sexual exploration and sexual intimacy as a natural right for all who have reached puberty. Pornography has never, in all history, been more accessible than it is today, being so readily available through the internet.

When we walk a sexual path which deviates from God's commands, the enemy is given increasing rights in our life to drive our thinking and our desires away from the liberating bond of love, and toward the ensnaring bondage of lust. Lust can also be associated with many other desires that become drivers of our thinking and our choices, defiling our relationships even within the Body of Christ.

> James 4:1–2... What is the source of quarrels and conflicts among you? Is not the source your pleasures that wage war in your members? You lust and do not have; so you commit murder. You are envious and cannot obtain; so you fight and quarrel. You do not have because you do not ask. (NASB)

Is it the right time to confess that lust has been allowed to pervade your desires contrary to God's commands? Is it time to forgive those who have looked upon your own sexuality with lust and not respect? Is it time to dispossess the enemy of this defiling hold on any of your close relationships, past and present? For God, the right time for truth is now, and He is always ready and willing to cleanse our hearts.

See Addiction, Adultery, Bondage, Desire, Idolatry, Intimacy, Obsession, Pornography, Sexual Sin

Manifestation (Manifest, Manifesting) – effect that we can see, which is demonstrating that there is an unseen cause.

Jesus gave a picture to His disciples to help them understand the seen and unseen activity of the Holy Spirit.

> John 3:8... The wind blows where it wishes and you hear the sound of it, but do not know where it comes from and where it is going; so is everyone who is born of the Spirit. (NASB)

While the variation in air pressure causing wind cannot itself be seen, the power of this unseen phenomenon is very evident in the movement of the things which we *do* see.

In a similar way, the unseen spiritual realm is constantly interacting with the physical realm, bringing change to our lives in both good and bad ways. Just as the energy of air pressure which surrounds our lives manifests its power in the swaying of trees and the wind in our face, so the omnipresent Holy Spirit manifests the power of God in the lives of those forming the Body of Christ on earth, by distributing supernatural and recognizable gifts.

> 1 Corinthians 12:7... But to each one is given the manifestation of the Spirit for the common good. (NASB)

At any one time, the particular manifestation of the presence and power of God will be different for each member of the Body of Christ, so that when all these abilities, distributed by the Holy Spirit, are combined, the Body will be able to carry out the plans of God.

Of course, there is another spiritual energy source at work on this earth, the one that Jesus refers to as the ruler of the world (John 14:30). Satan's power can be manifested in humankind through the rights we give to him when we walk in disobedience to God. The ruler of the earth manifests this power in us through unholy, unclean spirits, which are often seeking to counterfeit the work of the Holy Spirit. For this reason, we should not assume that all supernatural manifestation in a believer is necessarily from the Holy Spirit (2 Corinthians 11:14; 1 John 4:1).

However, we can guard against being deceived when we witness any supernatural manifestation. The enemy, although powerful, can never sustain a display of the fruit of the true character of Jesus (Matthew

7:15–16). Unclean spirits also tend to manifest in ways that simply replicate their effect in each person present, so that all have a similar experience, with no true distribution of gifting nor corporate equipping of the Body.

When unclean spirits are being being confronted by the Holy Spirit and expelled from someone's body, manifestation may occur, although it is by no means essential. For example, shouting, shaking, blowing, coughing, burping or yawning can happen. In general, such manifestations are less troublesome when all the enemy's rights to be there have been dealt with before the expulsion. It is wise to limit manifestation in this way. Few words, but full authority; these are the ways of Jesus.

> Luke 4:35... But Jesus rebuked him saying, "Be quiet and come out of him!" And when the demon had thrown him down in the midst of the people, he came out of him without doing him any harm. (NASB)

See Authority, Counterfeit, Deception, Deliverance, Discernment, Fruit, Gifts of the Holy Spirit, Power, Supernatural

Manipulation (Manipulate, Manipulative) – underhand control of people or situations.

Out of inner pain, and fueled by a carnal nature, many of us resort to manipulation in order to get others to do what we want. However, it is not the way relationships are meant to be in God's Kingdom. Manipulation is a form of coercive control over the free will of another person, and it is sin. It gives rights to the enemy to hold us bound by his power, and wrongly tied to the other people involved.

An end result, however praiseworthy, does not justify the method, if that method involves manipulation. Jesus never resorts to this way of persuasion, even though He longs to be given rule over our lives.

> Matthew 11:29–30... Take My yoke upon you and learn from Me, for I am gentle and humble in heart, and YOU WILL FIND REST FOR YOUR SOULS. For My yoke is easy and My burden is light. (NASB)

We may need to confess our own sin of manipulative behavior, or forgive others who have sought to control our lives in ungodly ways.

God will restore a heart crushed by control, and give us freedom from any resulting ungodly soul-ties and demonic bondage.

See Control, Freedom, Free Will, Jezebel, Soul-tie

Marriage (Marry, Marriage, Married) – union of one man with one woman, voluntarily entered into for life, to the exclusion of all others.

This definition of marriage has been written on a plaque on the wall of our town hall registry office for as long as anyone can remember. Although intended to be a secular statement, it fits very well with biblical principles, simply because that was where this definition of marriage was rooted. The world may choose to redefine marriage, but the Bible remains an unchanging plumb line of what God says is right.

We read in the Bible that God ordained marriage to be a special and sacred covenant, to deeply join two lives of the opposite sex, bringing precious companionship when honored, but unfortunately also bringing huge damage when abused (Malachi 2:14). Marriage is not just a negotiable human contract to meet perceived needs, however loving and well-intentioned the participants may be. Rather, it is an agreement to permanently share our lives, sealed through covenant vows, rituals and oaths. Any covenant made before God can only be altered by His personal intervention, not by the whim of human beings.

> Matthew 19:4–6… And [Jesus] answered and said, "Have you not read that He who created them from the beginning MADE THEM MALE AND FEMALE, and said, 'FOR THIS REASON A MAN SHALL LEAVE HIS FATHER AND MOTHER AND BE JOINED TO HIS WIFE, AND THE TWO SHALL BECOME ONE FLESH'? So they are no longer two, but one flesh. What therefore God has joined together, let no man separate." (NASB)

Recognizing the different attributes of men and women, God calls a wife to respect the leading of her husband, and for him to love his wife, with a heart of sacrifice (Ephesians 5:22–33). After careful consideration of these commitments before God, the covenant of marriage should be initiated by public ceremony (John 2:2), and then completed (consummated) in private through sexual intercourse. This covenant of marriage is the only safe place, spiritually and physically, to give oneself to another in this intimate way.

God also intended that a faithful marriage of a man and a woman would be an ideal and safe environment for the procreation and nurture of children, where they can be unconditionally loved, and wisely taught the ways of God. An essential aspect of marriage is that a man and woman will form a new family by fully leaving their parents. Of course, this is not a denial of important family bonds, but the establishing of a new order of relationship and leadership, or headship for all concerned.

Marriage is such a foundational concept of covenant union that God uses it to describe the eventual consummation of the relationship between the Body of Christ and Jesus Himself (Revelation 19:7–9). Sadly, the true meaning and the profound significance of marriage are being lost in these days. This precious institution was given to us by God as a foundation for a healthy society, and we surely tamper with it at our peril.

> Hebrews 13:4… Marriage is to be held in honor among all, and the marriage bed is to be undefiled; for fornicators and adulterers God will judge. (NASB)

See Adultery, Covenant, Divorce, Headship, Intimacy, Procreation, Sex, Sexual Sin

Martial Art – combative technique, most often associated with practices originating in South East Asia.

These techniques range from defensive styles (Tai Chi Chuan) to highly aggressive styles (Ninjutsu), but most are intended to strengthen the body both physically and spiritually.

For example, one of the Judo masters described Judo as *a union of body and soul, containing spiritual and physical factors put together.*[16]

The word *Judo* actually means *the way of submission (the ending '-do' in martial art techniques means 'the way')*. Judo comes from roots in the martial art of Jujutsu, an ancient samurai combat procedure. These techniques almost always followed a spiritual as well as a practical path of training. Where there is a spiritual foundation to any activity, it is important that we realize the likely negative consequence for us if that spiritual foundation is inconsistent with the Word of God.

When we seek spiritual empowering of our bodies outside the authority of Jesus, the enemy is always ready to take the opportunity to get a measure of control. Jesus knows our spiritual needs and declares Himself to be the only safe spiritual path to follow. In fact, He is the only way to the Father and also to the abundant spiritual life which God desires for each of His children. In His mercy, God will seek us out, even on a wrong spiritual path which we have taken, but He will only ever point us to the one true pathway, which is Jesus.

> John 14:6... Jesus said to him, "I am the way, and the truth, and the life; no one comes to the Father but through Me." (NASB)

See Alternative Medicine, Exercise, New Age Movement, Self-control, ˒ Violence

Martyr (Martyrdom) – one who suffers to the point of death for witnessing to their belief.

The Greek word *martyr* means witness. This hard journey has been, and will be, the experience of many followers of Jesus. However, He promises us that those who are persecuted for His sake will receive a great reward in heaven (Matthew 5:10–12).

Nevertheless, we must be careful not to see any suffering that we do face in this world as a necessary payment for our own redemption. Disciples of Jesus will know trouble in their lives, as they necessarily oppose the ways of this world, but the full payment for sin and the carrying of all iniquity have been taken by Jesus.

> John 16:33... These things I have spoken to you, so that in Me you may have peace. In the world you have tribulation, but take courage; I have overcome the world. (NASB)

See Death, Disciple, Forgiveness, Suffering, Witness

Masculinity (Masculine) – male identity.

All children are intended by God to develop a strong bonding with their parents. As a baby, a boy is closely linked to his mother and gradually develops a sense of his own individuality as he grows. During puberty, he develops increased confidence in his masculinity as he separates further from his mother and identifies with his father, from whom rightful encouragement and affirmation are so very important. The Bible often alludes to such a father-son relationship as being significant in the maturing of identity and destiny.

> Hosea 11:1... The LORD says, "When Israel was a child, I loved him and called him out of Egypt as my son." (GNB)

This maturing process can be seriously weakened, damaged or even halted if the father-son relationship in particular is unloving and unaffirming. For example, if the father is hostile, dismissive or rejecting toward him, the boy may reject the need for this fathering, and may then have difficulty embracing his own masculinity. This can lead to a strong desire to connect with and receive from other males, sometimes sexually.

When men face the truth of these issues, forgive their father for any lack of godly affirmation, and repent of their own ungodly ways of compensating, God is able to reach into the deep place of their human spirit to affirm and heal their masculinity.

See Affirmation, Destiny, Father, Homosexuality, Human Spirit, Identity, Sexuality, Transgender

Mask – self-created image that I present to those around me, as being the truth of who I am.

When our hearts have been damaged and distressed by wounding and sin, we naturally seek to hide this painful part of our being. We may try to run away or become a recluse, or we may just hide the dysfunction of our lives behind a mask of smiles and pleasantness, competence and efficiency, false peace and complacence, self-righteousness and judgment, or maybe even joking and laughter.

> Proverbs 14:13… Even in laughter the heart may be in pain, And the end of joy may be grief. (NASB)

Unfortunately, a mask denies the whole truth. It is unreality, it is a lie, it is enemy territory in our lives, governed by the father of lies. If what we present is not who we are, we are giving permission for a loss of personal integrity, and breaking the intended wholeness of the soul and human spirit.

All that Jesus said and did as He walked the earth was fully consistent with the thoughts and attitudes of His heart. He wants our lives to be the same. God will not heal a mask which *we* have created, for He can only love and will only heal the true person that *He* has created, however much damage needs repair. He waits for us to confess sinful behavior, and to remove the mask that seeks to hide the reality of our being from those around us, from ourselves and from Him.

See Coping Mechanism, Defense Mechanism, Dissociation, Hypocrite, Image, Integrity, Lie, Self-protection, Unreality

Masturbation (Masturbate) – self-stimulation to cause sexual arousal.

The self-focus of masturbation is not God's order for the lives of those who follow Jesus Christ. Unchallenged, it can become a compulsive or addictive behavior and is frequently fed by pornography or lustful fantasy.

God intended that through sensual acts of intimacy with our marriage partner, we would together enjoy pleasurable sexual experiences which would include sexual intercourse, the physical, emotional and spiritual union which affirms the marriage covenant and gives opportunity for procreation.

The strong desire for an intimate expression of our sexuality should ideally only be awakened at the time of marriage. Unfortunately, we live in a fallen world which tends to see the expression of sexual intimacy as an entitlement for everyone, from the time of adolescence. Much of society regards these desires essentially as a hunger to be fed, or a need of comfort to be met, in whatever way we might choose. But God has given us a challenging view of personal purity in His Kingdom, through the life and teaching of Jesus. He has called us into the radically new lifestyle of seeing our bodies as completely surrendered in service to Him.

MEDICINE

> Romans 6:13... Do not offer any part of yourself to sin as an instrument of wickedness, but rather offer yourselves to God as those who have been brought from death to life; and offer every part of yourself to him as an instrument of righteousness. (NIV)

Sadly, for many people there have been early sexual encounters in their lives which have distorted the process which God intended for the expression of their sexuality. These defiling experiences of a sexual nature can often be the door opener to later problems with issues such as masturbation. However, God understands all the dysfunction of our past, our desire for comfort, and the rightful expression of our sexuality.

He is able to meet every need, as we bring to Him the wounded places of our heart, forgiving those who have wrongly used us, and confessing the ways by which we have sought to comfort ourselves. He can deliver us from the stronghold of masturbation if we choose His way and acknowledge His supreme authority and power over every grip that the enemy might have had on our lives. Jesus walked this earth in perfect righteousness. He invites us each day to join Him in the wonder of His strength and His purity.

See Addiction, Bondage, Cleansing, Comfort, Compulsion, Defiling, Deliverance, Lust, Pornography, Purity, Sexual Sin, Sex

Medicine (Medicinal) – medication or therapy to restore the body from disorder.

Through centuries of human trial and error, God's wonderful provision has been discovered in a huge range of natural and synthesized substances which bring relief to the body when there is dysfunction. However, the Bible also recognizes the foundational significance of spiritual well-being in the health of the whole body.

> Proverbs 17:22... A joyful heart is good medicine, But a broken spirit dries up the bones. (NASB)

Medicine can be very helpful in assisting the healing process, provided that it is based in scientific principles that are quantifiable and repeatable. Of course, there are often unhelpful known chemical side effects which need to be considered along with the beneficial effects of any remedy.

It is always wise to commit any medicine to the Lord, seeking His protection from what may be harmful.

The problem comes when medication or therapy is deemed to have unexplainable power to heal, from energy which is apparently sourced in the spiritual realm. There are many examples of this among alternative medicines and therapies. Homeopathy is one example. Such medicine may well appear to relieve symptoms, but when the power to heal is unexplained and spiritual, there is a serious question as to whether the unseen and unknown spiritual side effects may be bringing harmful bondage. Homeopathy is not a herbal remedy but an occult practice based on unproven and unbiblical spiritual laws. The only truly safe source for spiritual restoration is in the teachings of Jesus and the ways of His Kingdom. The physical body will, in some measure, always reflect the condition of the human heart, so the healing process will invariably need the right medicine for both the human body and the human spirit.

> Matthew 5:3... Blessed are the poor in spirit, for theirs is the kingdom of heaven. (NASB)

See Alternative Medicine, Healing, Herbal Medicine, Holistic Healing, New Age Movement, Occult, Power, Quackery

Meditation (Meditate) – focusing the mind through a concentration on particular words, images or concepts.

Paul encourages the believers in Philippi to dwell on those things which will edify the mind.

> Philippians 4:8... Finally, brethren, whatever is true, whatever is honorable, whatever is right, whatever is pure, whatever is lovely, whatever is of good repute, if there is any excellence and if anything worthy of praise, dwell on these things. (NASB)

This is a recognition that many of the sounds and sights in this world, not least in today's media, can cause spiritual defilement if allowed to have a place in our lives, for example scenes of violence, pornography and dark fantasy. The Lord has called us to walk with Him in the freedom of a pure heart. We need to make clear choices as to what we take into our minds through our ears and eyes.

> Psalm 101:3... I will set no worthless thing before my eyes; I hate the work of those who fall away; It shall not fasten its grip on me. (NASB)

In a world which frequently advocates a holistic response to the disorder of our lives, there are many religious, New Age and occult practices which promote forms of meditation as a means of making connection with the spiritual realm, for example in transcendental meditation, yoga and Buddhism. The techniques involved in such meditation usually require emptying the mind of all but the particular object of focus, usually the self, while awaiting the mystical experience.

Sadly, an empty mind, not guarded by the lordship of Jesus, even when using practices not intended to have any religious connotation (such as with the practice called *mindfulness*, which actually has roots in Buddhism) can cause us to be spiritually vulnerable if unwisely pursued, and could open up participants to the demonic realm. If we have been involved in wrongful meditation, it will be important to confess this and seek the Lord's cleansing from any powers of darkness that have taken hold.

Meditation on the Word of God, under the direction of the Holy Spirit, is something very different and very beneficial (Psalm 119:97). Here the mind is fed and filled with truth and life as we think about and chew over the Bible verses we are reading (Joshua 1:8). This is the precious walk of a disciple of Jesus, and a way to amazing freedom for the human spirit, soul and body.

> John 8:32... If you continue in My word, then you are truly disciples of Mine; and you will know the truth, and the truth will make you free. (NASB)

See False Religion, Mindfulness, New Age Movement, Prayer, Yoga

Memory (Memorize, Remember, Remembrance) –
recollection of past experience or knowledge.

MEMORY

The storage and recall of information from the past is surely a wonderful but complex aspect of God's design for the human body. It requires intricate interaction between the physical senses, the brain, the soul and, not least, the human spirit.

> 1 Corinthians 2:11... It is only our own spirit within us that knows all about us; in the same way, only God's Spirit knows all about God. (GNB)

Brain dysfunction or severe trauma can cause a break to these physical and spiritual connections within the body, causing memory loss or distortion. Medical practices such as Electroconvulsive Treatment (ECT), sometimes used as emergency therapy for psychiatric disorders, can have the same effect. Also, we may make a conscious or unconscious choice to disconnect from painful memories, as a coping mechanism.

Any induced breaks in the rightful flow of memory, whether inflicted by a shock to the body or chosen in order to minimize pain or guilt, are contrary to God's order, and therefore can give specific rights to the enemy to control the complex systems of memory within the body, soul and human spirit.

Rightful remembrance should be part of normal life. It is even an instruction from God to His people that certain significant events should be particularly commemorated, to affirm God's faithfulness to His covenant promises (Deuteronomy 15:15; Luke 22:19). However, where there are memories which are painful, these can be brought to a place of peace with Jesus, when we choose not to allow brokenness to be the way (even unconsciously) of dealing with the wounds or sins of our past. Just choosing to forget them does not resolve them; it simply buries them in a place of spiritual isolation and darkness. God does not wipe out difficult memories but, through His healing of wounds and His forgiveness of sin, He removes the nagging remembrance of shame, guilt or pain.

> Isaiah 54:4... you will forget the shame of your youth, And the reproach of your widowhood you will remember no more. (NASB)

See Accident, Brokenness, Coping Mechanism, Denial, Dissociation, Full Fragmentation, Human Soul, Human Spirit, Partial Fragmentation, Trauma

Mercy (Merciful) – release given from due punishment.

When human or divine law is broken, justice will, as a rule, require punishment. At the end of a court case, a judge decides on the consequence of a guilty verdict for the accused. He does not normally have the authority to show mercy, although sometimes the head of state, such as a president, does have this prerogative.

When God's laws are broken by human disobedience, the spiritual consequence has been determined by Him – that it requires bloodshed (Ezekiel 18:20; Romans 6:23). This sounds harsh, but sin is extremely serious; sin leads to death (Genesis 3:2–3) and it destroys lives. However, the loving heart of God seeks to show mercy, provided that justice is rightfully acknowledged and fully met, and provided that similar mercy is extended to others.

> James 2:13... For judgment will be merciless to one who has shown no mercy; mercy triumphs over judgment. (NASB)

Under the Old Covenant, justice was met through the sacrifice of animals, when God's people carefully followed His instructions. The animals died instead of the people, and the death sentence caused by sin was removed. Under the New Covenant, this escape from the consequence of sin is only possible through our having a part in the payment made by Jesus' death on the cross. The cost of God's mercy was enormous, but it gave Him the ability to declare forgiveness once and for all. His Son was willing to pay everything necessary for each of us to be completely released from the punishment and death that is due from our sin. We can have this freedom if we accept Jesus as Savior.

What a Savior!

> John 3:16... For God so loved the world, that He gave His only begotten Son, that whoever believes in Him shall not perish, but have eternal life. (NASB)

See Blame, the Cross, Forgiveness, Guilt, Judgment, Justice, Punishment, Religion, Sin

Messiah (Messianic) – See Christ

Messianic Believer – phrase used to describe a Jew who has chosen to believe in, and follow, Jesus (Yeshua) as the Messiah.

See   Believer, Christ, Christian, Covenant

Mind (Mental) – place of thinking within the soul.

This part of our inner being is where we process our response to the world around us. Is this situation safe? Is this going to cause me pain? What is the truth in this conversation?

The mind can be damaged by the traumas of life. It can be overwhelmed, shattered or defiled when abused in ways which God never intended.

It is the repository of our stored impressions of life, out of which our will makes decisions of behavior. There are different levels of activity in the mind from the fully conscious to the deeply unconscious, this latter place being usually accessed more through dreams than in our daytime lives.

Mental disorder can be caused by chemical imbalance within the body, such as the side effect of a drug or by physical trauma or the degeneration of the brain in dementia. However, where there are no obvious physical causes, mental disorders will frequently have an emotional or spiritual root. If our mind has been fed or distorted with sexual images, violent or abusive activity, confusion, ungodly meditation, rejection, unbelief or unreality, for example, there will be a need for God's transformation and cleansing (Titus 1:15). This precious renewing of the mind is only truly possible through the presence and purity of Jesus in our lives, as we walk in agreement with Him. Under the anointing of the Holy Spirit, we can increasingly know the very mind of Christ (1 Corinthians 2:16).

> Romans 12:2... And do not be conformed to this world, but be transformed by the renewing of your mind, so that you may prove what the will of God is, that which is good and acceptable and perfect. (NASB)

MINDFULNESS

See Control, Meditation, Mindfulness, Mindset, Human Soul, Thinking, Transformation

Mindfulness – learned practice of focusing thoughts and emotions on the present.

This is becoming very fashionable these days and is seen by many as bringing well-being to their lives, as an aid to concentration and as a therapy for a wide range of psychological disorders, including anxiety. Actually, Jesus agrees that mental distraction caused by anxiety is indeed unhelpful to us.

> Matthew 6:34... So do not worry about tomorrow; it will have enough worries of its own. There is no need to add to the troubles each day brings. (GNB)

And the Bible encourages us to take captive under the authority of Jesus every thought that persists in opposing the truth of God.

> 2 Corinthians 10:5... we pull down every proud obstacle that is raised against the knowledge of God; we take every thought captive and make it obey Christ. (GNB)

However, Jesus would not endorse either the spiritual roots or many of the techniques associated with today's mindfulness programs. They are based on beliefs and methods derived from Buddhism, and participants are usually encouraged not to evaluate the rightness or wrongness of the thoughts that they are experiencing. Mindfulness is seen to be increased through various techniques such as meditation and yoga. In Buddhist tradition, it is part of a process which is intended to lead both to enlightenment and to detachment from the unhelpful cravings of this life.

Mindfulness training has been widely adapted for secular settings, in schools and hospitals, for example, intending such programs to be independent of any spiritual connection. However, as believers, we need to be very careful of soulish techniques, devoid of the authority of Jesus, which are used to deal with mind disorder, and the spiritual roots of mindfulness should not be ignored. Any mind activity which is likely to open us to a spiritual control other than the Holy Spirit has the potential for causing hidden bondage rather than bringing true freedom. Followers of Jesus can be fully confident that the Bible gives spiritually safe advice and practice to help tackle issues such as lack of concentration, unhelpful cravings, stress and anxiety.

> Philippians 4:6–9… Don't worry about anything, but in all your prayers ask God for what you need, always asking him with a thankful heart. And God's peace, which is far beyond human understanding, will keep your hearts and minds safe in union with Christ Jesus. In conclusion, my friends, fill your minds with those things that are good and that deserve praise: things that are true, noble, right, pure, lovely, and honorable. Put into practice what you learned and received from me, both from my words and from my actions. And the God who gives us peace will be with you. (GNB)

See Alternative Therapy, Anxiety, Meditation, Mind, Self-control

Mindset – attitude of heart, spiritually bound to the ways of God or to the ways of this world.

> Romans 8:5–6… For those who are according to the flesh set their minds on the things of the flesh, but those who are according to the Spirit, the things of the Spirit. For the mind set on the flesh is death, but the mind set on the Spirit is life and peace … (NASB)

Through wrong teaching or when we have been frequently or deeply hurt, and when pressed by our carnality, we can form sinful beliefs, attitudes and prejudices concerning ourselves and the world around us. They become strongly, sometimes unconsciously, entrenched, and they significantly affect the way we behave. These mindsets of response, especially towards any situation that resembles the events which have previously wounded us, can lock us into seeing life in a predetermined, obstinate, even intolerant way, in accordance with the spirit of this world rather than the Holy Spirit.

Jesus has come into this world to challenge and change these mindsets, if we are willing to let Him into our hearts. Through the leading of the Holy Spirit, we can be healed from the wounding of the past and choose to behave out of a mindset that is increasingly strengthened to be in agreement with Jesus. We need to allow Him to write His truth

MINISTRY

into our mind, replacing our erroneous beliefs (Matthew 5:21–48). The evidence of this change will be the fruit of the character of Christ being displayed in our responses to the challenges of life.

See Attitude, Belief, Behavior, Bondage, Carnal Nature, Judgment, Truth

Ministry (Minister) – service to others in the likeness of Jesus.

The Son of Man came to serve, not to be served (Matthew 20:28). It is an amazing truth that the one to whom all authority has been given in heaven and on earth came down to us to serve, even to wash the feet of His disciples. His ministry brought salvation to a world lost in the quagmire of sin. When directed and empowered by the Holy Spirit, Jesus moved into His personal destiny of a savior and a servant.

> Luke 3:23... When He began His ministry, Jesus Himself was about thirty years of age, being, as was supposed, the son of Joseph, the son of Eli ... (NASB)

Now, the followers of Jesus, walking in the prophecy of Isaiah 61, sealed in a new divine covenant, have become the Body of Christ. We, like Timothy, are called to continue the service that Jesus started (2 Timothy 4:5), for example, in evangelism, intercession, teaching, prophecy, exhortation, giving, leadership, healing and deliverance, equipped in all things by the Holy Spirit for the benefit of this needy world, so that God's Kingdom may come on earth. In fact, this has always been God's plan for His people.

> Isaiah 61:6a... But you will be called the priests of the LORD; You will be spoken of as ministers of our God... (NASB)

Many of us who are part of Ellel Ministries feel called particularly to serve the Body of Christ in the areas of hospitality, teaching and healing (Luke 9:11).

See Authority, Body of Christ, Disciple, Gifts of the Holy Spirit, Healing, Prayer Ministry

Miracle (Miraculous) – supernatural event dependent on spiritual power.

266

We would all like to see more miracles but, importantly, the safety of any manifestation of spiritual power will always depend on the righteousness of the one who exercises the spiritual authority.

> Matthew 7:22–23... Many will say to Me on that day, "LORD, LORD, did we not prophesy in Your name, and in Your name cast out demons, and in Your name perform many miracles?" And then I will declare to them, "I never knew you; DEPART FROM ME, YOU WHO PRACTICE LAWLESSNESS." (NASB)

The Body of Christ, when walking in true obedience to its Head, Jesus Christ, is gifted by the Holy Spirit to operate with supernatural ability which can bring dramatic change in this world.

> 1 Corinthians 12:7,10... But to each one is given the manifestation of the Spirit for the common good ... and to another the effecting of miracles ... (NASB)

The root meaning of this word *miracles* is simply *works of power*. Every time we see the power of the Spirit of God drive out the power of the enemy in deliverance, for example, we are witnessing a miracle of Kingdom change in the life of a believer (Matthew 12:28).

Whilst not being fearful of deception, we need to be mindful of the challenge of these end days. There will be increasing signs and wonders which will be miraculous, sometimes extraordinary, works of spiritual power, but not necessarily under the authority of Jesus.

> Matthew 24:24... For false messiahs and false prophets will appear and perform great signs and wonders to deceive, if possible, even the elect. (NIV)

For our walk with Jesus to be meaningful, we should see frequent miraculous changes in our own lives and in the lives of others within the Body of Christ, and it is important, through obedience to Jesus, to desire such supernatural activity in this dark world. However, when the disciples returned from ministry, rightfully full of excitement at the works of power which they had seen operating through them, Jesus gently brought them back to the central issue of true importance in their lives.

> Luke 10:20... Nevertheless do not rejoice in this, that the spirits are subject to you, but rejoice that your names are recorded in heaven. (NASB)

See Authority, Deception, Fruit, Gifts of the Holy Spirit, Manifestation, Power, Supernatural

Miscarriage (Miscarry) – unintended natural death of a child in the womb before the age at which it could survive independently.

At whatever stage a death in the womb has occurred, whether a miscarriage or a later stillbirth, it is an event which is outside God's intended order and purposes for humankind (Exodus 23:26). Fruitfulness was God's plan from the moment of creation (Genesis 1:28). It is an aspect of His nature. Unfortunately, the sinfulness of humanity has spoiled this plan of fruitfulness. From the Fall, there was a defilement in the generational inheritance which affected every aspect of human existence, including procreation, and so barrenness became part of the human story, including Abram's wife, Sarai (Genesis 16:1), until God intervened.

Unless there has been sin needing forgiveness (Exodus 21:22-23) or a lack of care by the mother for her unborn child, there is no need for her to carry any personal guilt for the loss of a child in her womb. There will be a reason, a root cause, possibly genetic and therefore likely to be related to generational iniquity, but often the exact cause remains completely unknown. What is certain is that such untimely deaths were never what God intended in His foundational covenant relationship with humanity, but they are the inevitable consequence of our corporate rebellion against His laws, down through history.

> Deuteronomy 28:15,18... But it shall come to pass, if you do not obey the voice of the LORD your God, to observe carefully all His commandments and His statutes which I command you today, that all these curses will come upon you and overtake you: ... Cursed shall be the fruit of your body and the produce of your land, the increase of your cattle and the offspring of your flocks. (NKJV)

For any woman who has suffered a miscarriage or a stillbirth, it can be helpful for there to be forgiveness of any ancestors in her own family line, or that of her husband, who have sinned and sown barrenness into the inheritance, especially if issues such as abortion or untimely deaths are known to have taken place in the past. It may also be helpful to ask the Lord for a name for the miscarried child before committing the human spirit of that little life into the hands of Jesus. He can carry all the deep pain of loss and also cleanse the womb from all demonic power, such as a spirit of death, which might have been given rights to be there, for example, through generational sin.

See Abortion, Cleansing, Committal, Curse, Death, Fruitfulness, Generational Iniquity, Healing, Human Spirit

Mother – female parent.

God's plan is that within the safety of a marriage covenant, a husband and wife should know each other in the intimacy of sexual intercourse. From this union, a child may be conceived and nurtured in the mother's womb. God planned that both mother and fetus would experience God's protection through the security of the marriage and the love of her husband.

The essential roles of a mother are bringing the baby to birth, followed by the unconditional care and nurture of the child in its early years, with the father affirming and guarding his growing family. While both parents should share in the raising of children, a mother's unconditional cherishing of her young child is of immeasurable importance to the well-being of his or her human spirit.

> Proverbs 4:3... I, too, was once a young boy in my father's house. And my mother loved me deeply. (NIRV)

Of course, the very close relationship of a mother and child must develop into healthy individuation, with no loss of love, but with increasing and liberating opportunities for the child to grow in his or her personal God-given identity. The absence of rightful early cherishing, or the bondage of a later controlling or codependent relationship between mother and child frequently brings disorder and deep inner damage in a child's life.

However, as we forgive our mother for the ways in which she came short of what God intended for the parenting of our lives, we can know a deep healing of our human spirit as we receive the unconditional love of God. He knows exactly the true role of a mother, as well as the depth of the unmet needs of our human heart, and He is ever ready to hear our cry.

> Isaiah 49:15... Can a mother forget her nursing child And have no compassion on the son of her womb? Even these may forget, but I will not forget you. (NASB)

See Bonding, Codependency, Conception, Control, Father, Marriage, Nurture

Mourning (Mourn) – process of walking through the pain of loss.

This can be particularly hard when dealing with the death of a loved one. It is a process which can take a long time, but can be fully shared with Jesus at every step. It will be different for each person, but will often include significant periods of despair, anger, pain, grief, depression, guilt and loneliness. It is important for us to mourn significant losses, and not to try to push aside the pain and press on with life immediately. Although mourning is very painful, it is a right and normal part of adjusting to loss.

For followers in Jesus Christ who are mourning the death of a family member or friend, the committal of their loved one's human spirit into

the hands and authority of God (Luke 23:46) is very important, whether or not the deceased was a believer. This committal, under the Lord's direction, can take place at a later time if it was not clearly carried out at the funeral. This can be especially helpful if it continues to be hard, even after a rightful time of mourning, to fully let go of the one who has died.

> Luke 23:46... And Jesus, crying out with a loud voice, said, "Father, INTO YOUR HANDS I COMMIT MY SPIRIT." Having said this, He breathed His last. (NASB)

Such committal allows a safe release, giving a secure closure of the relationship, however good (or bad) that relationship was while they were alive. As well as speaking out forgiveness for the ways in which they caused harm to others in their lifetime, it can be helpful to break any ungodly soul-ties which might be maintaining an unhealthy joining in the spiritual realm. This denies the enemy any opportunity to defile the living with any issues which had affected the one who has died.

Physical death is a dividing place between the realm of the living and the realm of the dead. It is right to value and honor every good memory and achievement of those who have died, but it is not right to seek to communicate with them in any way, however comforting such contact might seem to be. This practice is the dark world of spiritualism and necromancy but unfortunately, this idea of holding on to the dead is even encouraged by the words sometimes spoken at some funerals.

The fact that God forbids His people to consult with the dead confirms that such practice is actually possible by occult means. This is unsafe spiritual territory for those in God's family (Deuteronomy 18:11).

God is the true Comforter for all who are mourning. He has come, through Jesus and the power of the Holy Spirit, to completely turn around the hopelessness of human life. He alone can heal the distress of our human spirit.

> Isaiah 61:3... To grant those who mourn in Zion, Giving them a garland instead of ashes, The oil of gladness instead of mourning, The mantle of praise instead of a spirit of fainting. So they will be called oaks of righteousness, The planting of the LORD, that He may be glorified. (NASB)

See Comfort, Committal, Death, Depression, Grief, Human Spirit, Loss, Pain, Soul-tie, Spiritualism

Necromancy – seeking contact with the human spirit of a dead person for the purpose of information, direction, healing, comfort, power or worship.

There is no person who has died with whom God requires us to seek contact, whatever the purpose. It is right to honor the godliness of those who have had fruitful lives, but it is never right to invoke their help or guidance once they have died. This includes those regarded as saints and all people recorded in Scripture, however good their lives appeared to be.

It is Jesus alone who has died for us and now lives to be the Savior of humankind, the only mediator between God and humanity, and the only way to the Father. God has always banned necromancy for His covenant people.

> Deuteronomy 18:9–11... When you come into the land that the LORD your God is giving you, don't follow the disgusting practices of the nations that are there. Don't sacrifice your children in the fires on your altars; and don't let your people practice divination or look for omens or use spells or charms, and don't let them consult the spirits of the dead. (GNB)

God would not forbid something that is not possible, and these commands of His have not changed. Any practice of necromancy gives significant opportunity to the powers of darkness to bring bondage and disorder into the lives of those involved, as it will intensify any issues of generational iniquity. Praise God that when the Son sets us free, through confession and forgiveness, we are free indeed (John 8:36).

See Ancestral Worship, Commandment, Disobedience, Generational Iniquity, Soul-tie, Spiritualism

Neglect – disregard of need, lack of care.

Neglect by those who should have cared for our lives may have been the result of carelessness, weakness, ignorance, family trauma or deliberate fault. However it has occurred, a lack of emotional or spiritual nurture, affirmation and protection can be as exposing and harmful as active physical abuse. People have sometimes said that as a child, they would have even preferred times of parental aggression to the pain of being completely disregarded.

> Ezekiel 16:5... No eye looked with pity on you to do any of these things for you, to have compassion on you. Rather you were thrown out into the open field, for you were abhorred on the day you were born. (NASB)

God created us to receive protection and provision in every area of our lives, both physically and spiritually. Where this has been deficient, as compared with God's standards, we will need to forgive our parents, or whoever else has neglected our welfare, and then open our hearts to the restorative work of the Holy Spirit, for He clearly sees every need.

> Psalm 22:24... [God] does not neglect the poor or ignore their suffering; he does not turn away from them, but answers when they call for help. (GNB)

> Ezekiel 16:8a... Then I [God] passed by you and saw you, and behold, you were at the time for love; so I spread My skirt over you and covered your nakedness. (NASB)

See Abuse, Acceptance, Covering, Isolation, Parenthood, Protection, Rejection, Significance

New Age Movement – unstructured worldwide community involved in unbounded spiritual exploration and practice.

A lady called Helena Blavatsky, the founder of Theosophy in the late nineteenth century, is considered to have originated the concept of a *New Age* of spiritual enlightenment, borrowing from ancient beliefs such as Taoism and Hinduism, mixed with spiritualism and a wide range of occult practice. The phrase *New Age* became popular in the 1960s and began to include countless esoteric practices seeking, for example, spiritual knowledge, escape, healing, excitement or significance, and using many different techniques such as hypnotherapy, yoga, hallucinogenic drugs and spirit channeling. There was a sense within the movement that New Age spirituality had replaced or perhaps revitalized formal religion, including Christianity.

Unfortunately, New Age practices are creeping into many churches through activities such as yoga, meditation, healing and exercise therapies. However, almost all of the activities of the New Age movement can be categorized as occult or false religion, and therefore likely to give considerable rights to the enemy to control the participants with demonic bondage. All spiritual restoration that denies the need for God's forgiveness of our sin through the cross, is a deception.

> **See** Alternative Medicine, False Religion, Healing, Holistic Healing, Occult, Supernatural, Sin

New Covenant – See Covenant

Neurosis (Neurotic) – psychological state with considerable anxiety and loss of objectivity, but without specific mental illness.

> **See** Anxiety, Depression, Distress, Fear, Human Spirit, Mind, Obsession, Phobia

Nurture (Nurturing) – nourishment for the human spirit, soul and body.

From the moment of conception we need both physical and spiritual nourishment, most importantly through the actions, attitudes and words of our parents. From the earliest days of our lives, unconditional acceptance, affirming words and kind actions are received in the human spirit like water given to a tiny plant seedling. Such nurture helps our spirit, soul and body to grow in strength.

The love of a mother and the affirmation of a father are particularly important for the spiritual well-being of a young child. When John the Baptist was named, his father, Zacharias, was moved publicly to affirm the identity of his son and God's calling on the child's life. In this way, Zacharias fed and strengthened the spirit of this man of destiny.

> Luke 1:76... And you, child, will be called the prophet of the Most High; for you will go on BEFORE THE LORD TO PREPARE HIS WAYS ... (NASB)

How contrary are a parent's words which express disappointment with the appearance of a new life or, at worst, how destructive are the actions of an attempted abortion. These pollute the child's spirit with the contaminated water of neglect, disapproval and rejection (Ezekiel 16:5).

We carry, even from conception, a mixed spiritual legacy of both righteousness and iniquity, depending on the beliefs and behaviors of our parents and ancestors (Lamentations 5:7). A defiled inheritance does distort the spiritual order of our lives, but it is the quality of the day-by-day nurture of our body, soul and spirit, particularly in the early years, that most affects our well-being in later life.

Persistent neglect of emotional and spiritual needs can be as harmful as active abuse. God created us to receive protection and provision in every area of our lives. Where we have been deprived of true parental nurture, we will need to forgive our parents and then look to Jesus daily, letting Him provide the deep feeding of our human spirit, which we need so much. As we continue in this, we will grow strong in our God-given identity.

> John 6:35... Then Jesus declared, "I am the bread of life. Whoever comes to me will never go hungry, and whoever believes in me will never be thirsty." (NIV)

See Affirmation, Approval, Generational Iniquity, Human Spirit, Identity

Oath – statement or promise, given apparent credibility by invoking the witness of something or someone held as sacred.

"I swear on this Bible that I will tell the truth." "I will keep my promise, as heaven is my judge." "I swear on my mother's grave that I will repay you." The swearing of oaths is not uncommon and is often done with very little thought. However, the consequence of our invoking a spiritual witness to any statement that we make is that we are, in effect, giving authority to spiritual powers to control the issue and even bring punishment if the promise proves false, just as Queen Jezebel did, to her eventual cost.

> 1 Kings 19:2... Then Jezebel sent a messenger to Elijah, saying, "So may the gods do to me and even more, if I do not make your life as the life of one of them by tomorrow about this time." (NASB)

Jesus expressly tells His disciples not to use oaths of any kind, but simply to speak with simplicity and honesty. This is clearly the way of His Kingdom.

> Matthew 5:34–35,37... But I tell you, do not swear an oath at all: either by heaven, for it is God's throne; o r by the earth ... All you need to say is simply "Yes" or "No"; anything beyond this comes from the evil one. (NIV)

Oaths can indeed be spiritually dangerous territory. For example, Freemasons seal the vows they make in their membership degrees by oaths which invite divine assistance, and invoke curses for failure, with no acknowledgment of the lordship or teaching of Jesus. The consequence is that the enemy is given rights to hold the participant in bondage to the ungodly statements made in becoming members of the organization, and to further release curses upon those who break their vows.

Thank God that there is freedom for all of us who are willing to confess wrongful oaths made in the past. Receiving His forgiveness takes away all the rights the powers of darkness may have to hold us to defiling pronouncements which we have made in ignorance or even in rebellion.

See Bondage, Control, Covenant, Curse, Freemasonry, Pronouncement, Vow

Obedience (Obedient, Obey) – acting in agreement with God's commands, and also with godly human authority.

See Agreement, Authority, Commandment, Disobedience, Law

Obsession (Obsessed, Obsessive, Obsessional) – persistent and irrational focus of thoughts toward something or someone, associated with marked anxiety.

Out of the insecurity which arises due to inner wounding, dissociation or brokenness, obsessions can develop through an unconscious desire, very often, to find some form of comfort, escape or perceived safety.

The object of such an obsession can be, for example, an unhealthy fixation on exercise, computer games, diet, health, religious observance, checking things, avoiding contamination or hoarding things. Where dependence, even unconsciously, on certain things or people in order to alleviate inner distress, displaces the centrality of Jesus, a dangerous door can be opened to idolatry, compulsion and addiction. Paul considers the issue:

> 1 Corinthians 6:12... All things are lawful to me, but not all things are profitable. All things are lawful for me, but I will not be mastered by anything. (NASB)

There is no intrinsic harm in many of these pastimes or lifestyles, but what would be our response if denied the opportunity to pursue such activities for a period of time? Would the result be anxiety, anger, or turning to another form of escape? Sometimes others can see these obsessional characteristics better than we can.

The object of an obsession can also sometimes be an unwanted idea, image or impulse which repeatedly intrudes into a person's mind. It is usually completely opposed to the person's values and beliefs, and is often obscene. For example, a loving mother may be terrified by a recurrent fear that she might deliberately harm her baby. The nature of these impulses and the associated anxiety can give such thoughts a considerable focus, thus reinforcing the obsessive cycle. All types of obsessive thoughts are very likely to be empowered by the enemy, with this control strengthening as the obsessions persist. If we try to deal with the issue only through our own coping mechanisms of denial or avoidance, for example, we may experience temporary relief but we simply add to the damage and the spiritual hold that has developed.

Secular treatment depends mostly on antidepressant drugs or cognitive behavioral therapy, and these can certainly help control the irrational thoughts and resulting behaviors. However, Jesus wants to bring healing to the root issues of the underlying wounding. Among these roots there is often damage to the human spirit, perhaps sustained in the womb or caused by poor bonding with mother, or resulting from anxiety caused by early separation from mother. Prayerful help from trusted friends can be life-changing, as we confess to the Lord how wrong coping mechanisms and priorities have got a hold of our lives, and as we invite Jesus to once again have His rightful central place. See 2 Corinthians 10:5. Jesus will heal the wounding in our human spirit as we bring it to him. The enemy's grip can be dislodged and a new walk of freedom begun.

See Addiction, Anxiety, Bonding, Compulsion, Dependence, Idolatry, Phobia, Wound

Occult (Occultic) – invoking power from the unseen spiritual realm.

All spiritual power which is not under the direct authority of Jesus is in the control of the Evil One and those operating within his domain.

Humanity has always been conscious of supernatural power. In fact, God intended that we should be particular instruments of His power in this world, but Satan has forever seduced us to walk in his fascinating, perverse and defiling power, rather than that which God has planned for our destiny. We have the choice as to whom we serve and to whom we give authority by our submission; either the one who blesses or the one who curses human lives.

Unhealthy occult activities include witchcraft, charms, fantasy games, superstition, fortune telling, astrology, divination, martial arts, yoga, ungodly meditation, casting spells, spiritualism, telepathy, some dark areas of music and art, and much alternative medicine. Many of these occult practices come within the pursuits of the New Age movement.

Whether they are pursued for reasons of amusement, personal well-being or the control of others, God has forbidden His covenant people to participate in all spiritual activity not directed by Him. He knows the damage which can be caused by demonic power being carelessly invited into our lives.

> Deuteronomy 18:10–11... There shall not be found among you anyone who makes his son or his daughter pass through the fire, one who uses divination, one who practices witchcraft, or one who interprets omens, or a sorcerer, or one who casts a spell, or a medium, or a spiritist, or one who calls up the dead. (NASB)

Jesus sends His disciples out into this world with a significant measure of His spiritual authority and power (Luke 9:1). These are the antidotes to occult bondage, when we have got caught up in the enemy's power. There is nothing more effective than the lordship of Jesus in overcoming the holds of the Evil One. As we confess our sinful involvement in the occult, God is ready to forgive, to remove any demonic holds and to heal the damaged places in our lives.

See Authority, Alternative Medicine, Bondage, Deliverance, Fascination, New Age Movement, Power, Powers of Darkness, Ritual, Supernatural, Superstition

Offense (Offend, Offensive) – actual or perceived wrongdoing against someone's well-being.

When a person has sinned against me, it is important that I am clear about what the offense is for which I need to forgive them. Sometimes I may discover that there has been no true sin against me, but simply a wrongful attitude of my own heart which I need to confess! At other times there will clearly have been a sinful and painful offense which needs to be faced with reality as I consider forgiving the offender. Even when there has been sin against me, I need to take care not to hold offense in my heart.

As long as the process of forgiveness remains unfinished, I will still carry the distress of the offense. This can be a powerful root for pain, bitterness, anger and resentment, all giving rights to the enemy to torment me and defile my heart.

> Proverbs 18:19a... An offended friend is harder to win back than a fortified city. (NLT)

When the forgiveness is complete, all the burden of the offense will have been given to Jesus. It will no longer have a defiling hold on my life, no longer able to add fuel to the difficult issues of today, and no longer able to provide a justification for me to sow judgment. The continued carrying of an offense, holding on to a sense of being a victim as a form of comfort, can be the cause of much dysfunction in a person's life. What a relief to be free of this heavy load as we confess our sinful ways of trying to fix our own pain!

See Anger, Bitterness, Blame, Forgiveness, Freedom, Judgment, Victim

Old Covenant – See Covenant

Openness – willingness to allow others to know my thoughts, feelings and beliefs, and to let their fellowship affect me.

God created us to be very open and secure in relationships, particularly toward those with whom we are meant to be close (Genesis 2:25). The sinfulness of humanity, and the damage that it has caused, has spoiled this openness, leading to much self-protection. Both our sin, and sometimes the sin of others who carry a responsibility for us, can move us into a place where we are not fully under God's protective covering, and this leads to an uncomfortable feeling of vulnerability (Genesis 3:10).

Little children usually start life very open, but they learn to guard their thoughts and feelings as life becomes more hostile, especially when parenting has not provided the physical and emotional security that God intended. A parent who is controlling or who wants to live their life through a child can cause that child to feel emotionally unsafe.

Of course, as adults, it would not be right for us to have the same level of intimacy with everybody, and we do need to be guarded in our hearts from those who may truly mean us harm. Even Jesus needed to be careful in deciding whom He could trust (John 2:24–25). Nevertheless, being guarded with everyone will simply lead to painful loneliness and a lack of any rightful intimacy. Healthy, open relationships call for a willingness to risk revealing some of our ignorance, uncertainties, fears, vulnerabilities and weak places, as well as our strengths.

God wants to heal us from the wounds of the past and provide, in Himself, the perfect spiritual parenting and protection that allows us to be appropriately trusting and open with one another in a right level of intimacy, particularly in marriage, in families and in the Body of Christ. If we ask the Lord, He will give us the wisdom to know who can be trusted with our openness.

> 2 Corinthians 6:11–13... Dear friends in Corinth! We have spoken frankly to you; we have opened our hearts wide. It is not we who have closed our hearts to you; it is you who have closed your hearts to us. I speak now as though you were my children: show us the same feelings that we have for you. Open your hearts wide! (GNB)

See Defense Mechanism, Intimacy, Relationship, Self-protection, Trust

Oppression (Oppress, Oppressive) – burdensome power of enemy authority.

This could be the bullying of one person by another, but there is a much wider issue of spiritual oppression. In this world, Satan has been given authority through human sin (1 John 5:19). Jesus called him the ruler of the world (John 14:30) and he is able to exert his power in proportion to human disobedience before God. Places of idolatrous worship, for example, will be inhabited by powers of darkness, and it is not unusual for Christians to sense a disquieting spiritual oppression existing in such places.

> Isaiah 34:14... Wild animals will roam there, and demons will call to each other. The night monster will come there looking for a place to rest. (GNB)

Although, perhaps, more noticeable at specific locations, spiritual oppression is, in fact, the overall condition of this world (1 Peter 5:8), and it can particularly affect individual lives where personal iniquity has given the enemy a right, not only to oppress from outside of the person's life but rather to control from within, often causing specific infirmity and bondage. Thankfully, Jesus came to deal with the problem.

> Acts 10:38... You know of Jesus of Nazareth, how God anointed Him with the Holy Spirit and with power, and how He went about doing good and healing all who were oppressed by the devil, for God was with Him. (NASB)

God's wonderful plan, from the beginning, has been to bring freedom from all oppressive control, both physical and spiritual. As we walk in the forgiveness and righteousness secured by Jesus at the cross, we can know the fullness of this precious freedom, and help others to find the same.

> Isaiah 58:6... Is this not the fast which I choose, To loosen the bonds of wickedness, To undo the bands of the yoke, And to let the oppressed go free And break every yoke? (NASB)

See Bondage, Control, Darkness, Deliverance, Freedom, Occult, Powers of Darkness, Reclaiming Ground, Ruling Spirit, Unclean Spirit, Yoke

Order (God's Order) – alignment of creation with God's design.

We sometimes say that a car is *in good working order*, meaning that it is functioning as intended by the manufacturer. When all the parts of the car are complete and working in perfect harmony, it is good for the car and good for the driver.

When all the parts of God's creation, spiritual and physical, are working in accordance with the intent of His laws and commands, then His order is in place and there is true peace. Such order is necessary for our personal well-being and for all relationships, whether in families, in the Body of Christ or even in a nation.

> Proverbs 29:18... A nation without God's guidance is a nation without order. Happy are those who keep God's law! (GNB)

God intended that His delegated authority and His order should flow through all of creation: the headship of Christ over humankind, man's headship in marriage and family (1 Corinthians 11:3), the rule of humankind over land and animals (Psalm 8:6), and even the essential protocol within the Godhead itself.

> Isaiah 45:12... I have made the earth, and created man on it. I stretched out the heavens with My hands; and I have set all their host in order. (LITV)

These are not issues of status but matters of order, so as to ensure fulfillment of God's plans and purposes. Jesus, though equal with His Father, was willing to humble Himself and operate only in accordance with God's perfect order (Philippians 2:5-11).

Even within our own bodies, God intended His order: the Holy Spirit ruling over the human spirit, imparting God's truth to protect and comfort the soul (Psalm 42:5), which in turn directs the activity of the physical body.

> Romans 8:16... The Spirit Himself testifies with our spirit that we are children of God ... (NASB)

The healing ministry of Jesus can be described as the *restoration of God's created order*, bringing right spiritual authority throughout creation, wholeness and freedom for individuals, and right relationships in families and society. In fact, for each of us, it results in peace with God, peace with all others and peace within ourselves. The life of Jesus on earth gave witness to this perfect order, and gave the opportunity, through His death, for reconciliation of everything back to how it should be.

> Colossians 1:20... and through [Jesus] to reconcile all things to Himself, having made peace through the blood of His cross; through Him, I say, whether things on earth or things in heaven. (NASB)

See Authority, Brokenness, Commandment, Disorder, Freedom, Headship, Healing, Human Spirit, Law, Reconciliation, Restoration, Wholeness

Orientation – see Sexual Orientation

Orphan Spirit – distressed condition of the heart, sometimes demonically sustained, due to not knowing the security of belonging in God's family.

Jesus makes a strong statement to His disciples as He prepares to return to His Father in heaven:

> John 14:18… I will not leave you as orphans; I will come to you. (NASB)

Jesus knows that whether or not we've experienced the loss of earthly parents, there is a deep need in the human spirit to be certain of a place in God's family. The disciples had experienced wonderful fellowship with Jesus as He walked the earth, so He promised them that His presence and His Father's presence would be with them in a lasting and intimate way by means of the Holy Spirit, despite His physical departure.

No matter what rejection, abandonment or abuse we have experienced in our lives, and no matter how much the enemy has reinforced a deep sense of our being spiritually orphaned, there is true healing and deliverance from the enemy's control available through the Holy Spirit as we forgive those who have hurt us, and as we open our human spirit to the Father-heart of God. Whatever the lies of the enemy, followers of Jesus are not spiritual orphans but covenant children of God, cherished, provided for and protected by our heavenly Father.

> Romans 8:16… The Spirit Himself testifies with our spirit that we are children of God … (NASB)

See Abuse, Acceptance, Family, Father-heart, Foothold, Human Spirit, Isolation, Rejection, Unclean Spirit

Pain (Painful) – God-created discomfort, the result of wounding, which is intended to lead to rightful treatment.

Wounding may be in the physical body, the human soul or the human spirit, and each of these areas within us can experience profound pain, which is telling us that there is something unresolved in our being (Psalm 38:8). The fact that something hurts is essential to the process of

us acknowledging the problem and also finding the solution. The writer C.S. Lewis made an interesting comment: *"Pain insists upon being attended to. God whispers to us in our pleasures, speaks in our consciences, but shouts in our pains."*[17] From the beginning of human life on earth, we have experienced pain from wounds to the body, and have looked for relief. We have discovered substances such as opium which act as an analgesic, a powerful way of suppressing pain. It may bring a welcome relief, but unless the wound is healed the pain will return, often more intensely, once the means of chemical suppression has worn off.

Something similar happens with heartfelt pain. If we have experienced, for example, the wounding of loss, rejection or abuse, there will be strong feelings such as despair, grief or loneliness, which we will find very painful. It is common for people to develop coping mechanisms to suppress this pain, and defense mechanisms to protect the wounded place. Our ways of coping may include drug abuse, alcohol, overeating, obsessive exercise or work, pornography, denial, dissociation or even self-harming to override the inner pain, just like the Gerasene demoniac.

> Mark 5:5... Constantly, night and day, he was screaming among the tombs and in the mountains, and gashing himself with stones. (NASB)

Suppressing inner pain may give apparent relief but only adds to the problem, by denying the healing that comes through release of emotions. Pushing away the underlying issue just causes further distress. God wants us to come to Him to find true healing for the hurting place, and an exchange of our pain for His comfort (Isaiah 61:2–3), even though it may take time. Shedding tears can be very restorative when given to Jesus (Luke 7:44). As we forgive those who have caused the pain and confess our wrong ways of trying to deal with it, God starts to restore our lives to a place of peace. He is ready, at any time, to hear the cry of our hearts.

> Psalm 69:29... But I am in pain and despair; lift me up, O God, and save me! (GNB)

See Addiction, Coping Mechanism, Dissociation, Emotion, Human Spirit, Inner Healing, Partial Fragmentation, Suffering, Wound

Paranoia (Paranoid) – heightened state of inner anxiety which causes irrational and sometimes delusional beliefs and responses.

God has given us the emotion of fear to motivate a search for safety in times of true danger. If and when godly spiritual covering and physical protection are found, God intended that all the bodily systems initiated by the fear would soon be returned to a place of peace and order.

Unfortunately, many people have known acute or chronic times in their lives when they felt very unsafe and it was not possible to find peace, due to inadequate covering. The consequence was that the body, soul and human spirit were left overwhelmed by anxiety and fear. Such unresolved trauma can leave the whole body out of order, easily triggered into irrational fears and responses over any circumstances today which seem to touch into the original issue. The more we permit these irrational fears to have control over what we do, the more the enemy has opportunity to empower the intensity of paranoia, and the more the spiritual, emotional and chemical order within the body can be affected, sometimes even leading to distressing feelings of persecution.

> Psalm 116:3… The danger of death was all around me; the horrors of the grave closed in on me; I was filled with fear and anxiety. (GNB)

However, through the inner healing and wholeness which Jesus can bring deep into the human heart, there is a way to break into this debilitating cycle of distress and fear. By letting Him recover and comfort any spiritually exposed places within, and by making choices to trust Him in the difficult situations of today, there can be true freedom from the grip of paranoia, including deliverance from any hold of the enemy.

> Psalm 94:19… When my anxious thoughts multiply within me, Your consolations delight my soul. (NASB)

See Anxiety, Covering, Delusion, Fear, Foothold, Inner Healing, Peace, Trauma

Pardon – See Forgiveness

PARTIAL FRAGMENTATION

Parenthood (Parent, Parenting) – being a father or mother.

It is one of the greatest responsibilities given by God to men and women, to have children and to raise, nurture and protect those children. Before a child matures fully into making his or her own choices, it is godly parenting which secures the well-being of that growing child. Righteous parents provide God's spiritual covering, but an absence of that covering through parental sin or dysfunction is one of the most common roots of disorder in a person's life, often not fully apparent until their adult years.

Parenthood is hugely rewarding when God's ways are followed. To help and to witness a child become the person whom God intended them to be is a priceless compensation for the many challenges and heartaches that can happen in families. God is there to guide, to enable, to forgive and to comfort along the journey, remembering that parenthood was His idea from the start, and restoration from life's difficulties is always His desire.

> 2 Corinthians 12:14c... For the children ought not to lay up treasure for the parents, but the parents for the children. (LITV)

See Affirmation, Comfort, Covering, Father, Inheritance, Mother, Marriage, Nurture, Protection

Partial Fragmentation – An expression used by Ellel Ministries to describe a breaking within the soul due to severe physical or emotional overwhelm, the break being strengthened and sustained by a conscious, or more often subconscious, choice to detach from the trauma.

When somebody experiences a severe shock, such as an emotional trauma or an accident, and they are unable to receive God's immediate help, the person may feel hopelessly out of control. At that moment, the trauma can seem overwhelming, far too much to cope with.

> Psalm 142:4... Look to the right and see; For there is no one who regards me; There is no escape for me; No one cares for my soul. (NASB)

As a result, there can be a breaking on the inside as the person allows themselves to be detached from the event. When this happens, the immediate effects of the trauma will lie hidden inside, unhealed and locked into the moment of that incident. In this way the wounding becomes trapped in time and everything that was felt at the time of the trauma, including the physical pain, the stress and the sense of overwhelm are kept alive inside. Because the person has detached from it, the wound and all the effects of the trauma remain unhealed. As a result, the person may continue to feel physical pain in their body even when the physical injuries themselves are healed.

The human spirit will also be wounded by the trauma, and the soulish control which maintains the separation from the traumatic event and the wounding further crushes the spirit. All of this damage will affect the person's ability to express the fullness of who they are as a person, often causing debilitating problems around issues of trust, rejection, abandonment and security. However, this is not the same as full fragmentation, in which there is a breaking or detachment in the human spirit as well as the soul, which means that the whole personality is broken. In partial fragmentation, by contrast, the detachment is only in the soul area and the person's identity remains intact.

Partial fragmentation is not uncommon, because when someone experiences a shocking and painful situation, their natural response is to handle the distress somehow in their own strength, rather than depending on God. Without His comfort and without rightful human nurture at the time of the incident, this inner fracturing commonly occurs. Then life continues under our soulish control, without the shock being released and without the necessary healing being received. The coping mechanism of shutting off from these painful thoughts and feelings can seem the best way to move on, but there will always be a consequence for the whole person in trying to fix such issues by ourselves. Unwanted food locked in a cupboard for years may be out of sight, but the effects of that decision on the rest of the house will eventually become all too apparent.

A physical accident, sudden loss, overwhelming injustice or abuse can all lead to partial fragmentation. If, for example, a young child loses a parent because of death, and is not nurtured through the grieving process, the trauma of the experience can cause the child to break on the inside and to leave all the fear, anger, pain and trauma unresolved and hidden in a place of partial fragmentation.

This results in the loss of contact with a vital aspect of their own self, which is trapped in the trauma of losing the parent. The breaking gave an immediate comfort and a false sense of well-being, but coping with problems by breaking away from them can eventually become a highly addictive habit. It can even cause a person to adopt a lifestyle of building a fortress of self-protection around the wounded places in their soul and spirit (which is, in fact, dissociation). Unfortunately, any burying of unresolved issues in our lives, including buried anger, for example, is out of line with the good way that God has instructed for our lives. So partial fragmentation, and any consequential dissociation, will result in separation from God and we will be in spiritual darkness in that place, which provides an opportunity for the enemy.

> Ephesians 4:26–27… BE ANGRY, AND yet DO NOT SIN; do not let the sun go down on your anger, and do not give the devil an opportunity. (NASB)

There are many symptoms which might, though do not necessarily, point to a fragmentation in the soul, such as irrational or immature emotional responses, depression, anxiety attacks, unresolved physical disorders, irrational guilty or embarrassed feelings, a drivenness to control in relationships, or a history of mental breakdown.

We may have a memory of a traumatic incident which has occurred in our lives, one that we know is not fully resolved and which perhaps we recall without experiencing the appropriate distressing emotions. If this is the case, it will be helpful to confess that we have probably sought to fix the past by wrongly controlling our thoughts and feelings in order to minimize the pain. God is very willing and very able to repair our inner brokenness as we respond to His commands (Isaiah 61:1; Psalm 147:1–6). Forgiving those who have hurt us and confessing all our controlling choices, made in order to detach ourselves from the trauma, will be a powerful start to the precious process of His healing, deliverance and wholeness for our lives.

During prayer ministry, we can ask Jesus to come to the wounded place in the person, which is trapped at the time of the traumatic incident, asking Him to heal what remains injured, to lift the trauma from them, to deliver them from any demonic bondage, to bind up the broken heart and to heal any physical condition which resulted from the incident. The one receiving prayer may experience buried, unexpected or even childlike thoughts and emotions which were there at the time of the original incident. Thankfully, the Lord is always ready to hear and respond to the cry of our hearts:

> Psalm 142:7... Bring my soul out of prison, So that I may give thanks to Your name ... (NASB)

See Brokenness, Choice, Control, Coping Mechanism, Defense Mechanism, Dissociation, Distress, False Memory, Full Fragmentation, Pain, Self-protection, Soulishness, Trauma

Passivity (Passive) – lethargy of will and general suppression of emotional responses to the circumstances of life.

Passivity is an enemy of true peace. It makes us vulnerable to deception. It often hides in the dark what should be resolved in the light. For many people who have been wounded by issues in the past, passivity has become a way of life to avoid facing further emotional pain in today's difficult situations. However, this defense mechanism, while sometimes making the person seem very composed, submissive and calm, often hides the truth of unresolved inner distress.

God's order is that we would be able to respond with emotional reality to the events of life, bringing to Him the difficult choices and the hurts to be restored to a place of true peace, through confession of our own sin and the forgiveness of those who have hurt us. Jesus demonstrated the perfect combination of alertness and peace.

Passivity can occasionally be the result of side effects from medication, in which case it is good to seek the Lord for alertness in the spirit. It can also be a family trait, or a learned behavior from parents in how to deal with life. However, passivity is destructive to relationships because rightful emotional awareness and responses are important aspects of human communication.

Passivity can also be a powerful barrier to true intimacy with God. Many religious practices actually promote passivity while saying that they are providing a way to peace or serenity. Buddhism, Hinduism and many forms of meditation, for example, dull the spiritual and emotional responses of the body to the truth of God, while opening doors to the lies of the enemy. We have not infrequently seen strong, and even aggressive, emotional turmoil becoming exposed in a person's life when there is deliverance from demonic power which has been given rights to establish a false religious peace. This turmoil was there all the time, but could not be brought to God for healing while it was hidden under passivity.

It is important that we actively choose submission to the Prince of Peace, rather than giving any opportunity to a spirit of passivity through lethargy in the mind, will or emotions.

> 1 Peter 5:8... Be of sober spirit, be on the alert. Your adversary, the devil, prowls around like a roaring lion, seeking someone to devour. (NASB)

See Defense Mechanism, Fatalism, Mask, Meditation, Peace, False Religion, Will

Peace (Peaceful) – condition of calm which results from the absolute certainty of God's protection and provision, irrespective of circumstances.

Peace is the absence of conflict with God, with myself, and with others. It's a deep sense of well-being in the human spirit, a place of childlike trust.

The Hebrew word *shalom*, usually translated as *peace* in the Bible, essentially means *safety*. When we experience complete safety in our heart, there is indeed a deep inner peace which affects the whole of our being. Such peace is God's intention for our lives individually and corporately, as we abide in His law and order.

> Psalm 37:28... for the LORD loves what is right and does not abandon his faithful people. He protects them forever ... (GNB)

The Bible tells us that Jesus is the ultimate source of this peace.

> Isaiah 9:6... For a child will be born to us, a son will be given to us; And the government will rest on His shoulders; And His name will be called Wonderful Counselor, Mighty God, Eternal Father, Prince of Peace. (NASB)

Peace is the absence of fear, anxiety, anger, distress, pain, despair, conflict or confusion. It's part of the fruit which grows in the life of a

follower of Jesus as we confess sin and give Him the things that trouble us, choosing to let the presence of Jesus transform our hearts by the work of the Holy Spirit.

> John 14:27... Peace I leave you; My peace I give to you; not as the world gives do I give to you. Do not let your heart be troubled, nor let it be fearful. (NASB)

See Anxiety, Covering, Fruit, Order, Protection, Righteousness, Security, Trust

Pederasty – ongoing desire by an adult male for sexual intimacy with an adolescent boy.

Also known as ephebophilia, this aspect of homosexuality is rooted in causes similar to those which give rise to other homosexual attraction, but especially from the wounding and distorted desires that come from receiving sexual abuse in adolescence. These types of relationship were seen as normal in many ancient societies, such as Greece, and today there is, in some homosexual literature, a move to promote so-called 'intergenerational intimate relationships' as both desirable and harmless. The Bible does not agree, declaring all forms of fornication to be contrary to God's order, sinful and highly destructive (Genesis 19:1–28).

Thankfully, we serve a God who loves us and can redeem us from all unrighteousness, if we walk in His ways of truth and grace, forgiving those who have sown defilement into our lives and repenting of our own sinful beliefs and behaviors.

As with pedophilia, there will need to be strong accountability for those receiving help, and in particular they will need to take great care to avoid situations which could pose a risk of temptation in this particular area of vulnerability.

See Abuse, Forgiveness, Fornication, Homosexuality, Pedophilia, Sexual Orientation, Sexual Sin, Shame

Pedophilia (Pedophile) – ongoing desire by an adult for sexual intimacy with a child.

Such a desire is certainly not God's order for the expression of human sexuality, and is actually one of the few sexual activities which is still regarded by most of the world as perverted and wrong. This is because where the adult's dysfunction has led to physical contact with child victims, the children are unable to defend themselves, either physically or emotionally. In fact, in the UK, anyone having knowledge of current sexual activity between a child and adult is legally required to report the matter to an appropriate authority.

Any sexual attraction toward children will most likely be rooted in inner damage and defilement to the soul and human spirit from generational iniquity or from wounding, including abuse, within the person's own life. However, any choice that is made to respond to these desires, through pornography or direct child abuse, is clearly sin and will give the enemy rights to demonically strengthen and control the wrongful attraction and the behavior.

Although it was an act of incest rather than pedophilia, we see in the story of the rape of Tamar how Amnon allowed his distorted sexual desire toward his half-sister to lead him into devastating sexual sin. He was not willing to bring the wrongful desire before God for cleansing.

> 2 Samuel 13:2,14... Amnon was so frustrated because of his sister Tamar that he made himself ill, for she was a virgin, and it seemed hard to Amnon to do anything to her. ... However, he would not listen to her; since he was stronger than she, he violated her and lay with her. (NASB)

Such deep issues of sexual disorder are not quickly resolved, and where child abuse has already occurred, there will usually be necessary legal processes. The first step to healing is a true acknowledgment of the wounded heart and the sinful choices which have been made. Through the person's forgiveness of others and repentance of personal sin, God can bring restoration to their human spirit and deliverance from the enemy's defiling distortion of their sexual identity. There will need

PERFECTIONISM

to be strong accountability for the person receiving help, and careful permanent avoidance of situations which could pose a risk of temptation in this area of vulnerability.

Most people are disgusted by issues of pedophilia, particularly where there has actually been abuse of children, but it is not a disorder beyond God's ability to forgive and cleanse. There are countless instances of pedophilia coming to light these days, even involving church leaders. So much pain has been caused in so many young lives by this abuse being kept hidden through distorted loyalties or paralyzing fear. Jesus came into the world to bring absolute truth and boundless grace. If we honestly walk His way, He can restore the lives of both the victims and the perpetrators of this deeply damaging issue.

See Abuse, Addiction, Forgiveness, Fornication, Defilement, Perversion, Pornography, Sexuality, Sexual Orientation, Sexual Sin

Perfectionism (Perfectionist) – drivenness to get everything in order and to avoid making mistakes at all costs.

Many Christians struggle with trying to make everything perfect, and then beating themselves up when they fall short of a perceived required standard. They know this can't be God's way, because even their best efforts never feel good enough and regularly result in disappointment, further anxiety or even depression, the very opposites of what they are trying to achieve.

Perfectionism also damages relationships as we set the bar impossibly high for others to jump, frequently refusing their help because 'they won't do it right'. In the process, we diminish their sense of value, as well as our own. And yet, in the Bible we find these challenging words which Jesus spoke:

> Matthew 5:48...be perfect, just as your Father in heaven is perfect. (NKJV)

Importantly, there's a huge difference between the bondage of perfectionism and the liberating pursuit of excellence or perfection to which we are called in this verse. Perfectionism often comes out of desperation to shut down inner anxiety. The anxiety is rooted in a sense of being unworthy of love and acceptance. We strive to earn these by our own efforts and achievement, and thereby hope to find a sense of peace. Any failure just reinforces worthlessness and reconnects us to the inner anxiety. But the true pursuit of excellence comes from knowing we are loved and accepted by the Lord Jesus, not because we have earned it, but because He truly loves us for who we are. We may be  disappointed when we fail but, if we truly know His love in our hearts, failure need not alter the way we feel about ourselves. We're forgiven! We're loved anyway! We're accepted! Our peace can remain intact (John 14:27). The enemy delights in keeping us locked into perfectionism, and holding us back from the destiny and fruitfulness to which our heavenly Father has called us. As we turn our eyes to Him today to receive His love and acceptance, and allow a passion to rise up in us not to serve ourselves but to serve Him in the pursuit of excellence, we can find freedom and true peace. He wants our human ability to be fully surrendered to His divine ability.

See Acceptance, Anxiety, Coping Mechanism, Inadequacy, Failure, Religion, Value

Personality – combination of human traits that makes each one of us a unique individual, created that way by God.

Understanding my God-given identity is the answer to the question, *Who am I?* My personality is the particular way I express that identity. We each like *different* colors, different music, different pastimes. Some of us are more outgoing than others; some are more practical, some more academic. Of course, our personality can be distorted by the wounding of life, but God has created and wants to restore each one of us to be able to walk in our unique personality, so that together with others we will complete the rich tapestry of human existence. We are known in every relationship not simply by our looks, but by our personality.

> Jeremiah 1:5... Before I formed you in the womb I knew you ... (NASB)

Along with personality, each of us displays a character. God wants to make our character increasingly like the character of Jesus, if we will permit Him to do this extraordinary work within us. This is not to change our precious, God-given personality, but to enable us to bear fruit in this world which will reflect the integrity, truth and grace of the Son of God.

See Acceptance, Character, Fruit, Identity, Image, Sanctification, Wounding

Personhood – distinct combination of identity and personality in an individual.

See Character, Healing, Identity, Personality Restoration

Person-part – broken part of the personhood of someone who has experienced full fragmentation as a result of trauma.

See Full Fragmentation

Perversion (Perverse, Pervert) – distortion of what God has created and intended for good.

The word *perversion* is most frequently used in connection with any sinful distortion of what God intended for the human expression of sexuality. Although the world increasingly regards most forms of sexual behavior as acceptable, the Bible is clear that God's order is for the intimate expression of human sexuality to be only within the covenant of true marriage. Even here, there are activities such as penetrative oral or anal sex which cannot be regarded as truly glorifying God in the rightful use of the various parts of the human body which He has created (1 Corinthians 6:20; Romans 6:13).

Adult sexual attraction directed toward children, adolescents or toward those of the same sex, for example, is not God's order for human relationships. Such perversions do not stop God loving us but when we endorse and act upon these desires, as with all sinful behavior, this inevitably separates us from the blessings of His Kingdom.

> 1 Corinthians 6:9–10... Or do you not know that wrongdoers will not inherit the kingdom of God? Do not be deceived: Neither the sexually immoral nor idolaters nor adulterers nor men who have sex with men nor thieves nor the greedy nor drunkards nor slanderers nor swindlers will inherit the kingdom of God. (NIV)

All perversion directly reflects the enemy's character and gives the powers of darkness opportunity to hold those involved in bondage to the sin. Paul saw this perverted character of Satan operating through the false prophecy of Elymas the magician.

> Acts 13:10... [Paul said,] "You are a child of the devil and an enemy of everything that is right! You are full of all kinds of deceit and trickery. Will you never stop perverting the right ways of the LORD?" (NIV)

However, Jesus came to this earth full of grace and truth, never to condemn but to offer forgiveness and release, not least for all those caught up in the grip of perverted desires and behaviors.

See Abuse, Disorder, Forgiveness, Grace, Homosexuality, Iniquity, Lesbianism, Order, Pederasty, Pedophilia, Sexual Sin

Phobia (Phobic) – fear that has control over a particular part of our lives.

The God-given emotion of fear is intended to be a *servant* to the human body, causing us the look for God's protection in times of true danger. It is not intended to be a *master* of the body. When fear becomes a master, it controls our decisions in ways that are powerful, but often irrational. A phobia exists when fear (such as arachnophobia, fear of spiders) has been given the opportunity to be a master in our lives in a particular area.

Such control can be empowered by the enemy, resulting in a demonic stronghold behind a phobia. Some phobias have their roots in a traumatic incident in the person's past. Others can run in families, where rights have been given to the enemy through sins of the ancestors, such as occult activity, false religions, Freemasonry etc.

Jesus is perfect love and the Scripture tells us that perfect love casts out fear (1 John 4:18). When those who have brought fear into our lives have been forgiven, and when we have chosen not to be controlled by a particular phobia, the power of any spirit of fear can be broken and cast out, in the name of Jesus.

Jesus encouraged His disciples not to let their troubled hearts become gripped with fear. He is always ready to give us courage.

> Mark 6:50... For they all saw Him and were terrified. But immediately He spoke with them and said to them, "Take courage; it is I; do not be afraid" [Greek – phobeo] (NASB)

See Control, Fear, Partial Fragmentation, Power, Slavery, Unclean Spirit

Plumb Line – surveying instrument, comprising of a weight at the end of a string which hangs exactly vertical due to the action of gravity.

God used the example of a plumb line in Scripture to explain that we need to be in line with His laws, in order to know His blessing.

> Amos 7:8... The LORD said to me, "What do you see, Amos?" And I said, "A plumb line." Then the LORD said, "Behold I am about to put a plumb line in the midst of My people Israel. I will spare them no longer." (NASB)

These are serious words that God is saying to His people through Amos. They are heading for disaster because of their refusal to follow God's instructions for the safety and well-being of their lives. They have decided that they know best!

When a plumb line is held up alongside a wall under construction, there can be no doubt as to whether the wall has been built truly vertical. Walls which are out of line are very prone to collapse, and this picture can be used also for people, where iniquity (being out of line with God) has left their lives distorted and vulnerable.

> Isaiah 30:13... Therefore this iniquity will be to you Like a breach about to fall, A bulge in a high wall, Whose collapse comes suddenly in an instant ... (NASB)

A plumb line lies perfectly vertical because of the physical law of gravity. Using it requires only that the surveyor holds up the line and allows the weight to come to rest. Whenever God's people are leading lives which are out of line with Him and likely to bring destruction upon themselves, it is very important that someone lifts up the truth of God's Word to allow His spiritual laws to show the straight line. Except for Jesus Himself, those who hold up a biblical plumb line are not themselves the measure of truth, but merely God's surveyors whom He has equipped to show that straight line.

We live in days when humanity seems content to be their own arbiter of what is right, believing that human virtue can be achieved by human reason alone. This is humanism. Such thinking is like a wall deciding by itself whether it is truly vertical. God's Word offers us an external check on our lives by comparison with the perfect plumb line of His truth. Only with this can we safely assess our lives, not to be condemned but to be restored, if we so choose, by the precious work of the cross.

Some occult practitioners use a pendulum to diagnose spiritual imbalance, a form of divination, but such a moving line will never show the cause of human disorder, which is human sin. Disciples of Jesus will increasingly know God's truth, and it is this which leads to real freedom (John 8:31–32).

See Bible, Humanism, Iniquity, Justice, Law, Righteousness, Truth

Pornography (Pornographic) – use of erotic images or words for sexual stimulation.

Derived from the Greek word for a *prostitute*, pornography describes a means of sexual stimulation which is not God's plan for the way of exploring and expressing the intimate aspects of our sexuality. He intended for this activity to be within the covenant of marriage, where a man and his wife can enjoy sexual intimacy in a mutually supportive and safe environment.

Pornography, whether related to heterosexual or homosexual activity has, in the last few years, become substantially more accessible through the internet. It tends to promote personal isolation, low self-worth and dependence on fantasy, all giving the enemy increasing control in our lives. When we surrender our sexuality in a way that is out of line with God, it can provide a demonic foothold for unclean spirits to drive us into increasing dependence on such activity in order to meet a need for comfort, especially in any wounded places of our identity and our emotions. Pornography invariably leads to compulsive routines and addictive behaviors, including masturbation (Romans 6:13). It can be highly destructive to a marriage relationship and victimizes those participating in the production of the sexual images.

Intentionally dwelling on pornographic images is idolatry (Ephesians 5:3,5). Such images may actually be in front of our eyes or they may be in our minds. In subtle or overt ways, we are trying to find our identity and fulfillment in idolatrous images rather than in God and His provision. In addition, we are giving considerable ground to the demonic realm by financing the destruction of the lives of the people in the images when we purchase the pornographic material or use a pornographic website.

Freedom from pornography comes by first acknowledging the sinful behavior, preferably confessing this to another trusted Christian. Then we need to address the root issues which are leading us to be attracted to such material. Such root issues are often found to be in inappropriate sexual activity at a young age, sometimes involving others, and now most frequently linked to the internet. Even very young children can find themselves stumbling upon a pornographic website and having their sexuality awakened in a totally inappropriate way.

We need to forgive all those who have knowingly or carelessly defiled the sexual innocence of our childhood. We also need to confess and truly repent of our pursuit of sexual gratification outside of God's boundaries. We will need to recognize and avoid the situations and opportunities which today trigger the sinful behavior, and also make ourselves accountable to others who are willing to help.

> Psalm 101:3... I will set no worthless thing before my eyes; I hate the work of those who fall away; It shall not fasten its grip on me. (NASB)

If we are serious in being released from the defilement of pornography, God's forgiveness and cleansing are readily available. There will probably need to be a time when the authority and power of the enemy are clearly addressed in order to expel unclean spirits, and it will also be necessary to break the ungodly soul-ties with other people who have participated with us in the activity, as well as breaking spiritual ties with the source of the images, such as websites and magazines. Pornography is a source of false comfort, but our need for true comfort remains, and God Himself is both willing and able to pour His real comfort into our hearts through His Spirit.

See Addiction, Deliverance, Masturbation, Sexual Sin

Possession (Possess) – something owned.

This word can just mean something held by a person; for example, when a child clings to a treasured cuddly toy. However, possession usually implies ownership, the result of payment made, and this is very important for us, because spiritual ownership is a serious issue in the Bible. The spiritual possession of our lives changed at the cross, when Jesus purchased us back from the realm of darkness into His precious family. Now we belong to Him.

> Acts 20:28... Be on guard for yourselves and for all the flock ... to shepherd the church of God which He purchased with His own blood. (NASB)

This corporate redemption of humankind becomes a personal right when we receive Jesus as our Savior (John 1:12). We are owned by God and become His treasured possession.

> 1 Peter 2:9... But you are a chosen people, a royal priesthood, a holy nation, God's special possession, that you may declare the praises of him who called you out of darkness into his wonderful light. (NIV)

However, the owner of a car is not necessarily the driver. If we have allowed the powers of darkness access to part of our lives, the enemy may have spiritual authority, a right to drive or control that part, even though he does not have ownership. This is why Christians may still need deliverance, despite having given their lives to Jesus.

Some versions of the Bible confusingly translate 'have a demon' (demonic *occupation*) with the word *possession* in some verses (Luke 4:33). It is important to realize that to have an unclean spirit does not mean being owned by one. Through sin, the enemy may have been given rights to inhabit and control part of a Christian's life, but he does not have the title deeds. God has declared His possession of His people, which comes through a covenant relationship (Deuteronomy 26:18), now sealed for us today through the death of Jesus on the cross, together with our response.

See Authority, Control, Deliverance, Foothold, Power, Powers of Darkness, a Right, Unclean Spirit

Power (Powerful) – ability to achieve a purpose.

An understanding of the difference between spiritual authority and spiritual power is essential in recognizing and dealing with the spiritual warfare that surrounds every believer. Here's a simple picture which was used earlier in this book when we were looking at the topic of authority. A quarry manager may have been given permission (authority) by the landowner to remove rock from the ground, and legally that's very important, but it is only when he has dynamite (power) that he is able to complete the task!

All spiritual authority comes from God, but it has been misused by humankind and largely surrendered to the ruler of the world, through our rebellion against God and our agreement with the enemy. Satan was originally created to be a servant of God, but in his rebellion he lost the spiritual authority which God had given him (Revelation 12:7–9). God gave humankind authority over the earth (Genesis 1:28), but at the Fall and through every subsequent sinful generation, the human race has consistently surrendered the authority that God gave to it into the hands of the enemy (Luke 4:6). When we obey someone, we are choosing to come under their authority, and when we choose to obey Satan, we hand over our own authority and we come under his authority (Romans 6:16).

Satan was endowed with a lot of power when he was created as a servant of God. Now that he has authority over the earth, given to him by humanity through sin, this combination of power and authority has given the enemy an ability to control the life of human beings. The Greek word for *power*, used in the New Testament, is *dunamis*, from which we get the word *dynamite*. Unfortunately, explosive power in the wrong hands can be very dangerous!

Thankfully, Jesus has come with a supreme ability to overcome the enemy's power in our lives, bringing freedom and healing.

> Act 10:38… You know about Jesus of Nazareth and how God poured out on him the Holy Spirit and power. He went everywhere, doing good and healing all who were under the power of the Devil, for God was with him. (GNB)

Rightful spiritual power for a follower of Jesus comes through Holy Spirit gifting, enabling every believer to challenge and overcome the power of the enemy, which is manifested through unclean spirits. However, this challenge is only effective, and indeed only safe, if the authority, or right, through which the enemy has sought to keep control is overcome by the authority of Jesus. This authority of Jesus is established as we walk in obedience to Him through truth and forgiveness, under the anointing of the Holy Spirit, keeping alert to the deceptive ways of the enemy.

> Acts 1:8… but you will receive power when the Holy Spirit has come upon you; and you shall be My witnesses both in Jerusalem, and in all Judea and Samaria, and even to the remotest part of the earth. (NASB)

See Authority, Counterfeit, Deception, Discernment, Foothold, Gifts of the Holy Spirit, Miracle, Satan, Supernatural, Unclean Spirit

Powers of Darkness – spiritual beings that operate under the authority of Satan.

Jesus told Saul on the Damascus road that the dominion of Satan is a realm of spiritual darkness.

> Acts 26:18… turn from darkness to light and the dominion of Satan to God … (NASB)

The powers of this dark realm enable the character of Satan to be promoted in the lives of men and women. There is a hierarchy of fallen spiritual beings, some operating over geographical areas, some over particular types of sin and some that can inhabit the lives of people (Ephesians 6:12). When the enemy is given spiritual rights through

PRAISE

human disobedience, the holding of that ground (of authority) is maintained by demonic power.

> Luke 22:53… I was with you in the Temple every day, and you did not try to arrest me. But this is your hour to act, when the power of darkness rules. (GNB)

Thankfully, the power of God, through the Holy Spirit, is infinitely greater than all the powers of darkness (Revelation 20:10–11). The spiritual battle is not a power struggle between God and Satan, because God is all-powerful. The battle is for our free will choice, whether we will serve God or sin, and thus whose authority we will come under. Through His finished work on the cross, together with the response of human obedience (Revelation 12:11), the authority of Jesus overcomes the authority of the enemy on the earth. In this situation, the powers of darkness must depart from the spiritual ground which they have held, including in people's lives. This is how God's kingdom comes on earth, as it already exists in heaven (Matthew 12:28).

See Darkness, Deliverance, Enemy, Power, Spirit, Unclean Spirit

Praise – expression of admiration and commendation.

Receiving rightful praise for something which we have achieved or become feeds our human spirit, and it is a vital part of true relationship. Here's some good advice:

> Proverbs 27:2a… Let another praise you, and not your own mouth … (NASB)

Parental praise of children, in recognition of earnest endeavor, is so important to grow a sense of inner confidence and value. The absence of due praise starves the human spirit, leading eventually to hopelessness and even a sense of shame. If absence of praise has been our experience, we will need to forgive those who have not given us this much-needed spiritual food. God alone can fully restore His own children from the disapproval and shame of the past.

> Zephaniah 3:19… Behold, I am going to deal at that time With all your oppressors, I will save the lame And gather the outcast, And I will turn their shame into praise and renown In all the earth. (NASB)

God does not need our praises, but we need to praise Him! Due to our carnal nature, the default setting for humankind is to have communication channels with God virtually closed, while those with the evil ruler of the world appear wide open (Ephesians 2:1–2). The psalms are full of expressions of praise, embracing dialogue with God even in the midst of difficult circumstances. Praising God in words, in song, in creativity or in tongues, whether alone or with others, clears the spiritual airwaves, because heartfelt praise makes contact with His omnipresence.

> Psalm 22:3... But thou art holy, O thou that inhabitest the praises of Israel. (KJV)

See Affirmation, Prayer, Pride, Thankfulness, Tongues, Value, Worship

Prayer (Pray, Prayerful) – dialogue by humanity with God.

Prayer brings human beings together with their Maker. Jesus encouraged His disciples to talk to their heavenly Father, exalting His supreme position, proclaiming the spread of His Kingdom, acknowledging His forgiveness, and seeking Him for essential provision and protection.

> Matthew 6:9–13... Pray, then, in this way: "Our Father who is in heaven, Hallowed be Your name. Your Kingdom come. Your will be done, On earth as it is in heaven. Give us this day our daily bread. And forgive us our debts, as we also have forgiven our debtors. And do not lead us into temptation, but deliver us from evil. ..." (NASB)

The Holy Spirit has been given to us as believers in order to reveal to us everything about Jesus – His truth, His grace, His authority, His

PRAYER MINISTRY

power, His purpose and, indeed, His presence (John 16:13–15). As part of this, God wants the ease and effectiveness with which Jesus talks to His Father to be our personal experience here on earth. The Holy Spirit enables and facilitates this precious dialogue between God and humankind (sometimes through the use of tongues) as we surrender our will to His will (1 Corinthians 2:11–16; Romans 8:26). Without this essential help from the Holy Spirit, our prayers soon become soulish.

Jesus also tells us that there is particular power in prayer when the Holy Spirit draws us into agreement with others in the Body of Christ concerning issues which are on our hearts. This is very relevant in the healing ministry, when we are able to have another person alongside as we seek God's restoration, together finding the truth and grace of God. The walk of revelation, conviction, confession and finding freedom can often be secured more effectively when another trusted person stands in unity with us through the process.

> Matthew 18:19–29… Again I say to you, that if two of you agree on earth about anything that they may ask, it shall be done for them by My Father who is in heaven. For where two or three have gathered together in My name, I am there in their midst. (NASB)

> James 5:16… Confess your sins to each other and pray for each other so that you may be healed. The earnest prayer of a righteous person has great power and produces wonderful results. (NLT)

See Agreement, Conviction, Holy Spirit, Intercession, Ministry, Prayer Ministry, Soulishness, Tongues, Unanswered Prayer

Prayer Ministry – being alongside a fellow believer, together seeking God for His truth and grace, and helping to bring God's healing into the person's life.

While Jesus walked the earth He brought healing, including deliverance, to many people's lives, overcoming the spiritual power which the enemy had over them. Through sin, humankind has given Satan rights to exert this power ever since the Fall of humanity.

> Acts 10:38… You know of Jesus of Nazareth, how God anointed Him with the Holy Spirit and with power, and how He went about

doing good and healing all who were oppressed by the devil, for God was with Him. (NASB)

In His victory over Satan, through His sinlessness and sacrificial death, Jesus was able to start a restoration ministry for humankind, which has now been delegated to His followers in the Body of Christ. Jesus instructed His first disciples to make more disciples who would obey the same divine commands given to them, including teaching about the Kingdom of God, healing the sick and casting out demons.

> Matthew 28:19–20... Go, then, to all peoples everywhere and make them my disciples: baptize them in the name of the Father, the Son, and the Holy Spirit, and teach them to obey everything I have commanded you. And I will be with you always, to the end of the age. (GNB)

Within the Body of Christ there are different abilities, enabled by the Holy Spirit (1 Corinthians 12:5–7). As we work together, yielded to Jesus, all these gifts and ministries enable the purposes of God to be fulfilled on earth. The ministry of healing and deliverance, restoring lives that are wounded, broken or in spiritual bondage, is often referred to as prayer ministry. The teams of Ellel Ministries around the world feel particularly called to serve in the areas of hospitality, teaching and prayer ministry (Luke 9:11), helping to bring the healing and character of Jesus to a hurting and damaged world today.

See Agreement, Gifts of the Holy Spirit, Healing, Ministry, Prayer, Restoration, Tongues, Truth

Prejudice – strongly held opinion, usually negative, driven by previous experiences rather than based on the current situation.

See Discernment, Forgiveness, Grace, Judgment

Pride (Proud) – desire for self-promotion of my importance, my ability and my achievements.

The Bible says that everything which we achieve of lasting value in this life depends on Jesus enabling us through the Holy Spirit.

> John 15:5... I am the vine; you are the branches. The one who remains in me – and I in him – bears much fruit, because apart from me you can accomplish nothing. (NET)

Pride is at the root of the carnal nature of humanity, in our rejection of the wisdom of God in favor of human wisdom. Along with fear and unbelief, pride is a foundational weapon in Satan's attack on the Body of Christ. It is a primary characteristic of the enemy's domain. Isaiah clearly sees the arrogant King of Babylon manifesting this proud spirit, in the extreme nature of his character.

> Isaiah 14:13–14... But you said in your heart, "I will ascend to heaven; I will raise my throne above the stars of God, And I will sit on the mount of assembly In the recesses of the north. I will ascend above the heights of the clouds; I will make myself like the Most High." (NASB)

C.S. Lewis once said, *"pride is spiritual cancer: it eats up the very possibility of love, or contentment, or even common sense."* [18]

Human pride is the basis of humanism, which believes that human virtue can be achieved by human reason alone. Self-importance, self-promotion, self-sufficiency, self-improvement are not the ways of God's Kingdom, and it is important to face the reality of these seductive character traits in our lives (Proverbs 16:18; James 4:6–7). Jesus never stands in condemnation, but merely wants us to face the truth that without Him, we can do nothing of true value!

> 1 John 2:16... Everything that belongs to the world – what the sinful self desires, what people see and want, and everything in this world

that people are so proud of – none of this comes from the Father; it all comes from the world. (GNB)

See   Carnal Nature, Humanism, Humility, Self-righteousness, Wisdom

Principality – See Ruling Spirit

Proclamation – See Pronouncement

Procrastination (Procrastinate) – putting off a task or putting off decision-making.

This can just be a lifestyle of apathy or laziness (Proverbs 24:30–34), but here we are particularly considering the type of procrastination which is really a coping mechanism rooted in a fear of expected painful consequences from making the wrong choice.

It is sometimes right to postpone a decision while awaiting further information or a clearer direction from the Lord. However, previous bad experiences of condemnation or ridicule, for example, when we have sought to choose a right pathway for ourselves or for others, can create an opening for an underlying fear which controls our choices today. Such a place of fear can give opportunity for the enemy to drive the behavior of procrastination. Jesus made clear choices at the right time as He walked in harmony with His Father.

> John 12:27–28a… Now My soul has become troubled; and what shall I say, "Father, save Me from this hour"? But for this purpose I came to this hour. Father, glorify Your name. (NASB)

As we deal with the wounds of the past and let the Holy Spirit restore our courage in the decision-making process, we can, with increasing confidence, be men and women who respond to the issues of life in a timely way.

> Ephesians 5:15–16… Therefore be careful how you walk, not as unwise men but as wise, making the most of your time, because the days are evil. (NASB)

See   Choice, Coping Mechanism, Fear, Free Will, Passivity

Procreation (Procreate) – God's creation of a child through the agency of human beings.

God planned that the conception of a new human being would be through a sperm from a man joining with an egg in a woman, with God's impartation of a life-giving human spirit. All this would follow sexual intercourse within the safe environment of a marriage covenant (Genesis 4:1).

Of course, much procreation occurs outside of any such covenant, which does not in any way diminish the significant value and purpose which God sees in every created individual, but it sometimes leads to deep issues of insecurity for a child so conceived. In addition, medical intervention has now made it possible for conception to occur without sexual union. Increasingly, there are opportunities for manipulation of the process for fertilizing an egg and implanting this within the womb through sophisticated procedures.

No doubt science will progressively develop further complex biological procedures to synthesize the constituent parts needed for procreation. However, there remains an important question for Christians: what effect will man-made techniques like this have on the unique and precious human spirit of the children so conceived (Zechariah 12:1b)? Will there be trauma or spiritual distortion occurring to the human spirit and the sense of identity of these children?

It is surely wise to bring any process of procreation which deviates, for whatever reason, from God's foundational design, before the true Creator for His direction over the methods proposed, or for His cleansing for any spiritually doubtful procedures from the past. This includes bringing before God spiritual issues to do with how any surplus, unwanted embryos were disposed of. It will be important to first receive His forgiveness for any actions which were taken independently of His direction. Abraham caused untold damage in His family by seeking a son in a way that was not what God had planned (Genesis 16:2).

Amazingly, procreation of human beings has been entrusted to men and women by the Creator of the universe. It is an utterly remarkable process. We need to acknowledge and follow His divine oversight and ensure that it is *His* will that always takes precedence, and not *ours*.

The consequence of such surrender was once particularly miraculous!

> Luke 1:38… And Mary said, "Behold the bondslave of the LORD; may it be done to me according to your word." And the angel departed from her. (NASB)

See Abortion, Conception, Contraception, Covering, Family, Human Spirit, Marriage, Parenthood, Miscarriage

Promiscuity (Promiscuous) – indiscriminate indulgence in sexual relationships.

God intended that the intimacy of sexual relationship would be within the safety of the covenant of marriage. The world encourages a completely different viewpoint, telling us that sex is an answer to our need for affirmation, for comfort, for escape, for excitement, for acceptance, for discovery of our identity or for simply meeting a sexual hunger. Viewed in this way, sexual relationships, and the promiscuity that can develop, are similar to drug-taking. We may feel intense pleasure in the act of such intimacy, but afterwards the deep needs which we were trying to meet will still be unresolved and, indeed, become even stronger.

Human relationships are precious and important in the journey of life, but they will never fully meet the deepest cries of the heart for affirmation, security, belonging and true comfort. We all need these things, and the cry of our heart for them will be particularly strong when they have not been adequately experienced during the early part of our lives. It is only God, through the intimate presence of the Holy Spirit, who can fill the empty love tank inside us which has been deprived by the wounding of the past. This has always been God's desire for His people. He alone truly answers the heart cry for connectedness and love.

> Ezekiel 16:8… "As I passed by again, I saw that the time had come for you to fall in love. I covered your naked body with my coat and promised to love you. Yes, I made a marriage covenant with you, and you became mine." This is what the Sovereign LORD says. (GNB)

See Affirmation, Comfort, Coping Mechanism, Identity, Intimacy, Love, Lust, Marriage, Rejection, Sexuality, Sexual Sin, Virginity

PROMISE

Promise – See Vow

Pronouncement (Pronounce) – strong statement of position, intention or belief, made either audibly or in the heart.

Of course, pronouncements such as *Jesus is my Lord* can be life-changing in a very positive way (Romans 10:9–10). Statements made by others, intended to edify our lives, can also be very significant to our well-being (Luke 3:22). Jesus said that His own words, spoken to His disciples, were spiritually powerful and life-giving.

> John 6:63... It is the Spirit who gives life; the flesh profits nothing; the words that I have spoken to you are spirit and are life. (NASB)

However, this truth concerning the significance of words also means that any pronouncement over our lives which disagrees with God, made either by ourselves (Proverbs 18:7) or by people carrying authority over our lives (Proverbs 12:18), can bring a curse rather than a blessing. Words of disapproval, such as *No one will ever want to marry you!* strongly spoken by a father over a teenage girl, would give opportunity to the enemy to undermine the God-given identity and destiny of that young woman.

The power of an ungodly pronouncement of this kind needs to be broken by the woman's forgiveness of her father, and by renouncing the lie which has given any right to the enemy to oppose God's plans for her life.

In the same way, an ungodly self-pronouncement out of the heart (Luke 6:45), such as *I'd be better off dead,* particularly where there has been any suicidal behavior, will give ongoing rights to the enemy to exert destructive power over our lives. Confession, together with a clear renouncing statement in agreement with God, using Scripture where appropriate (Psalm 118:17–18), will take away those rights and restore the lordship of Jesus over all the days of our earthly lives.

Destructive self-pronouncements are made during the ceremonial degrees of membership in Freemasonry and similar organizations such as the Orange Order. The vows spoken, declaring an ungodly covenant with the organization, are spiritually strengthened by rituals and oaths. These hold the participants and their families bound into powerful curses over their bodies. Those who are seeking freedom from the enemy's bondage will need to make clear and systematic renunciation of these pronouncements. With the help of Jesus, Peter, the disciple, needed to clearly renounce his three statements of not knowing the Lord, which had been empowered by cursing and swearing (Matthew 26:74). To deal with these destructive pronouncements, Jesus encouraged Peter to speak out three times that he loved Him (John 21:15–17). This counteracted Peter's denials, because declaring love is a very special way of knowing someone.

Pronouncements which are driven by a strong attitude of the heart, especially when confirmed by our actions, can be extremely powerful, bringing spiritual life or death to the person targeted by the words spoken, depending on whether such words agree or disagree with the truths and commands of God.

> Proverbs 18:21... Death and life are in the power of the tongue ... (NASB)

See Blessing, Curse, Foothold, Freemasonry, Oath, Ritual, Vow, Word

Prophecy (Prophesy, Prophet) – spoken revelation coming from the heart of God, through a gift of the Holy Spirit, into the heart of human beings.

God has spoken to humankind through the Bible, and He highlights His truth for today by drawing our attention to particular words of Scripture. He also affirms His word through spiritual gifts such as prophecy, revealing specific truth into the Body of Christ in order to give confirmation, conviction or direction for the fulfillment of His plans and purposes. True prophecy will always be fully consistent with biblical truth. It simply connects human beings with the heart of God, in the reality of our lives today. It can be very significant in the healing and deliverance ministry as truth exposes the works of darkness.

As with all manifestations of spiritual power, it is important to carefully discern the source and weigh the truth of the revelation. Jesus tells us that whenever there is a display of any supernatural power, we will know that He is the originator if the fruit of His character is truly evident (Matthew 7:15–23). Of course, any prophecy, which speaks of future events, will also need to be clearly fulfilled, in order for it to be confirmed as truly from God (Deuteronomy 18:22; Ezekiel 13:3–6). If we believe that we have received a false prophecy, there should be forgiveness of the one who prophesied. All those affected by the prophecy should be released from the power of the words spoken and from any ungodly soul-tie to the speaker.

Prophecy is a vital part of the full functioning of the Body of Christ, always to be tested, particularly by those in leadership. It should be valued in all those whom God has gifted in this way, whilst encouraging clear accountability for everything that is spoken.

> 1 Thessalonians 5:19–21... Do not quench the Spirit; do not despise prophetic utterances. But examine everything carefully; hold fast to that which is good ... (NASB)

The prophets, those who frequently minister through this gift, should never be seen as a kind of oracle, available to give us a word whenever we feel the need. God speaks through true prophecy only when *He* chooses, and when *He* desires to impart revelation of His heart into a specific moment of human need (Amos 3:7).

See Deception, Discernment, Gifts of the Holy Spirit, Manifestation, Revelation, Soulishness, Supernatural

Protection (Protect) – place of safety, through covenant relationship with God.

The Bible tells us that God provides a spiritual covering around the lives of those who are walking in obedience to His commands.

> Psalm 91:1–2... Whoever goes to the LORD for safety, whoever remains under the protection of the Almighty, can say to him, "You are my defender and protector. You are my God; in you I trust." (GNB)

John 14:23... Jesus replied, "Anyone who loves me will obey my teaching. My Father will love them, and we will come to them and make our home with them." (NIV)

In this fallen world, full of sin, we will not be fully immune from trouble, as Jesus warns us (John 16:33). However, there is a place of peace for every true follower of Jesus in the midst of the challenges of life, for He is above every trial. Satan is hostile to us and is described by Jesus as a thief and a murderer (John 10:10). But every area of our lives that is brought under the lordship of Jesus is removed from the destructive hands of the enemy and placed into the protective hands of the Lord. He can provide spiritual safety and peace beyond our understanding, affecting the emotional and physical well-being of our lives, in ways that sometimes only He can see.

He simply asks us to completely trust Him with our lives in order that nothing of what God has prepared for us will be stolen or destroyed by the Evil One. We may need to forgive those who have not given us the protection that God intended, particularly as children. We may also need to confess the ways in which we have been careless with our own lives, not fully valuing the priceless work of creation that God knit together in our mother's womb (Psalm 139:14).

There is no doubt that in God's eyes, we are truly worth His fighting for our safety (Deuteronomy 1:30) and worth His painstaking restoration when we do get damaged by the inevitable knocks of this sinful world.

Ezekiel 16:8... "Then I passed by you and saw you, and behold, you were at the time for love; so I spread My skirt over you and covered your nakedness. I also swore to you and entered into a covenant with you so that you became Mine," declares the LORD God. (NASB)

Psalm 37:28... for the LORD loves what is right and does not abandon his faithful people. He protects them forever ... (GNB)

See Commandment, Covenant, Covering, Parenthood, Security, Value

Pruning (Prune) – removing what is not full of life in order to increase fruitfulness.

Pruning is a well-known principle to a gardener caring for fruit trees and vines, but Jesus tells us that this is also necessary in our personal lives.

> John 15:1–2... I am the true vine, and My Father is the vinedresser. Every branch in Me that does not bear fruit, He takes away; and every branch that bears fruit, He prunes it so that it may bear more fruit. (NASB)

Like the diseased branches of a tree, many of the beliefs and attitudes of our hearts, which have grown out of the hurts of the past, are not displaying the fruit of the Holy Spirit, but rather the deathly character of the enemy.

The hurts will need healing, which begins with us forgiving others, but the dead wood of our lives will need to be removed through confession of sin and repentance if we are to be truly fruitful. When we have lived for many years with familiar mindsets and coping mechanisms, even though unhealthy, it can seem painful to let them be pruned, but this is essential for the most important purpose which Jesus has for our lives.

> John 15:16... You did not choose Me but I chose you, and appointed you that you would go and bear fruit, and that your fruit would remain, so that whatever you ask of the Father in My name He may give to you. (NASB)

Let's trust the Father as the perfect vinedresser (or gardener) of our lives, and be willing to look with Him at the true condition of our hearts.

See Character, Cleansing, Fruit, Healing, Holy Spirit, Mindset

Punishment (Punish) – painful consequence of disobedience.

God is not sitting in heaven deciding how to make life difficult for His naughty children. He created an amazing world with critically important spiritual laws which were designed by Him to make our lives safe, satisfying and significant. Unfortunately, humankind has constantly rebelled against these laws and discovered that God was truthful when He told us about the unpleasant consequence of disobedience: spiritual death and disorder (Genesis 3:3; Romans 6:23).

> Romans 1:27b… Men do shameful things with each other, and as a result they bring upon themselves the punishment they deserve for their wrongdoing. (GNB)

If I ignore a warning sign that says 'keep off the railway track' and I get hit by a train, it would be foolish of me to blame the railway company for my punishment – the damage that I receive for my disobedience.

Thankfully, sin has not wiped out the human race, because a divine Savior has come to take the full punishment for every sinner, allowing each of us to know freedom and healing from the consequence of our disobedience. Our part is to admit the wrong in our own lives, forgive others for their sin against us, and accept that Jesus has indeed taken all the punishment. If I choose to deny sin or to deny that the death of Jesus on the cross was necessary or sufficient to pay all the cost of my sin, then the enemy can take full advantage of my denial. He may seek to make sure that I receive the full measure of the suffering that is due.

God absolutely loves every sinner and hates the destructive works of the enemy (1 John 3:8) but it remains our choice as to whether we accept the wonderful offer of God's saving love (John 3:16).

See Commandment, Disobedience, Forgiveness, Grace, Iniquity, Justice, Law, Martyr, Pain, Sin, Suffering

Purity (Pure, Purification) – spiritual cleanness.

It is the condition of being undefiled, with nothing present that is not meant to be there. This quality is sought in precious metals; their value is determined by how little intrusion there is of other elements. For this reason, metals go through a refining process, which usually involves great heat. God declares that we are truly valuable just as we are, even though we are all, to some extent, defiled by sinful beliefs and behaviors. But He knows that we were made by Him to be spiritually pure (Jeremiah 9:7), for in this lies the fullness of our intimacy with Him.

> Matthew 5:8... Blessed are the pure in heart, for they shall see God. (NASB)

The sin of this world has spiritually defiled every human being. Only one person has walked this earth completely uncontaminated by darkness. Jesus has made it possible that if we confess our own impurity and walk in His purity, we will become all that God planned for us to be, a part of the perfect bride for the King of kings (2 Corinthians 11:2).

> Ephesians 5:25–27... Husbands, love your wives just as Christ loved the church and gave his life for it. He did this to dedicate the church to God by his word, after making it clean by washing it in water, in order to present the church to himself in all its beauty – pure and faultless, without spot or wrinkle or any other imperfection. (GNB)

Living and speaking in purity is not possible by our own effort, but rather it comes as we surrender to the One who is utterly pure. In Him we will find the joy of how our lives were meant to be, cleansed from all sin and ready for our destiny in God.

> Jeremiah 15:19...If you return, then I will restore you – before Me you will stand; And if you extract the precious from the worthless, you will become My spokesman. (NASB)

See Behavior, Cleansing, Defilement, Righteousness, Sexual Sin, Sin

Quackery – medical treatment that is a deception.

Throughout history, medical treatments have been offered by charlatans who have pretended to have knowledge and expertise. We still find them today, especially on internet websites. Countless potions and pills have been purchased by people desperate for healing, and many of these treatments have at the least been ineffective, but at worst they have been dangerous. Thank God that the worldwide medical profession is today mostly very well regulated and based on the God-given laws of nature (science).

However, there does need to be a note of caution. This is in the field of alternative medicine which claims to apply some form of spiritual power, life force or energy to our healing needs, but this power is outside the safe authority of Jesus. Practitioners of alternative medicine, some even with a Christian commitment, may be very well-meaning, but sincerity does not necessarily protect them, nor ourselves, from deception. Any form of alternative medicine which claims to be beneficial to our spirit is, in effect, offering spiritual restoration. Such spiritual restoration which ignores the need for our forgiveness at the cross and which speaks about power (or energy) that is not God's power should be viewed with considerable suspicion. The effect in the long term is likely to lead us further from Jesus, our true healer.

> Acts 13:8... But Elymas the magician (for so his name is translated) was opposing them [Paul], seeking to turn the proconsul away from the faith. (NASB)

See Alternative Medicine, Counterfeit, Deception, Discernment, Falsehood, Healing, Holistic Healing, Medicine

Rape – forced sexual intercourse on another adult or on a child.

God sees sexual assault as extremely serious, in fact, worthy of the death penalty, when the victim is entirely innocent (Deuteronomy 22:25–27). A similar assessment could be made for those aiding sexual violence; for example, someone participating in sex trafficking. It will be very hard for the victim of rape to forgive the perpetrator, and indeed those who should have provided protection, when the violation of personhood is so very deep.

Reconciliation will be very rare and is impossible if there is no repentance by the rapist, but forgiveness is both possible and profoundly restorative for the victim with God's help. Equally, there are many stories of rapists turning to the Lord, in the conviction of their gross sin, and finding God's forgiveness and peace.

See Abuse, Forgiveness, Personhood, Sexual Sin, Shame, Trauma, Violence

Reality (Real) – See Truth

Reason – God-given human ability to seek meaning and well-being for our lives.

God wants us, as He spoke through Isaiah, to consider such things always in the light of His Word and His truth about our lives.

> Isaiah 1:18... "Come now, and let us reason together," Says the LORD, "Though your sins are as scarlet, They will be as white as snow; Though they are red like crimson, They will be like wool." (NASB)

Human reason without divine revelation will never result in spiritual truth (1 Corinthians 2:14). If we decide that human ability to reason by ourselves is the ultimate source of wisdom, we have stepped into the realm of humanism, which is idolatry and rebellion against God. During the French Revolution, some of the leaders even proposed a new cult for the worship of *Reason*, intending it to replace the much discredited Christian practices of the day. This cult may have died out in name, but not in practice. Biblical truth, acknowledged for thousands of years, is now daily being set aside by governments around the world in favor of a distorted truth based simply on human reason. How effective this is in giving destructive license to the spiritual ruler of the world!

God has given humankind an extraordinary intellect, with some individuals experiencing exceptional gifting. However, if we fail to come to the same conclusion as Job, namely that we can never fully fathom the wisdom of God, we are very vulnerable indeed to all the spiritual damage that can result from the grip of pride.

> Job 42:1–6... Then Job answered the LORD. I know, LORD, that you are all-powerful; that you can do everything you want. You ask how I dare question your wisdom when I am so very ignorant. I talked about things I did not understand, about marvels too great for me to know. You told me to listen while you spoke and to try to answer your questions. In the past I knew only what others had told me,

but now I have seen you with my own eyes. So I am ashamed of all I have said and repent in dust and ashes. (GNB)

See Enlightenment, False Religion, Humanism, Pride, Revelation, Truth, Wisdom

Rebellion (Rebel, Rebellious) – disobeying rightful authority, in particular, disobeying the commands of God.

God has created humankind to operate under His spiritual authority, and also under the authority He has delegated to certain people who are called to give direction over the lives of others, such as parents, and leaders of nations and communities.

> Exodus 6:13... The LORD commanded Moses and Aaron: "Tell the Israelites and the king of Egypt that I have ordered you to lead the Israelites out of Egypt." (GNB)

All positions of rightful authority have come from God (Romans 13:1), for example, the position of father, church leader or the leader of a nation. Sadly, humankind has defiled that God-given authority through sin. However, we should all respect these institutions of authority, even while sometimes, if necessary, confronting the sin issues in one another's lives (Matthew 23:1–3). The existence of rightful authority should not be an excuse for harshness by the one who is ruling, nor an excuse for insincere submission by the one being ruled (Ephesians 6:5–9).

When our will is in rebellion to God-ordained authority, we are exercising spiritual control which gives powerful rights to the enemy, and the Bible describes this as witchcraft.

> 1 Samuel 15:23... For rebellion is as the sin of witchcraft, And stubbornness is as iniquity and idolatry. Because you have rejected the word of the LORD, He also has rejected you from being king. (NKJV)

Rebellion strongly breaks covenant with God and has always carried a serious consequence (Deuteronomy 21:18–21), but Jesus has come with God's mercy which triumphs over judgment, for all who acknowledge sin and receive forgiveness. The story of the prodigal son declares the heart of God, even in the face of rebellion against Him, and shows the opportunity for divine reconciliation once repentance occurs.

RECLAIM GROUND

> Luke 15:32... But we had to celebrate and rejoice, for this brother of yours was dead and has begun to live, and was lost and has been found. (NASB)

See Authority, Commandment, Disobedience, Independence, Witchcraft

Reclaim Ground – remove land or buildings out from the spiritual control of the powers of darkness.

From the moment of the Fall in the Garden of Eden, the earth that we live on has been under a curse (Genesis 3:17), suffering the spiritual rule of Satan (Luke 4:6; John 14:30). C.S. Lewis wrote: *"There is no neutral ground in the universe. Every square inch, every split second, is claimed by God and counterclaimed by Satan."*[19] Human disobedience defiles not only our own lives, but the ground which we occupy (Isaiah 24:5–6; Hosea 4:1–3). This causes the ground, or the buildings, affected by human sin, to be spiritually hostile to the occupants (Leviticus 18:24–25).

This defilement can be empowered by territorial spirits, stealing the peace and fruitfulness which God has purposed for the earth He has given to us. This was true, for example, of the land of Edom, demonized by the disobedience of the people of that land.

> Isaiah 34:14... Wild animals will roam there, and demons will call to each other. The night monster will come there looking for a place to rest. (GNB)

We sometimes recognize that certain buildings or places carry an unseen but noticeable spiritual darkness, such as an accident blackspot on a road, where there has been an unexplained high frequency of mishaps. Similar spiritual darkness can affect our homes or church buildings through sin committed in the past, but when those who carry legitimate responsibility for particular ground choose to confess the sin which has defiled the place, and forgive those who have been the cause of this in the past, they can seek God for cleansing of the land and expulsion of all the powers of darkness which have been given rights to control ground.

It was just so for the land which God had given to the Children of Israel:

> Leviticus 26:40,42... If they confess their iniquity and the iniquity of their forefathers, in their unfaithfulness which they committed against Me, and also in their acting with hostility against Me ... then

> I will remember My covenant with Jacob, and I will remember also
> My covenant with Isaac, and My covenant with Abraham as well,
> and I will remember the land. (NASB)

This is an important principle in bringing cleansing to our homes, work environments and places of worship, where the enemy has been given rights in the past through, for example, sexual sin, false religion, broken covenants or violence, and this may well be bringing harm to the occupants today (Lamentations 5:7–18).

King Hezekiah cleansed the temple in Jerusalem, reclaiming it to be known once again as a place of God's presence by directing the people to walk in obedience to God's laws and by removing all the idols which had been erected inside (2 Chronicles 29:5). Much later, Jesus overturned the tables of the moneychangers, through which the enemy had been given rights to defile the temple precincts. He was seeking to reclaim the ground for His Father's true purposes (Matthew 21:12–13).

When we get right with God concerning sinful practices on land or in buildings, we bring blessing both into our own lives and onto any ground which we rightfully possess. The rule of the enemy can then be challenged and removed, restoring well-being to the inhabitants and peace to the land (2 Chronicles 7:14). This can, on occasions, be a very important step in bringing healing and deliverance to those afflicted by disorders which have, perhaps, been associated with spiritually defiled and hostile locations. See Leviticus 18:26–30.

See Curse, Defilement, Deliverance, Iniquity, Ruler of the World, Ruling Spirit

Reconciliation (Reconcile) – restoration of harmony in a broken relationship.

Sin damages relationships; in particular, the intimacy of our relationship with God. He does not stop loving us when we disobey His commands, but our ability to know and experience His love is seriously affected by sin. However, the break can be resolved when we receive the forgiveness declared by Jesus at the cross. When sin is confessed and we allow ourselves to receive God's forgiveness, we are assured of full reconciliation with Him. Amazingly, our walk with Him can then be as if the sin has been completely washed away (John 1:29).

It is a similar principle when there has been a breakdown in human relationships as a consequence of sinful behavior. Even though we may rightly have forgiven someone for their sin against us, and we find ourselves willing to accept them unconditionally, there can be no true reconciliation without that person being willing to deal with their sin. We can choose to have a measure of relationship with them, but unresolved sin will always be a barrier. Of course, the same would be the case if we were unwilling to deal with our own sin against somebody else.

It is clear from the Bible that a primary ministry of Jesus is indeed that of reconciliation, both for humanity with God and for humanity with each other. In these end times particularly, there will be a specific and strategic reconciliation in the Messiah, Jesus, between Jew and Gentile, an abolishing of enmity. Paul refers to this as the making of the *one new man* (Ephesians 2:11–22).

Followers of Jesus today have the privilege of walking in the ministry of reconciliation, under the anointing of the Holy Spirit, in a world much divided by prejudice and hatred.

> 2 Corinthians 5:18... Now all these things are from God, who reconciled us to Himself through Christ and gave us the ministry of reconciliation ... (NASB)

See Acceptance, Confession, Forgiveness, Relationship, Restoration

Redemption (Redeem) – returning to the original owner something that had been held by someone who had a right of possession.

For example, if a woman sells a valuable diamond ring to a pawnbroker, the pawnbroker has the right to possess the ring forever unless the woman redeems the ring within the time agreed. To redeem it, she needs to make a payment which is usually larger than the price she originally received.

Redemption is precisely what has happened to each person who receives Jesus as Savior of their lives. From the moment of the Fall, humanity's sin has given Satan, the ruler of the world, a right to hold our lives in his domain. The wages of sin is death (Romans 6:23), so the price of our redemption was death – a price which Jesus paid on our behalf. Each person has a choice whether or not they want to receive the benefit of this amazing redemption – God's forgiveness given at the cross. For each believer there comes a moment when we make that choice, and at this point of decision we are transferred from the domain of darkness into the Kingdom of God. We are restored into the possession of the One who made us and loved us enough to pay the huge cost of redemption, namely, the death of Jesus.

> Colossians 1:13–14... For He rescued us from the domain of darkness, and transferred us to the kingdom of His beloved Son, in whom we have redemption, the forgiveness of sins. (NASB)

While in the spiritual hands of the enemy, we were vulnerable to all the defilement that can result from a careless and abusive owner. When born again of the Holy Spirit, we are re-established as God's possession, sealed as His child, but inevitably we carry some of the spiritual damage of the past. Redemption fully changes the spiritual ownership of our lives, but it does not necessarily deal with the specific areas of spiritual authority which were given to the enemy through any unresolved issues relating to our own past sin, or the sin of those who carried responsibility for our lives, such as parents. There may need to be repentance or forgiveness of others relating to particular past issues in order that we can know the fullness of God's cleansing from the enemy's defilement.

If the valuable diamond ring is eventually redeemed by its owner, through a costly payment to a pawnbroker, it may be brought home with joy but it probably carries considerable dirt from where it has been. Thank God that He not only forgives and redeems His children, but cleanses us from all the unrighteousness of the past, if we open our hearts to Him (1 John 1:9).

See Authority, Cleansing, the Cross, Darkness, Forgiveness, Possession, Power, Transformation

Refining – See Testing

Rejection (Reject) – deeply painful condition of feeling unwanted and unacceptable.

Once established in a person's life, rejection can become an enslaving mindset which even seems to define something of their identity – as a rejected person. Rejection is the way of the world, not of God's Kingdom.

Think of harvested apples on a conveyor belt destined for the supermarket. An apple may be of the sweetest flavor but can be rejected simply because it does not meet some imposed standard of shape or color. Life can certainly feel a bit like that! Frequently the world seems to draw a circle and count us out, whereas God draws a circle and always welcomes us in, if we choose to accept Him.

God has never rejected us, but as humankind, we have consistently rejected Him ever since the Fall, which leaves us feeling excluded and unloved at the core of our being. In this world, we can receive much rejection, even from the moment of conception, and each experience can build into us a belief system that rejection is to be expected as an inevitable part of who we are.

This is painful, so we develop coping mechanisms (controlling, striving or withdrawing, for example) to try to minimize the feelings of rejection and to win some acceptance in our relationships. Inevitably, our own ways of trying to fix the problem don't work! In fact, we just give the enemy more opportunity to empower his holds in our life, in the areas of rejection, fear of rejection and self-rejection. But God has a solution!

Firstly, we can bring to Him the times of rejection in our lives, forgiving those who have hurt us (very often our parents), and so receive the healing and comfort that God can supernaturally pour into our damaged heart. Secondly, we can make a choice to believe that what God says about us is true: as followers of Jesus, we are wanted and highly valued in His family just as we are, despite our need for healing and cleansing. We know for certain that this is what Jesus says about our value, not least from His story of the prodigal son, who was unconditionally loved by his father even when the son was in his most repulsive condition returning home.

> Luke 15:20... And he arose, and came to his father. But when he was yet a great way off, his father saw him, and had compassion, and ran, and fell on his neck, and kissed him. (KJV)

As we choose to act out of this belief in the unending love of God, behaving as sons and daughters in His family and not as slaves to the fear of rejection (Romans 8:15–16), God can bring supernatural revelation of His love and restore our hearts to a mindset where we know, without any doubt, our value and the unconditional acceptance that is declared by our Father in heaven. This decision to agree with God removes the bondage of rejection and fear, and leads to disempowerment of all the enemy's spiritual holds.

See Acceptance, Belief System, Fear, Mindset, Pain, Self-rejection, Slavery, Unclean Spirit, Unconditional

Relationship (Relate, Relational) – interaction with God and with other people.

God created us for relationship with Him, for relationship with each other, and for rule over His creation (Genesis 1:26–28). Human relationships can be the source of the deepest joy for humankind, but also the deepest pain. In a perfect covenant agreement with God, human beings would know true peace in all relationships, but sin has caused huge damage.

The ministry of Jesus was, and still is, primarily one of reconciliation (2 Corinthians 5:18). It was heralded by John the Baptist, who came to prepare for this ministry in the same spiritual gifting as Elijah (Matthew 11:14).

> Malachi 4:5–6... Behold, I am going to send you Elijah the prophet ... He will restore the hearts of the fathers to their children and the hearts of the children to their fathers, so that I will not come and smite the land with a curse. (NASB)

The first priority in reconciliation must be our relationship with God, which can be restored by our surrender to Jesus and our confession of sin. We are then increasingly able to walk in the perfect obedience, mutual love and peaceful harmony which Jesus enjoyed with His Father.

RELIGION

In that place of a growing heart security, we can find a restoration of peace in all the human relationships which have caused us wounding and pain. As we forgive others and confess our own wrong behaviors, God pardons, cleanses and brings deep healing to the places of distress and bondage. It may not be possible for us to be fully reconciled to those who have not acknowledged their sin against us, but we can walk in personal peace and freedom.

In addition, where there has been wrongful control or wrongful intimacy in a relationship, it will often be necessary for us to seek God for release from ungodly soul-ties. Ungodly ties to other people can pull us away from the deep bond of love which God wants to have with all His children. Relationships are intended by God to be life-enhancing, while the truth is that many have been life-draining.

Human relationships cannot replace the deep intimacy which God has purposed for us as the Father of our human spirit (Hebrews 12:9), but He knows that it is not good for man to live alone (Genesis 2:18), so healthy relationships, in different degrees of appropriate intimacy, are essential for our well-being and for the effectiveness of the Body of Christ.

> John 13:35... By this all men will know that you are My disciples, if you have love for one another. (NASB)

See Codependence, Control, Covering, Interdependence, Intimacy, Love, Lust, Marriage, Openness, Reconciliation, Soul-tie, Sexual Sin

Religion (Religious) – spiritual belief system held by a group of adherents, usually following a set of rules or rituals to win divine favor or find personal well-being.

Christianity is arguably not a religion by this definition! That is because we have chosen to follow *someone* who has been completely obedient to God's commands, rather than trying to follow a set of divine rules by ourselves. During His time on earth, Jesus represented humankind perfectly by walking in unbroken relationship with His heavenly Father, something that has proved to be totally impossible for every other human being.

Under the Old Covenant, God gave the Jews written laws, the Torah, to keep them right with His created order. Under the New

Covenant, Jesus has explained and demonstrated the significance, intent and spirit of those laws (John 1:17). He is able to completely fulfill all the laws of God on our behalf (Matthew 5:17–18), and He has even paid the full cost of all the sin which we have committed. Jesus does not ask us to win His or His Father's favor by rigid adherence to rules, but rather by loving Him sufficiently to want to follow all His ways (John 14:23–24).

> John 21:15... So when they had finished breakfast, Jesus said to Simon Peter, "Simon, son of John, do you love Me more than these?" He said to Him, "Yes, LORD; You know that I love You." He said to him, "Tend My lambs." (NASB)

As soon as we simply pursue rules in trying to win God's favor, we are no longer dependent on His grace and on the righteousness of Jesus; instead, we are trying to get right with Him by our own effort (Colossians 2:20-23). The consequence of breaking God's foundational laws given under the Old Covenant still stands, but the way of keeping right with these laws is now through the forgiveness and atonement of the cross, not through legalism. Legalistic ways of life, or religious ministry practices, are not just ineffective but they are actually dangerous, as the enemy seeks to trip us up on any rule we break (James 2:10). Paul warned the believers in Galatia that this kind of religious practice would give rights to religious spirits to control and defile their lives.

> Galatians 4:9,10... But now that you know God – or I should say, now that God knows you – how is it that you want to turn back to those weak and pitiful ruling spirits? Why do you want to become their slaves all over again? You pay special attention to certain days, months, seasons, and years. (GNB)

God is not impressed with religious practice (Amos 5:21–24). Rather, He looks for a heart relationship with His children, encouraging them to walk in obedience to Him simply because of the power of love. Of course, a true love-relationship with Jesus will inevitably be manifested in a lifestyle of increasing kindness and purity.

> James 1:27... Pure and undefiled religion in the sight of our God and Father is this: to visit orphans and widows in their distress, and to keep oneself unstained by the world. (NASB)

See Belief System, False Religion, False Religious Practice, Law, Legalism, Religious Spirit, Ritual

Religious Spirit – unclean spirit defiling the lives of those people who have followed false religious practices or false gods, rather than following Jesus.

Such spirits are active in all false religions. People who become believers in Jesus from a background of false religious practice can be vulnerable to their Christian walk being influenced by deceiving religious spirits. Where there has been involvement in other religions and past wrong beliefs, these need to be fully dealt with, through confession, repentance and deliverance.

Sincere Christians from various denominational backgrounds can also be affected by religious spirits where the traditions of these denominations have, in some measure, turned away from dependence upon the grace of God and the righteousness of Christ, and replaced these with man-made procedures for salvation. It doesn't matter how well-meaning the practices were. The enemy knows that he has rights to have some authority over churches, and to defile the lives of believers, where religious observance has been allowed to have precedence over true relationship with Jesus.

> Galatians 4:9–10… But now that you know God – or, I should say, now that God knows you – how is it that you want to turn back to those weak and pitiful ruling spirits? Why do you want to become their slaves all over again? You pay special attention to certain days, months, seasons, and years. (GNB)

See Deception, False Religion, False Religious Practice, Grace, Legalism, Religion, Ritual, Ruling Spirit, Unclean Spirit

Remembrance – See Memory

Renunciation (Renouncement, Renounce, Renouncing) – statement of retraction from a previous pronouncement of the person's belief or position.

Words are powerful! Sometimes we have spoken out agreement with the lies of the enemy, whether in active rebellion against the Word of God or simply in ignorance. Whatever our reasons were, such words remain in a spiritual 'debit account' (Matthew 12:36–37), which gives the powers of darkness a foothold to act against us in those areas.

> Proverbs 12:13... Evildoers are trapped by their sinful talk, and so the innocent escape trouble. (NIV)

In fear, Peter spoke out three times that he had no relationship with Jesus. Later, when he met Jesus on a beach after the resurrection, Jesus made a point of encouraging Peter to actively renounce these lies (John 21:15–17), which would have left him very vulnerable had they remained unresolved. Jesus had previously warned His disciples of the huge spiritual consequence of speaking out denial of Him.

> Matthew 10:33... But whoever denies Me before men, I will also deny him before My Father who is in heaven. (NASB)

These words of Jesus to His disciples were not uttered as a threat, but simply as a fact of spiritual reality of just how significant our statements are, made through words and actions. Thankfully, Peter responded to Jesus on the beach by clearly stating his relationship with, and indeed his love for, the One who actually loved him too much to leave the foolish words of the past without them being fully renounced.

What have we spoken out or acted out in the past in agreement with the enemy, about ourselves or about others, or even about God? What have we believed and voiced that today should be renounced? This will remove any foothold we have previously given to the enemy for him to act upon our past mistakes. Jesus has come to each one of us to forgive us, to settle all spiritual debts and to fully untie us from the mistakes of the past, so equipping us for our destiny in His Kingdom.

> John 21:17b... And [Peter] said to Him, "LORD, you know all things; You know that I love You." Jesus said to him, "Tend My sheep." (NASB)

See Confession, Forgiveness, Pronouncement, Word

Repentance (Repent) – turning to God in thought, word and deed, away from a sinful activity.

When we confess sin and receive God's forgiveness and cleansing, it is important that our desire to turn away from previous behavior is clearly demonstrated, because this is noticed in the spiritual realms. The power of the Holy Spirit is available to strengthen us in every battle against sin, but in the fight for our freedom and wholeness we must make it very clear which side we are supporting!

To give up smoking and keep a packet of cigarettes hidden somewhere 'just in case' simply tells the enemy that he has a good chance of tempting us back. Decisions made in agreement with Jesus need to be backed up with determined words and clear actions which give the Holy Spirit an open door to empower us. With Him, we can surely hold the reclaimed ground of our lives, ensuring that all the powers of darkness are evicted.

Confession is agreement with God concerning sin and it wonderfully attracts His forgiveness (1 John 1:9). Repentance declares that we are determined to walk in a new direction under the spiritual authority of Jesus, and no longer under the ruler of the world (Hebrews 6:1). Thankfully, this releases divine power to defeat the enemy. These principles are truly contested by the enemy, as Paul knew only too well.

> Acts 26:19–21... So, King Agrippa, I did not prove disobedient to the heavenly vision, but kept declaring both to those of Damascus first, and also at Jerusalem and then throughout all the region of Judea, and even to the Gentiles, that they should repent and turn to God, performing deeds appropriate to repentance. For this reason some Jews seized me in the temple and tried to put me to death. (NASB)

See Confession, Deliverance, Forgiveness, Righteousness

Resentment (Resent, Resentful) – deep sense of offense or injury concerning someone.

Whatever the cause, this is essentially a problem of unforgiveness in our hearts and, if unresolved, can be very damaging to our well-being, and to the Body of Christ. Some people have carried this defiling issue for

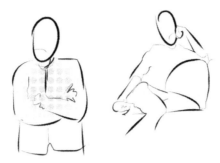

years, but Jesus has given us His Kingdom solution to our holding such an attitude toward another person.

> Mark 11:25… Whenever you stand praying, forgive, if you have anything against anyone, so that your Father who is in heaven will also forgive you your transgressions. (NASB)

The world will probably say we have every right to continue to feel aggrieved, but holding resentment will hurt us much more than it hurts the person we are resenting. God will not deny the wounding which has caused our pain, nor will He deny the need, at times, for godly confrontation, but He offers a radical way for us to find true peace and complete freedom from the cancer of resentment: the key is forgiveness.

See Bitterness, Confrontation, Emotion, Forgiveness, Judgment, Offense, Reconciliation, Unforgiveness

Respect (Respectful) – valuing and esteeming of someone's personal qualities and abilities.

The word *respect* conveys a strong sense of the worth in a person. When we respect someone we will avoid insulting, offending, degrading or injuring them or their feelings. Respect tries to spare the person unnecessary trouble, interference or interruption. When we respect someone, we will want to listen carefully to what they say and to understand their point of view. Respect can be shown in simple things such as giving a person your time, a smile, a thank you, in some cultures maybe a bow, and particularly by focusing on what is praiseworthy in their lives.

The Bible teaches that respect of others does not require us to ignore their sinful behavior (1 Thessalonians 5:14–15) but to value the person whom God has made, their gifting and their rightful position, in government or in marriage, for example.

> 1 Peter 2:17... Respect everyone, love other believers, honor God, and respect the Emperor. (GNB)

> Ephesians 5:33... However, each one of you also must love his wife as he loves himself, and the wife must respect her husband. (NIV)

> 1 Peter 3:7a... Husbands, in the same way be considerate as you live with your wives, and treat them with respect ... (NIV)

See Affirmation, Boundary, Honor, Praise, Thankfulness, Value

Restitution – recompense for any loss caused by sin.

The cost of sin in the heavenly realm has been fully paid by Jesus. As we receive God's forgiveness, we can walk free from all the spiritual debt that is due from our sin.

However, the Bible reminds us that to help meet human justice, the person who has been wronged should be compensated in an appropriate way, even going beyond the recognized cost (Luke 19:8). Not only does this bring a measure of restoration for the one who has been wronged, but it also gives opportunity for the one who has sinned to truly face the human cost of their wrongdoing.

> Numbers 5:6–7... Speak to the sons of Israel, "When a man or woman commits any of the sins of mankind, acting unfaithfully against the LORD, and that person is guilty, then he shall confess his sins which he has committed, and he shall make restitution in full for his wrong and add to it one-fifth of it, and give it to him whom he has wronged." (NASB)

Restitution is not a means of gaining God's pardon, which we cannot earn by good works. Equally, the forgiveness given by the victim of sin should not depend on any receipt of recompense. Only the death of Jesus is sufficient to pay the debt of all sin, but to graciously recompense in some way the one who has been wronged, if that is possible, can be an effective way of expressing, and walking in, true repentance.

>   **See** Debt, Forgiveness, Punishment, Reconciliation, Repentance, Restoration

Restoration (Restorative, Restore, Restoring) – bringing lives back to the place of freedom and created order which God intended for them.

The heart of God is always to restore his children from all that has damaged and gripped their lives as a result of sin. He looks, sometimes in vain, for those who will be instruments of this rescue mission.

> Isaiah 42:22... But this is a people robbed and plundered; All of them are snared in holes, And they are hidden in prison houses; They are for prey, and no one delivers; For plunder, and no one says, "Restore!" (NKJV)

In recent history we have seen the miracle of restoration which God had promised for the nation of Israel, and which He is now bringing to fulfillment (Ezekiel 36:23–28). When God makes covenant with humanity, He cannot break His promises.

If God can restore nations, and this is surely on His agenda (Isaiah 49:6), He can certainly be trusted to restore the individual lives of all those in covenant with Him through Jesus Christ (Matthew 8:17).

RESURRECTION

God has put within the human heart a deep delight in seeing fine things restored to their former glory, whether these be paintings, houses or even vintage cars! How much more rewarding is the restoration of a life that has been broken and bound by walking in the darkness of this world.

True restoration demands expertise and time. Thankfully, God has these without limit, and He chooses to use the followers of Jesus, enabled by the Holy Spirit, to participate in this amazing work. Today, as we look at a world of hurting lives, let's declare with God, "Restore!"

See Bondage, Covenant, Deliverance, Freedom, Healing, Order, Sin, Wholeness

Resurrection (Resurrect) – rising from the dead.

The resurrection of Jesus in bodily form is central and essential to the Christian faith and therefore to the healing ministry.

> 1 Corinthians 15:17... and if Christ has not been raised, your faith is worthless; you are still in your sins. (NASB)

But there is even more than *His* resurrection. Jesus has promised that true belief in Him will result in a resurrected life for each one of us after physical death. We have His personal assurance, spoken to Martha, for example, as she sought Jesus for the life of her brother Lazarus.

> John 11:25... Jesus said to her, "I am the resurrection and the life; he who believes in Me will live even if he dies ..." (NASB)

Actually, there will be a resurrection not just for followers of Jesus, but for every human being who has died. However, for those who have rejected Him in this life, the consequence will not be precious fellowship with God, but divine judgment and eternal separation from Him.

> John 5:29... and will come forth; those who did the good deeds to a resurrection of life, those who committed the evil deeds to a resurrection of judgment. (NASB)

Contrary to much thinking in the world, and even within the church, Jesus does not say that rebellion against God results in annihilation after physical death, nor in a final divine compromise of reconciliation. Jesus proved His own resurrection to life when He was seen by well over 500 people (1 Corinthians 15:6). Actually death could not hold someone who had not sinned (Acts 2:24), and now He has offered to humankind the opportunity, spiritually, to be part of both His death and His rising to life.

The healing and deliverance ministry is just the start of this restored existence for every believer. Let us be confident in saying *"He is risen!"* and that in Him, each of us will have a new, resurrected, imperishable body (1 Corinthians 15:42), eternally at peace with our Maker.

See   Death, Deliverance, Eternity, Faith, Jesus, Kingdom, Life, Sinlessness

Revelation (Reveal, Revelatory) – significant and often unexpected understanding, received not by human reason but through the Holy Spirit.

God has given humankind an extraordinary mind; one that is able to explore, analyze and understand much of the physical world in which we live. However, there is also a spiritual realm, with divine truths and laws which significantly affect our lives. This realm can only be truly understood by revelation, which is given by the Holy Spirit and received in the human spirit.

> 1 Corinthians 2:10… these are the things God has revealed to us by his Spirit. (NIV)

> Romans 8:16… The Spirit Himself testifies with our spirit that we are children of God … (NASB)

We should always remember that what the Spirit of God reveals to our hearts will always be consistent with the written word of the Bible, for He is the author of both.

God directs and empowers the Body of Christ on earth through the gifts of the Holy Spirit. When we meet together in small groups, perhaps for the healing ministry, or in larger groups, perhaps for worship, God will impart His gifts through the members of the Body, in order that we might be truly effective in helping to establish His Kingdom on earth.

Together we can receive, test and weigh the validity of the revelations and manifestations of the Spirit, ensuring that lives are built up and not torn down.

> 1 Corinthians 14:26... This is what I mean, my friends. When you meet for worship, one person has a hymn, another a teaching, another a revelation from God, another a message in strange tongues, and still another the explanation of what is said. Everything must be of help to the church. (GNB)

See Gifts of the Holy Spirit, Holy Spirit, Manifestation, Reason, Supernatural, Truth, Vision

Revenge (Vengeance) – bitter pursuit of some form of payment from someone who is guilty of wrongdoing.

Revenge is a very understandable form of justice, but it is not the way of God's Kingdom under the New Covenant sealed by Jesus on the cross. The problem with adopting vengeance as my system of justice is that I must be willing to receive it as well as give it. Jesus gave that warning to the scribes and Pharisees, who were determined to exercise their own judgment on the woman caught in adultery and were demanding that she pay with her life.

> John 8:7... But when they persisted in asking Him, He straightened up, and said to them, "He who is without sin among you, let him be the first to throw a stone at her." (NASB)

Jesus has come with a radical new system of justice. He has been willing to bear all the suffering due for humanity's sin and has issued a pardon for all of us who make the choice to be obedient to His way of forgiveness, rather than the world's way of vengeance toward those who have wronged us. In this way we leave God to be the ultimate judge of human hearts.

> Romans 12:19... Never take your own revenge, beloved, but leave room for the wrath of God, for it is written, "VENGEANCE IS MINE, I WILL REPAY," says the LORD. (NASB)

See Bitterness, Blame, Debt, Forgiveness, Guilt, Judgment, Justice, Resentment

Rhema – See Word

Ridicule – mocking form of dishonor.

See Abuse, Affirmation, Honor, Rejection, Shame, Value

Right (Rightful) – in line with God's laws and commandments, in thoughts, words and actions.

The original meaning of the English word *right* is *straight*. When we hold up the plumb line of God's Word, we can see whether our lives are in line with what He says. Under the Old Covenant, God gave a written law to His children to show them what was right (Romans 3:20). Under the New Covenant, we have a revelation of the truth of God, fulfilled and given through Jesus (John 1:17). Interestingly, He strongly challenged the self-righteousness of the Pharisees.

> Luke 18:14… "I tell you," said Jesus, "the tax collector, and not the Pharisee, was in the right with God when he went home. For those who make themselves great will be humbled, and those who humble themselves will be made great." (GNB)

Because Jesus is the only One to have ever been completely right with God, true surrender to Jesus is now the way to come back in line with God. This is achieved through our confession and His forgiveness. The Holy Spirit has written God's laws on the hearts of followers of Jesus (Hebrews 8:10), so now we can know clearly what is right, if we are open to the Holy Spirit's conviction. We should always remember that what the Spirit of God reveals to our hearts will always be consistent with the written word of the Bible, for He is the author of both.

> John 16:8… And when [the Holy Spirit] comes, he will prove to the people of the world that they are wrong about sin and about what is right and about God's judgment. (GNB)

In this spiritually hostile world, where the concepts of right and wrong seem simply to follow fashion, it is so precious that God has given us His unchangeable laws and commandments which keep us safe from harm. In the same way that a wall cannot determine its own straightness, but needs the external check of someone holding

A RIGHT

a plumb line, so humankind cannot, by itself, know what is right without the plumb line of God's truth given through the Holy Spirit, the perfect Counselor.

> Proverbs 12:15... The way of the fool is right in his own eyes, But a wise man is he who listens to counsel. (NASB)

See Commandment, Iniquity, Law, Plumb Line, Wrong, Righteousness, Sin

a Right – authority, license or entitlement which is given.

A claim of entitlement is only legitimate if it is conferred by someone else who carries true authority which they can delegate. For example, the pilot of an airplane has the right to fly it because authority has been delegated (given) to him by the airline company. A gunman on that airplane may claim a right to redirect the flight, but he does so only by using force, and he has no legitimate right.

God is in supreme authority over His entire creation (Romans 13:1), but He also delegated authority over the earth to humankind (Genesis 1:26–28). If we obey God, we are coming under His authority. In other words, we maintain His righteous rule over our lives (Romans 6:16). However, when we sin, we are giving rulership to the one we obey – Satan. This is why Jesus calls Satan the ruler of the world (John 14:30). By coming under Satan's authority, we are surrendering the authority that God gave to us.

So if we persist in an area of sin, including unforgiveness, the enemy can claim a legal right to control that part of our lives (2 Corinthians 2:10–11), because we have given him that right. We have surrendered authority to him by agreeing to follow his ways, rather than the ways of God. In deliverance ministry, this right is often referred to as a *foothold*.

> Ephesians 4:26–27... And "don't sin by letting anger control you." Don't let the sun go down while you are still angry, for anger gives a foothold to the devil. (NLT)

In the wider sense of the issue of rights, we live in a world where various entitlements and rights are perceived by many as obvious aspects of natural justice. Interestingly, *The United States Declaration of Independence* (1776) states that it is self-evident that humanity has been endowed by our Creator with certain rights, namely life, liberty and the pursuit of happiness. Despite this being biblically incorrect, much international justice these days is based on these so-called inalienable rights. *Inalienable* means that humankind has apparently had these natural rights from birth and that they cannot be taken away.

Those of the world can agree with one another, if they so choose, in man-made constitutional rights and privileges, but God has declared a very different form of justice for His children. God is indeed the Creator, and the One who has all authority, but He has only conferred rights to humanity within the boundaries of a divine covenant, which is now effective only through a personal relationship with Jesus, and through the confession of sin.

> John 1:12... as many as received [Jesus], to them He gave the right to become children of God, even to those who believe in His name. (NASB)

> Revelation 22:14... Blessed are those who wash their robes, so that they may have the right to the tree of life, and may enter by the gates into the city. (NASB)

Without receiving Jesus as Savior, we cannot keep the commands of God. In breaking covenant with Him and by following the ungodly ways of the world, we give over rights (authority) to the enemy to spiritually rule the world and to control our lives (Luke 4:6).

In many nations now, the declaration of humanity's apparent rights has largely replaced the acknowledgment of God's foundational laws and the recognition of human sin. True justice can never be found by human beings just claiming our rights, but only by our being convicted of our wrongs, through the Holy Spirit. God has declared in His Word that humankind has inalienable value (John 3:16), but He does not say that humanity has inalienable rights. God's conferring of rights can come only as we walk in obedience to the terms of His covenant, these being His commandments to believe in Jesus Christ and to love one another (1 John 3:23).

See Authority, Covenant, Deliverance, Foothold, Humanism, Law, Power

Righteousness (Righteous) – heart condition of being right with God.

This is how the condition of our lives was meant to be – in line with God's laws and commands. The original meaning of the English word *right* is straight, or in line. It is in this place of right-ness or righteousness that we can know the fullness of God's love, His protection and His provision.

Sin changes this condition and causes us to walk in unrighteousness or iniquity, which means that we are out of line with God and therefore outside of His protective spiritual covering. He will faithfully direct us onto the pathway of righteousness if we choose to walk in obedience to Him (Psalm 23:1–3). However, our sinful nature is always pressing for another direction, often in accordance with what the world says is right, but the world's righteousness is actually like a filthy garment in God's eyes (Isaiah 64:6).

Thankfully, when we do sin, there is a complete answer to the inevitable condition in which we then find ourselves. Jesus has made it possible for us to be fully restored.

> 1 John 1:9... If we confess our sins, He is faithful and righteous to forgive us our sins and to cleanse us from all unrighteousness. (NASB)

We sometimes hear a reformed convict declaring his intention to *go straight* in the future. He is actually saying that from that time onwards, he wants his life to be right. For all of humankind, if we so choose, getting right with God is possible, because of Jesus.

See Carnal Nature, Commandment, Covering, Iniquity, Plumb Line, Self-righteousness, Sin, Right

RITUAL

Ritual (Rite, Ritualistic) – ceremonial behavior to empower beliefs or vows.

When the physical body is used in some form of ceremonial behavior to reinforce words spoken, there is a strong spiritual significance to this, which may be good or bad. In rightful obedience to the instructions of Jesus, His followers powerfully identify with the consequence of His death by routinely eating bread and drinking wine, a ritual which symbolically equates to receiving the body and blood of Jesus into their personal lives. This act of Holy Communion does not of itself bring salvation, but it visibly declares a desire to be surrendered to Jesus and to all that He did at the cross.

When we participate in this with honest hearts, it can be a precious place of revelation and healing. However, there is a serious warning in the Bible that, when such ritual is entered into without the true lordship of Jesus, it can be very harmful.

> 1 Corinthians 11:27... Therefore whoever eats the bread or drinks the cup of the LORD in an unworthy manner, shall be guilty of the body and the blood of the LORD. (NASB)

The effect of defiling rituals is seen in countless false religious practices (Galatians 4:8–10) and false religions, such as Freemasonry, for example, which requires the participants to speak out and act out ungodly vows and oaths which effectively curse their bodies, their lives and even their families. The different progressions of membership in Freemasonry are known as *rites*, such as the Scottish or York rite, and such rituals establish spiritual covenants, strengthening the enemy's grip when these practices are not in line with the will of God (Matthew 5:34–37).

Even more sinister rituals are sometimes found in the occult or satanic abuse of individuals, including children. These involve sexual or traumatizing acts, often with religious overtones. In such rituals, the power of Satan's realm of darkness will be invoked, if not overtly then certainly by the enemy being given significant license through the perverse nature of the ungodly ceremonies.

For those who have been caught up in ungodly rituals, the way of healing is found through confession of personal sin, forgiveness of others involved, and a clear renouncing of all that has been spoken and enacted in the ritual procedures. Ungodly soul-ties may have been formed with the other participants and need to be broken. God's heart is to restore us from the deeply wounding and defiling experiences of our past so that we can enjoy the future of a unique covenant relationship and destiny in Him, free from the bondage of false religious practices and defiling rituals.

See Covenant, False Religion, Freemasonry, Grace, Legalism, Occult, Pronouncement, Religion, Satanism, Soul-tie

Root – source, cause or origin of the good or bad fruit in people's lives.

Our wrong behaviors or bodily disorders are rarely just the result of today's issues. We display the bad fruit of all that has previously distorted our lives: the past wounds, sins and spiritual bondage. Without understanding the root issues in our lives, we will not see the problems fully resolved, and we will only be able to manage the symptoms.

Consider a weed, like a dandelion. If we only cut off the flowers, the root remains intact underground and ready to send up further shoots. Likewise, we need to acknowledge and deal with the roots in our lives which are producing the unwanted fruit of our symptoms. Facing, with Jesus, the truth of our past can be a very liberating step into our future (John 4:29).

It has been rightly said that the healing and deliverance ministry of Jesus frequently starts on the inside of our lives and ends on the outside. This is another way of saying that our physical bodies usually reflect the condition of our hearts. When past issues are unresolved in the soul and human spirit, the body today demonstrates the effect of the inner damage. Jesus confirmed this truth to His disciples one day in the synagogue, when he met a woman whose body reflected her spiritual state.

> Luke 13:11,16... And there was a woman who for eighteen years had had a sickness caused by a spirit; and she was bent double, and could not straighten up at all. ...

> "And this woman, a daughter of Abraham as she is, whom Satan has bound for eighteen long years, should she not have been released from this bond on the Sabbath day?" (NASB)

The sinful ways in which people behave today are most often rooted in the wounding of the past. Where unforgiveness has led to a judgmental and bitter heart, for example, the consequence today can be very defiling, both to the person and to those with whom they have relationship. It is no good just telling them to behave better; the roots of the problem must be tackled in order to bring true cleansing.

> Hebrews 12:15… See to it that no one falls short of the grace of God and that no bitter root grows up to cause trouble and defile many. (NIV)

See Behavior, Belief, Bitter Root Judgment, Core Belief, Fruit, Healing, Sin, Truth, Unforgiveness, Wound

Ruler of the World – one of the names for Satan, used by Jesus.

> John 14:30… I will not speak much more with you, for the ruler of the world is coming, and he has nothing in Me … (NASB)

Human beings were created to rule over the earth (Genesis 1:28), but we handed over this God-given authority to Satan. When you obey someone, you give them a right to rule over you (Romans 6:16). So, from the time that humanity followed the instruction of Satan to eat the fruit forbidden by God, we surrendered our authority to rule the earth over to Satan. This was confirmed by Satan's words to Jesus in the wilderness.

> Luke 4:5–6… And [the devil] led [Jesus] up and showed Him all the kingdoms of the world in a moment of time. And the devil said to Him, "I will give you all this domain and its glory; for it has been handed over to me, and I give it to whomever I wish." (NASB)

The earth has been spiritually defiled by human sin and the consequent rule of Satan (Genesis 3:17). However, as we walk in obedience to Jesus, the spiritual authority of the ruler of the world is diminished, and the ground which God has given to humankind can be reclaimed and restored into fruitfulness.

See Authority, Barrenness, Enemy, the Fall, Reclaim Ground, Rebellion, a Right, Ruling Spirit, Satan, World

Ruling Spirit – spiritual being, with a domain of authority.

Sometimes translated in the Bible as *principality*, this can refer to spiritual powers either obedient or disobedient to God (Colossians 1:16), but most often when the Bible mentions them, these are powers of darkness. The Bible is clear on the existence of a hierarchy of spiritual beings in the enemy's realm of darkness, including those referred to as ruling spirits or rulers (Greek – *arche*).

> Ephesians 6:12... For we are not fighting against human beings but against the wicked spiritual forces in the heavenly world, the rulers, authorities, and cosmic powers of this dark age. (GNB)

It is less clear what particular roles each of these levels of the demonic realm have over either spiritual territory or over other spirits. However, this network of spirits, which appear to gain some measure of strength from each other, needs to be considered when carrying out deliverance in someone's life. The Holy Spirit may prompt us that there is a need to deal with a ruling spirit governing the particular unclean spirit which is being evicted from a person's life.

For example, a spirit of addiction to nicotine, controlling someone's life, may be linked to ruling spirits operating in the organizations who manufacture and supply the cigarettes. When we are delivering the person of the spirit which is driving their personal addiction, it may well be helpful to bind the ruling spirits, to be held by the authority of Jesus, while this particular minion in their network is driven out of the person being set free.

> Matthew 12:29... Or how can anyone enter the strong man's house and carry off his property, unless he first binds the strong man? And then he will plunder his house. (NASB)

Places of false worship will be governed by ruling spirits (sometimes called *territorial spirits*) which have been given their authority through the idolatry of those people worshipping in that place. When helping people to be set free from unclean spirits of false religion, for example, it may be necessary to bind, and break the link to, ruling spirits which have governed the relevant temples, religious sites, congregations or the false belief systems. When we are in a rightful place of authority under Jesus and as directed by the Holy Spirit, we have an entitlement to bind His enemies (Psalm 149:5–9). It is important that we do seek that authority. For example, a group of church leaders operating in unity will have significant spiritual authority over the enemy in their area.

See Angel, Authority, Binding, Control, Darkness, Deliverance, Powers of Darkness, Reclaim Ground, a Right, Spirit

Sacrifice (Sacrificial) – surrender of a life for a spiritual purpose.

Throughout the Old Testament, God required of His people the sacrifice of many animals to provide a physical and spiritual payment for the cost of their sin. This was in substitution for their own lives, because the result of sin is always death (Romans 6:23). They needed to know that God could not ignore the requirements of divine justice, in particular the need for bloodshed, so that He could forgive sin.

> Hebrews 9:22... In fact, the law requires that nearly everything be cleansed with blood, and without the shedding of blood there is no forgiveness. (NIV)

Now, under the New Covenant, only one sacrifice is effective. It is the sacrifice which God has provided, the blood shed by Jesus at the cross. All other blood sacrifice, which is contrary to God's commands, simply gives rights to the powers of darkness to gain control in the lives of those participating.

> 1 Corinthians 10:20... What I am saying is that what is sacrificed on pagan altars is offered to demons, not to God. And I do not want you to be partners with demons. (GNB)

Sacrifice was always an important part of sealing a covenant in the Bible. In fact, the Hebrew word for *covenant* implies the cutting of flesh. So the use of sacrifice, when part of an ungodly covenant, pronouncement or religious practice, strongly empowers the enemy in his spiritual hold over any vows which are being proclaimed. For this reason, in false religions, witchcraft, the occult or Satanism, there may be sacrificial acts to invoke spiritual power (Deuteronomy 32:17), sometimes using play-acting (as in some rituals of Freemasonry), sometimes the killing of a live animal, and even, on occasions, the taking of human life.

Whatever our involvement has been in such things, we can come to the Lord today for complete cleansing from all the defilement of the past. We can now depend on the one perfect sacrifice of Jesus, who restores true covenant with God and pays for all the cost of our sin. Our part is to present our bodies to Him as a *living* and holy sacrifice (Romans 12:1), surrendering our lives wholeheartedly to the lordship of Jesus, the perfect Lamb of God.

> Revelation 12:11… And they overcame [Satan] because of the blood of the Lamb and because of the word of their testimony, and they did not love their life even when faced with death. (NASB)

See Atonement, Blood, Covenant, the Cross, False Religion, Occult, Satanism

Sadness (Sad) – lack of joy.

See Emotion, Depression, Despair, Grief, Joy

Safety (Safe) – See Security

Safe Sex – sexual intimacy according to God's order, only within a faithful marriage.

The world believes that safety from transmitted disease in sexual intercourse can be found in using a contraceptive condom. This does not actually give full physical protection and certainly gives no spiritual protection. Of course, if God's laws and commands were fully followed by humankind, there could be no sexually transmitted disease. Thankfully, God does not stand in condemnation of our sinful ways but rather He invites us to know His forgiveness and to seek His cleansing.

See Contraception, Order, Marriage, Protection, Sexual Sin, Soul-tie

SANCTIFICATION

Salvation – saving of human life from spiritual destruction.

The process of God's salvation of our lives can be compared with the rescue of a seabird from an oil spill. First the bird is taken out of the oil, then the oil is taken out of the bird, and finally the bird is restored into its full freedom. Our Savior, Jesus Christ, has rescued us from the domain of spiritual darkness (Colossians 1:13), He is removing that darkness from our lives, and He is preparing us for full liberation into eternal life (Isaiah 51:6).

Since Jesus has fully paid the cost of humanity's sin, the right that the ruler of the world has to hold ownership of our lives is removed, but only *if* we choose to receive this truth (Romans 1:16). Then God's healing and deliverance can begin, for this is the next step of salvation. The enemy's defilement of our lives can be washed away as his spiritual authority is removed. That authority is taken away as we obey God and deal with specific sin issues.

> Philippians 2:12… Therefore, my dear friends, as you have always obeyed – not only in my presence, but now much more in my absence – continue to work out your salvation with fear and trembling … (NIV)

Finally and gloriously, we shall know the fullness of salvation when we meet Jesus face to face (1 John 3:2; Hebrews 5:9). So God's salvation covers the past, the present and the future!

Someone has said that salvation is primarily to save us from ourselves. Without the coming of Jesus, the entire world would have been lost to the control of our carnal natures and to the hold of the Evil One. Thank God for the Savior who has come to rescue us!

> Acts 4:12… And there is salvation in no one else; for there is no other name under heaven that has been given among men by which we must be saved. (NASB)

See Born Again, the Cross, Deliverance, Freedom, Forgiveness, Healing, Sanctification, Satan, Sin

Sanctification (Sanctify) – supernatural process by which followers of Jesus become more like Him.

God has given each of us a unique personality, the essence of which He does not want to change, but the holiness of the character of Jesus needs to grow within our lives as we allow the Holy Spirit to challenge and change us.

> 2 Thessalonians 2:13... But we should always give thanks to God for you, brethren beloved by the LORD, because God has chosen you from the beginning for salvation through sanctification by the Spirit and faith in the truth. (NASB)

Sanctification and holiness sound like outdated words, but this process is a necessary and extraordinary adventure of conviction, confession, repentance and divine cleansing, sometimes including eviction of the enemy's power, where his defiling grip has controlled some part of our lives. Such a journey defines what it is to be a true follower of Jesus (Hebrews 10:14), more and more able to move into the fullness of the destiny and peace for which God has created us.

Actually, He chose each one of us precisely in order that we would bear lasting fruit, that is, the holy character of Christ.

> John 15:16... You did not choose Me but I chose you, and appointed you that you would go and bear fruit, and that your fruit would remain, so that whatever you ask of the Father in My name He may give you. (NASB)
>
> Galatians 5:22–23... But the fruit of the Spirit is love, joy, peace, patience, kindness, goodness, faithfulness, gentleness, self-control ... (NASB)

See Cleansing, Deliverance, Destiny, Fruit, Holiness, Transformation

Satan (Satanic) – ruler of the realm of spiritual darkness, in eternal rebellion against the will of God.

Satan, which means adversary (of God), has many other names and descriptions of his character in Scripture: a liar, a murderer, a thief, a deceiver, a serpent, a tempter, an accuser, the devil, the destroyer, the lord of the flies (Beelzebub), the enemy and the Evil One.

SATAN

He is a created spiritual being, limited in location, knowledge and power, and he is in no way comparable with Almighty God (Job 2:1–2). However, his rebellion against God, when he was followed by other powers of darkness (Revelation 12:9), together with the authority given to him through the Fall (Luke 4:6), has allowed him to operate with a title which even Jesus uses to refer to this enemy – *the ruler of the world* (John 14:30). This authority to rule the world of God's creation was given to Satan by humanity when Adam and Eve chose to disobey God; they followed the advice of the serpent to eat the fruit of the tree of good and evil. When you obey someone, you come under their authority, so humankind came under Satan's authority.

Even today, the enemy's authority is either increased by our disobedience toward God or decreased by our obedience, as followers of Jesus.

> Luke 10:17–19… The seventy-two men came back in great joy. "LORD," they said, "even the demons obeyed us when we gave them a command in your name!" Jesus answered them, "I saw Satan fall like lightning from heaven. Listen! I have given you authority, so that you can walk on snakes and scorpions and overcome all the power of the Enemy, and nothing will hurt you." (GNB)

Satan himself may not be directly involved in every sinner's life, but the powers of darkness which operate under his direction (Acts 26:18) do look for a right, through iniquity, to exercise a measure of spiritual control in the lives of men and women. These demonic powers operate in a network of lies and fear, with the character of Satan at the heart of the web. By His sinless death on the cross, Jesus has defeated the authority of Satan and totally disarmed the power of Satan's realm, all on behalf of those who truly acknowledge and follow Jesus as Lord and Savior.

In Christ, and only in Him, we can, like the seventy-two early disciples, overcome the destructive might of the Satan's demonic realm. As we walk in the truth and guidance of the Holy Spirit, the Body of Christ will see increasing healing and deliverance, just as Jesus demonstrated to us while He walked the earth.

> Acts 10:38... You know about Jesus of Nazareth and how God poured out on him the Holy Spirit and power. He went everywhere, doing good and healing all who were under the power of the Devil, for God was with him. (GNB)

Followers of Jesus should be *aware* of Satan and his tactics, and *impressed* by God and His ways, but not the other way round.

See Authority, Darkness, Disobedience, Evil, the Fall, Powers of Darkness, Rebellion, a Right, Unclean Spirit, World

Satanism – active submission to the rule of the Evil One.

Such a lifestyle may be personally chosen in overt rebellion against God, or it may be the consequence of abusive coercion (sometimes of children) into the deep occult practices of a family or a coven. A coven is a group of people who are demonically bonded together for the purpose of opposing God's kingdom, actively serving Satan and the powers of darkness. We are told that a wrong focus on Satan had even been operating in the church at Thyatira (Revelation 2:24).

People get involved in witchcraft in order to invoke personal demonic power to enable them to control other people or their environment. But a group fully involved in Satanism goes much further, in leading an utterly perverted and defiling lifestyle where every belief and behavior is in complete opposition to the commands and the ways of Jesus. They use distorted sexual, religious and traumatizing rituals, together with much occult symbolism, in order to establish networks of power through demons, and to obtain wrongful control of the human spirit in the lives of individuals.

Thankfully, Jesus is far above every power and principality, including Satan himself (Ephesians 1:21). In Jesus, those who have been caught up in Satanism can find freedom and cleansing as they walk with the Lord, and with trusted Christian friends, through the process of bringing every part of their broken and defiled lives into the power of His forgiveness and restoration. It may take time, but God is utterly faithful, and willing to journey with us over every hurdle of healing, through to the finish.

> Acts 26:18... to open their eyes so that they may turn from darkness to light and from the dominion of Satan to God, that they may receive forgiveness of sins and an inheritance among those who have been sanctified by faith in Me. (NASB)

See Control, Deliverance, Freedom, Healing, Occult, Rebellion, Ritual, Satan, Unclean Spirit, Witchcraft

Savior (Save) – one who rescues another from harm.

See the Cross, Jesus, Salvation

Scripture (Scriptural) – words in the Bible.

See Bible, Truth, Word

Secrecy (Secret) – concealing of truth.

There is a rightful limit to how much truth should be shared at any particular time. For example, a young child can be overwhelmed if a parent shares too much detail of a family problem or marital squabble. Jesus had boundaries to how much truth he shared in various circumstances, because He knew that human hearts were frequently not ready or able to hear. That is one of the reasons why he spoke in parables (Matthew 13:13).

However, there are times when secrecy is chosen or imposed in situations when the truth should be told. This can be spiritually dangerous territory, because sustaining such a lie gives authority to the enemy, who is the father of lies (John 8:44) and operates in the realm of darkness.

Sometimes an adult who has abused a child will force the victim, through intimidation, to keep the issue a secret. When the one who was abused comes, perhaps much later in life, to an opportunity for receiving God's healing, they can find it very hard to break the secret, because of seemingly irrational difficulties concerning loyalty and fear. There will be strong enemy pressure to keep things in the dark.

Personal sin, especially where there is shame, will also often give rise to wrongful secrecy. When we cover up any unresolved issues of the past, we are burying them alive rather than putting those sins to death at the cross with Jesus. The Bible gives very good advice to ensure that every hold of secrecy being used by the enemy is rooted out.

> James 5:16a... Therefore, confess your sins to one another, and pray for one another so that you may be healed. (NASB)

The pathway to the grace of God's healing will always be through a gateway of truth. The enemy will fight hard in order not to be exposed. However, walking closely with Jesus will always ensure that breaking ungodly secrecy is both safe and liberating.

> John 8:31b–32... If you continue in My word, then you are truly disciples of Mine; and you will know the truth, and the truth will make you free. (NASB)

See Abuse, Coping Mechanism, Darkness, Fear, Lie, Loyalty, Truth

Security (Secure) – confidence of safety.

Although we generally seek security for our physical well-being, it is even more deeply needed for our human spirit.

Right from the very beginning of our lives, God meant us to know, at the core of our being, the security of His protection and His provision, in a covenant relationship with Him. However, everything changed at the Fall.

It was a sudden and overwhelming sense of insecurity that Adam and Eve felt, as they reaped the consequence of their disobedience to God's command concerning the Tree of the Knowledge of Good and Evil (Genesis 3:7–10). One moment they were dwelling in spiritual intimacy and safety with God, and the next moment they experienced fearful isolation and exposure.

Their attempts to establish their own security by hiding and covering themselves were completely ineffective in meeting the inner need. True security is essential for the human spirit, and if such security is not known through our trusting God we look for substitutes, such as relying on other people, or relying on finance, knowledge, reason, religion, body image, employment, fantasy or independence. None of our substitutes meet our inner need.

Thankfully, Jesus has come. He came to earth to make it possible for our human spirit to be reborn into the light, life and perfect security of a restored covenant relationship with our heavenly Father. The security which Jesus knows in the Father can be *our* security.

> Psalm 61:4... Let me live in your sanctuary all my life; let me find safety under your wings. (GNB)

God's spiritual covering is available for all His children, giving us protection and an opportunity to resolve the insecurity of the past. For despite spiritual rebirth we may still carry much wounding, both from the original wounds which left us feeling insecure and also from

the effect of our attempts to make ourselves feel secure. Just as when a baby is born into the world it carries with it any damage sustained during the months from conception, so we bring into our newborn Christian life the damaging effects of unsafe times in our past.

As we forgive those who have not provided rightful safety for our lives, and as we confess our own ways of ungodly self-protection (false security), we can make a choice to trust in the absolute faithfulness of God. This may take a while if we have suffered the carelessness or betrayal of others, but these steps of faith will open the door for God's healing and will be life-transforming for those who have walked in the deep insecurity of an anxious spirit.

> Isaiah 32:15–17... But once more God will send us his spirit. The wasteland will become fertile, and fields will produce rich crops. Everywhere in the land righteousness and justice will be done. Because everyone will do what is right, there will be peace and security forever. (GNB)

SEDUCTION

See Anxiety, Confidence, Covenant, Covering, Faith, Father, Protection, Self-protection, Trust

Seduction (Seductive) – persuasive temptation or deception often associated with sexual sin.

See Deception, Sexual Sin, Temptation

Self-centeredness (Self-centered) – See Selfishness

Self-comfort – seeking relief from pain or distress, without God.

See Comfort, Self-pity

Self-confidence – deep assurance of personal identity and worth.

It can be extremely difficult to know this assurance if we have received very little personal affirmation in our lives. Of course, it is possible to display a mask of self-confidence (1 Timothy 1:7) often hiding unresolved insecurity in the heart, but for most people this unreality becomes exhausting and it is often the cause of emotional and physical disorder.

As followers of Jesus we have been given, through the witness of the Holy Spirit, a wonderful assurance that irrespective of life's knocks, we are secure and significant children of our heavenly Father. Furthermore, He has prepared a destiny for our lives and will gift us with all that we need to fulfill that destiny, provided that we completely trust Him.

> Proverbs 14:26... Reverence for the LORD gives confidence and security to a man and his family. (GNB)

The truth is that however the *world* chooses to assess us, *we* can choose to walk in complete confidence in who we are in God's family. We may need to forgive those who have undermined our self-confidence, but we can ask the Lord to rewrite His truth on our hearts.

> Romans 8:16... The Spirit Himself testifies with our spirit that we are children of God ... (NASB)

356

See Affirmation, Destiny, Faith, Identity, Mask, Security, Value

Self-control – control over my own body, soul and human spirit.

When there is control of my mind, will and emotions through the rule of the Holy Spirit, directing my human spirit in accordance with the will of God, this self-control is a precious fruit of the Spirit, maintaining right order within my body (Galatians 5:22–23).

Control of myself under God's guidance is good. However, there can also be ungodly and destructive self-control when my will, governed by my carnal nature, seeks to suppress the right leading of my spirit.

> Romans 8:6... To be controlled by human nature results in death; to be controlled by the Spirit results in life and peace. (GNB)

As an example, it is ungodly to deny rightful emotional responses. This would be the case if I deal with my anger about injustice by denying that I feel it, rather than taking it to God. If I choose to dissociate from the reality of (say) a shameful identity, this also is ungodly control of myself and can lead to brokenness and spiritual bondage.

Jesus wants to be king over our lives, but ungodly self-control puts *me* on the throne. We wrongly control ourselves through suppressing emotions, denying the reality of our sin and wounds, abandoning part of our true identity, and by giving a wrong place to fear.

Godly self-control, on the other hand, recognizes and feels emotions, but controls the inappropriate expression of those feelings, not shifting

SELF-HARM

them onto others in a destructive way, but holding them until there is an opportunity to pour out our heart to the Lord, as the psalmist did (Psalm 62:8).

Self-control must never replace our submission to God. Control in the right hands is truly good for us, and the best hands we can submit to are those of Father, through Jesus Christ.

> 1 Peter 4:2... From now on, then, you must live the rest of your earthly lives controlled by God's will and not by human desires. (GNB)

See Control, Coping Mechanism, Defense Mechanism, Dissociation, Fruit, Soulishness

Self-harm (Self-harming) – intentional infliction of damage to one's own body, in response to inner pain.

When Jesus met the Gerasene man afflicted with a legion of demons, He was clearly meeting someone suffering from extreme distress. The Bible describes the man's dysfunctional and compulsive behavior, including the fact that he was in the habit of cutting himself.

> Mark 5:5... Constantly, night and day, he was screaming among the tombs and in the mountains, and gashing himself with stones. (NASB)

The man certainly needed deliverance, but he also desperately needed deep healing for his soul and human spirit. Some people, suffering with extreme and irresolvable inner pain, find that cutting or otherwise harming themselves can bring a measure of temporary relief. It can also be a contradictory cry for help or attention, for example, toward parents or medical personnel. Self-inflicted rituals involving trauma, physical pain or discomfort, including eating disorders, can be a way of dissociating from an emotionally painful place inside. Sometimes, when there is strong self-hatred, shame or guilt, even false guilt, then inflicting punishment on oneself through pain or disfigurement, not least when blood is seen, can seem a suitable response.

Of course, all self-harming is contrary to God's intentions for our well-being. It just adds to inner pain and guilt, and it gives significant rights to the enemy to strengthen the destructive mindsets and behaviors with his power, frequently driving the person into addictive routines. Jesus can meet the deepest of our deep inner needs. He can comfort the most extreme of emotional pain, and He can evict the enemy from all the places where he has had a defiling grip on our lives, just as Jesus did, so powerfully, for the troubled Gerasene man.

> Mark 5:15... They came to Jesus and observed the man who had been demon-possessed sitting down, clothed and in his right mind, the very man who had had the "legion"; and they became frightened. (NASB)

See Body Piercing, Control, Coping Mechanism, Pain, Punishment, Rejection, Self-rejection, Shame

Self-hatred – extreme despising and rejection of oneself.

It is not unusual for people who have experienced deep wounding, rejection and particularly abuse, to carry considerable shame and self-hatred, frequently believing themselves to be somehow guilty for what has happened, even if that is untrue. These issues are very often compounded by the sinful coping mechanisms they may have developed to deal with the inner pain, such as self-harming, addictions, promiscuity or eating disorders. These reinforce the low self-esteem, the self-rejection and self-loathing.

The person may also choose to dissociate from this 'bad' and hated part of their own identity, instead presenting an image of themselves which appears more acceptable to friends and family. Alternatively, the self-hatred may be more evident in the person's lifestyle, clothing or general behavior, all of which may be intentionally degrading the attractiveness of the person's God-given identity or sexuality. Sadly, for some, the spiral of self-hatred can finish in the violence of suicide.

The Bible declares strongly that each one of us is of immense value to God, irrespective of the circumstances of our lives. His love for us is unconditional and unending. He sees us as His treasured children, and longs for us to be able to know these truths deep within our soul and spirit, by walking with Jesus. Confessing self-hatred and choosing to see ourselves as God sees us can radically change the life of anyone trapped in these issues, and give opportunity to expel the spiritual power that the enemy has exerted over our beliefs and behaviors.

> Psalm 139:13–14… For You formed my inward parts; You wove me in my mother's womb. I will give thanks to You, for I am fearfully and wonderfully made; Wonderful are Your works, And my soul knows it very well. (NASB)

See Badness, Belief System, Despising, Punishment, Self-rejection, Sexuality, Suicide, Value

Selfishness (Selfish) – focus on self, demonstrated in attitudes and behaviors.

This is the default setting of all human beings driven by the carnal nature (2 Timothy 3:2). Until our human spirit is born again of the Holy Spirit, through belief in Jesus, it is not possible for God to be the true focus of our being.

In whatever way we present our lives, we will be mostly serving ourselves, albeit in a concealed way, seeking inner comfort and safety, especially when the wounding of the past remains unhealed. Of course, there are many examples of altruism among non-believers; people who have realized from instinct or learning that there can be a deep inner fulfillment through helping other human beings. Most parents, for example, show a remarkably selfless regard for their children's well-being. Selfishness may be the default setting, but it is not inevitable, and we always have personal choice.

However, for a true follower of Jesus Christ, if we are open to change, the whole focus of our lives is being daily and radically transformed. As we receive healing and deliverance from the disorders of the past, we become more able to declare, like Jesus, "Father … not My will, but Yours be done" (Luke 22:42). Truly walking according to God's instructions will inevitably result in a growing unselfishness, although for many of us, especially those who still carry unresolved inner pain, the choice to be God-focused rather than self-focused does not come easily. Maybe we need to ask the Lord today what He wants to do next to help us deal with the grip of selfishness that can steal the fulfillment of our God-given destiny.

> Proverbs 28:25... Selfishness only causes trouble. You are much better off to trust the LORD. (GNB)

See Behavior, Carnal Nature, Comfort, Fall, Sin, Soulishness, Transformation

Self-pity – unhealthy compassion for oneself.

When we have experienced injustice or wounding, we rightly look for someone to show compassion and bring us comfort. However, in the absence of knowing God's answer to our needs, our carnality can lead us to become gripped by self-pity.

> Psalm 13:1–2... How much longer will you forget me, LORD? Forever? How much longer will you hide yourself from me? How long must I endure trouble? How long will sorrow fill my heart day and night? How long will my enemies triumph over me? (GNB)

Unfortunately, this self-pity becomes a barrier to the true comfort and healing that God wants to give us. Unchallenged, self-pity can develop into a judgment against friends, family and even God, so we believe and expect that no one will care sufficiently for our well-being. Holding on to self-pity is a sin and it can give rights to the enemy to lock us in to resentment and hopelessness.

However, if we are willing to walk in forgiveness of those who have hurt us, and in acknowledgment of our self-centered ways, Jesus is there for us with His life-giving pity and His powerful healing.

> Mark 1:41... Jesus was filled with pity, and reached out and touched him. "I do want to," He answered. "Be clean!" (GNB)

See Bitterness, Comfort, Coping Mechanism, Jealousy, Resentment, Unforgiveness, Wound

Self-pronouncement – See Pronouncement

Self-protection – harmful self-guarding of the human heart.

It is right for us to take care of the whole person that God has created us to be, not putting ourselves in unnecessary danger. God's order within the human body is that by the inspiration of the Holy Spirit, our human spirit should give direction to our soul and body, so that we walk in safety, both spiritually and physically.

> Job 32:8–9... But it is the spirit in a person, the breath of the Almighty, that gives them understanding. It is not only the old who are wise, nor only the aged who understand what is right. (NIV)

However, where there has been deep inner wounding affecting our human spirit, our carnal nature seeks to protect and even hide the wound. Our soul rises up to guard the place of insecurity in our identity. Self-protection can involve many types of defense mechanism, such as independence, denial, dissociation, control, religious ritual or excessive dependence on man-made security and wealth (Proverbs 18:11). All such behaviors are simply trying to self-fix the insecurity of the heart. Imagining that such things can truly protect us is a fantasy which plays right into the enemy's hands. The only way in which we can be brought into authentic spiritual safety is through confession of our ungodly self-protection, inviting God to heal our hearts, and allowing Him to witness anew into our spirits (Romans 8:16) that we are covenant-protected children of God.

> 2 Thessalonians 3:3... But the LORD is faithful, and He will strengthen and protect you from the evil one. (NASB)

See Covering, Defense Mechanism, Dissociation, Protection, Self-control, Soulishness

Self-rejection – personal agreement with the rejection we experience from the world.

People try to cope with the pain of rejection in different ways. Some become rebellious while others find it less painful to just agree with the deceiving spirit of this world, which declares that they are not acceptable as they are, they do not fit, that they are not meeting the standard of intelligence or appearance or whatever else is perceived to be desirable.

However, God says the complete opposite, and He wants us to choose a position of agreement with Him.

> Psalm 139:14... I will give thanks to You, for I am fearfully and wonderfully made; Wonderful are Your works, And my soul knows it very well. (NASB)

Self-rejection can be very destructive, leading to self-hatred and sometimes even to suicide. The enemy seeks to strengthen any mindset and choice which opposes the truth of God. But when we confess this sinful self-rejecting attitude of heart and receive the forgiveness of God, He can strengthen our sense of self-worth, help us to know His unconditional acceptance of us, and expel any unclean spirit which has been driving and reinforcing the self-rejection.

See Acceptance, Rebellion, Rejection, Self-hatred, Unconditional, Value

Self-righteousness (Self-righteous) – righteousness sought through human effort.

The Bible has strong words to say about self-righteousness.

> Isaiah 64:6... For all of us have become like one who is unclean, And all our righteous deeds are like a filthy garment; And all of us wither like a leaf, And our iniquities, like the wind, take us away. (NASB)

God's view of righteousness is completely different from humanity's view (Matthew 5:20). Humanism promotes the belief that humankind can achieve goodness by the use of human ability alone. God says it is only achieved by letting the One who is completely righteous live in us and through us.

> Jeremiah 23:6... In [Messiah's] days Judah will be saved, And Israel will dwell securely; And this is His name by which He will be called, "The LORD our righteousness." (NASB)

Self-righteousness is independence from God. It is the outworking of pride, it breeds arrogance, it defiles the heart, it is simply unrighteousness by another name and it needs to be confessed as sin.

> 1 John 1:9... If we confess our sins, He is faithful and righteous to forgive us our sins and to cleanse us from all unrighteousness. (NASB)

See Carnal Nature, Humanism, Pride, Righteousness, Unrighteousness, Wisdom

Sex (Sexual) –

(1) gender: male or female – **See** Femininity, Masculinity, Sexuality.

(2) intimate sexual activity, usually with another person, in particular sexual intercourse.

God invented sex! He created us male and female and designed the human body so that there could be safe, intimate and pleasurable joining for those who have entered into a covenant of marriage.

Sexual intercourse not only creates and endorses the special 'one flesh' relationship of marriage, but gives opportunity for the procreation of children within a physically and spiritually protected environment. Jesus affirmed this God-ordained joining of a man and a woman.

> Matthew 19:4–6... And [Jesus] answered and said, "Have you not read that He who created them from the beginning MADE THEM MALE AND FEMALE, and said, 'FOR THIS REASON A MAN SHALL LEAVE HIS FATHER AND MOTHER AND BE JOINED TO HIS WIFE, AND THE TWO SHALL BECOME ONE FLESH'? So they are no longer two, but one flesh. What therefore God has joined together, let no man separate." (NASB)

Unfortunately, the world has mostly decided to ignore God's ways. Sex is now regarded by many people as just one of many desirable pastimes, and simply a transient act of the physical body. There is no understanding of the emotional and spiritual ties which will inevitably be established from an intimate union which God intended to bond two people together for life. Paul reminds the Christians at Corinth that their lax attitude toward sex ignores the damaging and lasting spiritual effects of sexual sin.

> 1 Corinthians 6:15–17... Do you not know that your bodies are members of Christ? Shall I then take away the members of Christ and make them members of a prostitute? May it never be! Or do you not know that the one who joins himself to a prostitute is one body with her? For He says, "THE TWO SHALL BECOME ONE FLESH." But the one who joins himself to the LORD is one spirit with Him. (NASB)

In a world that clamors for sexual freedom, in sometimes very perverse forms, it is important that followers of Jesus stand up for sexual purity (Ephesians 5:3). God is ready to forgive and cleanse us from all the defilement of the past if we acknowledge our sin and choose His ways. How wonderful it would be to live in a world surrendered to God's truth concerning sex. May His Kingdom come!

See Intimacy, Marriage, Purity, Sexuality, Sexual Orientation, Sexual Sin, Soul-tie

Sexuality – that part of our God-created identity which exhibits masculinity or femininity.

God made us male and female (Genesis 1:27). These two forms of a human being complement each other in wonderful ways with differing abilities which together allow God's purpose for humankind to be fulfilled, not least in procreation. Alongside the more obvious physical differences, there are other God-given characteristics which become apparent, for example, in family life, where women tend toward a more nurturing role and men tend to adopt a more protective role.

The knowledge of our sexuality is rooted in our human spirit, which is imparted by God into the body at conception.

> 1 Corinthians 2:11... It is only our own spirit within us that knows all about us ... (GNB)

However, there is much opportunity through generational iniquity, parental sin, abuse and personal wrongdoing, for damage to occur in a person's sexuality, causing distorted sexual attraction, confusion of gender and a range of dysfunctions. Thankfully, God can restore the deepest places of inner wounding in our lives when we come to Him in obedience to His ways. Whilst not forcing themselves into any man-made stereotypes, it is good for followers of Jesus, both men and women, to seek the Lord's help to be as complete in their God-given sexuality as possible, through receiving His healing from past wounds, and His empowering for future destiny. God sees much deeper than just outward appearance.

> Proverbs 31:30... Charm is deceitful and beauty is vain, But a woman who fears the LORD, she shall be praised. (NASB)

Jesus walked the earth in His masculinity to perfection, without distortion and without sin. He had no need to express that masculinity through sexual intercourse, as this was not part of God's plan for Him. The life of Jesus proves that singleness, viewed from God's perspective, does not deny the opportunity for a powerful and authentic expression of sexuality; it simply denies the most intimate form of that expression. Singleness may indeed be a rightful and fulfilling destiny for some, as they seek God's path for their lives.

See Femininity, Identity, Masculinity, Personhood, Singleness, Sex, Sexual Orientation, Sexual Sin, Transgender

SEXUAL ORIENTATION

Sexual Orientation – direction of attraction regarding sexual intimacy.

The word *orientation* is a term which is not found in the Bible, but which the world has come to use for what is assumed to be an innate and fixed human condition of sexual identity and attraction. It is similar to saying that the needle in a navigator's compass does not necessarily have a north-pointing orientation, but we would clearly recognize this as contrary to the laws of physics.

The Bible says that God's design (God's law) for a man and a woman is for them to be rightfully attracted to the opposite sex, and for this attraction to be intimately consummated only within the covenant of marriage (Matthew 19:5). The human body is clearly designed such that the sexual organs of adult men and women can safely join in a way that gives pleasure and can result in the fusion of a sperm and an egg, to give opportunity for the procreation of a new life.

The Bible also teaches that the existence of sexual attraction outside of God's order, for example, men to men, women to women, or adults to children, is rooted in the corporate sin which has been sown into this world through generations of rebellion and idolatry (Romans 1:20–27). Within these verses, distorted attraction is described as degrading, and therefore dishonoring, to the precious human beings God has created.

> Romans 1:26–27... For this reason God gave them over to degrading passions; for their women exchanged the natural function for that which is unnatural, and in the same way also the men abandoned the natural function of the woman and burned in their desire for one another, men with men committing indecent acts ... (NASB)

Any sexual attraction not intended by God is a condition which needs His love and His healing, together with determined new choices by those affected, rather than endorsement of the disorder, which is what is commonly demanded in the world today. This world-view, which says that sexual orientation cannot change and that almost any sexual orientation is acceptable, simply empowers the ruler of the world in his deceptions, not least in driving more and more young people, often struggling with issues of personal identity, into further confusion and dysfunction in their sexuality.

It is commonly believed that sexual orientation is genetically determined and therefore unchangeable, but this assumption is not based on fact. Studies have shown that social and environmental factors play a larger part in the development of homosexual attraction than genetic factors do. If one of two identical twins (with the same DNA) has this attraction, there is only a 20 to 30 per cent chance of the other being the same. If it was entirely genetically determined, that figure would be closer to 100 per cent.[20] We do carry certain spiritually inherited tendencies, for the Bible tells us that we are all born carrying generational iniquity (Psalm 51:5), but it is during our lives that wounding most often occurs.[21]

Even though it may be very hard at times not to give in to a distorted sexual attraction, or indeed to any other wrong compulsion, seeking to abide by God's created order will always be the right thing to do. God unconditionally loves all people, irrespective of their so-called sexual orientation, but His desire is to restore His order through His healing, not to encourage human disorder. Many disagree with this biblical point of view, but God's laws and commands, if they were truly acknowledged and embraced, would result in a world of remarkable well-being for humankind, not least in the area of sexual identity.

See Bisexuality, Homosexuality, Human Spirit, Identity, Lesbianism, Pedophilia, Sexuality, Sexual Sin, Transgender

Sexual Sin – behaviors and attitudes which are contrary to God's commands for the expression of our sexuality.

The Bible clearly states that some sexual activities are sinful, such as fornication, homosexual behavior and adultery. Whilst acknowledging these, Jesus challenges His followers to an even higher standard of sexual purity as they allow His righteousness increasingly to change and cleanse their lives.

> Matthew 5:27–28... You have heard that it was said, "YOU SHALL NOT COMMIT ADULTERY"; but I say to you that everyone who looks at a woman with lust for her has already committed adultery with her in his heart. (NASB)

Other areas of sexual sin are less explicitly mentioned in the Bible, although for those who are truly seeking sexual purity, it is not hard

SEXUAL SIN

to understand which sexual attractions and activities are not right with God. He wants us always to be spiritually well covered for our protection, not least when we are sexually exposed. We are fully responsible for our sin, but it is clear that generations of iniquity, particularly idolatry, have defiled our lives today and brought disorder and pressure in sexual attraction and practice.

> Romans 1:20–24... For since the creation of the world His invisible attributes, His eternal power and divine nature, have been clearly seen ... even though they knew God, they did not honor Him ... and their foolish heart was darkened. ... they became fools, and exchanged the glory of the incorruptible God for an image in the form of corruptible man and of birds and four-footed animals and crawling creatures. Therefore God gave them over in the lusts of their hearts to impurity, so that their bodies would be dishonored among them. (NASB)

Our bodies are dishonored, even within marriage, when they are used in ways for which God clearly did not design them. This would be the case for penetrative anal or oral sex, for example. There is even increasing medical evidence that these activities can be harmful, for example causing mouth cancer by transmitting the HPV virus.[22] There is also the significant issue of spiritual bondage. We have many times seen deliverance in people's lives when there has been confession of this type of sexual intimacy which has been dishonoring to God's creation of our bodies.

> 1 Corinthians 6:20... For you have been bought with a price: therefore glorify God in your body. (NASB)

When someone is struggling with drivenness to sexual sin, in order to help them to be truly free, very often it will be important to look behind the driven behaviors of today to discover the wounding and sexual distortion which has occurred through their early years.

I remember praying with a young man who was terribly controlled by masturbation and sexual fantasy. From the age of six, he had frequently been sat in front of pornographic videos by an auntie who looked after him when his parents were working. The process of God's healing started with a deep and difficult forgiveness of both his parents and the auntie for so carelessly corrupting his sexuality at such a young age. As he then received God's forgiveness for his own sin, he found a wonderful new freedom and release from the demonic bondage that had so defiled his life.

See Adultery, Covenant, Fornication, Homosexuality, Lesbianism, Marriage, Masturbation, Pedophilia, Pornography, Sex, Sexual Orientation, Soul-tie

Sexually Transmitted Disease – physical infection passed from one person to another through sexual intimacy.

There are more than thirty forms of bacterial or viral disorders that can be transmitted through sexual intimacy.[23] Not all of these are prevented by the use of a condom. The world increasingly laughs at rightful sexual abstinence, but if all humankind operated according to God's laws and commands, there would only be godly sexual intimacy within a faithful marriage, and no opportunity for transmission of such diseases.

However, unfortunately there is much sin in this area of human activity and much physical consequence, not least in the serious damage to reproductive organs in some who may wish to have children in the future. God has provided help through wonderful medical treatment to counteract disease, but we also need to come to Him for cleansing from spiritual defilement which may well have deeper and more lasting effects, not just on ourselves but on our offspring. Sexual sin sows iniquity into the lives of those affected, and also into their generational inheritance.

Only through the forgiveness of God can this unrighteousness be completely put right:

> 1 John 1:8–9... If we say that we have no sin, we are deceiving ourselves and the truth is not in us. If we confess our sins, He is faithful and righteous to forgive us our sins and to cleanse us from all unrighteousness. (NASB)

See Cleansing, Contraception, Marriage, Order, Safe Sex, Sexual Sin, Soul-tie

Shame (Shameful) – deep emotion in response to spiritual or physical exposure.

Shame is more a condition of the human spirit than just a feeling in the soul. It may start as an emotion, but if left unresolved, can soon become a hold on a person's identity, leading them to believe that they are actually a shameful person.

Exposure which leads me to experience shame can come from a number of sources: my own sin, my apparent inadequacy, the revealing of my mistakes, the abuse of others, the ridicule of others, the betrayal of others, or from my carrying the burden of family sin or humiliation (in the area of poverty, for example).

> Proverbs 12:4... An excellent wife is the crown of her husband, But she who shames him is like rottenness in his bones. (NASB)

Shame can affect every part of our being, including our beliefs, our relationships, our security in the Lord, and even our physical posture. It can sometimes lead to self-harming, people-pleasing, withdrawal, and loss of creativity and joy.

> Ezra 9:6... O my God, I am ashamed and embarrassed to lift up my face to You, my God, for our iniquities have risen above our heads and our guilt has grown even to the heavens. (NASB)

However, it is very important to be sure of the source of the shame which we carry. Where it is truly the result of our own sin, our confession and God's forgiveness will bring precious release, but where the sin really belongs to the behavior of others who have imposed a cloak of shame on us, we need to acknowledge and renounce the false garment which we have been wearing and forgive those who have been the cause of our exposure. A burden of shame can also come to us from historical abuse which was suffered by, or perpetrated by, our family or even our nation, for example, by those connected with slavery or war crimes.

Jesus was very willing to carry the guilt and shame of sinful humanity, but He rejected the shame which those around the cross wrongly tried to heap onto Him, in the humiliating exposure of His body.

> Hebrews 12:2… fixing our eyes on Jesus, the author and perfecter of faith, who for the joy set before Him endured the cross, despising the shame, and has sat down at the right hand of the throne of God. (NASB)

See Addiction, Core Belief, Covering, Emotion, Guilt, Humiliation, Identity, Inadequacy, Sin

Sickness (Sick) – disease in any part of the human body, contrary to God's order.

It is clear from the Bible that disease is not God's desire for His children. His covenant promises have always included the removal of sickness from His people (Deuteronomy 7:12–15). This was affirmed through the prophets (Isaiah 53:4-5), and then fulfilled, and clearly demonstrated, through Jesus.

> Matthew 8:17… He did this to make come true what the prophet Isaiah had said, "He himself took our sickness and carried away our diseases." (GNB)

Ever since the Fall, there has been contamination of God's creation through humankind's constant rejection of God's commandments. This has been continued by every person who has lived on earth, with the exception of Jesus. That is why death could not hold Jesus after the cross, but there is an inevitable physical deterioration for all other human beings culminating, at some point, in physical death. By God's grace, medical treatment has wonderfully constrained the effects of disease, but only Jesus can truly restore God's spiritual order in the human body (Matthew 5:3), and this gives opportunity for divine deliverance and healing. Of course, God can heal anyone through His sovereign choice, but when Jesus restores God's spiritual order in our lives, very often physical healing will follow as a natural consequence.

Today, each one of us is reaping, spiritually and physically, the consequence of the corporate human iniquity that was sown over past generations, with our own iniquity added to it. At some point, sickness in the body will end in death, but before that time, God is glorified when we come to Him in faith and seek His restoration of divine order and thus His healing of the lives of His children (John 11:4). The mysteries of the spiritual and physical realms mean that God alone knows why sometimes we see His healing and sometimes we do not. Therefore, we can only trust that God fully knows what is truly right, and that He will always answer the essence of our prayers in His way.

See Body, Covenant, Deliverance, Generational Iniquity, Healing, Order

Significance (Significant) – importance and purpose.

God created us to be highly significant. We were designed to walk in His delegated authority as rulers of this created world.

> Psalm 8:4–6... What is man that You take thought of him, And the son of man that You care for him? Yet You have made him a little lower than God, And you crown him with glory and majesty! You make him to rule over the works of Your hands; You have put all things under his feet ... (NASB)

At the Fall, humankind gave that authority over to Satan and sin separated us from an intimate walk with God. Consequently, the true knowledge of our significance in God's creation was lost to us, in the darkness that enveloped our human spirits.

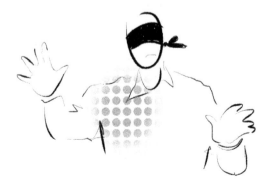

Unconscious of this fallen condition, people without Jesus strive to find a substitute for the significance for which we were all created, but when limited to human wisdom, this striving is directed at goals such as status, position, wealth, control, prestige, image, celebrity, notoriety, intellect, or perceived success of family or friendships. Through the cross, our true significance has been redeemed and made known to us through the Holy Spirit.

> Romans 8:16... The Spirit Himself testifies with our spirit that we are children of God ... (NASB)

In Christ Jesus, we are covenant children of God, a royal priesthood with direct access to the King of kings, anointed members of the Body of Christ on earth, operating with His authority and power to further God's Kingdom and take spiritual ground from the evil ruler of the world (Luke 10:18–19).

Whatever the wounding experiences of life have taught us to the contrary, we *are* hugely significant as followers of Jesus. We have nothing to prove to the world about our importance, and we may need to confess and be cleansed from the sinful strivings of the past. We can simply rest in a deepening conviction that as children of God, we are part of an amazing divine purpose, each with a special place and special gifting. May the Lord heal each one of us from the past so that we can move into the fullness of our future destiny.

See Carnal Nature, Destiny, the Fall, Fruit, Gifts of the Holy Spirit, Image, Value

Sin (Sinful, Sinfulness) – belief or behavior which opposes God's laws and commands.

> 1 John 3:4... Everyone who practices sin also practices lawlessness; and sin is lawlessness. (NASB)

Sin is not an acceptable concept for most of the world today because it requires a belief that divine law is the arbiter of what is right, rather than human reason. When we are determining justice, humanism and the declaration of humanity's apparent natural rights have largely replaced the biblical notion of sin. But without an external plumb line, a wall cannot be assessed for vertical straightness. So it is with humankind; without the plumb line of God's truth about sin, there is no way we can determine what is actually right or wrong (Romans 7:7). Sin not only places humankind outside of the covenant protection of God and separates us from God (Isaiah 59:2), but it can also lead to spiritual slavery (John 8:34) and demonic bondage. Actually, sin is a life-stealer!

> Ephesians 2:1–2... And you were dead in your trespasses and sins, in which you formerly walked according to the course of this world, according to the prince of the power of the air, of the spirit that is now working in the sons of disobedience. (NASB)

Sin has deeply damaged and defiled God's creation. All disorder, sickness and natural disasters are rooted in the corporate sin of humankind since the Fall (Genesis 3:17; Leviticus 18:24–25; Leviticus 26:14–16; Hosea 4:1–3; John 5:14; Revelation 21:3–4).

The good news is that God has provided an answer through His Son, Jesus. All the spiritual cost and consequence of sin has been met by Him at the cross. If we accept that He represented us there, and if we confess the reality of our sin and turn from it, we can be completely forgiven and He is able to cleanse us from all the unrighteousness that is affecting our lives (1 John 1:9).

Hundreds of New Age and alternative therapies purport to improve our spiritual condition, but not one of them deals with the root issue, which is sin. Society prefers to excuse sin rather than to confront it. Humanist thinking concludes that we should be able to do whatever we like provided that it does not harm others, but sin is like a poison which contaminates the public reservoir, lowering the spiritual health of families and, indeed, whole communities.

Thank God that Jesus, who did *not* sin, was willing to be punished on behalf of all of us who *have* sinned, so that we can go free. Jesus has rightly been called the friend of sinners but the enemy of sin.

> 1 John 3:5... You know that He appeared in order to take away sins; and in Him there is no sin. (NASB)

See Commandment, Confession, Debt, Defilement, Forgiveness, Freedom, Iniquity, Justice, Law, Punishment, Rebellion, a Right, Righteousness

SINFUL NATURE

Sinful Nature – see Carnal Nature

Sinlessness (Sinless) – condition of being completely right with God, in all beliefs and behaviors.

Only one person has walked the earth in this condition, namely Jesus Christ who, though tempted as we are, did not sin (Hebrews 4:15). He alone was able to say that the enemy had absolutely no foothold in His life through which to control Him.

> John 14:30… I will not speak much more with you, for the ruler of the world is coming, and he has nothing in Me … (NASB)

The Bible records Job as blameless (Job 2:3) seemingly because He kept a short account with God in all his activities, but he was not sinless. Indeed, he eventually admitted that he had been trying to argue his position with God from a place of arrogance concerning his own wisdom (Job 42:1–6). Owning our sinfulness is the first step to finding freedom and cleansing.

> 1 John 1:8–9… If we say that we have no sin, we are deceiving ourselves and the truth is not in us. If we confess our sins, He is faithful and righteous to forgive us our sins and to cleanse us from all unrighteousness. (NASB)

See Blame, Confession, Foothold, Righteousness, Sin, Temptation

Singleness – condition of being unmarried.

There are many attitudes toward the issue of singleness, and some of these can be unhelpful and even harmful. It is interesting to note that no one will be given in marriage throughout our eternal resurrected existence, except, of course, as part of the bride of the Lamb. In his belief that the days were urgent for committed service to the Lord, Paul addressed the issue of singleness. In a very forthright way, he wrestled with the cost and the benefit of married life. He did not oppose marriage, but concluded that the state of singleness, such as his own, could be an advantage.

> 1 Corinthians 7:32–34a… I would like you to be free from worry. An unmarried man concerns himself with the LORD's work, because

SINGLENESS

> he is trying to please the LORD. But a married man concerns himself
> with worldly matters, because he wants to please his wife; and so he
> is pulled in two directions... (GNB)

Earlier in the same chapter, Paul implies that his own ability to be
settled with, and indeed delight in, a life of singleness was a personal
gift from God. A specific gifting for this way of living may indeed be
experienced by some believers as they seek to walk in the destiny of
their lives. However, for many single people such a calling and gifting
are not personally evident, as they hold in their hearts a rightful
desire to be married, whether this is for the first time or after loss of
a spouse.

Marriage is good, God-ordained, an expression of covenant and a safe
place for procreation. It is not wrong to look forward to these things,
but the challenge is to find true peace with God whether in singleness or
in marriage. In fact, it is important within the Body of Christ for all of
us to fully respect both states, seeing neither as inferior nor undesirable,
but fully welcoming each other as valid members of God's family. We
all need kindness and sometimes help from one another, in both words
and actions.

One thing should be made particularly clear: an unmarried person is
no less complete in their personal identity and no less spiritually covered
than a married person. Our completeness in God and the extent of His
protection over our lives are a consequence of our covenant relationship
with Him within the Body of Christ, not dependent on our conjugal
state. Marriage brings a special and very intimate relationship with
another person of the opposite sex, providing a new place of God's
covering, not least through His intended order between a husband and
his wife (Ephesians 5:22–33). However, Jesus does not say that marriage
is the ultimate fulfillment of our earthly lives. He was the most complete
man ever to have walked the earth, experiencing all the normal human
desires, but he remained single.

Sometimes singleness has become wrongly settled in people's lives,
for example, through the wounding of abuse, the fear of intimacy, the
unresolved pain of previous betrayal, an imagined gift of singleness,
or occasionally through pronouncements and curses coming from
themselves or others, including ancestors. It is good for single people to
forgive those who have spoken out or acted toward them in opposition
to God's ordinance for marriage, also confessing unhelpful personal

377

fears and attitudes. This opens the door to all that God has prepared for their lives.

> Jeremiah 29:11... I alone know the plans I have for you, plans to bring you prosperity and not disaster, plans to bring about the future you hope for. (GNB)

For those walking in singleness but retaining a desire for marriage, there will often be pain associated with loneliness, disappointment, the unfulfilled hope for sexual intimacy and parenthood, and often a sense of isolation even within the church. Jesus understands all these difficult areas. He asks those troubled by such issues to place their singleness fully into His hands, seeking God's perfect plan for their comfort, fruitfulness and fulfillment of destiny.

See Covering, Destiny, Disappointment, Fruitfulness, Gifting, Identity, Intimacy, Loneliness, Marriage, Pronouncement, Sexuality, Virginity

Slavery – possession and control of a human life by someone else.

Any abusive control by a person over another human being is contrary to God's order (Ephesians 6:9). Throughout history, there has frequently been ownership of slaves by those who gained power over others, whether by victory in battle or by forceful abduction. The Bible does, in fact, consider the possibility of someone choosing to continue to be enslaved to a benevolent master, as a way of ensuring provision and protection (Deuteronomy 15:16–17), but it is almost inevitable that any practice of slavery will license abuse, and lead to profound degradation for the one who is owned. God will never condone this. There is slavery in many parts of the world today, even the developed world, particularly through issues such as people trafficking for prostitution, and we would do well to pray and work against this.

Where a person has a family history of slavery, they may well find themselves carrying some associated generational spiritual effects, such as difficulties with identity, rejection, rebellion, anger or shame. God can cleanse this disabling inheritance as

we walk in the grace of forgiveness and the transforming truth that we are God's sons and daughters.

In our present world, many modern forms of slavery exist in the dark, but at the time when Jesus walked the earth it was acknowledged as a very common and visible fact of life in a world of Roman supremacy. At that time, Jesus and Paul did not directly challenge the existence of slavery, although Paul clearly taught that all men are of equal status before God (Galatians 3:28). Rather, the divine challenge which they considered most important to bring was about human hearts. They spoke to those who, for whatever reason, were involved in this way of life, about how it so easily encouraged wrongful attitudes (Philemon 1:10–18). Many of the same challenges will face employers and employees today (Ephesians 6:5–9).

As well as physical slavery, there is also the important issue of spiritual slavery, which is the result of sin.

> John 8:34...Jesus answered them, "Truly, truly, I say to you, everyone who commits sin is the slave of sin." (NASB)

When we allow any sinful practice to control and direct an area of our lives, we effectively take that part of ourselves out of the hands of our heavenly Father and place it into the hands, or under the spiritual authority, of the rebellious ruler of the world (Romans 6:16). Satan is, without doubt, a slave master, using his army of slave drivers, the powers of darkness, to hold us in obedience to his demands (2 Peter 2:19).

But God did not create us to be fearful slaves of a condemning and destructive enemy, but rather to be secure sons and daughters of the One who loves us unconditionally (Romans 8:15). It is our choice as to whether we walk as slaves or sons in every area of our lives.

> Galatians 4:8–11... In the past you did not know God, and so you were slaves of beings who are not gods. But now that you know God – or, I should say, now that God knows you – how is it that you want to turn back to those weak and pitiful ruling spirits? Why do you want to become their slaves all over again? You pay special attention to certain days, months, seasons, and years. I am worried about you! Can it be that all my work for you has been for nothing? (GNB)

SMOKING

We know that complete freedom comes when we confess sinful mind-sets and behaviors, and so receive God's forgiveness and deliverance.

> Galatians 5:1... It was for freedom that Christ set us free; therefore keep standing firm and do not be subject again to a yoke of slavery. (NASB)

See Body Piercing, Condemnation, Control, Deliverance, Fear, Foothold, Freedom, Phobia, False Religious Practice, Shame, Sin, Soul-tie, Yoke

Smoking (Smoke) – breathing in the smoke of a burning substance in order to experience some pleasurable effect.

Smoking has long been associated, in many ancient cultures, with providing a means of connection to the spirit realm. While today's smokers may not be seeking any such spiritual hold on their lives, they do make themselves vulnerable to both physical and spiritual damage through a behavior which is known to be contrary to the well-being of the body.

Depending on the substance used, most commonly tobacco, smoking can be highly addictive due to chemical and emotional dependence, and also due to spiritual bondage. This spiritual bondage is the result of rights which the person has given to the enemy through implied rebellion against God by their choice to repeatedly harm a precious human body which God has created (1 Corinthians 6:20). Thank God that Jesus has authority over all that would seek to hold our lives captive, and so true healing, deliverance and release from the 'family of smokers' is available for all those who are ready to confess and repent of this destructive habit.

> 1 Corinthians 6:12... All things are lawful for me, but not all things are profitable. All things are lawful for me, but I will not be mastered by anything. (NASB)

It will be helpful to reflect on the reason, the place and the people associated with the start of any smoking habit. This will allow us an opportunity to forgive others as appropriate and to release soul-ties in the spiritual realms with anyone who was involved, including with the tobacco suppliers. There is no condemnation from God, nor should there be from fellow believers, if we are finding it hard to stop smoking. However, God loves us too much to leave this damaging activity unchallenged and unchanged.

See Addiction, Comfort, Dependence, Rebellion, Self-hatred, Shame, Soul-tie

Son of God – one of the messianic titles for Jesus, affirming His divinity.

He is one of the three persons who make up the Trinity, and was sent into the world to save humankind from the consequence of sin (John 3:16–17). He is the exact representation of the nature of God (Hebrews 1:3), holding supreme authority in heaven and on earth (Matthew 28:18), high above the evil ruler of the world, and able to pardon and cleanse all those who recognize and follow Him.

> Matthew 16:16–17... Simon Peter answered, "You are the Christ, the Son of the living God." And Jesus said to him, "Blessed are you, Simon Barjona, because flesh and blood did not reveal this to you, but My Father who is in heaven." (NASB)

I have heard it described that Jesus, as He walked the earth, was all of God that could be poured into a human life without disrupting its perfect humanity (Colossians 2:9). The divinity of Jesus was essential because He had to truly represent God in the forgiveness released at the cross. In doing so, He established the New Covenant between God and humanity. He was the perfect representative of God, as well as of humankind, at the moment that this wonderful covenant was sealed. The death of just a good man was not enough.

See Christ, Covenant, God, Jesus, Salvation, Trinity

Son of Man – one of the messianic titles for Jesus, affirming His humanity.

The Bible tells us that Jesus was born as a human being, a legitimate (although not necessarily genetic) descendant of Adam (Luke 3:23–38; 1 Corinthians 15:45,47), for only such a person could undo the mistake that Adam had made. In the same way, Jesus was also a legitimate descendent of King David and so He fulfilled the prophecy that there would be one in David's family line with whom God would establish an everlasting kingdom (2 Samuel 7:12–13). God became a member of the human family through Jesus Christ. As He walked the earth, He was the perfect representative of humankind, how God intended each one of us to be, fully obedient to His heavenly Father, the complete image of God in a man. He represented us at the cross, paying for our sin with His death, and establishing a New Covenant between God and humanity.

> Luke 18:31... Then [Jesus] took the twelve aside and said to them, "Behold, we are going up to Jerusalem, and all things which are written through the prophets about the Son of Man will be accomplished." (NASB)

See   Christ, Covenant, God, Jesus, Salvation, Trinity

Soul – See Human Soul

Soulishness (Soulish) – giving dominance to the sinful attitudes of our soul rather than to God's wisdom through our human spirit.

> James 3:14–15... But if in your heart you are jealous, bitter, and selfish, don't sin against the truth by boasting of your wisdom. Such wisdom does not come down from heaven; it belongs to the world, it is unspiritual and demonic. (GNB)

The word *unspiritual* in this passage is a translation of the Greek word *psuchikos* (from *psuche* meaning *soul*), referring to the responses in humanity which come more from the self-centered human *soul* than from the God-centered human *spirit*.

The soul expresses our earth-centered life, including our mind, will and emotions. Our soul is designed by God to be submitted to the direction of our human spirit, which receives life and truth through the Holy Spirit (Job 32:7-8).

The problem is that from the wounding experiences of life, the human spirit can be defiled (2 Corinthians 7:1), crushed and broken (Psalm 34:18), even though we have been born again of the Holy Spirit. Driven by our carnal nature, the soul then takes over leadership of our lives in place of our damaged human spirit. The soul uses human wisdom to try to make sense of and to compensate for the distorted beliefs and damaged identity which are rooted in the human spirit. Our soul tends to assume a place of dominance and self-protection, thus opposing the truth and direction of the Holy Spirit. This tendency can be termed as soulish and, if sustained, it will give the enemy an opportunity. He will use his power to strengthen our unrighteous beliefs and behaviors, eventually doing considerable damage to our lives.

When we recognize that our carnal nature will always try to draw us into making soulish responses to the painful experiences of life, we can increasingly make determined choices to follow the wisdom of God, seeking His comfort and His protection rather than following human wisdom. For many of us, it has become an unconscious and damaging lifestyle to self-comfort and self-protect rather than to face our deep inner wounds with the help of the Holy Spirit, who truly knows our needs.

> 1 Corinthians 2:12,14... But we have not received the spirit of the world, but the Spirit from God ... But a natural [soulish] man does not receive the things of the Spirit of God, for they are foolishness to him ... (LITV)

See Carnal Nature, Human Spirit, Human Soul, Selfishness, Self-protection

Soul-tie – unseen spiritual bond which joins people in relationships.

Such bonds can be *good*, as with David in his covenant agreement with his friend Jonathan:

> 1 Samuel 18:1... the soul of Jonathan was knitted with the soul of David; and Jonathan loved him as his own soul. (LITV)

or *bad*, as with Jacob in the wrong dependency on his favorite son, Benjamin:

> Genesis 44:30–31... [Jacob's] soul being bound to [Benjamin's] soul, it will be when [Jacob] sees that the youth [Benjamin] is not [with us], he [Jacob] will die. ... (LITV)

Good (godly) soul-ties are healthy. They become established in good relationships such as rightful marriage, sincere friendships, and particularly through the loving bonds intended within the Body of Christ (Philippians 2:1–2).

Bad (ungodly) soul-ties are unhealthy (Proverbs 5:22). They are a consequence of wrong relationships which are contrary to God's order, regardless of whether or not the person had a choice about the relationship.

These spiritually damaging bonds can be established where there has been, for example, wrong control, intimidation, sexual sin, pornography, unhealthy emotional dependence, false healing techniques, unlawful conspiracy, blood exchange, shared worship of false gods, occult rituals, ungodly covenants, shared addictive behavior or an ungodly connection with someone at the time of their death.

Bad ties, particularly, control the human soul (the way we think, how we feel, the choices we make), but can also cause significant damage to the human spirit and the physical body (Proverbs 5:3,8–9; Proverbs 14:30). Such ties can cause anxiety, spiritual defilement, emotional distress, mental confusion and physical disorder. Although unseen, these soul-ties can be felt by the participants. For Christians, good soul-ties will strengthen their walk with God, especially in relationship with others in the Body of Christ, but where the ties are bad, they will pull them away from their unity in Christ.

Release from an ungodly soul-tie is like the removal of an unseen oppressive yoke, which has been pushing and pulling us through the wrong linking to another person. The controlling relationship between Jacob and Esau, for example, is described as a yoke (Genesis 27:40). As we confess our own sin in any wrong relationship in the past or present, and forgive those who have had a wrongful control over our lives, we can lay claim to the freedom that Jesus has provided for us at the cross. We may also need to seek the Lord's restoration to the soul and human spirit where the tie has distorted our thinking, feelings, choices or personal identity. The enemy can demonically empower the spiritual darkness of ungodly soul-ties, so once the bondage is broken, deliverance from controlling demons may be necessary. Physical healing can also follow from this new place of spiritual freedom.

> Isaiah 58:6... Is not this the fast that I have chosen? to loose the bands of wickedness, to undo the heavy burdens, and to let the oppressed go free, and that ye break every yoke? (KJV)

See Bondage, Codependence, Control, Freedom, Loosing, Relationship, Sexual Sin, Unclean Spirit

Spell – See Charm, Curse

Spirit – a being in the eternal, heavenly, invisible realm.

God, who is Himself Spirit (John 4:24), has created every being, whether in heaven or on earth (Colossians 1:16). Through rebellion against His commands, the spiritual realm is partly in darkness, inhabited by a hierarchy of fallen spiritual beings, including Satan, angels and unclean spirits (Ephesians 6:12).

> Jude 6 ... And angels who did not keep their own domain, but abandoned their proper abode, He has kept in eternal bonds under darkness for the judgment of the great day ... (NASB)

The majority of spiritual beings in the heavenly realm are not fallen. They are living in light, and this angelic host serves God in true obedience to His commands.

> Hebrews 1:14... What are the angels, then? They are spirits who serve God and are sent by him to help those who are to receive salvation. (GNB)

SPIRITUAL

While in this life, human beings are created to operate in both the spiritual realm and in the physical world. C.S. Lewis wrote: *"It is since Christians have largely ceased to think of the other world that they have become so ineffective in this."*[24] God breathed into each one of us a human spirit (Zechariah 12:1) which, because of the Fall, exists in spiritual darkness until we are born again of the Holy Spirit. Salvation is the process of rescuing us from spiritual darkness and then removing the residual darkness from the whole of our being, expelling any unclean spirits which are inhabiting that darkness (Acts 26:18; 1 John 2:9).

See Angel, Holy Spirit, Human Spirit, Ruling Spirit, Unclean Spirit.

Spiritual – existing in the non-physical realm, the eternal realm of God's creation.

Our covenant relationship with God through Jesus Christ takes us, individually and corporately, beyond just our physical existence into a significant interaction with God in the eternal realm. We are citizens now of the Kingdom of His Son, transferred from out of the enemy's spiritual domain, the realm of the powers of darkness (Colossians 1:13).

> 1 Peter 2:5... you also, as living stones, are being built up as a spiritual house for a holy priesthood, to offer up spiritual sacrifices acceptable to God through Jesus Christ. (NASB)

See Angel, Darkness, Eternal, Kingdom, Light, Spirit, Unclean Spirit

Spiritualism (Spiritism) – occult practice, interpreting spiritual phenomena through the use of a medium.

This practice is frequently associated with seeking to make contact with dead relatives for the purpose of bringing comfort or guidance. It is most likely that if the medium is not actively deceiving the clients, he or she is actually linking with demonic powers which have some knowledge of the person who has died. To participate in spiritualism, and in particular to act as a medium for the powers of darkness, or possibly for the human spirit of a dead person, is spiritually dangerous and defiling territory, and is strictly forbidden by God for His covenant people. Those who have been affected by these practices can, of course, always come to the Lord for His forgiveness and cleansing.

> Deuteronomy 18:10–11... There shall not be found among you anyone who ... casts a spell, or a medium, or a spiritist, or one who calls up the dead. (NASB)

See Ancestral Worship, False Religion, Human Spirit, Necromancy, Occult, Powers of Darkness, Unclean Spirit

Spiritual Warfare (Spiritual Battle) – battle for freedom from the powers of darkness.

When Jesus was teaching His disciples how to pray, He made it very clear that they would be part of a serious battle – a battle for their freedom from the spiritual domain of the Evil One, and so become progressively secure in God's Kingdom on earth.

> Matthew 6:10,13... may your Kingdom come; may your will be done on earth as it is in heaven. ... Do not bring us to hard testing, but keep us safe from the Evil One. (GNB)

> Ephesians 6:12... For we are not fighting against flesh-and-blood enemies, but against evil rulers and authorities of the unseen world, against mighty powers in this dark world, and against evil spirits in the heavenly places. (NLT)

The battle and victory against the unseen ruler of the world belongs to the Lord (2 Chronicles 20:15), but our response to God, through proclamation of truth, through confession of sin and through intercession, can significantly affect the enemy's spiritual authority over people's lives. Jesus has secured a complete defeat over the enemy (Colossians 2:15), but at the present time, the powers of darkness still have the right to control that part of human life which opposes the commands of God (Ephesians 4:26–27). Satan demanded such a right to sift Peter's life in order to expose the reality of his uncertain relationship with Jesus.

> Luke 22:31... Simon, Simon, behold, Satan has demanded permission to sift you like wheat ... (NASB)

It can be painful to face sin issues in our lives and to become aware of the defiling presence of the enemy, but this can also be a precious opportunity to let the conviction and forgiveness of God bring another powerful step in His victory over enemy-held ground. When the authority of the enemy is removed, all demonic power can also be expelled. Furthermore, if we carry spiritual responsibility for families, fellowships, places or even nations, our personal agreement with God about our sin can bring opportunity for further freedom for all those under our spiritual covering.

Intercession, which is dialogue and agreement with God on behalf of others, is always a safe and powerful instrument of spiritual warfare. However, direct challenges to the powers of darkness should only be undertaken when the enemy's authority has been clearly overruled, through God's forgiveness being received by those who have confessed relevant personal sin issues.

It is not the strength or complexity of our words that defeat the enemy, but only our complete surrender to the One who does have all knowledge, authority and power over Satan. Christians can regard themselves more as soldiers than civilians (2 Timothy 2:3). It is a military principle that to be *in* rightful authority we must be *under* rightful authority (Luke 7:8). By following and obeying Jesus, we come under the One who has been given all authority in heaven and on earth (Matthew 28:18).

See Authority, Deliverance, Intercession, Kingdom, Power, Powers of Darkness, Satan, Tongues

Stress (Stressful) – condition of the human spirit, soul or body resulting from carrying a burden.

It is inevitable that the weighty issues of life will cause tension or pressure and therefore stress in our bodies, but if we carry these loads simply in our own strength, the consequence can be that we become distressed or overstressed, and therefore damaged.

The burdens which we carry can be spiritual, mental, emotional or physical, but we need to make sure that we are not carrying responsibilities which Jesus has not given us to carry. He explains this by the picture of a yoke, an age-old method by which loads have been carried by people and animals. He encourages us to put down all that we may have wrongly carried in the past. Instead, He calls us to take up the yoke and loading which are fully under His authority and which are right for our bodies.

> Matthew 11:28–30... Come to me, all of you who are tired from carrying heavy loads, and I will give you rest. Take my yoke and put it on you, and learn from me, because I am gentle and humble in spirit; and you will find rest. For the yoke I will give you is easy, and the load I will put on you is light. (GNB)

Even if we are carrying the right loads today, inner distress can also occur as a result of unresolved past damage in our soul and spirit. Take the example of a steel beam carrying a heavy load, which can become overstressed if there are tiny cracks or impurities in the microscopic structure of the steel. These cracks are usually only discovered by special instruments or, unfortunately, by collapse! In the same way, the wholeness and purity of our hearts can be damaged through the wounds we have received, together with our wrong choices; for example, wounding through abuse or the wrong choice of an addictive practice.

Only God is able to see and show us the condition of our hearts, damaged by the iniquity of this world. Like the hidden weak spots in a steel beam, these places of damage to our soul and spirit affect the integrity of our whole being and reduce our ability to withstand the pressures of life.

> Proverbs 18:14... The spirit of a man will sustain his infirmity; but a wounded spirit who can bear? (KJV)

Thankfully, God not only knows our hearts, but He is able and willing to repair and bring peace to the places where integrity and purity have been lost. As He shows us the wounds, the sins and the enemy holds, we can forgive and be forgiven, be cleansed and strengthened in these inner parts so that the yoke and burdens of Jesus are indeed easy, light and not stressful.

Psalm 118:5... In my distress I called to the LORD; he answered me and set me free. (GNB)

See Brokenness, Burnout, Distress, Human Soul, Human Spirit, Iniquity, Peace, Sin, Wounding, Yoke

Stronghold – significant place of iniquity in our personal or corporate lives, which the enemy holds under his spiritual authority.

Often, as a result of the wounding that we have experienced in life, we can become bound into beliefs and behaviors which are out of line with God, but which have become our way of coping with distress or our way of seeking to defend ourselves from further damage. The carnal nature draws us toward fear, unbelief, pride, rebellion, cynicism, rejection or self-pity, for example. When these become our established ways of response to life, the enemy is given license to strengthen these problems with demonic power and to establish strongholds in these sinful aspects of our character. Any change from this position can seem hopelessly impossible. A stronghold has been described in this way: *a mindset impregnated with hopelessness that causes us to accept as unchangeable situations that we know are contrary to the will of God*[25].

From a geographical view of the spiritual battle, the concept of strongholds, governed by ruling spirits, may relate to spiritual territory given over to the enemy as a result of corporate sin, such as a city area of prostitution or a location where various New Age establishments are grouped together in a particular place.

In our personal lives, simply trying to behave better will only mask the underlying issues. We need the strength of God to oppose these enemy fortresses (Psalm 9:9). As we truly acknowledge sin, receive the forgiveness of God, and allow the Holy Spirit to heal the wounds and renew our minds, the strongholds can indeed be torn down. The battle and victory belong to the Lord but we need to demonstrate very clearly, individually and sometimes corporately, whom we follow on the battlefield.

2 Corinthians 10:4–5... (For the weapons of our warfare are not carnal, but mighty through God to the pulling down of strong holds;) Casting down imaginations, and every high thing that exalteth itself against the knowledge of God, and bringing into captivity every thought to the obedience of Christ ... (KJV)

See Carnal Nature, Coping Mechanism, Defense Mechanism, Deliverance, Foothold, Mindset, Ruling Spirit, Spiritual Warfare

Success (Successful) – meeting a standard, whether in appearance, ability or behavior.

Jesus has declared a completely different measure of success from that of the world. He says that by following Him and His teaching, we become increasingly successful by the criteria of His Kingdom, and we can be completely free from all the pain and shame of failure in the past. He invites us to identify ourselves with Himself, the One who has been completely successful.

> 2 Chronicles 31:21… [Hezekiah] was successful, because everything he did for the Temple or in observance of the Law, he did in a spirit of complete loyalty and devotion to his God. (GNB)

C.S. Lewis wrote: *"It is not your business to succeed, but to do right: when you have done so the rest lies with God."*[26]

See Destiny, Failure, Identity, Self-confidence, Significance, Value, Vision

Suffering (Suffer) – painful consequence of disorder in this world.

We suffer because of the Fall, because of the sinful actions of others, because of accidents, because of loss and because of our own sin. Jesus suffered on the cross to the point of death because of His choice to pay the full cost of human sin and to carry all the resulting suffering and pain on behalf of the entire human race.

> Isaiah 53:4–5... But he endured the suffering that should have been ours, the pain that we should have borne. All the while we thought that his suffering was punishment sent by God. But because of our sins he was wounded, beaten because of the evil we did. We are healed by the punishment he suffered, made whole by the blows he received. (GNB)

Jesus does not promise His followers a life that is free of trouble (John 16:33), but He says that under His rule we can know a deep peace even while carrying the toughest burdens.

> Matthew 11:29... Take My yoke upon you and learn from Me, for I am gentle and humble in heart, and YOU WILL FIND REST FOR YOUR SOULS. (NASB)

To be a disciple of Jesus sets our lives squarely against the enemy, which can well mean spiritual hostility from the powers of darkness (Revelation 12:17). However, we need to be careful not to give them any unnecessary opportunity or rights to harm us. Nor should we blame the enemy for our own or other people's carelessness or wrongdoing, and the painful consequences which follow. Satan certainly tempts us to sin and takes advantage of our sin, but we alone make the choices.

Some Christians also believe that willfully exposing themselves to forms of suffering will somehow help atone for sin and identify their lives more fully with Jesus. This is unbiblical and dangerous. It gives the enemy a right to strengthen such a choice with demonic power because by desiring to suffer, they are declaring that without their participation, the suffering and death of Jesus on the cross was somehow insufficient.

Sinful beliefs and behaviors need to be brought to God so that we can receive His forgiveness. All suffering needs to be brought to Him for His healing and comfort, and should not be embraced or endured in an attempt to win His favor. No true father enjoys seeing His children suffer, even though they will inevitably get hurt through disobedience. Suffering is the consequence of all the iniquity in this world, but our heavenly Father will never ask us to make penitential payment to receive His forgiveness and His comfort, because He has loved us so much that the total cost of human sin has been put onto His Son's account (John 3:16).

See Atonement, Comfort, Disobedience, False Guilt, Forgiveness, Healing, Iniquity, Pain, Punishment

Suicide (Suicidal) – death caused by a person intentionally killing themselves.

The Bible says that it is for God, not humanity, to appoint the time of our departure from this earthly life (Ecclesiastes 3:2). The enemy seeks to have power over the life and death of humankind, but for those who walk in agreement with the truths and commands of God, Jesus has made it possible for Satan to be rendered powerless (Hebrews 2:14).

Making a choice to end our lives as a way of dealing with pain or distress is not a decision which agrees with God. It does not stop His love for us but it does put us, in some measure, outside His spiritual covering. It is a choice made in agreement with the enemy, which means it gives him rights to bring his destructive power to bear on all those affected, not just the person who dies or attempts to die. Suicide and attempted suicide will sow iniquity into the spiritual inheritance of families. It also puts the person's loved ones through a major trauma in their bereavement. It is an extreme act of self-rejection or an extreme coping mechanism to deal with pain, often linked to depression, but it is contrary to all that Jesus has declared over our lives.

> John 10:10... The thief comes only to steal and kill and destroy; I came that they may have life, and have it abundantly. (NASB)

To seek to take control of the timing of our death is to hand over spiritual authority to the enemy and to give him a right to empower his control with, say, an unclean spirit of death. To ask others to assist in the ending of our lives is a defilement of their lives, making them vulnerable to the enemy's grip. If we have contemplated or tried suicide, God is always ready to forgive and to cleanse us from all unrighteousness (1 John 1:9). The enemy's power can be expelled once we get right with God.

At times life can be very tough, painful, seemingly hopeless and with no sign of God's rescue from all that assails us. If a person is feeling suicidal, it is important to seek, with God, the roots of these feelings – for example, there may be suppressed anger (Jonah 4:9) – and to find, with the help of trusted Christian brothers and sisters, the deep healing that God can bring. Asking if someone feels suicidal and talking with others about these issues does not increase the likelihood of a person committing suicide. We can join with the psalmist who chose to see things from God's point of view, recognizing that he was dearly and deeply loved despite all the circumstances of life. This scripture can be hugely powerful for those dealing with past or present suicidal thoughts:

> Psalm 118:17–18... I will not die, but live, and tell of the works of the LORD. The LORD has disciplined me severely, but He has not given me over to death. (NASB)

See Death, Depression, Despair, Hopelessness, Life, Pronouncement, Self-rejection

Supernatural – according to spiritual laws, rather than physical laws.

Humankind has been created to exist at the interface of the spiritual and physical realms. When we walk in obedience to God, our Creator, it should not be surprising if we regularly experience the supernatural intervention of God into the earthly realm, for example, with revelation, miraculous healing or deliverance.

Supernatural gifts of the Holy Spirit are distributed among believers in Jesus to benefit the Body of Christ on earth in the fulfillment of its destiny (1 Corinthians 12:7). It is indeed very rewarding to be instruments of this divine power (Luke 10:17), and such gifting should be earnestly desired in our daily walk with the Lord (1 Corinthians 14:1).

Unfortunately, human sin has also given authority to Satan and to the powers of darkness to move in supernatural ways through the lives of those walking in disobedience to God. Jesus warns that such deceiving manifestations of the supernatural will increase in these end times, counterfeiting the true signs and wonders of God.

> Matthew 24:24... For false Christs and false prophets will arise and will show great signs and wonders, so as to mislead, if possible, even the elect. (NASB)

Church life in some congregations can be largely devoid of any evidence of the miraculous, so that when a supernatural event does occur it is immediately assumed to be of God. However, it is important to be alert to the schemes of the Evil One (2 Corinthians 2:11), and to seek discernment (1 John 4:1). The enemy is not remotely as powerful as the God of the universe, and the fruit of his character is utterly contrary to that of Jesus (Matthew 7:15–16). However, Satan can give an impressive supernatural display, albeit an eventually destructive one, if we give him license through our naivety or disobedience.

> 1 Peter 5:8... Be of sober spirit, be on the alert. Your adversary, the devil, prowls around like a roaring lion, seeking someone to devour. (NASB)

See Authority, Counterfeit, Deception, Discernment, Gifts of the Holy Spirit, Manifestation, Miracle, Power, Spiritual

Superstition (Superstitious) – seeking to affect the course of our lives by putting our faith in particular rituals, practices or objects.

Through the superstitious use of such routines or charms, we can give rights to the powers of darkness to exercise a measure of control over our lives, even as Christians.

> Galatians 4:9–10... how is it that you want to turn back to those weak and pitiful ruling spirits? Why do you want to become their slaves all over again? You pay special attention to certain days, months, seasons, and years. (GNB)

When we rely on horoscopes, fortune-telling, lucky charms, ritual behaviors, alternative healing techniques or religious practices, these all have the potential of bringing cursing rather than blessing to us. True Holy Spirit protection, guidance and restoration for our lives come only through faith in Jesus Christ.

> John 14:16–17... I will ask the Father, and He will give you another Helper, that He may be with you forever; that is the Spirit of truth, whom the world cannot receive, because it does not see Him or know Him, but you know Him because He abides with you and will be in you. (NASB)

It is always worth seeking the LORD, asking Him to show us the truth about any practice or object in which we have put our faith in the past. He is ready with forgiveness and cleansing for every wrong pathway that we have taken.

> See Alternative Medicine, Charm, Cure, Deliverance, False Religion, False Religious Practice, Foothold, Occult, Ritual

Swearing (Swear) – See Oath

Tattooing (Tattoo) – ink-marking the body under the skin.

As well as being for a decorative purpose and occasionally for medical identification, tattooing has long been associated with a declaration of commitment or submission to a particular person or an organization, a visible and permanent demonstration of a vow or agreement.

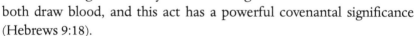

In biblical times, branding or cutting the body was sometimes used to confirm a covenant, this being a part of a sometimes painful ritual to declare the serious and unending nature of the agreement being made. Cutting the body or tattooing both draw blood, and this act has a powerful covenantal significance (Hebrews 9:18).

God instructed the Children of Israel that these practices, used with ritual significance, were contrary to His will for the rightful surrender of their lives to His authority. Body piercing and tattooing have been used throughout history as a mark of slavery, and God wanted His children to walk in freedom from every potential hold of the enemy.

> Leviticus 19:28... You shall not make any cuts in your body for the dead nor make any tattoo marks on yourselves: I am the LORD. (NASB)

European sailors and pilgrims in the Middle Ages witnessed the practice of tattooing while on their foreign travels, and they frequently returned home carrying words and pictures inscribed on their bodies. Increasingly

TEACHING

this became a fashionable practice among both the aristocracy and ordinary people.

Today, in many countries, there has been an explosion in the practice of tattooing, not least among young adults. Unfortunately, such permanent marks on the precious body that God has created can sometimes defile the person both emotionally and spiritually. Tattoos, especially those associated with rebellious, aggressive or occult themes, may declare, even unconsciously, ungodly and harmful agreements with the enemy.

Those confessing and repenting of tattoos from the past may not easily be able to have them physically removed, but God can fully cleanse us from all unrighteousness and deliver us from every power of darkness which may have attached itself to the practice. In Christ there is never condemnation, but there is often a need for His conviction of our carelessness in how we have used our bodies in the past.

See Body Piercing, Defilement, Cleansing, Covenant, Foothold, Rebellion, Slavery

Teaching (Teach, Taught) – explaining the truth of God's Word.

Secular teaching is primarily aimed at giving knowledge to the mind, whereas Christian teaching is seeking divine wisdom for both the human spirit and the soul. The ways of God's Kingdom are completely different from the ways of the world. Jesus spent much of His time during His ministry on earth helping people to understand the truths of this Kingdom, which He had received from His Father (John 7:16) and demonstrating the restoration that is available to people whose lives are spiritually broken and held captive.

> Luke 9:11… But the crowds found out where he was going, and they followed him. He welcomed them and taught them about the Kingdom of God, and he healed those who were sick. (NLT)

In Ellel Ministries, we see this verse as foundational to our understanding of the process for God's healing. Continuing in the ministry of Jesus, the Body of Christ has been empowered by the Holy Spirit to offer teaching and healing to this needy world (John 14:26). As the truths of God's Word are carefully explained, there is opportunity for people to receive revelation, to consider the spiritual condition of their own lives, and so

397

respond to God's call for confession, repentance and forgiveness, which are among the essentials of His Kingdom, in order that they can walk into the wholeness and freedom that God has prepared.

See Bible, Healing, Ministry, Revelation, Truth, Word

Temporal – subject to time.

The physical world in which we live is constrained by time, whereas the spiritual realms are eternal. The human body, in this life, is a meeting place of the eternal and temporal realms because we have a physical body changing with time (and eventually returning to the dust of the earth), together with a human spirit which is our unique and eternal God-given identity.

> Ecclesiastes 12:7... then the dust will return to the earth as it was, and the spirit will return to God who gave it. (NASB)

Our lifespan in this physical, temporal world is a gift of God, which provides an opportunity for us to be reconciled with Him. We need

this because of humankind's separation from God which occurred at the Fall (Genesis 3:24). Such redemption is not possible for rebellious beings confined to the spiritual, eternal realms (Jude 6).

We need the Lord's help to recognize the reality of both our temporal and eternal existence. The affliction which we may now endure in the physical realm will be gloriously superseded by the joy of eternal life.

> 2 Corinthians 4:16–18... Therefore we do not lose heart, but though our outer man is decaying, yet our inner man is being renewed day by day. For momentary, light affliction is producing for us an eternal weight of glory far beyond all comparison, while we look not at the things which are seen, but at the things which are not seen; for the things which are seen are temporal, but the things which are not seen are eternal. (NASB)

See Conception, Death, Eternal, Life, Spiritual, Supernatural

Temptation (Tempt, Tempting) – sin opportunity that attracts the attention of our carnal nature.

For a follower of Jesus, there is always a choice of whether to walk according to the direction of the Holy Spirit or to give way to our carnality (Romans 8:5). Each choice gives opportunity for more strength to come from the Holy Spirit, or further bondage from the powers of darkness. God can use the temptations that we experience as an opportunity to test and strengthen our faith in Him when we walk His way, and so we find a deeper place of peace and security. Inevitably, however, the enemy prowls around believers, suggesting his ways of self-comfort, self-importance and compromise, just as he did with Jesus in the wilderness (Luke 4:1–13).

The more we resist a particular temptation, the more we deny license to our carnal nature and we weaken the enemy's grip in that area of our lives. The deeper our relationship with Jesus, the more His own character and His own resolve, through the Holy Spirit, will direct our lives and help us to walk in righteousness. Amazingly, Jesus was tempted in just the same way as we are (Hebrews 4:15), so He knows how it feels to make difficult choices in times of huge pressure (Hebrews 2:18), but He always chose to walk in loving agreement with His Father.

> John 12:27–28... Now My soul has become troubled; and what shall I say, "Father, save Me from this hour"? But for this purpose I came to this hour. Father, glorify Your name ... (NASB)

Temptation to sin will always be with us, but we can trust God to steer us away from the hardest issues (Matthew 6:13), knowing with certainty that He will not allow us to be tested beyond our ability to resist the attraction of sin, if we depend on Him.

> 1 Corinthians 10:13... No temptation has overtaken you but such as is common to man; and God is faithful, who will not allow you to be tempted beyond what you are able, but with the temptation will provide the way of escape also, so that you will be able to endure it. (NASB)

See Carnal Nature, Choice, Conscience, Evil, Free Will, Power, Sin, Satan, Testing

Territorial Spirit – see Ruling Spirit (and Reclaim Ground)

Testimony – spoken or written evidence of the truth, grace and power of God.

Interestingly, we are told in the Bible that our personal testimony of what Jesus has done seals specific defeat of the enemy in our lives.

> Revelation 12:11... And they overcame [Satan] because of the blood of the Lamb and because of the word of their testimony, and they did not love their life even when faced with death. (NASB)

Jesus disabled the enemy's overall hold on humankind through God's release of forgiveness at the cross. His victory becomes reality in our own lives through the personal response which we make to this amazing gift of God. The more that we give acknowledgment to what God is doing in our lives, the more we set a seal on our walk of freedom and wholeness in Him.

Testimony not only secures victory in our own lives, but it is also a powerful challenge and encouragement to others in the Body of Christ. Saved from spiritual death we truly have something to speak about, no matter how tough the journey.

> Psalm 118:17... I will not die, but live, And tell of the works of the LORD. (NASB)

See Martyr, Thankfulness, Truth, Witness, Word

Testing a Revelation – discerning the source and validity of a spiritual manifestation, such as prophecy.

The ability to discern or distinguish between spirits is listed by Paul as a gift of the Holy Spirit (1 Corinthians 12:10). This gives us an indication that such discernment is not obvious, but requires vigilance and the help of the Holy Spirit (1 John 4:1).

See Counterfeit, Deception, Discernment, Gifts of the Holy Spirit, Manifestation, Prophecy, Revelation

Testing (Test, Testing Time) – challenging time in our lives, used by God to refine us.

In a world which is largely in rebellion against God, there will inevitably be many temptations, troubles and much testing in our lives (Deuteronomy 8:2). The ruler of the world thrives on disorder. Jesus tells His followers that this will be so, but He invites them to join Him in His victory over every work of darkness in the world, and to know a supernatural peace and courage.

> John 16:33... These things I have spoken to you, so that in Me you may have peace. In the world you have tribulation, but take courage; I have overcome the world. (NASB)

Every time we face a difficult challenge in life, it is an opportunity to reject the way of the world and to be tested in our resolve to walk in obedience to God (Judges 3:1–4). Today, we can choose a way of life which is guided and empowered by the Holy Spirit. Each decision we make in line with God brings a refining and strengthening of our character, so we become more like Jesus and so walk in a greater measure of His authority. It has been well said that "man's extremity is God's opportunity".[27]

The pruning of fruit trees can often seem extremely harsh but the resultant fruitfulness is frequently amazing. We are not promised an easy walk, and sadly some will fall away (Luke 8:13), so Jesus encourages His disciples to seek God's direction and protection in times of testing. These are situations when the enemy is sure to try to take advantage of any vulnerable issues in our lives.

> Matthew 6:13... Do not bring us to hard testing, but keep us safe from the Evil One. (GNB)

See Fruit, Peace, Pruning, Sin, Spiritual Warfare, Suffering, Temptation

Thankfulness (Thank, Thankful) – gratitude from the heart.

This is so much more than just politeness! Thankfulness toward one another in the Body of Christ values each other's gifting, strengthens unity and encourages selflessness.

A heart of thankfulness toward God (Colossians 3:16-17) for all that He is and all that He has done in our lives deepens our relationship with Him, feeds our human spirit, rightly proclaims Him as the ultimate source of all goodness, and keeps the door open for His blessing and direction.

> Psalm 92:1... It is good to give thanks to the LORD And to sing praises to Your name, O Most High ... (NASB)

See Praise, Self-pity, Testimony

Thinking (Think, Thought) – activity of the mind, to process the experiences of life.

Unless we are sleeping (and even then there is some level of cognitive activity), we are always thinking. Sometimes we are at peace, sometimes troubled by current events (Daniel 5:6), and sometimes distressed by unresolved issues from the past (Psalm 139:23). Our carnal nature is always pressing on our thoughts, trying to make us walk in accordance with the world. But Jesus wants us to surrender our human thoughts to His divine thoughts, so that we will deny the enemy any license to direct our choices of behavior.

> 2 Corinthians 10:5... We are destroying speculations and every lofty thing raised up against the knowledge of God, and we are taking every thought captive to the obedience of Christ ... (NASB)

When a person experiences brokenness and damage to their thinking processes, it is likely to be due to a lack of godly spiritual covering in their generational line or during their own lifetime (Matthew 9:36). The

Lord knows about our troubled minds and He is ready to give us His forgiveness, comfort, healing and peace, as we come into agreement with His ways, forgiving those who have left us exposed to distress in our thinking.

> Isaiah 55:9... For as the heavens are higher than the earth, So are My ways higher than your ways And My thoughts than your thoughts. (NASB)

See Anxiety, Choice, Conscience, Meditation, Mind, Mindfulness, Human Soul

Tongues – gift of the Holy Spirit, allowing believers to express words to God in a language directed by their human spirit rather than from the mind.

> 1 Corinthians 14:14... If I pray in a tongue, my spirit prays, but my mind is unfruitful. (NASB)

The gift of tongues gives us an opportunity to dialogue with God when our own language seems insufficient, not least in times of intercession, spiritual warfare and prayer ministry (Romans 8:26). The language God gives can be completely unknown to us or, on occasions, be a known earthly language, as on the day of Pentecost (Acts 2:8). Of course, tongues will not be necessary after the return of Jesus, when the perfect relationship with God comes (1 Corinthians 13:8-10), but it is a valuable gift for our lives now.

In our daily lives it is common for the human soul within us to take a dominant position as we seek to comfort and protect ourselves. As a result, we often neglect the One who wants to direct us. This was something that Jesus never did (John 14:10). Exercising the gift of tongues allows God to give us a voice by the direction of the Holy Spirit through our human spirit. Interestingly, a research project in 2006 at the University of Pennsylvania showed that the part of the brain which deals with personal control of behavior became less active while Christians were speaking in tongues.[28]

Such Spirit-led dialogue often seems to release other divine gifts such as prophecy, wisdom and faith. Speaking or singing in tongues (1 Corinthians 14:15) is not a measure of spiritual maturity, but rather

TRANSFORMATION

an aid to our fellowship with Him. God knows also that when tongues are used in a public setting, particularly where unbelievers are present, it is helpful for there to be an understanding of the essence of what is being spoken. For this reason He frequently gives others the gift of interpreting the tongue in order that His purpose can be revealed more clearly, and so build up the Body of Christ (1 Corinthians 14:26).

The release of this gift in an individual frequently follows closely on baptism in the Holy Spirit, but it is not a necessary proof of receiving the baptism, as some are baptized in the Spirit without speaking in tongues (1 Corinthians 12:30). However, as with all the gifts of the Holy Spirit, speaking in tongues should be earnestly desired by every believer (1 Corinthians 14:1), whether for personal edification (1 Corinthians 14:4), for exalting God (Acts 10:46), or for use in the fellowship of believers (1 Corinthians 14:26), so that we may increasingly walk in the fullness of God.

Of course, there will be excesses and abuses connected with speaking in tongues, and many have had poor teaching or bad experiences concerning this gift, but let us graciously help one another not to neglect this significant and supernatural gift of God. It can be an amazing daily door-opener to exploring more of God's will for our lives (Romans 8:26-27). The apostle Paul certainly found this gift of tongues very useful (1 Corinthians 14:18).

See Gifts of the Holy Spirit, Human Spirit, Intercession, Prayer, Prayer Ministry, Spiritual Warfare, Supernatural

Transformation (Transform) – deep and noticeable change in the character of a person or a group of people.

Some behaviors in people's lives may be changed for the better by human effort or strong discipline, but true transformation of the sinful heart is a supernatural work of the Holy Spirit (2 Corinthians 3:18). He can cause us to become progressively more like Jesus as we surrender to Him every part of our lives. Every born-again believer in Jesus has been *transferred* in spiritual location from darkness to light (Colossians 1:13), restored into our true spiritual identity as a child of God (John 1:12) and a citizen of His Kingdom (Matthew 13:37–38). However, each one of us still needs to be *transformed* in our spiritual condition from an image that conforms to the world to an image that conforms to Christ.

> Romans 12:2... do not be conformed to this world, but be transformed by the renewing of your mind, so that you may prove what the will of God is, that which is good and acceptable and perfect. (NASB)

The Greek word which is translated as *transformed* in this verse also gives us the word *metamorphosis*, used in biology to describe, for example, the extraordinary change which happens when a caterpillar turns into a butterfly. It's a transformation even more remarkable than this which God desires to bring about in each of our lives. A change so big that the old me is being completely replaced by a new me, able to reveal an image of Christ to others.

> 2 Corinthians 5:17... Therefore if anyone is in Christ, he is a new creature; the old things passed away; behold, new things have come. (NASB)

Our part in the process is to present to God every sinful and damaged part of our lives for deep metamorphosis into men and women of holiness and wholeness. We need to choose for the shaping of our image to be done by the hands of the Divine Potter, and not by our carnality and the relationships which have wrongly influenced our lives. Beware also of the world's counterfeits: there are hundreds of alternative remedies purporting to transform our inner condition, but only Jesus deals with the sin of the world, which is the root issue. As each individual believer yields to the One who truly can work miracles, the transformation of whole communities is even possible. Humanism says that virtuous lives can be achieved simply by human reason and human effort. Such ideas are well-meaning but will never lead to a transformed world.

See Carnal Nature, Character, Conviction, Fruit, Holiness, Identity, Image, Wholeness

Transgenderism (Transgender) – condition of gender identity in which a person chooses to be regarded as being of the opposite sex to that of their innate bodily appearance and their DNA.

Such a person used to be described as transsexual, and some people still prefer that term. A transgender person may carry out this desire through clothing and make-up, or may choose to pursue medical procedures which alter the shape and characteristics of the body. Sexuality, meaning our masculinity or femininity, is a significant aspect of our human identity, determined in the human spirit (1 Corinthians 2:11), expressed in the soul and demonstrated in the shape and functioning of the physical body.

Damage, particularly to the human spirit, from generational iniquity and from the wounding and sin issues connected with people's lives, can result in serious inner defilement and brokenness, sometimes leading to disharmony between physical appearance and the inner 'voice' of sexual identity.

Wounding which contributes to such damage may occur in the womb or during childhood. Some examples in the womb would be negative parental pronouncements about the anticipated gender of the child, fetal trauma from accidents or attempted abortion, or spiritual defilement from occult activity or a previous death in the womb. During childhood, the contributing issues may be sexual abuse, poor role-modeling and sexual guidance, inadequate or inappropriate bonding with mother or father, or a lack of godly parental affirmation of a child's sexuality.

The 'shape' of our sexual identity, rooted in the human spirit, is not only distorted by past wounding but also by the ungodly choices which we have made to try to fix our own needs, sometimes leading to a form of self-idolatry. In addition, where we have chosen to act against God's order for our lives, the enemy has a right to demonically empower that disorder and so strengthen any false identity that we have adopted. God in no way rejects any person with transgender feelings, but His desire for their lives is restoration of His created order, not the promotion of disorder through adopting a false sexual image (Deuteronomy 22:5).

God completely understands the profound sexual confusion and distress of those who feel unhappy living within their bodies, and He knows the deep issues which need to be dealt with to bring peace. His ways require confession of personal sin and forgiveness of all those who have contributed to the inner wounding, in order to open the door for God's healing, deliverance and redemption of the abundant life which He purposed for us from our mother's womb.

> Psalm 139:13–14... For You formed my inward parts; You wove me in my mother's womb. I will give thanks to You, for I am fearfully and wonderfully made; Wonderful are Your works, And my soul knows it very well. (NASB)

See Abortion, Femininity, Homosexuality, Human Spirit, Identity, Lesbianism, Masculinity, Miscarriage, Order, Sexuality, Transvestitism

Transvestitism (Transvestite) – clothing oneself in order to appear to be of the opposite sex.

This issue is not about pantomime characters who entertain children, but about recognizing that a choice to cross-dress is frequently the outworking of confusion or denial concerning our God-given sexual identity. So the practice needs God's restoration rather than human endorsement. Meeting areas of inner distress or dysfunction by wearing clothes appropriate to the opposite sex gives a right to the enemy to strengthen the disorder with demonic power, promote compulsion, and bring bondage to any distortion of sexual identity. The Bible says clearly that transvestitism is out of line with God's order.

> Deuteronomy 22:5... A woman shall not wear man's clothing, nor shall a man put on a woman's clothing; for whoever does these things is an abomination to the LORD your God. (NASB)

The roots of such behavior will often be in issues such as rejection, isolation, abuse and disapproval in early life. The affirmation of our sexual identity is a very important parental role, particularly of a father, though sadly it is often neglected. Generational iniquity and poor parenting cause damage to the human spirit, the core of our sexual identity. Some transvestites (especially entertainers) carry a hatred of the opposite sex as a result of early wounding, and so their parodies are intended more to mock than to mimic.

Restoration starts with forgiveness of those who have failed to nurture our God-given identity, as well as personal acknowledgment of sinful practices which have been an attempt to meet our inner needs for comfort or significance. Without doubt, our sexual identity is very important to God, to be honored and valued as He intended.

> 1 Corinthians 6:20... For you have been bought with a price: therefore glorify God in your body. (NASB)

See Affirmation, Comfort, Human Spirit, Identity, Transgender, Value, Wounding

Trauma (Traumatize, Traumatic) – severe wounding.

In a well-known story told by Jesus, a good Samaritan came upon a man lying by the side of the road, desperately in need of help. Religious leaders had just walked on by. It was the Samaritan, the one displaying the heart of Jesus, who took the time to apply first aid and then to transport the wounded man to a place that would be safe for him to find full recovery.

> Luke 10:34... and [the Samaritan] came to him and bandaged up his wounds [Greek word – trauma], pouring oil and wine on them; and he put him on his own beast, and brought him to an inn and took care of him. (NASB)

Jesus calls the Body of Christ on earth today to be those who notice the traumas which others have experienced, to care where others are unwilling, to help remove the person from the spiritually hostile territory of the enemy, and to bring them to a place of safety for complete restoration in Jesus.

People can be traumatized and broken in body, soul and human spirit as a result of this sinful world. Breaking in the soul and spirit is sometimes called fragmentation, and this can be a significant problem when someone has experienced trauma. Wonderful physical and emotional transformation can result from God's healing of such an injury. What a precious ministry to be able, today, to be an instrument of God's re-covering and healing of wounded people.

See Accident, Full Fragmentation, Partial Fragmentation, Wholeness, Wounding

Trinity – threefold nature of God.

Although it is a theologically challenging concept, it is very important for a Christian to believe that the one God whom we serve exists in the divine relationship of Father, Son and Holy Spirit.

> Matthew 28:19... Go therefore and make disciples of all the nations, baptizing them in the name of the Father and the Son and the Holy Spirit ... (NASB)

This relationship of equality also contains a divine protocol regarding their respective roles. We read in the Bible how the Holy Spirit reveals the glory of Jesus (John 16:14), and Jesus reveals the way to the Father (John 14:6). The threefold nature of God also expresses an important diversity in the way human beings are to experience Him. God wants us to know Him, for example, as our Father (Ephesians 4:6), our Friend (John 15:14) and our Counselor (John 14:16).

The undermining of the biblical truth of the Trinity is a significant area of deception which will be empowered by the enemy if we give him license. For example, Christians may respect the sincerity of Muslims, and we can love them as our neighbors, but we cannot agree that they worship the same God as those who are believers in Jesus Christ. Around the outside of the Dome of the Rock, the Muslim shrine on the Temple Mount in Jerusalem, are written powerful proclamations which include the words *God has no son*. These words are intended to directly challenge Christian belief.

The actual word *Trinity* is not found in the Bible, but the concept itself is clearly affirmed in the New Testament (1 Peter 1:2). It is an essential concept if we accept the divinity of Jesus. Over 2,000 years, Christians have sought ways of describing the mystery of the Trinity. For example, our sun is, at the same time, a burning mass of molecules which we believe as fact, a light source by which we are able to see, and a heat source which we can feel. In a similar way, we believe in the all-powerful heavenly Father, we believe that Jesus reveals to us what the Father is like, and we feel the warmth of His love through the Holy Spirit. However, no human picture will give an adequate revelation of the precious truth of the three-in-one nature of the God of the Bible.

Importantly, we are also warned that any demonstration of spiritual power which denies the true relationship of the Godhead comes not from the Holy Spirit, but from an antichrist spirit which is unwilling

TRUST

to acknowledge Jesus as the Son of God and the true Messiah. This deception can be found even in Christian movements and meetings today, where the fullness of the Godhead is actively sidelined through a wrongful focus on spiritual impartation or manifestation.

> 1 John 2:22–23... Who is the liar but the one who denies that Jesus is the Christ? This is the antichrist, the one who denies the Father and the Son. Whoever denies the Son does not have the Father; the one who confesses the Son has the Father also. (NASB)

See Antichrist, Deception, Discernment, Father, God, Holy Spirit, Jesus

Trust (Trusting, Trustworthy) – choice to depend on the faithfulness of another person.

Trust is a process of learning appropriate dependence on someone, and is the basis of all authentic relationships. As we choose to trust God and find Him to be faithful, confidence in Him becomes rooted in our hearts, so that trusting Him becomes a normal way of life, a mindset and a place of deep security.

> Jeremiah 17:7... Blessed is the man who trusts in the LORD, And whose trust is the LORD. (NASB)

Trusting God is primarily a decision of the soul, which is helped by growing evidence of His trustworthiness, whereas faith in God is more a progressive condition of the human spirit and a gift of God (1 Corinthians 12:9). Both result in blessing. Conversely, the Bible tells us that to trust only in the ability of humanity leads to cursing of our lives.

> Jeremiah 17:5... Cursed is the man who trusts in mankind And makes flesh his strength, And whose heart turns away from the LORD. (NASB)

However, there is a need for rightful interdependence with one another, not least in the Body of Christ. We need to grow in our trust of others, as the fruit of the Holy Spirit increasingly establishes the character of Jesus in all of our lives. This can take time, and though we are commanded to love, accept and forgive one another, we are not commanded to trust others without applying caution. Trust has to be earned. Even Jesus, who completely trusted His Father and followed His instructions, did not entrust Himself to everyone on earth.

> John 2:24... But Jesus, on Hs part, was not entrusting Himself to them, for He knew all men ... (NASB)

It's very likely that each of us has known unreliability, dishonesty, injustice and betrayal in our own lives, so trusting can be difficult. In Christ, we can forgive those who have hurt us and begin to walk in the trust which Jesus has in His Father. We can also learn to trust people with appropriate levels of intimacy, as the Holy Spirit leads. Through Him, we will be able to discern the spiritual authority operating over the lives of others, and this will rightly affect our willingness to trust them. We trust the pilot when we choose to travel by airplane, because we believe that he or she is operating under right authority and has been trained to do the job. That is why the followers of Jesus were able to trust Him. Like the centurion with the sick slave (Luke 7:8–9), they saw that Jesus was *in* right authority because He was *under* right authority, the authority of the Father (John 14:10).

As with the demolition of a tall brick chimney, breaking trust can happen very quickly, whereas building it can be a long process. In the Body of Christ, those who are becoming truly trustworthy will be the people who have surrendered their lives to Jesus, to be increasingly conformed to His image.

See Betrayal, Codependence, Discernment, Faith, Dependence, Interdependence, Intimacy, Security

Truth (Truthful, True, Truly) – that which agrees with God in all physical and spiritual matters.

Philosophers have argued for centuries over the question of *what is truth*. Pilate asked Jesus the same question (John 18:38), but the answer had already been given to His disciples when Jesus described Himself as *the* Truth (John 14:6). Everything He is and everything He speaks is absolute truth. He also describes the Holy Spirit as the *Spirit of Truth* (John 14:17), the One who brings revelation to followers of Jesus about the reality of their lives and their relationship with God. Our battle against the enemy, and the restoration of our lives, starts with establishing truth (Ephesians 6:14), by exposing sin, disorder, spiritual darkness and unreality. Jesus calls the devil *a liar* and, indeed, the *father of lies* (John 8:44), meaning that where truth is absent, Satan's domain holds spiritual authority.

John the disciple described Jesus as being *"the Word [who] became flesh ... full of grace and truth"* (John 1:14, NASB). Wherever the lordship of Jesus is established, through obedience to His teaching, truth becomes inevitable. However, truth without grace simply leads to condemnation. If we are willing to acknowledge and respond to the truth about the righteousness of God and the iniquity of our lives, the enemy becomes exposed. Then the grace of God's forgiveness can take away this hostile authority, leading to freedom and healing.

> John 8:31–32... So Jesus was saying to those Jews who had believed Him, "If you continue in My word, then you are truly disciples of Mine; and you will know the truth, and the truth will make you free." (NASB)

On many occasions, while praying for others, we have seen the breakthrough come when truth has been revealed, acknowledged and spoken out in agreement with God (Psalm 51:6). I remember a lady who had experienced a very dysfunctional and abusive family as she grew up. She realized that loyalty within the family had always been seen to be more important than truth, and this covering up of sinful behavior had been a root cause of the deep anxiety which she experienced. As she acknowledged and faced the truth of what had really happened, she began to walk into amazing healing.

We live in dangerous times when truth is not seen as precious (2 Thessalonians 2:8–10). Someone has rightly said: *"The further a society drifts from the truth the more it will hate those who speak it."*[29] To fully walk in truth means no hiding, no cover-up, no unreality, no fantasy, no holding on to pride, no false loyalty, no pretense, no darkness, no masks, no distortion, no dissociation, no deviation, no compromise, and no added lies. Today, we can ask the Lord to put this love of truth deep within our hearts.

> Proverbs 16:6... Iniquity is covered by mercy and truth, and in the fear of Jehovah, men turn aside from evil. (LITV)

See Counterfeit, Deception, Freedom, Grace, Holy Spirit, Lie, Teaching

Unanswered Prayer – prayer that seems to receive no response from God.

This is not an unusual issue! The psalmists in the Bible frequently commented on God's apparent silence (Psalm 83:1), and even Jesus went through the experience of feeling utterly forsaken on the cross (Matthew 27:46), as He cried out, quoting the first few words of a psalm; Jesus truly knows how we feel.

> Psalm 22:1–2… My God, my God, why have You forsaken me? Far from my deliverance are the words of my groaning. O my God, I cry by day, but You do not answer; And by night, but I have no rest. (NASB)

However, our not hearing an answer from God does not mean that He is not listening. C.S. Lewis knew the challenge of unanswered prayer and wrote: *"I know now, Lord, why you utter no answer. You are yourself the answer. Before your face questions die away. What other answer would suffice?"*[30] Our

relationship with God is essentially one of faith which requires us to walk in the assurance of God's Word before it is seen as fact. This can be hard, but it can also be a precious opportunity to grow in our knowledge of truth about Him, and truth about ourselves.

Here are some examples of truths that God may want to reveal to us as we wait for His answer to prayer, particularly prayer for healing. These points are to help, not to condemn us, and perhaps to challenge us in some of the areas that could be giving the enemy an opportunity to resist the healing that God has for us.

- Maybe there is unbelief in me or those around me, not accepting that Jesus heals and delivers in people's lives today (Luke 9:41).

UNANSWERED PRAYER

- Maybe there is ignorance or denial about the root causes of the problem (John 8:31–44).

- Maybe there is unforgiveness in my heart toward others or even toward myself (Matthew 18:23–35).

- Maybe there is unresolved wounding or brokenness in my heart which is holding me trapped in the disorder (Isaiah 61:1).

- Maybe there is unconfessed sin (1 John 1:8).

- Maybe there is a wrong spiritual inheritance from my ancestors affecting my life (1 Peter 1:18–19).

- Maybe there are ungodly soul-ties which need to be broken (Romans 6:16).

- Maybe there is spiritual contention far beyond my understanding, and only God knows the perfect timing for my restoration (Luke 22:31).

I'm sure that Daniel was impatient to receive an answer to his prayer for explanation of the vision which he had received, but he was probably very surprised at the reason given to him for the delay in receiving God's answer.

> Daniel 10:12–13... Then [the angel] said to me, "Do not be afraid, Daniel, for from the first day that you set your heart on understanding this and on humbling yourself before your God, your words were heard, and I have come in response to your words. But the prince of the kingdom of Persia was withstanding me for twenty-one days ..." (NASB)

Our part on the journey of wholeness and freedom is to humble ourselves before God, make our requests known with persistence (Luke 18:7), walk in the truths that He reveals, and wait for Him to respond how and when He decides it is appropriate to answer the essence of our prayer. Unlike Daniel, we are seldom going to be aware of the significant contention in the heavenly realms that surely exists over every step forward that we make with God.

See Brokenness, Denial, Faith, Generational Iniquity, Healing, Prayer, Sin, Soul-tie, Truth, Unbelief, Unforgiveness

UNCLEAN SPIRIT

Unbelief (Unbelieving) – heart attitude that opposes faith in God and His Word.

Unbelief is established when doubt is given opportunity to become wrongly rooted in the heart (Mark 11:23). This can affect a follower of Jesus, especially if unbelief has been sown into someone's life through a family background of false religion or the occult, for example. Jesus met this particular stronghold of the enemy in the father of the epileptic boy. In preparation for deliverance of the boy, Jesus gave the father the opportunity to resolve this defiling bondage which was operating within the family.

> Mark 9:22–23… "It has often thrown him into the fire and into the water to destroy him. But if You can do anything, take pity on us and help us!" And Jesus said to him, "'If You can?' All things are possible to him who believes." (NASB)

It has been said that pride, fear and unbelief are three of the most powerful weapons in the enemy's arsenal. Indeed, we should not be ignorant of Satan's tactics as he seeks to destroy the works of God's Kingdom (Matthew 13:58). Unbelief stands in clear opposition to faith, the most important shield that we have to resist the powers of darkness (Ephesians 6:16).

If the Holy Spirit reveals unbelief in our hearts (Hebrews 3:12), we simply need to confess this to the Lord and let Him lovingly cleanse and transform us to be newly empowered with faith.

> Mark 9:24… Immediately the boy's father cried out and said, "I do believe; help my unbelief." (NASB)

See Attitude, Doubt, Faith, False Religion, Fear, Judgment, Pride, Truth

Uncertainty – See Doubt

Unclean Spirit – spiritual being, also called an evil spirit or a demon, which operates in the realm of darkness, ruled by Satan.

It is not clear from the Bible where unclean spirits come from, but they are part of God's creation, although they are fallen and utterly opposed to His will. Some of these satanic powers have the ability to dwell within a person, defiling and distorting the human spirit, soul and body.

> Matthew 12:43–45... When an evil spirit goes out of a person, it travels over dry country looking for a place to rest. If it can't find one, it says to itself, "I will go back to my house." So it goes back and finds the house empty, clean, and all fixed up. Then it goes out and brings along seven other spirits even worse than itself, and they come and live there. So when it is all over, that person is in worse shape than at the beginning. ... (GNB)

Jesus endorsed the reality of unclean spirits in this picture of the enemy's tactics and, more directly, as He delivered many people from demonic control. From these encounters, we know for certain that these powers of darkness both hear and respond to the direct commands of Jesus (Luke 4:33-35). They know Him, but are in rebellion against His Kingdom. They experience fear (James 2:19), they torment those whom they infest (Mark 5:5), they can show supernatural strength (Luke 8:29), they promote Satan's character, they can cause specific disorders such as infirmity (Luke 13:11), they sometimes work in groups, and they know the rights which they have (Acts 19:15): rights which come from human sin.

The right or authority which an unclean spirit has to operate in or through someone's life is conferred by the sinful choices made by humankind in rebelling against the commands of God. When we follow the ways of the world, rather than the instructions of Jesus, we give spiritual authority over our lives to the ruler of the world (as Jesus calls Satan) and to the powers of darkness which are subject to this evil ruler.

Unclean spirits cannot possess (own) a follower of Jesus. Jesus owns us. His ownership of our lives is secured when we accept Him as Lord and Savior. However, where there is unresolved iniquity in our lives, that is, a place which continues to be out of line with God, the enemy can hold spiritual authority over that part of our lives (2 Corinthians 2:10-11), and empower this by an unclean spirit.

Indications that demonic activity may be holding part of a person's life can be a sense of drivenness in some area of sin (such an obsession or addiction), self-destructive tendencies, tormenting thoughts or fears, occult attraction or persistent infirmities.

Examples of ways in which the enemy might get an opportunity for spiritual control in our lives are: occult activity, idolatry, immorality, wrong dependence, false beliefs, unforgiveness, controlling fears, generational iniquity, false healings, traumas, violence, or even unresolved buried anger.

> Ephesians 4:26–27... BE ANGRY, AND yet DO NOT SIN; do not let the sun go down on your anger, and do not give the devil an opportunity. (NASB)

Just as He gave His first disciples the authority and power to drive out unclean spirits, so today Jesus has enabled His followers to expose the authority of the enemy through revelation given by the Holy Spirit and to expel the powers of darkness by His gifting distributed to the Body of Christ (2 Timothy 2:26). Usually with the support of a prayer ministry pair alongside, the general process of deliverance, evicting an unclean spirit from a person's life, is:

1. Confess and repent of iniquity, including unforgiveness, as the Holy Spirit brings relevant conviction.

2. Receive God's forgiveness and in this way remove the enemy's spiritual authority.

3. Under the authority of Jesus, directly address any unclean spirit, and (empowered by the Holy Spirit) command the spirit to leave quietly.

    > Luke 4:35... Jesus ordered the spirit, "Be quiet and come out of the man!" The demon threw the man down in front of them and went out of him without doing him any harm. (GNB)

In our experience, the more thoroughly the enemy's rights are removed before the unclean spirit is addressed, the more quietly and quickly it leaves.

See Authority, Control, Darkness, Deliverance, Foothold, Fruit, Generational Iniquity, Power, Powers of Darkness, Satan, a Right, Spirit, Truth

Unconditional – not dependent on our effort, our ability or our righteousness.

The salvation which Jesus bought for us on the cross is unconditional. It does not depend on our efforts or on our good behavior. We simply receive it by faith. It is a gift of love, freely given by the One who loves each of us unconditionally.

We were designed by God to receive completely unconditional love, both from Him and from each other, not least from our parents, from the moment they knew of our existence. Such unconditional love (which includes affirmation, kindness and care) nurtures and strengthens our human spirit.

> Luke 6:35... Love your enemies and do good to them; lend and expect nothing back. You will then have a great reward, and you will be children of the Most High God. For he is good to the ungrateful and the wicked. (GNB)

God's *giving* of acceptance and love to each one of us is unconditional (Hosea 3:1). However, for us to fully *receive* that love, as well as the blessings which God has prepared for those in covenant with Him, we must obey His foundational commands. These commands are to believe in Jesus Christ and to love one another (1 John 3:23). Any iniquity in our hearts will separate us, in some measure, from being able to receive and feel the boundless grace and loving-kindness which is flowing from the heart of God (Isaiah 59:2).

We also see here that God commands us, as followers of Jesus, to love one another unconditionally. Unconditional love does not deny the importance of godly discipline or correction, because it rightly differentiates between the inalienable value of each person and the destructive nature of their sin.

See Acceptance, Blessing, Grace, Law, Love, Loving-kindness, Value

Unforgiveness (Unforgiving) – heart condition resulting from a decision by one who has been wronged not to release the offender from the debt that is due.

When someone has sinned against me, I will inevitably have a strong feeling that some recompense is due for all the pain that they have caused me. They surely need to pay (an eye for an eye) for what they've done! Arguably, this issue can be the greatest obstacle to the fullness of God's healing and deliverance in our lives.

It has been said that unforgiveness between two people is like locked horns between two fighting animals. There can be neither spiritual nor emotional release until the issue is resolved. The New Covenant between God and humanity is founded on the forgiveness which was released at the cross by Jesus. This was possible because the ultimate payment for sin was made by Jesus on behalf of all those who accept Him as Savior. Our ability to receive that forgiveness, however, is dependent on our agreement with God concerning our sin, and also our willingness to forgive those who have sinned against us.

> Matthew 6:12... And forgive us our debts, as we also have forgiven our debtors. (NASB)

Jesus emphasized the importance of this issue by telling a shocking parable about a king's servant who loses release from a huge debt owed to his master, because he is unwilling to forgive a fellow servant a much smaller sum of money (Matthew 18:23–35). The result in this story is a tortuous imprisonment for the unforgiving servant, clearly intended to represent spiritual captivity by the enemy.

> Matthew 18:34–35... And his LORD, moved with anger, handed him over to the torturers until he should repay all that was owed him. My heavenly Father will also do the same to you, if each of you does not forgive his brother from your heart. (NASB)

Unless we fully enter into the conditions of God's covenant of forgiveness for His children (2 Corinthians 2:10–11; Matthew 6:15), the enemy can retain a right to hold part of our lives bound until there is payment of the spiritual debt due (Colossians 2:14–15, NASB). Forgiving those people who have sinned against us is rarely easy. It needs to happen not through the persuasion of others, but through the conviction and help of God, revealing that His way of forgiveness is the most extraordinary key to divine healing that has ever existed.

See Choice, Debt, Blame, Forgiveness, Judgment, Offense, Resentment, Wound

Ungodliness (Ungodly) – not in accordance with God's ways.

> Titus 2:11–12... For the grace of God has appeared, bringing salvation to all men, instructing us to deny ungodliness and worldly desires and to live sensibly, righteously and godly in the present age ... (NASB)

See Iniquity, Sin, Unrighteousness

Unity (Unite) – oneness in truth and purpose with God and with other people.

Unity is very important to the progress of the Kingdom of God on earth, for it is this oneness of purpose among God's people which releases the anointing and empowering of the Holy Spirit to bring about God's will.

> Psalm 133:1,3b... Behold how good and how pleasant it is For brothers to dwell together in unity! ... For there the LORD commanded the blessing – life forever. (NASB)

Disunity in marriages, families, communities and, not least, in the Body of Christ, is a significant weapon for the enemy, as it effectively disempowers the true purposes of God. No human body could achieve anything if each hand worked with a different purpose from the other. It is very important that we confess the disunity that so easily grows out of the self-centeredness of our carnal nature. Then God's forgiveness and cleansing can restore the effectiveness of our walk together as followers of Jesus.

> Philippians 2:2... make my joy complete by being of the same mind, maintaining the same love, united in spirit, intent on one purpose. (NASB)

Unity is also important when considering the integrity of the body, soul and human spirit within the individual human being (Isaiah 61:1). Our

hearts can be deeply broken by the sins and wounds of life but, through God's forgiveness and healing released at the cross, Jesus has come to restore one-ness. So unity is important in our personal lives (Psalm 86:11, NASB), in our relationships with one another and, particularly, in our relationship with God, so that each of us can know for ourselves the wonderful unity that Jesus knew with the Father in all these areas.

> John 17:23... I in them and You in Me, that they may be perfected in unity, so that the world may know that You sent Me, and loved them, even as You have loved Me. (NASB)

See Agreement, Body of Christ, Brokenness, Holy Spirit, Integrity, Soul-tie, Wholeness

Unjust – See Injustice

Unreality (Unreal) – state of mind which is not dwelling in truth.

This is frequently a coping mechanism established to deal with the distress or pain of past events. Of course, looking at things in a positive way may be helpful in certain circumstances, but not if we are avoiding truth. When we are on the journey toward resolution of difficult issues and for healing from past wounding, it is essential that we seek the whole truth as God sees it. This is a precious work of the Holy Spirit (John 16:13) in our lives, if we open our hearts to Him.

Unfortunately there is an enemy, whom Jesus calls the *father of lies*, and this means that wherever there is an absence of truth, not least through unreality, the powers of darkness have authority to hold the spiritual ground and promote deception. When we are praying for one another for healing and deliverance, it is very important that we expose any unreality, although we should do it with much grace. Unreality may present, for example, in the form of a false memory, inappropriate emotional responses, denial, behavioral masks, or inappropriate religious behavior.

> Colossians 2:17... These things were like a shadow of what was to come. But what is true and real has come and is found in Christ. (NCV)

God will not heal what He did not make. Our unreality is not His creation. If we have sought to fix our problems by creating an unreal image or lifestyle, we will need to confess and turn away from this before we can receive God's true restoration.

See Coping Mechanism, Deception, Denial, Fantasy, Falsehood, Lie, Mask, False Religion, Satan, Truth

Unrighteousness (Unrighteous) – heart condition of being not right with God.

> 1 John 1:9... If we confess our sins, He is faithful and righteous to forgive us our sins and to cleanse us from all unrighteousness. (NASB)

See Iniquity, Righteousness, Sin

Value (Valued, Valuable) – worth of each person.

The Bible confirms that every individual has hugely significant innate value (Psalm 139:14), simply by virtue of being created by God in His likeness.

> Genesis 1:26... And God said, "Let Us make man in Our image, after Our likeness ..." (KJV)

At the Fall, human value was not lost, but our awareness of, and the fulfillment of, that value was defiled through separation from our Creator. Jesus came to earth and died on the cross to bring reconciliation between Father God and His children, so that we might once again realize and enjoy the full value of our God-created identity and destiny. Sadly, without an understanding of sin, forgiveness and true identity, the world makes a distorted assessment of value by promoting human endeavors such as celebrity, status, wealth, image or intellect, goals which simply lead, for many, to extremes of striving or despair.

In contrast, God declares each person's true value to be worth the agony and death of His only Son, a price that He was willing to pay to rescue each one of us. Though God fully knows our true value, it can lie hidden from human realization. Like silver and gold that has yet to be mined from the ground, our God-created condition needs to be unearthed and purified. The sin of the world has contaminated humanity, and the Bible is full of references to God's desire to purify His people (Malachi 3:3). Through Jesus, this is entirely possible.

For us to fully realize our true value, which is wholly present from our conception, followers of Jesus are being daily transformed into His likeness through the work of the Holy Spirit (2 Corinthians 3:18), removing the distortion that has hidden our true value due to our sinful nature (Romans 7:24 – 8:2). We are also given supernatural gifts, which through our interdependence in the Body of Christ empower us to appreciate the true value in ourselves and in one another (Romans 12:4–8). The ministry of healing and deliverance is very important in dealing with the old defiling mindsets.

God loves even rebellious people, because they are precious to Him (Luke 6:35) and therefore worth the death of His Son, but Jesus also told His disciples (John 15:16) that He had chosen them in order that they would go and bear fruit, in other words, that they would be restored in effectiveness through His character growing in their lives. We are each a priceless work of divine creation, immensely valuable, but God wants to cultivate that value, if we are willing, by redeeming us from the damage which sin has caused, and by growing in us His lasting fruit.

See Destiny, Failure, Fruit, Inner Healing, Identity, Image, Pruning, Purity, Rejection, Significance, Success, Testing

Vengeance – See Revenge

Victim (Victimization) – one who receives abuse.

Many of us have experienced wounding as a consequence of the sinful behavior of others. Jesus knows the severe pain which this causes and He longs to comfort and heal our inner distress, as we find ourselves able to forgive those who have abused us or not protected us.

He also wants each of us to live as those who have overcome the evil of the world (Romans 12:21), not as a victim, for this is not the identity of a child of the King of kings. We may have known times of being the victim of abuse, when choice was taken from us, but now we do have a powerful choice. We can either agree with the spiritual ruler of the world, who readily endorses sinful beliefs like those which had defiled the heart of Mephibosheth (2 Samuel 9:8), or we can agree with the Creator of the world, who declares us to be His rightful and hugely significant children (John 1:12).

The choice not to walk in the identity of a victim can be life-changing. As we make this choice, increasingly we will be empowered by the Holy Spirit, rather than being driven by unclean spirits, which can distort our view of the world so as to fit with a victim mentality. Jesus gives His disciples amazing power over the intimidating work of the enemy. He calls us to walk *under* His loving authority and so be *in* authority over all that would seek to harm us.

> Luke 10:19... Behold, I have given you authority to tread on serpents and scorpions, and over all the power of the enemy, and nothing will injure you. (NASB)

See Abuse, Belief System, Comfort, Core Belief, Identity, Mindset, Significance

Violence (Violent) – force used to exert extreme physical or emotional control and abuse.

Such abuse can happen at any time in our lives, even in the womb through attempted abortion. The Kingdom of God is ruled by the Prince of Peace (Isaiah 9:6), and violence against people, for whatever reason, is not His way under the New Covenant with humankind (Matthew 5:39).

> Luke 22:50–51... And one of [the disciples] struck the slave of the high priest and cut off his right ear. But Jesus answered and said, "Stop! No more of this." And He touched his ear and healed him. (NASB)

All violence suffered at any time in our lives can cause us deep wounding and brokenness, as well as giving opportunity to the enemy to control us, in some measure, through unclean spirits of intimidation, infirmity and even death. The way of restoration, through Jesus Christ, is for us to walk in God's truth and grace (John 1:17). However, forgiveness of the perpetrator of serious violence, such as rape, will not be easy. It is very important that the victim is fully heard and believed by those seeking to help resolve the inner

damage caused by violence and, with time, God can heal even the deepest brokenness and pain.

> Psalm 147:3... He heals the broken-hearted and bandages their wounds. (GNB)

See Abortion, Abuse, Control, Foothold, Intimidation, Martial Art, Rape

Virginity (Virgin) – condition of a person who has had no sexual intercourse.

God intended that both men and women would remain virgins until they experienced sexual intercourse within the covenant relationship of marriage. This act of sexual intimacy is meant to be the moment of consummation of that covenant, even accompanied by the shedding of blood, as the woman's hymen is broken (Deuteronomy 22:13–19).

Virginity is rarely valued these days. Sexual intercourse is common outside marriage and sexually transmitted diseases are part of the consequence. Whatever the views of the world, this is not God's created order. Only our confession of wrongdoing and His forgiveness, through Jesus Christ, can restore the spiritual integrity of our lives when we have disregarded His laws. At Ellel Ministries, we have witnessed this kind of confession being the start of significant healing in many people's lives, when they admit that God's ways are right and that human ways are wrong, not least in this area of sexual purity. The Bible reveals to us the remarkable truth that God sees all His people as a virgin bride, being prepared and cleansed for a divine marriage (Isaiah 62:5). Paul endorses this picture of our being part of the bride of Christ when he writes to believers in Corinth.

VISION

> 2 Corinthians 11:2... I am jealous for you with a godly jealousy; for I betrothed you to one husband, so that to Christ I might present you as a pure virgin. (NASB)

See Confession, Covenant, Marriage, Purity, Sexual Sin, Sexually Transmitted Disease, Singleness

Vision – revelation in the heart, seeing things from God's viewpoint.

Through the gifting of the Holy Spirit, God gives revelation to His children in order to bring about His plans and purposes on earth (1 Corinthians 14:26). Sometimes a recognizable picture is given through the 'eyes' of the human spirit to impart God's knowledge or wisdom concerning a particular issue (Ephesians 1:18).

This revelation may need to be shared and tested with others in the Body of Christ, in order for true understanding to be received. Perhaps it is a picture which is relevant in (say) a moment of prayer ministry, or it may be a strategic glimpse of the future. One man we know saw, in 1976, a clear pictorial vision of the Ellel Ministries center at Glyndley Manor, although he did not then know the property. Several years later, he unexpectedly visited the actual building and he realized that God wanted him to purchase it, along with others, for particular Christian work.

Sometimes the vision which God gives is better described as a strong and persistent impression in the heart, by which He directs the thoughts, or even the destiny, of a particular individual or a group of believers. All vision needs to be consistent with the Word of God and subjected to the discernment of other mature believers. This type of vision was given to Peter Horrobin, the founder of Ellel Ministries, which led him to pray with others for the establishing of a center for a healing ministry based on Luke 9:11 in the north-west of England.

The Bible is full of examples of God's people being directed by vision, received both day and night (Acts 16:9). Whether revealing big or small issues, our experiencing of ongoing godly vision which motivates our lives is hugely important for our well-being, because without it, despair and hopelessness can grow.

> Proverbs 29:18... Where there is no vision, the people perish ... (KJV)

God designed us to be men and women of vision and destiny, knowing godly desire and purpose in our hearts. We may make mistakes or experience some failures in the eyes of the world, but success in God's family is simply a matter of walking in obedience to all that we believe the Lord has spoken into our lives, while we also walk in a place of right accountability to others in the Body of Christ (Ephesians 5:21). It is never too late to seek the Lord, asking Him to impart vision for the next step of our journey with Him, however this comes, whether as heart impressions, pictures or even dreams!

> Acts 2:17… "AND IT SHALL BE IN THE LAST DAYS," God says, "THAT I WILL POUR FORTH MY SPIRIT ON ALL MANKIND; AND YOUR SONS AND DAUGHTERS SHALL PROPHESY, AND YOUR YOUNG MEN SHALL SEE VISIONS, AND YOUR OLD MEN SHALL DREAM DREAMS … " (NASB)

See Desire, Destiny, Discernment, Gifts of the Holy Spirit, Hopelessness, Human Spirit, Revelation

Vow – significant promise, whether privately or publicly declared.

Words spoken out, or just voiced in our hearts, carry spiritual power (Proverbs 18:21). Every word which Jesus spoke was life-giving (John 6:63) and every promise that God has made, He will not break.

> Titus 1:2… In the hope of eternal life, which God, who cannot lie, promised long ages ago. (NASB)

A higher spiritual authority is often called upon to witness a vow, and this type of declaration is sometimes called an oath (Hebrews 6:16). Interestingly, God can only make such a promise by His own authority, for there is none higher!

> Hebrews 6:13… When God made his promise to Abraham, he made a vow to do what he had promised. Since there was no one greater than himself, he used his own name when he made his vow. (GNB)

Vows can be very significant, particularly when linked to oaths and covenants. Jesus teaches us that we should be very careful about oaths which invite spiritual oversight; it is better to simply make clear statements of intent.

> Matthew 5:34,37... But I tell you, do not swear an oath at all ... All you need to say is simply "Yes" or "No"; anything beyond this comes from the evil one. (NIV)

When we speak in agreement with God, our promises are empowered by the Holy Spirit to bring blessing. The Holy Spirit will no doubt endorse the promises made at a godly wedding, for example. But when our promises are spoken in disobedience to the commands of God, they can be held by the enemy to bring cursing. For example, an unclean spirit can empower the defiling vows made during ungodly religious rituals, such as within Freemasonry.

Vows from the past which we believe may be wrongly affecting us today can be brought before the Lord by confessing our own mistakes, and forgiving those whose words have defiled our lives. Scriptures spoken out today, in agreement with God's view of our lives, can be very powerful in overwriting, in the spiritual realm, the words of harmful vows from the past. The Lord is ready to cleanse us from any powers of darkness which have taken advantage of wrongful words we have used.

See Covenant, Curse, Freemasonry, Oath, Pronouncement, Word

Wedding – See Marriage

Wholeness – integrity of the body, soul and human spirit, as God intended.

When we are careless with our possessions, things get broken. In this spiritually hostile world, made unsafe by the sinfulness of humanity, lives get broken; not just physically, but emotionally and spiritually as well. Abuse and traumas fracture the soul and spirit, damaging the inner integrity, or wholeness, which sustains our lives (Proverbs 18:14).

Inner brokenness can also be caused by our responses to wounding. When our lives have been damaged by the sinful behavior of others, we can compromise the integrity of our being through coping mechanisms such as unreality, deception, dissociation, or addictive practices, including, for example, drug abuse.

Thankfully, Jesus has come to bind up the brokenhearted, regardless of how this damage has occurred (Isaiah 61:1). He alone sees the lack of integrity within our lives and can restore the wholeness that He intended. Our forgiveness of others and God's forgiveness of our own wrong behaviors are the basis for repairing the cracks. Wholeness and holiness are God's desire for every follower of Jesus.

> 1 Thessalonians 5:23... May God himself, the God who makes everything holy and whole, make you holy and whole, put you together – spirit, soul and body – and keep you fit for the coming of our Master, Jesus Christ. (The Message)

See Brokenness, Dissociation, Full Fragmentation, Integrity, Partial Fragmentation, Unity

Will (Willing, Willingness) – place within a person where choices are made.

This is arguably the most significant part of our soul, for it is here that we make the choice about spiritual rule over every circumstance of our lives. In His humanity, the will of Jesus did not want to go through the agony of the cross, but He chose to submit His will to that of the Father, and this tough decision radically changed the course of human history.

> Mark 14:36... And [Jesus] was saying, "Abba! Father! All things are possible for You; remove this cup from Me; yet not what I will, but what You will." (NASB)

Our own decisions in life do not have quite such a cosmic outcome but, hour by hour, we do have a contest of choices in our will, whether to walk in obedience to the conviction of the Holy Spirit or whether to walk in accordance with the ways of the world (Romans 7:19).

Unfortunately, the functioning of the will can be damaged by many things; for example, inappropriate decisions demanded of us at an early age, use of medical or recreational drugs, ungodly healing methods such as hypnotherapy, the effects of addictive behavior, being subject to ungodly control, irrational fears, torture and physical trauma. In addition, demonic holds can result in drivenness that may seem to deny our ability to choose although, in reality, our freedom to decide to walk God's way can never be completely taken from us, no matter how difficult it may seem.

It is important that we seek the Lord's healing for the things which have damaged our will. As we allow Him to resolve these issues of the past, we will have more strength to oppose our carnal nature and make right choices in the future. Every time we walk in agreement with Jesus, surrendering our will to the will of the Father, we become further empowered by the Holy Spirit to overcome the pressure of the enemy, and more able to enter into our God-given destiny.

Interestingly, in secular treatments for addiction, it is not uncommon for addicts to be encouraged to submit their will to the will of some higher unseen power. Thankfully, we know the highest power that exists!

> Matthew 6:9–10... Pray, then, this way: "Our Father who is in heaven, Hallowed be Your name. Your kingdom come. Your will be done, On earth as it is in heaven." (NASB)

See Addiction, Carnal Nature, Choice, Control, Conviction, Decision, Drug Abuse, Fear, Free Will, Holy Spirit, Human Soul, Phobia

Wisdom (Wise) – mature understanding.

Through the experiences of life we gain knowledge, though we may not necessarily act wisely.

Leading a life which is just dependent on human wisdom will not necessarily ensure good character nor good behavior (1 Corinthians 3:19). Such a soulish lifestyle is very vulnerable to our carnal nature, and even to demonic intrusion.

> James 3:15... This wisdom is not that which comes down from above, but is earthly, natural, demonic. (NASB)

Amazingly, God has given followers of Jesus access to divine wisdom, which is gifted to us by the Holy Spirit, when required for the Body of Christ on earth.

> 1 Corinthians 12:7–8… But to each one is given the manifestation of the Spirit for the common good. For to one is given the word of wisdom through the Spirit, and to another the word of knowledge according to the same Spirit … (NASB)

This supernatural wisdom allows us to have a glimpse of how God sees particular issues (James 3:17). It can radically affect the way we respond to the circumstances of life, helping us deal more effectively with the spiritual battle in and around us. Whenever we feel a need for God's wisdom, we can ask Him. He is pleased to direct our lives, and for us to teach and advise others, based on His boundless heavenly insight, rather than our very limited earthly experience.

> James 1:5… If any of you lacks wisdom, you should ask God, who gives generously to all without finding fault, and it will be given to you. (NIV)

See Gifts of the Holy Spirit, Humanism, Reason, Revelation, Soulishness

Witchcraft – invoking of spiritual power outside of the authority of Jesus.

There are countless practices which have been used down through the ages which are intended to establish unseen control by individuals. This control may be sought over objects, land, events and people, in order to obtain power, health, destruction of others, foresight and even increase of possessions. These practices frequently involve ritual, sacrifice, oaths, charms and potions, all directed toward receiving demonic empowerment.

Even without the use of these devices of witchcraft, demonic powers can be given rights to operate through individuals who seek to control others through ungodly domination or manipulation. This will often occur where there is an absence of godly authority and direction. We see this very clearly in the life of Queen Jezebel, who was recognized

WITNESS

by others to be operating far beyond just the strength of her sinful character.

> 2 Kings 9:22... When Joram saw Jehu he asked, "Have you come in peace, Jehu?"
>
> "How can there be peace," Jehu replied, "as long as all the idolatry and witchcraft of your mother Jezebel abound?" (NIV)

Witchcraft may be seen as harmless fun in some children's books and at Halloween parties, but any dabbling with demonic power, however innocently intended, can open dangerous doors to the spiritual realms, so God has forbidden His people to be involved with such practices, for very good reasons. We will need to come to the Lord for His forgiveness and cleansing if we have disobeyed His commands or been affected by others in this area.

> Deuteronomy 18:9–10... When you enter the land which the LORD your God gives you, you shall not learn to imitate the detestable things of those nations. There shall not be found among you anyone who makes his son or his daughter pass through the fire, one who uses divination, one who practices witchcraft, or one who interprets omens, or a sorcerer ... (NASB)

See Commandment, Control, Jezebel, Occult, Power, Powers of Darkness, Rebellion, Ritual

Witness (Witnessing) – one who gives evidence of what has been seen or heard.

The clearest sign that a follower of Jesus has been baptized in the Holy Spirit is an empowered ability to be a witness to God's truth and character.

> Acts 1:8... but you will receive power when the Holy Spirit has come upon you; and you shall be My witnesses both in Jerusalem, and in all Judea and Samaria, and even to the remotest part of the earth. (NASB)

Empowered by the Holy Spirit, we are not simply speaking about Jesus but, as a part of the Body of Christ, we are able to supernaturally reveal

His authority and power which is operating through our lives on this earth.

It is often pointed out that the Greek word which is translated *witness* in the verse above also means *martyr*, which certainly adds an extra challenge. We are warned of something similar in the book of Revelation, because the evil ruler of the world, though disarmed at the cross, can still influence our lives. He continues to have places of spiritual authority over each of us in those specific areas where we have not obeyed Jesus (Ephesians 4:27). And he only loses those footholds through our personal obedience to the teaching of Jesus, even to the point, perhaps, of giving up our earthly lives (Revelation 12:11; Hebrews 12:4).

I clearly need to count the cost of being a true witness of Jesus. Even though He has come to give me abundant life, it is Himself, and not my life, which will need to be the focus of my love.

> John 12:25... He who loves his life loses it, and he who hates his life in this world will keep it to life eternal. (NASB)

See Baptism in the Holy Spirit, Body of Christ, Disciple, Martyr, Obedience, Testimony

Word – something spoken or written by God or by human beings.

In all that Jesus said and did as He walked the earth, He so completely expressed the heart and character of God, that John calls Jesus *the* Word (in Greek, *Logos*).

> John 1:1... In the beginning was the Word, and the Word was with God, and the Word was God. (NASB)

Jesus was a living representation on earth of all the words of God. Every word He uttered was wholly true and spiritually life-giving (John 6:63). In addition to Jesus, the Living Word, God has given us, through the inspiration of the Holy Spirit, His written Word in

WORLD

the form of the Bible. When read under the anointing of the Holy Spirit, it speaks truth to us straight from the heart of God (Psalm 119:160a).

Words are very powerful. The words of God brought the whole of creation into being (Genesis 1:3). Particular words from the Bible, when prompted by the Holy Spirit today can supernaturally overcome the power of the enemy, not least during times of prayer ministry (Psalm 107:20). Although not always used in this way in the New Testament, the Greek word *rhema* is often used by believers to mean a direct and powerful spoken word from God, particularly appropriate for the current moment.

> Ephesians 6:17... And take THE HELMET OF SALVATION, and the sword of the Spirit, which is the word [rhema] of God. (NASB)

Our own words, or words spoken to us or about us by those with whom we have a significant relationship, can also be opportunities for powerful blessing, if they are in agreement with God. They can also be opportunities for demonic cursing if spoken in rebellion to God's Word.

> Ecclesiastes 10:20... Also, do not curse a king in your thought; and do not curse the rich in your bedrooms; for a bird of the heavens may carry the voice; yea, the LORD of wings may tell the matter. (LITV)

We need to take much care what we say and what words we receive into our hearts from others (Proverbs 15:4; 18:21). It may be necessary to seek the Lord for healing and cleansing from the effect of cursing words spoken in the past, forgiving others and confessing our own mistakes, renouncing that which has been said in disagreement with God's truth.

See Bible, Blessing, Cursing, Jesus, Pronouncement, Renunciation, Vow

World (Worldly) – physically, planet earth and humanity; spiritually, all that is not of the eternal Kingdom of God.

> John 18:36a... Jesus answered, "My Kingdom is not of this world. ..." (NASB)

Jesus says that His disciples also are not of the world, and that they must expect hostility from the world.

> John 15:19... If you were of the world, the world would love its own; but because you are not of the world, but I chose you out of the world, because of this the world hates you. (NASB)

Followers of Jesus live in this physical world but their spiritual allegiance is not to this world, nor to the ruler of the world.

> 1 John 2:15... Do not love the world or the things in the world. The love of the Father is not in those who love the world ... (NRSV)

> 1 Corinthians 2:12... Now we have received, not the spirit of the world, but the Spirit who is from God, so that we may know the things freely given to us by God ... (NASB)

See Darkness, Kingdom of God, Light, Ruler of the World

Worship – heartfelt honor, adoration, value and service given to something or someone.

God has made humankind with a deep desire to worship. He, of course, intended that the highest place of value and honor would be given to Himself, because this would bring security and meaning to our lives, affirming our identity and destiny. Jesus explained that worship is essentially a spiritual experience.

> John 4:24... God is spirit, and those who worship Him must worship in spirit and truth. (NASB)

False worship in a Christian organization can occur when there is undue focus on seeking some form of spiritual impartation into the lives of the worshippers at the expense of a rightful honoring of God, the Father, Son and Holy Spirit. Similarly, worship of angels (Colossians 2:18–19) and addressing historical or biblical persons (Deuteronomy 18:11), during times of worship or intercession, are not permitted in Scripture; these would give significant license for deception by the enemy.

False worship can also occur as a consequence of soulishness in those who are leading if, even with good intentions, they deny the true direction of the Holy Spirit by seeking to manipulate the way a congregation gives worship to God. True worship of God is only possible when our human spirit is led by the Holy Spirit, and so directed into glorifying Jesus and our heavenly Father (John 16:13–15).

Worship involves the whole of our being. We worship when we are surrendered to God in our thinking, emotions, choices, actions and words. Mere lip service and tradition are not pleasing to God (Isaiah 29:13). Singing and music are recognized in the Bible as powerful expressions of worship, engaging the human spirit but, in fact, everything that we say and do in agreement with God, under the anointing of the Holy Spirit, is a form of worship.

It is not wrong to give honor to living people, provided that God is above all whom we choose to serve (Ephesians 5:21). The Anglican marriage service traditionally included a promise for the husband and wife to worship each other with their bodies, which is a rightful honoring and valuing of the marriage partner, to include surrender of themselves in sexual intimacy, all under the lordship of Jesus.

Unfortunately, humanity's carnal nature draws us into worship of many things which are unhelpful and even dangerous. Satan tried to seduce Jesus away from serving His heavenly Father, and we are certainly going to be tempted in a similar way.

> Luke 4:5–8... And [the devil] led Him up and showed Him all the kingdoms of the world in a moment of time. And the devil said to Him, "I will give You all this domain and its glory; for it has been handed over to me, and I give it to whomever I wish. Therefore if You worship before me, it shall all be Yours." Jesus answered him, "It is written, 'YOU SHALL WORSHIP THE LORD YOUR GOD AND SERVE HIM ONLY.'" (NASB)

The world invites us to worship false gods, success, health, exercise, sport, status, celebrity, money or intellect, for example, all potentially leading us to idolatry. The trouble is that we inevitably take on the character of whatever we worship. It is a spiritual law:

> Psalm 115:8... Those who make [idols] will become like them ... (NASB)

When we give honor and value to the evil ruler of the world, and his ways, we actually display something of his character. However, the good news is that when God, through Jesus Christ, is the focus of our worship, the Holy Spirit grows us into His likeness. We will bear the fruit of His character, a prime purpose for which Jesus chose us (John 15:16).

WOUND

See Authority, False Religion, Honor, Idolatry, Lordship, Soulishness, Value

Worth (Worthy) – see Value

Worthlessness (Worthless) – being of no value.

See Value

Wound (Woundedness, Wounding) – damage inflicted on the body, soul or human spirit.

Just as the flesh and bones of our physical bodies can be cut, crushed, broken or disabled, so too there can be damage to the inner places of our mind, will, emotions and human spirit, caused by the sinful treatment we have received from others or even from ourselves.

God has given us pain as an indicator of injury so that we will look for healing of our wounds, whether physical, spiritual or emotional. Sometimes these just need a little time to heal through the natural processes which God has designed. However, if we do not know His ways for dealing with the wounds of the soul and spirit, we may try to fix the pain ourselves, often making the situation worse and still leaving it unresolved. Thankfully, there is healing and deliverance available in Jesus today for these issues of the past, often coming through prayer ministry in the Body of Christ (Acts 5:16).

When ministering healing, it is important that we differentiate between sins, unclean spirits and wounds. It is surprising how often we try unsuccessfully to repent of a wound, heal a demon or cast out a sin! Sins need to be confessed so that the forgiveness and cleansing of God can be received. Unclean spirits need to be expelled once the rights of the enemy have been removed through confession and forgiveness of sin. However, wounds need divine repair to restore wholeness and function. This healing process usually starts as we forgive those who were responsible for causing the wounds, and probably by also confessing the wrong ways, the coping mechanisms, by which we have tried, in our own strength, to deal with inner pain.

Then, as we bring the wounded places of our lives to the exchange of the cross, pouring out our hearts to Him, the wounds which Jesus carried in His body become the means by which we can receive healing for the wounds which we have carried within our own bodies. What a Savior!

> 1 Peter 2:24… and He Himself bore our sins in His body on the cross, so that we might die to sin and live to righteousness; for by His wounds you were healed. (NASB)

See Brokenness, Coping Mechanism, Emotion, Forgiveness, Human Soul, Human Spirit, Inner Healing, Mind, Pain, Trauma, Wholeness, Will

Wrongfulness (Wrongdoing, Wrong, Wrongful) – thoughts, words or actions out of line with God's laws and commandments.

The Bible tells us what is right and wrong, and this is personally confirmed by the conviction of the Holy Spirit in the heart of every follower of Jesus. Since the Fall of humankind, our carnal nature has drawn us toward believing and doing what is wrong and, sadly, there is a consequence to walking this way.

> Colossians 3:25… For he who does wrong will receive the consequences of the wrong which he has done, and that without partiality. (NASB)

Praise God that forgiveness and cleansing are always there for us when we confess our wrongdoing, and the Holy Spirit is ready to empower us to turn toward what is right when we surrender our will to the will of the Father.

See Badness, Carnal Nature, Evil, Iniquity, Sin, Unrighteousness

X-P – Greek letters *chi-rho*.

It seemed important to have at least one entry in this book for every letter of the alphabet, so I took the liberty here of borrowing the Greek letter X! *Chi-rho*, the first two letters from the Greek word for *Christ* have been used since the time of the early church to represent the Lord. Whenever we see these two letters, sometimes written one over the other, we can remember that Jesus is indeed the promised Messiah, the Anointed One, who came to earth to bind up the brokenhearted and set captives free (Isaiah 61:1). Thank You, Lord!

See Anointing, Christ

Yoga – foundationally, a religious practice intended to bring a person progressively into spiritual union with a supreme deity of Hinduism.

The ritual process includes a series of steps, involving meditation, breathing exercises and demanding body postures (frequently resembling animals). Many people use these body positions as a form of physical exercise, believing that they are completely free from any spiritual connections. Yoga is an example of the countless alternative therapies promoted today for our well-being. They seem to be well-meaning but they actually invoke spiritual power outside of the authority of Jesus.

Interestingly, the word *yoga* means *union* or *yoke*, because in its Hindu origins this religious practice is intended to bring increasing spiritual receptivity to, and union with, the spiritual realms. To believe that we can follow some of the ritual practice of a false religion without any possibility of spiritual defilement is surely unwise. Many Christians have found that confessing and renouncing the practice of yoga, and seeking the Lord's cleansing from all demonic holds on the body, soul and human spirit, have resulted in remarkable freedom.

If we are looking for a safe yoke and true healing, Jesus has the perfect answer!

> Matthew 11:29… Take My yoke upon you and learn from Me, for I am gentle and humble in heart, and YOU WILL FIND REST FOR YOUR SOULS. (NASB)

See Alternative Medicine, Defilement, Exercise, False Religion, Meditation, New Age Movement, Occult, Yoke

Yoke – cross-piece of wood or iron fastened over the necks of animals or humans in order to restrain them or to carry a load, and hence a biblical symbol for control.

Throughout the Bible, the picture of a yoke on people's backs is used to describe strong control, usually oppressive, especially by harsh enemies, coming as a result of the disobedience of God's people to His

commands. Interestingly, the word *subjugate*, meaning to conquer or dominate, comes from a Latin origin meaning *to bring under the yoke*.

> Deuteronomy 28:48... therefore you shall serve your enemies whom the LORD will send against you, in hunger, in thirst, in nakedness, and in the lack of all things; and He will put an iron yoke on your neck until He has destroyed you. (NASB)

God's promise to His people under the Old Covenant was that He would release them from oppression, removing the spiritual yoke, if they would walk in obedience to His commands. Restoration of God's people to true freedom has always been His heart.

> Ezekiel 34:27b... Then they will know that I am the LORD, when I have broken the bars of their yoke and have delivered them from the hand of those who enslaved them. (NASB)

Under the New Covenant, there comes a final fulfillment of this freedom as Jesus offers an amazing new yoke, not oppressive and harmful, but a wonderful divine control available for humankind, which brings a new relationship with God and a true and lasting peace.

> Matthew 11:29... Take My yoke upon you and learn from Me, for I am gentle and humble in heart, and YOU WILL FIND REST FOR YOUR SOULS. (NASB)

Throughout history, yokes have been used to join together animals, and sometimes even people (especially slaves). A yoke is a very good representation of a soul-tie. This is something which holds those yoked together in a controlling bond of relationship, which can be good (Philippians 4:3, KJV) or bad (Genesis 27:40).

As we forgive those who have oppressed our lives, and as we receive God's forgiveness for our own sinful behaviors, God will lift every spiritual yoke from our lives, removing not only the wrongful control but also the ungodly ties that have wrongly bound us to others.

> Galatians 5:1... It was for freedom that Christ set us free; therefore keep standing firm and do not be subject again to a yoke of slavery. (NASB)

See Control, Freedom, Oppression, Slavery, Soul-tie

Zap – colloquial expression for an instant manifestation of spiritual power.

Often Jesus seemed to heal people very quickly, although usually there was important dialogue first, in order to establish the truth of the person's relationship with Him. He was able to know their hearts after just a few words. Knowing the truth about our relationship with God and the truth about ourselves is a vital doorway to healing.

> John 8:31–32... So Jesus was saying to those Jews who had believed in Him, "If you continue in My word, then you are truly disciples of Mine; and you will know the truth, and the truth will make you free." (NASB)

Unfortunately, the process of our arriving at that truth today can take time, even with others alongside, because of the perversity of our carnal nature and the fact that our hearts can deceive us (Jeremiah 17:9). As we open our lives to the Holy Spirit, He leads us into the truth and

He gives us the opportunity to respond with appropriate confession or forgiveness, which then leads to freedom.

We may wish that God would just zap us with healing, either directly or through some gifted minister but, more often than not, God will want to take us on a journey with the Holy Spirit, discovering more truth of Jesus and more truth about ourselves as we move into a new place of wholeness, holiness and healing. His ultimate purpose in our lives is to build character, to progressively transform each one of us into the image of Christ (2 Corinthians 3:18). There is no short cut to such transformation.

> 1 Thessalonians 5:23... May God himself, the God who makes everything holy and whole, make you holy and whole, put you together – spirit, soul and body – and keep you fit for the coming of our Master, Jesus Christ. (The Message)

See Healing, Holiness, Jesus, Transformation, Wholeness

Notes

1 *A Grief Observed* by CS Lewis © copyright CS Lewis Pte Ltd 1961, pp. 20–21.

2 The ancient Greek manuscripts of the New Testament, which are the source of our English translations, vary in whether or not they include "bind the broken-hearted" in this verse. The majority of Greek manuscripts do contain it, which is why the words are found in the King James Bible and others. However, some English translations follow one of the Greek manuscripts which do not contain these words and so they are omitted in these versions (e.g. NIV). It seems likely that the translations which do include these words in Luke's Gospel are more accurate, since it is clearly stated that Jesus read the words from the book of Isaiah, and Isaiah does begin with this statement about healing the brokenhearted.

3 *Mere Christianity* by CS Lewis © copyright CS Lewis Pte Ltd 1942, 1943, 1944, 1952, p. 202.

4 *The Problem Of Pain* by CS Lewis © copyright CS Lewis Pte Ltd 1940, chapter 6, "Human Pain".

5 *Mere Christianity* by CS Lewis © copyright CS Lewis Pte Ltd 1942, 1943, 1944, 1952, pp. 136–137.

6 *The Great Divorce* by CS Lewis © copyright CS Lewis Pte Ltd 1946, chapter 11, pp. 97–98.

7 The Collected Letters III by CS Lewis © copyright CS Lewis Pte Ltd 2006, p 109.

8 Joan R. Kahn and Kathryn A. London, "Premarital Sex and the Risk of Divorce", *Journal of Marriage and the Family*, 53 (1991): 845–855.

   Edward O. Laumann et al., *The Social Organization of Sexuality: Sexual Practices in the United States* (Chicago: University of Chicago Press, 1994), pp. 503–505.

   Tim B. Heaton, "Factors Contributing to Increasing Marital Stability in the United States", *Journal of Family Issues*, 23 (2002): 392–409, pp. 401,407.

   Jay Teachman, "Premarital Sex, Premarital Cohabitation, and the Risk of Subsequent Marital Dissolution Among Women", *Journal of Marriage and Family*, 65 (2003): 444–455, p. 454.

   Anthony Paik, "Adolescent Sexuality and Risk of Marital Dissolution", *Journal of Marriage and Family*, 73 (2011): 472–485, pp. 483,484.

9 *Mere Christianity* by CS Lewis © copyright CS Lewis Pte Ltd 1942, 1943, 1944, 1952, p.48.

10 http://link.springer.com/article/10.1007%2Fs10508-008-9386-1 (accessed 2 October 2015).

NOTES

https://en.wikipedia.org/wiki/Biology_and_sexual_orientation#cite_note-22 (accessed 2 October 2015).

11 Studies* have shown that the more older male siblings a boy has, the greater his chances of developing same-sex attraction. Even in the womb, a boy may detect his mother's strong desire for him to be female, which is one of many potential woundings in the human spirit that can cause gender confusion.

*R. Blanchard (1997), "Birth order and sibling sex ratio in homosexual versus heterosexual males and females", *The Annual Review of Sexual Research* 8: 27–67. PMID 10051890 (Academic journal)

12 http://iheu.org/humanism/the-amsterdam-declaration (accessed 23 November 2015)

13 *Mere Christianity* by CS Lewis © copyright CS Lewis Pte Ltd 1942, 1943, 1944, 1952, p.226.

14 St Augustine, Confessions, book 4, quoted in C.S. Lewis, The Four Loves chapter 6, (1960; London: HarperCollins 2002) p.145

15 *The Weight Of Glory* by CS Lewis © copyright CS Lewis Pte Ltd 1949, p. 170.

16 Kyuzo Mifune quoted in various websites, for example, www.neworleansjudo.org/philosophy.htm (accessed 6 November 2015).

17 *The Problem Of Pain* by CS Lewis © copyright CS Lewis Pte Ltd 1940, chapter 6, "Human Will".

18 *Mere Christianity* by CS Lewis © copyright CS Lewis Pte Ltd 1942, 1943, 1944, 1952, p.125.

19 *Christian Reflections* by CS Lewis © copyright CS Lewis Pte Ltd 1967, 1980, p.52.

20 http://link.springer.com/article/10.1007%2Fs10508-008-9386-1 (accessed 2 October 2015).

https://en.wikipedia.org/wiki/Biology_and_sexual_orientation#cite_note-22 (accessed 2 October 2015).

21 Studies* have shown that the more older male siblings a boy has, the greater his chances of developing same-sex attraction. Even in the womb, a boy may detect his mother's strong desire for him to be female, which is one of many potential woundings in the human spirit that can cause gender confusion.

*R. Blanchard (1997), "Birth order and sibling sex ratio in homosexual versus heterosexual males and females", *The Annual Review of Sexual Research* 8: 27–67. PMID 10051890 (Academic journal)

22 www.nhs.uk/Livewell/STIs/Pages/oral-sex-and-cancer.aspx#oral (accessed 16 November 2015)

www.oralcancerfoundation.org/hpv

D'Souza G, Cullen K, Bowie J, Thorpe R, Fakhry C (2014) Differences in Oral Sexual Behaviors by Gender, Age, and Race Explain Observed Differences in Prevalence of Oral Human Papillomavirus Infection. PLoS ONE 9(1): e86023. doi:10.1371/journal.pone.0086023

23   *Mere Christianity* by CS Lewis © copyright CS Lewis Pte Ltd 1942, 1943, 1944, 1952, p.134

24   Lewis, *Mere Christianity*, p. 134.

25   Ed Silvoso, *That None Should Perish* (Ventura: Regal, 1994), p.155.

26   *The Collected Letters* II by CS Lewis © copyright CS Lewis Pte Ltd 2004, p.174.

27   John Flavel (1627–91), *The Whole Works of the Rev. Mr John Flavel*, Vol 4 (London: W Baynes & Son, 1820), "Wonderful Sea-Deliverances", p. 507.

28   Andrew B. Newberg, Nancy A. Wintering, Donna Morgan, Mark R. Waldman, "The Measurement of Regional Cerebral Blood Flow during Glossolalia: A Preliminary SPECT Study", *Psychiatry Research: Neuroimaging*, Volume 148, Issue 1, 22 November 2006, pp. 67–71.

29   This quotation is widely attributed to George Orwell, although it has not been found in his writings, so it is not clear who first said it.

30   *Till We Have Faces* by CS Lewis © copyright CS Lewis Pte Ltd 1956, p.269

ABOUT THE AUTHOR

David Cross is Deputy International Director for Ellel Ministries and Regional Director for the Ministry in Western Europe.

He graduated from Nottingham University in 1969 and qualified as a chartered civil engineer, leading to a varied working career. This included building roads and bridges in the Highlands of Scotland and, in the early 1980's, overseeing the construction of new town development in the New Territories area of Hong Kong. It was here that he had a personal encounter with God and a huge change of direction occurred when he gave his life to Jesus.

When David, and his wife Denise, returned to Scotland, they became very active in church life and David led ski tours in the Cairngorm Mountains. In order to further the Christian healing ministry in the Highlands, as an elder in the Church of Scotland, he and others in the local church made contact with Ellel Ministries in 1991, and two years later David and Denise joined the Ministry at the international headquarters of Ellel Grange, near Lancaster.

Both David and Denise have been Ellel Centre Directors and are now two of the senior leaders of the ministry, serving as members of the International Executive Leadership.

David and Denise have three children and eight grandchildren, all giving much joy in the midst of their very busy lives. Besides the thrill of sharing God's truth through teaching and writing, David loves walking and photography. His authoritative teaching from God's word has brought understanding and healing to many who have been confused and damaged by the ungodly ideologies of today's world. David has written four other books: *Soul-Ties, God's Covering, Trapped by Control, The Dangers of Alternative Ways to Healing* (with John Berry) and *What's Wrong with Human Rights?*

Other Books by David Cross

www.sovereignworld.com

Soul Ties

Providing unique insight, this book looks discerningly at what a soul tie is, both of a good and bad kind, and the impact this invisible bond has on us in our everyday life.
Paperback 128 pages ISBN 978-185240-451-2

The Dangers of Alternative Ways to Healing
David Cross and John Berry

Many forms of alternative therapies are available today and this book provides fascinating coverage of what they are with clear guidelines on how spiritually safe or unsafe they might be.
Paperback 176 pages ISBN 978-185240-537-3

Trapped by Control

This book takes a closer look at who or what can control people's lives and how to escape from ungodly control by others.
Paperback 112 pages ISBN 978-185240-501-4

God's Covering – A Place of Healing

Seeks to explain the reality of what can happen when we move out from under God's covering and become spiritually exposed.
Paperback 192 pages ISBN 978-185240-485-7

'What's wrong with Human Rights'

The concept of universal human rights exists without any divine endorsement from a biblical point of view. This book claims that they are best described as a man-made religion, and therefore a false religion.
Paperback 192pages ISBN 978-185240-873-2

Other titles in the Truth & Freedom series

Healing from the Consequences of Accident, Shock and Trauma
Peter Horrobin

Accidents and traumas are the root cause of many unhealed symptoms. Filled with testimonies of healing, this ground breaking book provides wonderful keys and encouragement to those still struggling with longstanding problems.
Paperback 160 pages ISBN 978-1-85240-743-8

Rescue from Rejection
Denise Cross

Use this book to walk a path of self-acceptance and breathe new life into your relationship with others and with God!
Paperback 160 pages ISBN 978-185240-538-0

Hope and Healing for the Abused
Paul and Liz Griffin

This book is for those who have been affected by abuse of any kind or anyone involved in pastoral ministry.
Paperback 128 pages ISBN 978-185240-480-2

Intercession & Healing
Fiona Horrobin

This book is for ordinary people in their walk with an extraordinary God. It is about breaking through with God in the most difficult of life's issues.
Paperback 176 pages ISBN 978-185240-500-7

OTHER BOOKS BY ELLEL MINISTRIES

Anger – How Do You Handle It?
Paul and Liz Griffin

This book will help you to differentiate between righteous and unrighteous anger, identify the root causes of the anger you experience and overcome the problem.
Paperback 112 pages ISBN 978-18524-0450-5

Stepping Stones to the Father Heart of God
Margaret Silvester

As you move along the stepping stones described in this book, you will journey from a distorted self-image based on abandonment, neglect, rejection or abuse to an image of Father God based on the Word of God and revelation from the Holy Spirit.
Paperback 176 pages ISBN 978-185240-623-3

Other reference material from Ellel Ministries

Healing Through Deliverance
– The Foundation and Practice of Deliverance Ministry
Peter Horrobin

In this ground-breaking book, Peter Horrobin draw on his thirty years of experience of ministry to lay out the biblical basis for healing through deliverance. He provides safe guidelines for ministry, helps the reader identify demonic entry points and teaches how we can be delivered and healed from the effects of demonic power. His prayer for the reader is that their commitment to Christ will be deepened and that they will respond afresh to God's call to heal the broken-hearted and set the captives free.
Hardback 630 pages ISBN 978-1-852404-98-7

THE WORK OF

Ellel Ministries International

Ellel Ministries was first established at Ellel Grange in the UK. The word Ellel is simply the name of the community in which Ellel Grange was built in the nineteenth century. In old English the word Ellel was *"All hail"* – meaning Praise God! In Hebrew it means *"towards God"* and in old Chinese the words mean *"Love flowing outwards"*.

For thirty years now God's love has been flowing outwards through the work bringing His healing to those in need and providing teaching and training for the Body of Christ. In the early days of the work people came from overseas and on returning home they began the work of establishing a local Ellel Center in their own country. Each one has the same vision to minister healing and to teach and train people to fulfil God's great commission in their local church.

Current list of centres, addresses and contact details:

UK Centers

Ellel Grange (& International HQ) Bay Horse, Lancaster, Lancashire, LA2 0HN
Tel: 01524 751 651   *Email:* info.grange@ellelministries.org

Ellel Glyndley Manor, Stone Cross, Pevensey, East Sussex, BN24 5BS
Tel: 01323 440 440   *Email:* info.glyndley@ellelministries.org

Ellel Pierrepont, Frensham, Farnham, Surrey, GU10 3DL
Tel: 01252 794 060   *Email:* info.pierrepont@ellelministries.org

Ellel Scotland, Blairmore House, Glass, Huntly, Aberdeenshire, AB54 4XH
Tel: 01466 799 102   *Email:* info.scotland@ellelministries.org

ELLEL MINISTRIES

Ellel Ireland, 35 Beanstown Road, Lisburn, County Antrim, BT28 3JQS, Northern Ireland
Tel: +44 (0) 28 9260 7162 / 07545 696 750   *Email:* info.northernireland@ ellelministries.org

Ellel Ministries Overseas Centers

Ellel Ministries Africa, PO Box 39569, Faerie Glen 0043, Pretoria, South Africa
Tel: +27 12 809 0031 / 1172   *Email:* info.africa@ellelministries.org

Ellel Kwazulu-Natal, PO Box 12, Winklespruit, 4145, KwaZulu-Natal, South Africa
Tel: +27 (0)31 916 2134   *Email:* bookingskzn@ellel.org.za

Ellel Ministries Australia (Sydney) Gilbulla, 710 Moreton Park Road, Menangle 2568, NSW, Australia
Tel: +61 02 4633 8102   *Email:* info.gilbulla@ellelministries.org

Ellel Ministries (Perth) PO Box 277, Gosnells, WA 6990, Australia
Tel: ++61 (0)8 9398 4648   *Email:* info@wa.ellel.org.au

Ellel Ministries Canada in Ontario, 183 Hanna Road, RR#2, Westport, Ontario, K0G 1X0, Canada
Tel: +1 613 273 8700   *Email:* info.emc@ellelministries.org

Ellel Ministries Canada West, Prairie Winds Centre, RR1, Site 15, Comp. 42, Didsbury, Alberta, T0M 0W0 Canada
Tel: +1 403 335 4900   *Email:* info.calgary@ellelministries.org

Ellel Ministries France (La FraternitéChrétienne), 10 Avenue Jules Ferry, 38380 Saint Laurent du Pont, France
Tel: +33 47 65 54 266   *Email:* info.france@ellelministries.org

Ellel Ministries Germany e.V., Bahnhofstr. 45-47, 72213 Altensteig, Germany
Tel: +49 7453 275 51   *Email:* buero@ellelgerman.de

Ellel Ministries Hungary, Veresegyhaz, PF17, 2112, Hungary,
Tel/Fax: +36 28 362 396   *Email:* info.hungary@ellelministries.org

ELLEL MINISTRIES

Ellel Ministries India, 502 Orchid Holy Cross Road, I. C. Colony, Borivili West, Mumbai, 400103, India
Mob: +91 93 2224 5209   *Email:* info.india@ellelministries.org

Ellel Ministries Malaysia - KL/Klang Valley, 9 & 11 Jalan Dendang 1, Kawasan 16, BerkeleyTown Center, 41300 Klang, Selangor D.E, Malaysia
Tel: +60 33 3599 011   *Email:* info.kl.malaysia@ellelministries.org

Ellel Ministries Malaysia - Sabah, Lot 10 and 12, First Floor, Wisma Leven, LorongMargosa 2, Luyang Phase 8, 88300 Kota Kinabalu, Sabah, Malaysia
Tel: +60 88 265 800   *Email:* info.malaysia@ellelministries.org

Ellel Ministries Netherlands, Wichmondseweg 19, 7223 LH Baak, The Netherlands
Tel: +31 575 441 452   *Email:* info.netherlands@ellelministries.org

Ellel Ministries New Zealand, PO Box 17690, Sumner, Christchurch 8840, New Zealand
Mob: +64 21 269 8384   *Email:* info.newzealand@ellelministries.org

Ellel Ministries Norway, Stiftelsen Ellel Ministries Norge, Grosås Senter, 4724 Iveland, Norge
Tel: +47 6741 3150   *Email:* post@ellelnorge.no

Ellel Papua New Guinea, C/o Boroko Baptist Church, PO Box 1689, Boroko, National Capital District 111, Papua New Guinea
Tel: +675 7161 3587/+675 767 33255 *Email:* info.png@ellelministries.org

Ellel Romania, Trotusului nr. 4, Oradea, 410242, Bihor, Romania
Tel: +40 731 351 445   *Email:* contact@ellelromania.ro

Ellel Ministries Rwanda, P.O. Box 2964, Kigali, Rwanda,
Tel: +250 789 501 986   *Email:* bookingsrwanda@ellel.org.za

Ellel Ministries Singapore, 39A JalanPemimpin, #05-01A, Halcyon Building, Singapore 577183
Tel: +65 6252 4234   *Email:* info@zion-ellel.org.sg

Ellel Ministries Sweden, Kvarnbackavägen 4 B, 711 92 Vedevåg, Sweden
Tel: +46 581 930 36   *Email:* info.sweden@ellelministries.org

Ellel Ministries Switzerland, Spitalweg 20, 4125 Riehen, Switzerland
Tel: +41 61 645 42 17   *Email:* info.switzerland@ellelministries.org

Ellel Ministries USA, 1708 English Acres Drive, Lithia, Florida 33547, USA
Tel: +1 813 737 4848   *Email:* info.usa@ellelministries.org

Would You Join With Us To Bless the Nations?

At the Sovereign World Trust, our mandate and passion is to send books, like the one you've just read, to *faithful leaders who can equip others* (2 Tim 2:2).

The 'Good News' is that in all of the poorest nations we reach, the Kingdom of God is growing in an accelerated way but, to further this Great Commission work, the Pastors and Leaders in these countries need good teaching resources in order to provide sound Biblical doctrine to their flock, their future generations and especially new converts.

If you could donate a copy of this or other titles from Sovereign World Ltd, you will be helping to supply much-needed resources to Pastors and Leaders in many countries.

Contact us for more information on (+44)(0)1732 851150 or visit our website www.sovereignworldtrust.org.uk

> *"I have all it takes to further my studies. Sovereign is making it all possible for me"*
>
> **Rev. Akfred Keyas – Kenya**

> *"My ministry is rising up gradually since I have been teaching people from these books"*
>
> **Pastor John Obaseki – Nigeria**

For more information about the worldwide work
of Ellel Ministries please visit:

www.ellel.org

Lightning Source UK Ltd.
Milton Keynes UK
UKHW020743150822
407177UK00005B/99